Protein Interaction Networks: Computational Analysis

The analysis of protein–protein interactions is fundamental to the understanding of cellular organization, processes, and functions. Proteins seldom act as single isolated species; rather, proteins involved in the same cellular processes often interact with each other. Functions of uncharacterized proteins may be predicted through comparison with the interactions of similar known proteins. Recent large-scale investigations of protein–protein interactions using such techniques as two-hybrid systems, mass spectrometry, and protein microarrays have enriched the available protein interaction data and facilitated the construction of integrated protein–protein interaction networks. The resulting large volume of protein–protein interaction data has posed a challenge to experimental investigation.

This book provides a comprehensive understanding of the computational methods available for the analysis of protein–protein interaction networks. It offers an in-depth survey of a range of approaches, including statistical, topological, data-mining, and ontology-based methods. The author discusses the fundamental principles underlying each of these approaches and their respective benefits and drawbacks, and she offers suggestions for future research.

Aidong Zhang is a professor in the Department of Computer Science and Engineering at the State University of New York at Buffalo and the director of the Buffalo Center for Biomedical Computing (BCBC). She is an author of more than 200 research publications and has served on the editorial boards of the *International Journal of Bioinformatics Research and Applications* (IJBRA), *ACM Multimedia Systems*, the *International Journal of Multimedia Tools and Applications*, the *International Journal of Distributed and Parallel Databases*, and *ACM SIGMOD DiSC* (Digital Symposium Collection). Dr. Zhang is a recipient of the National Science Foundation CAREER Award and SUNY (State University of New York) Chancellor's Research Recognition Award. Dr. Zhang is an IEEE Fellow.

PROTEIN INTERACTION
NETWORKS

Computational Analysis

Aidong Zhang
State University of New York, Buffalo

CAMBRIDGE
UNIVERSITY PRESS

Shaftesbury Road, Cambridge CB2 8EA, United Kingdom

One Liberty Plaza, 20th Floor, New York, NY 10006, USA

477 Williamstown Road, Port Melbourne, VIC 3207, Australia

314–321, 3rd Floor, Plot 3, Splendor Forum, Jasola District Centre, New Delhi – 110025, India

103 Penang Road, #05–06/07, Visioncrest Commercial, Singapore 238467

Cambridge University Press is part of Cambridge University Press & Assessment,
a department of the University of Cambridge.

We share the University's mission to contribute to society through the pursuit of
education, learning and research at the highest international levels of excellence.

www.cambridge.org
Information on this title: www.cambridge.org/9780521888950

First published 2009

A catalogue record for this publication is available from the British Library

Library of Congress Cataloging-in-Publication data
Zhang, Aidong, 1961–
    Protein interaction networks : computational analysis / Aidong Zhang.
        p. cm.
    Includes bibliographical references and index.
    ISBN 978-0-521-88895-0 (hardback)
    1. Protein-protein interactions – Data processing.   2. Protein-protein
    interactions – Mathematical models.   I. Title.
    [DNLM: 1. Protein Binding – physiology.   2. Protein Interaction Mapping –
    methods.   3. Computational Biology – methods. QU 55 Z625p 2009]
    QP551.5.Z53   2009
    572´.64–dc22   2009002688

ISBN   978-0-521-88895-0   Hardback

To my daughter, Cathy

Contents

Color plates follow page 82

Preface

I am pleased to offer the research community my second book-length contribution to the field of bioinformatics. My first book, *Advanced Analysis of Gene Expression Microarray Data*, was published in 2006 by World Scientific as part of its Science, Engineering, and Biology Informatics (SEBI) series. I first became involved in the study of bioinformatics in 1998 and, over the ensuing decade, have been struck by the enormous quantity of data being generated and the need for effective approaches to its analysis.

The analysis of protein–protein interactions (PPIs) is fundamental to the understanding of cellular organizations, processes, and functions. It has been observed that proteins seldom act as single isolated species in the performance of their functions; rather, proteins involved in the same cellular processes often interact with each other. Therefore, the functions of uncharacterized proteins can be predicted through comparison with the interactions of similar known proteins. A detailed examination of a PPI network can thus yield significant new insights into protein functions. These interactions have traditionally been examined via intensive small-scale investigations of a small set of proteins of interest, each yielding information about a limited number of PPIs. The existing databases of PPIs have been compiled from such small-scale screens, presented in individual research papers. Because these data were subject to stringent controls and evaluation in the peer-review process, they can be considered to be fairly reliable. However, each experiment observes only a few interactions and yields a data set of very limited size. Recent large-scale investigations of PPIs using such techniques as two-hybrid systems, mass spectrometry, and protein microarrays have enriched the available protein interaction data and facilitated the construction of integrated PPI networks. The resulting large volume of PPI data has posed a challenge to experimental investigation. Consequently, computational analysis of the networks has become a necessary tool for the determination of functionally associated proteins.

This book is intended to provide a comprehensive understanding of the computational methods available for the analysis of PPI networks. It offers an in-depth survey of a range of approaches to this analysis, including statistical, topological, data-mining, and ontology-based methods. The fundamental principles underlying each of these approaches are discussed, along with their respective benefits and drawbacks. Suggestions for future research are also offered. In total, this book is intended to offer bioinformatics researchers a comprehensive and practical guide to the analysis of PPI networks, which will assist and stimulate their further investigation.

Some knowledge on the part of the reader in the fields of molecular biology, data mining, and statistics is assumed. Apart from this, the book is designed to be self-contained, as it includes introductions to the fundamental concepts underlying data generation and analysis. Thus, this book is expected to be of interest to a variety of researchers. It can be used as a textbook for advanced graduate courses in bioinformatics, and most of its content has been tested in the author's graduate-level course in this field. In addition, it can serve as a resource for graduate students seeking topics for investigation. The book will also be useful to researchers involved in computational biology in universities, organizations, and industry. For this audience, it will provide guidance on the techniques available for analysis of PPI networks. Research professionals interested in expanding their knowledge base can draw upon the material presented here to gain an understanding of principles and methods involved in this growing and highly significant field.

ACKNOWLEDGMENTS

I would like to express my deepest thanks to my doctoral students, Pritam Chanda, Young-rae Cho, Woo-chang Hwang, Taehyong Kim, and Lei Shi, for their excellent technical contributions. I am also highly appreciative of the editorial work of Rachel Ramadhyani.

The inspiration for this book was an invitation from Ms. Lauren Cowles, a senior editor from Cambridge University Press. I would like to express my special thanks to her.

Aidong Zhang
Buffalo, New York

1

Introduction

1.1 RAPID GROWTH OF PROTEIN–PROTEIN INTERACTION DATA

Since the sequencing of the human genome was brought to fruition [154,310], the field of genetics now stands on the threshold of significant theoretical and practical advances. Crucial to furthering these investigations is a comprehensive understanding of the expression, function, and regulation of the proteins encoded by an organism [345]. This understanding is the subject of the discipline of proteomics. Proteomics encompasses a wide range of approaches and applications intended to explicate how complex biological processes occur at a molecular level, how they differ in various cell types, and how they are altered in disease states.

Defined succinctly, proteomics is the systematic study of the many and diverse properties of proteins with the aim of providing detailed descriptions of the structure, function, and control of biological systems in health and disease [241]. The field has burst onto the scientific scene with stunning rapidity over the past several years. Figure 1–1 shows the trend of the number of occurrences of the term "proteome" found in PubMed bioinformatics citations over the past decade. This figure strikingly illustrates the rapidly increasing role played by proteomics in bioinformatics research in recent years.

A particular focus of the field of proteomics is the nature and role of interactions between proteins. Protein–protein interactions (PPIs) regulate a wide array of biological processes, including transcriptional activation/repression; immune, endocrine, and pharmacological signaling; cell-to-cell interactions; and metabolic and developmental control [9,139,167,184]. PPIs play diverse roles in biology and differ based on the composition, affinity, and lifetime of the association. Noncovalent contacts between residue side chains are the basis for protein folding, protein assembly, and PPI [232]. These contacts facilitate a variety of interactions and associations within and between proteins. Based on their diverse structural and functional characteristics, PPIs can be categorized in several ways [230]. On the basis of their interaction surface, they may be homo- or hetero-oligomeric; as judged by their stability, they may be obligate or nonobligate; and as measured by their persistence, they may be transient or permanent. A given PPI can fall into any combination of these three categorical pairs. An interaction may also require reclassification under certain

1

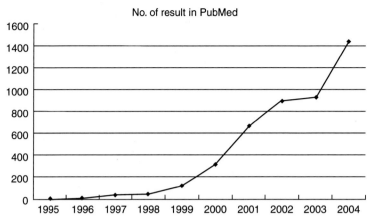

No. of result in PubMed

Figure 1–1 Number of results found in PubMed for the term "proteome." (Reprinted from [200] with permission of John Wiley & Sons, Inc.)

conditions; for example, it may be mainly transient in vivo but become permanent under certain cellular conditions.

It has been observed that proteins seldom act as single isolated species while performing their functions in vivo [330]. The analysis of annotated proteins reveals that proteins involved in the same cellular processes often interact with each other [312]. The function of unknown proteins may be postulated on the basis of their interaction with a known protein target of known function. Mapping PPIs has not only provided insight into protein function but also facilitated the modeling of functional pathways to elucidate the molecular mechanisms of cellular processes. The study of PPIs is fundamental to understanding how proteins function within the cell. Characterizing the interactions of proteins in a given cellular proteome will be the next milestone along the road to understand the biochemistry of the cell.

The result of two or more proteins interacting with a specific functional objective can be demonstrated in several different ways. The measurable effects of PPIs have been outlined by Phizicky and Fields [254]. PPIs can:

- alter the kinetic properties of enzymes; this may be the result of subtle changes at the level of substrate binding or at the level of an allosteric effect;
- act as a common mechanism to allow for substrate channeling;
- create a new binding site, typically for small effector molecules;
- inactivate or destroy a protein; or
- change the specificity of a protein for its substrate through interaction with different binding partners; for example, demonstrate a new function that neither protein can exhibit alone.

PPIs are much more widespread than once suspected, and the degree of regulation that they confer is large. To properly understand their significance in the cell, one needs to identify the different interactions, understand the extent to which they take place in the cell, and determine the consequences of the interactions.

In recent years, PPI data have been enriched by high-throughput experimental methods, such as two-hybrid systems [155,307], mass spectrometry [113,144], and protein chip technology [114,205,346]. Integrated PPI networks have been built from these heterogeneous data sources. However, the large volume of PPI data currently available has posed a challenge to experimental investigation. Computational analysis of PPI networks has become a necessary supplemental tool for understanding the functions of uncharacterized proteins.

1.2 COMPUTATIONAL ANALYSIS OF PPI NETWORKS

A PPI network can be described as a complex system of proteins linked by interactions. The computational analysis of PPI networks begins with the representation of the PPI network structure. The simplest representation takes the form of a mathematical graph consisting of nodes and edges [314]. Proteins are represented as nodes in such a graph; two proteins that interact physically are represented as adjacent nodes connected by an edge. Based on this graphic representation, various computational approaches, such as data mining, machine learning, and statistical approaches, can be designed to reveal the organization of PPI networks at different levels. An examination of the graphic form of the network can yield a variety of insights. For example, neighboring proteins in the graph are generally considered to share functions ("guilt by association"). Thus, the functions of a protein may be predicted by looking at the proteins with which it interacts and the protein complexes to which it belongs. In addition, densely connected subgraphs in the network are likely to form protein complexes that function as a unit in a certain biological process. An investigation of the topological features of the network (e.g., whether it is scale-free, a small network, or governed by the power law) can also enhance our understanding of the biological system [5].

In general, the computational analysis of PPI networks is challenging, with these major difficulties being commonly encountered:

- *The protein interactions are not reliable.* Large-scale experiments have yielded numerous false positives. For example, as reported in [288], high-throughput yeast two-hybrid (Y2H) assays are ~50% reliable. It is also likely that there are many false negatives in the PPI networks currently under study.
- *A protein can have several different functions.* A protein may be included in one or more functional groups. Therefore, overlapping clusters should be identified in the PPI networks. Since conventional clustering methods generally produce pairwise disjoint clusters, they may not be effective when applied to PPI networks.
- *Two proteins with different functions frequently interact with each other.* Such frequent, random connections between the proteins in different functional groups expand the topological complexity of the PPI networks, posing difficulties to the detection of unambiguous partitions.

Recent studies of complex systems [5,227] have attempted to understand and characterize the structural behaviors of such systems from a topological perspective. Such features as small-world properties [319], scale-free degree distributions [28,29], and hierarchical modularity [261] have been observed in complex systems, elements that are also characteristic of PPI networks. Therefore, topological methods can be used to address the challenges mentioned earlier and to facilitate the efficient and accurate analysis of PPI networks.

1.2.1 Topological Features of PPI Networks

Barabasi and Oltvai [29] introduced the concept of degree distribution, $P(k)$, to quantify the probability that a selected node in a network will have exactly k links. Networks of different types can be distinguished by their degree distributions. For example, a random network follows a Poisson distribution. In contrast, a scale-free network has a power-law degree distribution, $P(k) \sim k^{-\gamma}$, indicating that a few hubs bind numerous small nodes. When $2 \leq \gamma \leq 3$, the hubs play a significant role in the network [29]. Recent publications have indicated that PPI networks have the features of a scale-free network [121,161,198,313]; therefore, their degree distribution approximates a power law, $P(k) \sim k^{-\gamma}$. In scale-free networks, most proteins participate in only a few interactions, while a small set of hubs participate in dozens of interactions.

PPI networks also have a characteristic property known as the "small-world effect," which states that any two nodes can be connected via a short path of a few links. The small-world phenomenon was first investigated as a concept in sociology [217] and is a feature of a range of networks arising in both nature and technology, including the Internet [5], scientific collaboration networks [224], the English lexicon [280], metabolic networks [106], and PPI networks [284,313]. Although the small-world effect is a property of random networks, the path length in scale-free networks is much shorter than that predicted by the small-world effect [74,75]. Therefore, scale-free networks are "ultra-small." This short path length indicates that local perturbations in metabolite concentrations could permeate an entire network very quickly. In PPI networks, highly connected nodes (hubs) seldom directly link to each other [211]. This differs from the assortative nature of social networks, in which well-connected individuals tend to have direct connections to each other. In contrast, biological networks have the property of disassortativity, in which highly connected nodes are only infrequently linked.

A number of recent publications have proposed the use of centrality indices, including node degree, pagerank, clustering coefficient, betweenness centrality, and bridging centrality metrics, as measurements of the importance of components in a network [47,53,103,110,226,268,319]. For instance, betweenness centrality [225] was proposed to detect the optimal location for partitioning a network [122,145]. The modified betweenness cut approach has been suggested for use with weighted PPI networks that integrate gene expression [61]. Jeong's group has espoused the degree of a node as a key basis for the identification of essential network components [161]. In this model, power-law networks are very robust to random attacks but highly vulnerable to targeted attacks [7]. Hahn's group identified differences in degree, betweenness, and closeness centrality between essential and nonessential genes in three eukaryotic PPI networks (yeast, worm, and fly) [131]. Estrada's group introduced a new subgraph centrality measure to characterize the participation of each node in all subgraphs in a network [103,102]. Palumbo's group sought to identify lethal nodes by arc deletion, thus facilitating the isolation of network subcomponents [239]. Guimera's group devised a clustering method to identify functional modules in metabolic pathways and categorized the role of each component in the pathway according to its topological location relative to detected functional modules [129].

As we will subsequently discuss in greater detail, the unique topological features found to be characteristic of PPI networks will play significant roles in the computational analysis of these networks.

1.2.2 Modularity Analysis

The idea of functional modules, introduced in [139], offers a major conceptual tool for the systematic analysis of a biological system. A functional module in a PPI network represents a maximal set of functionally associated proteins. In other words, it is composed of those proteins that are mutually involved in a given biological process or function. A wide range of graph-theoretic approaches have been employed to identify functional modules in PPI networks. However, these approaches have tended to be limited in accuracy due to the presence of unreliable interactions and the complex connectivity of the networks [288]. In particular, the topological complexity of PPI networks, arising from the overlapping patterns of modules and cross talks between modules, poses challenges to the identification of functional modules. Because a protein generally performs different biological processes or functions in different environments, real functional modules are overlapping. Moreover, the frequent, dynamic cross connections between different functions are biologically meaningful and must be taken into account [274].

In an attempt to parse this complexity, the hierarchical organization of modules in biological networks has been recently proposed [261]. The architecture of this model is based on a scale-free topology with embedded modularity. In this model, the significance of a few hub nodes is emphasized, and these nodes are viewed as the determinants of survival during network perturbations and as the essential backbone of the hierarchical structure. This hierarchical network model can plausibly be applied to PPI networks because cellular functionality is typically hierarchical in nature, and PPI networks include a few hub nodes that are biologically lethal.

The identification of functional modules in PPI networks or modularity analysis can be successfully accomplished through the use of cluster analysis. Cluster analysis is invaluable in elucidating network topological structure and the relationships among network components. Typically, clustering approaches focus on detecting densely connected subgraphs within the graphic representation of a PPI network. For example, the maximum clique algorithm [286] is used to detect fully connected, complete subgraphs. To compensate for the high-density threshold imposed by this algorithm, relatively dense subgraphs can be identified in lieu of complete subgraphs, either by using a density threshold or by optimizing an objective density function [56,286]. A number of density-based clustering algorithms using alternative density functions have been presented [12,24,247].

As noted, hierarchical clustering approaches can plausibly be applied to biological networks because of the hierarchical nature of functional modules [261,297]. These approaches iteratively merge nodes or recursively divide a graph into two or more subgraphs. To merge nodes iteratively, the similarity or distance between two nodes or two groups of nodes is measured and a pair is selected for merger in each iteration [17,263]. Recursive division of a graph involves the selection of nodes or edges to be cut. Partition-based approaches have also been applied to biological networks. One partition-based clustering approach, the Restricted Neighborhood Search Clustering (RNSC) algorithm [180], determines the best partition using a cost function. In addition, other approaches have been applied to biological networks. For example, the Markov Clustering Algorithm (MCL) finds clusters using iterative rounds of expansion and inflation that, respectively, prefer the strongly connected regions and weaken the sparsely connected regions [308]. The line graph generation method [250] transforms a network of proteins connected by interactions into a network of connected interactions and then uses the MCL algorithm to cluster the PPI network. Samantha and Liang [272] applied a statistical approach to the clustering of proteins based on the premise that a pair of proteins sharing a significantly greater number of common neighbors will have a high functional similarity. The recently introduced STM algorithm [148] votes a representative of a cluster for each node.

Topological metrics can be incorporated into the modularity analysis of PPI networks. From our studies, we have observed that the bridging nodes identified in PPI networks serve as the connecting nodes between protein modules; therefore, removing the bridging nodes preserves the structural integrity of the network. Such findings can play an important role in the modularity analysis of PPI networks. Removal of the bridging nodes yields a set of components disconnected from the network. Thus, using bridging centrality to remove the bridging nodes can be an excellent preprocessing procedure to estimate the number and location of modules in the PPI network. Results of this research [151,152] have shown that such approaches can generate larger modules that discard fewer proteins, permitting more accurate functional detection than other current methods.

1.2.3 Prediction of Protein Functions in PPI Networks

Predicting protein function can be, in itself, the ultimate objective of the analysis of a PPI network. Despite the many extensive studies of yeast that have been undertaken, there are still a number of functionally uncharacterized proteins in the yeast database. The functional annotation of human proteins can provide a strong foundation for the complete understanding of cell mechanisms, information that is invaluable for drug discovery and development. The increased interest in and availability of PPI networks have catalyzed the development of computational methods to elucidate protein functions.

Protein functions may be predicted on the basis of modularization algorithms. If an unknown protein is included in a functional module, it is expected to contribute toward the function that the module represents. The generated functional modules may thus provide a framework within which to predict the functions of unknown proteins. Each generated module may contain a few uncharacterized proteins along with a larger number of known proteins. It can be assumed that the unknown proteins play a positive role in realizing the function of the generated module. However, predictions arrived at through these means may be inaccurate, since the accuracy of the modularization process itself is typically low. For greater reliability, protein functions should be predicted directly from the topology or connectivity of PPI networks.

Several topology-based approaches that predict protein function on the basis of PPI networks have been introduced. At the simplest level, the "neighbor counting method" predicts the function of an unknown protein by the frequency of known functions of the immediate neighbor proteins [274]. The majority of functions of the immediate neighbors can be statistically assessed [143]. The function of a protein can be assumed to be independent of all other proteins, given the functions of its immediate neighbors. This assumption gives rise to a Markov random field model [85,196]. Recently, the number of common neighbors of the known protein and the unknown protein has been taken as the basis for the prediction of function [201].

Machine learning has been widely applied to the analysis of PPI networks, and, in particular, to the prediction of protein functions. A variety of methods have been developed to predict protein function on the basis of different information sources. Some of the inputs used by these methods include protein structure and sequence, protein domain, PPIs, genetic interactions, and gene expression analysis. The accuracy of prediction can be enhanced by drawing upon multiple sources of information. The Gene Ontology (GO) database [84] is one example of such semantic integration.

1.2.4 Integration of Domain Knowledge

As noted, the accuracy of results obtained from computational approaches can be compromised by the inclusion of false connections and the high complexity of networks. The reliability of this process can be improved by the integration of other functional information. Initially, the identification of similarities in gene sequence can be a primary indicator of a functional association between two genes. Additionally, genome-level methods for functional inference, such as gene fusion events and phylogenetic profiling, can generate useful data pointing to functional linkages. Beyond this, we know that genes with correlated expression profiles determined through microarray experiments are likely to be functionally related. Many studies [65,66,153,304] have investigated the integration of PPI networks with gene expression data to improve the accuracy of the functional modules identified. Finally, as briefly noted earlier, GO [18,301] can be a useful data source to combine with the PPI networks. GO is currently one of the most comprehensive and well-curated ontology databases in the bioinformatics community. It represents a collaborative effort to address the need for consistent descriptions of genes and gene products. The GO database includes GO terms and their relationships. The former are well-defined biological terms organized into three general conceptual categories that are shared across different organisms: biological processes, molecular functions, and cellular components. The GO database also provides annotations to each GO term, and each gene can be annotated on one or more GO terms. The GO database and its annotations can thus be a significant resource for the discovery of functional knowledge. These tools have been employed to facilitate the analysis of gene expression data [89,105,147] and have been integrated with unreliable PPI networks to accurately predict functions of unknown proteins [84] and identify functional modules [68,70].

1.3 SIGNIFICANT APPLICATIONS

The systematic analysis of PPIs can enable a better understanding of cellular organization, processes, and functions. Functional modules can be identified from the

PPI networks that have been derived from experimental data sets. There are many significant applications following this analysis. In this book, the following principal applications to which this analysis can be applied will be discussed:

■ *Predicting protein function.* As noted earlier, the most basic application of PPI networks is the use of topological analysis to predict protein function. The generated functional modules can serve as a framework within which to predict the functions of unknown proteins. Each generated module may contain a few uncharacterized proteins. By associating unknown proteins with the known proteins, we can suggest that those proteins participate positively in performing the functions assigned to the modules.

■ *Lethality analysis.* The topological analysis of PPI networks can be used to systematically assess the biological importance of bridging and other nodes in a PPI network [65,66,70,148]. Lethality, a crucial factor in characterizing the biological indispensability of a protein, is determined by examining whether a module is functionally disrupted when the protein is eliminated. Information regarding lethality is compiled in most PPI databases. For example, the MIPS database [214] indicates the lethality or viability of each included protein. Such sources allow the researcher to compare the lethality of nodes with high bridging-score values to that associated with other competing network parameters in the PPI networks. These comparisons reveal that nodes with the highest bridging scores are less lethal than both randomly selected nodes and nodes with high degree centrality. However, the average lethality of the neighbors of the nodes with the highest bridging scores is greater than that of a randomly selected subset. Our research has indicated that bridging nodes have relatively low lethality; interconnecting nodes are characterized by higher lethality; and modular nodes and peripheral nodes have, respectively, the highest and lowest proportion of lethal proteins. These results imply that many of the bridging nodes do not perform tasks critical to biological functions [151,152]. As a result, these nodes would serve as good targets for drugs, as discussed later.

■ *Assessing the druggability of molecular targets from network topology.* Translating the societal investments in the Human Genome Project and other similar large-scale efforts into therapies for human diseases is an important scientific imperative in the post–human-genome era. The efficacy, specificity/selectivity, and side-effect characteristics of well-designed drugs depend largely on the appropriate choice of pharmacological target. For this reason, the identification of molecular targets is a very early and critical step in the drug discovery and development process. The goal of the target identification process is to arrive at a very limited subset of biological molecules that will become the principal focus for the subsequent discovery research, development, and clinical trials. Pharmacological targets can span the range of biological molecules from DNA and lipids to metabolites. In fact, though, the majority of pharmacological targets are proteins. Effective pharmacological intervention with the target protein should significantly impact the key molecular processes in which the protein participates, and the resultant perturbation should be successful in modulating the pathophysiological process of interest. Another important consideration that is sometimes overlooked during the target identification step is the potential for side effects.

Ideally, an appropriate balance should be found among efficacy, selectivity, and side effects. In practice, however, compromises are often required in the areas of specificity/selectivity and side effects, since pharmacological interventions with proteins that are central to key processes will likely affect many biological pathways. We have observed that the biological correlates of the nodes with the highest bridging scores indicate that these nodes are less lethal than other nodes in PPI networks. Thus, they are promising drug targets from the standpoints of efficacy and side effects.

1.4 ORGANIZATION OF THIS BOOK

This book is intended to provide an in-depth examination of computational analysis as applied to PPI networks, offering perspectives from data mining, machine learning, graph theory, and statistics. The remainder of this book is organized as follows:

- Chapter 2 introduces the three principal experimental approaches that are currently used for generating PPI data: the Y2H system [121,156,307], mass spectrometry (MS) [113,120,144,187,210,303], and protein microarray methods [114,346].
- Chapter 3 discusses various computational approaches to the prediction of protein interactions, including genomic-scale, sequence-based, structure-based, learning-sequence-based, and network topology-based techniques.
- Chapter 4 introduces the basic properties of and metrics applied to PPI networks. Basic concepts in graphic representation employed to characterize various properties of PPI networks are defined for use throughout the balance of the book.
- Chapter 5 discusses the modularity analysis of PPI networks. Various modularity analysis algorithms used to identify modules in PPI networks are discussed, and an overview of the validation methods for modularity analysis is presented.
- Chapter 6 explores the topological analysis of PPI networks. Various metrics used for assessing specific topological features of PPI networks are presented and discussed.
- Chapter 7 focuses on greater detail on one type of modularity algorithm, specifically, the distance-based modularity analysis of PPI networks.
- Chapter 8 focuses on greater detail on graph-theoretic approaches for modularity analysis of PPI networks.
- Chapter 9 discusses the flow-based analysis of PPI networks.
- Chapter 10 examines statistical- and machine learning-based analysis of PPI networks.
- Chapter 11 discusses the integration of domain knowledge into the analysis of PPI networks.
- Chapter 12 presents some of the more recent approaches that have been developed for incorporating diverse biological information into the explorative analysis of PPI networks.
- Chapter 13 offers a synthesis of the methods and concepts discussed throughout the book and reflections on potential directions for future research and applications.

1.5 SUMMARY

The analysis of PPI networks poses many challenges, given the inherent complexity of these networks, the high noise level characteristic of the data, and the presence of unusual topological phenomena. As discussed in this chapter, effective approaches are required to analyze PPI data and the resulting PPI networks. Recently, a variety of data-mining and statistical techniques have been applied to this end, with varying degrees of success. This book is intended to provide researchers with a working knowledge of many of the advanced approaches currently available for this purpose. (Some of the material in this chapter is reprinted from [200] with permission of John Wiley & Sons, Inc.)

2

Experimental Approaches to Generation of Protein–Protein Interaction Data

2.1 INTRODUCTION

Proteins and their interactions lie at the heart of most fundamental biological processes. Typically, proteins seldom act in isolation but rather execute their functions through interaction with other biomolecular units. Consequently, an examination of these protein–protein interactions (PPIs) is essential to understanding the molecular mechanisms of underlying biological processes [79]. This chapter is intended to provide an overview of the more common experimental methods currently used to generate PPI data.

In the past, PPIs were typically examined via intensive small-scale investigations of restricted sets of proteins of interest, each yielding information regarding a limited number of PPIs. The existing databases of PPIs have been compiled from the results of such small-scale screens presented in individual research papers. Since these data are subject to stringent controls and evaluation in the peer-review process, they can be considered to be fairly reliable. However, each experiment observes only a few interactions and provides a data set of limited size.

Recent high-throughput approaches involve genome-wide detection of protein interactions. Studies using the yeast two-hybrid (Y2H) system [121,156,307], mass spectrometry (MS) [113,120,144,187,210,303], and protein microarrays [114,346] have generated large amounts of interaction data. The Y2H system takes a bottom-up genomic approach to detecting possible binary interactions between any two proteins encoded in the genome of interest. In contrast, mass spectrometric analysis adopts a top-down proteomic approach by analyzing the composition of protein complexes. The protein microarray technology simultaneously captures the expression of thousands of proteins.

2.2 THE Y2H SYSTEM

One of the most common approaches to the detection of pairs of interacting proteins in vivo is the Y2H system [21,155]. The Y2H system, first introduced in 1989 [107], is a molecular–genetic tool that facilitates the study of PPI. The interaction of two proteins transcriptionally activates a reporter gene, and a color reaction is seen

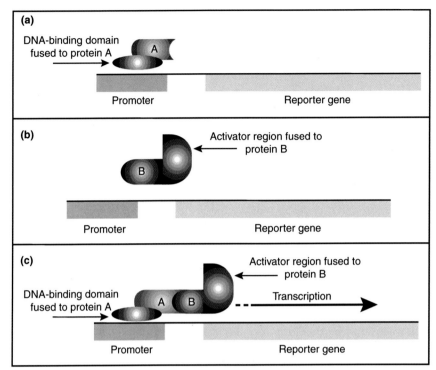

(a)

DNA-binding domain
fused to protein A

A

Promoter   Reporter gene

(b)

Activator region fused to
protein B

B

Promoter   Reporter gene

(c)

Activator region fused to
protein B

DNA-binding domain
fused to protein A   Transcription

A B

Promoter   Reporter gene

Figure 2–1 Y2H system applied to the detection of binary protein interactions.
(Reprinted by permission from Macmillan Publishers Ltd: Nature [233], copyright 2000.)

on specific media. This indication can track the interaction between two proteins, revealing "prey" proteins that interact with a known "bait" protein.

Two-hybrid procedures are typically carried out by screening a protein of interest against a random library of potential protein partners. Figure 2–1 [233] depicts the Y2H process. In Figure 2–1(a), we see that the fusion of the "bait" protein and the DNA-binding domain of the transcriptional activator does not turn on the reporter gene; no color change occurs; and the interaction cannot be tracked. Figure 2–1(b) shows that, similarly, the fusion of the "prey" protein and the activating region of the transcriptional activator is also insufficient to switch on the reporter gene. In Figure 2–1(c), the "bait" and the "prey" associate, bringing the DNA-binding domain and activator region into sufficiently close proximity to switch on the reporter gene. The result is gene transcription and a color change that can be monitored.

The Y2H system enables both highly sensitive detection of PPIs and screening of genome libraries to ascertain the interaction partners of certain proteins. The system can also be used to pinpoint protein regions mediating the interactions [157]. However, the classic Y2H system has several limitations. First, it cannot, by definition, detect interactions involving three or more proteins and those depending on posttranslational modifications (PTMs) except those applied to the budding yeast itself [157]. Second, since some proteins (e.g., membrane proteins) cannot be reconstructed in the nucleus, the Y2H system is not suitable for the detection of interactions involving these proteins. Finally, the method does not guarantee that an interaction indicated by Y2H actually takes place physiologically. Given these limitations, the Y2H system is most suitable for the detection of binary interactions, particularly those that are transient and unstable.

Despite these drawbacks, the Y2H system has become established as a standard technique in molecular biology and serves as an important method for proteomics analysis [240]. High-throughput Y2H screens have been applied to *Escherichia coli* [31], hepatitis C virus [108], Vaccinia virus [213], *Saccharomyces cerevisiae* [156,307], *Helicobacter pylori* [259], and *Caenorhabditis elegans* [198,315], *Drosophila melanogaster* [121], and *Homo sapiens* [76,266].

Recently, numerous modifications of the Y2H approach have been proposed that characterize PPI networks by screening each protein expressed in a eukaryotic cell [109]. Drees [92] has proposed a variant that includes the genetic information of a third protein. Zhang et al. [342] have suggested the use of RNA for the investigation of RNA–protein interactions. Vidal et al. [311] used the *URA3* gene instead of *GAL4* as the reporter gene; this two-hybrid system can be used to screen for ligand inhibition or to dissociate such complexes. Johnson and Varshavsky [166] have proposed a cytoplasmic two-hybrid system that can be used for screening of membrane protein interactions.

Despite the various limitations of the Y2H system, this approach has revealed a wealth of novel interactions and has helped illuminate the magnitude of the protein interactome. In principle, it could be applied in a more comprehensive fashion to examine all possible binary combinations between the proteins encoded by any single genome.

2.3 MASS SPECTROMETRY (MS) APPROACHES

Another traditional approach to PPI detection uses quantitative MS to analyze the composition of a partially purified protein complex together with a control purification in which the complex of interest is not enriched.

Mass spectrometry analysis proceeds in three steps: bait presentation, affinity purification of the complex, and analysis of the bound proteins [2]. Two large-scale studies [113,144], that apply MS analysis to the PPI network in yeast have been published. Each study attempted to identify all the components that were present in "naturally generated" protein complexes, taking as their subject essentially pure preparations of each complex [188]. In both approaches, bait proteins were generated that carried a particular affinity tag. In the case studied by Gavin et al. [113], 1,739 TAP-tagged (Tandem Affinity Purification) genes were introduced into the yeast genome by homologous recombination. Ho et al. [144] expressed 725 proteins modified to carry the FLAG epitope. In both cases, the proteins were expressed in yeast cells, and complexes were purified using a single immunoaffinity purification step. Both groups resolved the components of each purified complex with a one-dimensional denaturing polyacrylamide gel electrophoresis (PAGE) step. From the 1,167 yeast strains generated by Gavin et al. [113], 589 protein complexes were purified, 232 of which were unique. Ho et al. [144] used 725 protein baits and detected 3,617 interactions that involved 1,578 different proteins.

Figure 2–2 illustrates the process of mass spectrometric analysis [188]. In step (1), an "affinity tag" is attached to a target protein (the "bait"). As illustrated in

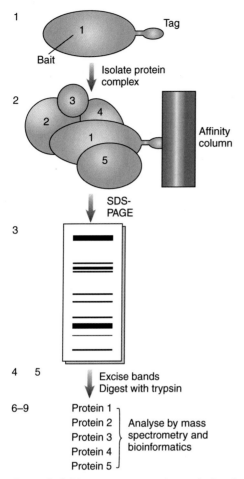

Figure 2–2 Mass spectrometric analysis of protein complexes. (Reprinted by permission from Macmillan Publishers Ltd: Nature [188], copyright 2002.)

Figure 2–2(2), bait proteins are systematically precipitated, along with any associated proteins, onto an "affinity column." In Figure 2–2(3), purified protein complexes are resolved by one-dimensional SDS-PAGE, so that proteins become separated according to mass. Step (4) entails the separating of protein bands by protein size; in step (5), protein bands are digested with trypsin. In steps (6–9), component proteins are detected by MS and bioinformatic analysis.

Mass-spectrometry-based proteomics can be applied not only to identify and quantify individual proteins [77,189,249,318] but also to protein analysis, including protein profiling [192], PTMs [206,207], and, in particular, identification of PPIs.

In general, mass spectrometric analysis is more physiological than the Y2H system. Actual molecular assemblies composed of all combinations of direct and cooperative interactions are analyzed in vivo, as opposed to the examination of reconstituted bimolecular interactions ex vivo or in vitro. MS can detect more complex interactions and is not limited to binary interactions, permitting the isolation of large protein complexes and the detection of networks of interactions. However, the technique is best applied to interactions of high abundance and stability, while two-hybrid approaches are able to reliably detect transient and weak interactions.

2.4 PROTEIN MICROARRAYS

Microarray-based analysis is a relatively high-throughput technology, that allows the simultaneous analysis of thousands of parameters within a single experiment. The key advantage of the microarray format is the use of a nonporous solid surface, such as glass, that permits precise deposition of capturing molecules (probes) in a highly dense and ordered fashion. The early applications of microarrays and detection technologies were largely centered on DNA-based applications. Today, DNA microarray technology is a robust and reliable method for the analysis of gene function [40]. However, gene expression arrays provide no information on protein PTMs (such as phosphorylation or glycosylation) that affect cell function. To examine expression at the protein level and acquire quantitative and qualitative information about proteins of interest, the protein microarray was developed.

A protein microarray is a piece of glass on which various molecules of protein have been affixed at separate locations in an ordered manner, forming a microscopic array [205]. These are used to identify PPIs, the substrates of protein kinases, or the targets of biologically active small molecules. The experimental procedure for protein microarray analysis involves choosing solid supports, arraying proteins on the solid supports, and screening for PPIs.

Experiments with the yeast proteome microarray have revealed a number of PPIs that had not previously been identified through Y2H or MS-based approaches. Global protein interaction studies were performed with a yeast proteome chip. Ge [114] has described a universal protein array, that permits quantitative detection of protein interactions with a range of proteins, nucleic acids, and small molecules. Zhu et al. [346] generated a yeast proteome chip from recombinant protein probes of 5,800 open-reading frames.

2.5 PUBLIC PPI DATA AND THEIR RELIABILITY

2.5.1 Experimental PPI Data Sets

PPIs within the *S. cerevisiae* have been the subject of extensive study due to the simplicity of the organism, and an abundance of data is currently available. Below is a partial list of the interaction data that have been generated for yeast via two of the high-throughput experimental methods discussed earlier, the Y2H system and mass spectrometric purification of protein complexes:

- *Ito full data* and *Ito core data*: In [156], Ito and colleagues applied the Y2H system to 3,275 proteins, detecting 4,392 interactions. From this "full data set," they selected a "core set" consisting of those proteins that appeared at least three times. This set comprised 758 interactions among 790 proteins.
- *Uetz data*: In [307], application of Y2H by Uetz and colleagues detected 1,459 interactions among 1,353 proteins.
- *Gavin complexes*: In [113], a comprehensive MS protein complex purification was conducted on yeast proteins, resulting in 589 purifications. These purifications

Table 2.1 Overlaps of Different PPI Data Sets

Data	Ito		Uetz	Gavin		Ho	
	Full	Core		Spoke	Matrix	Spoke	Matrix
Ito Full	4392	758	186	55	107	64	95
Ito Core	758	758	133	40	69	41	56
Uetz	186	133	1459	58	100	60	86
Gavin Spoke	55	40	58	3815	3815	292	842
Gavin Matrix	107	69	100	3815	18793	563	2264
Ho Spoke	64	41	60	292	563	4108	4108
Ho Matrix	95	56	86	842	2264	4108	28172

were further manually curated into 232 protein complexes [113], covering 1,310 proteins. The original purifications and the curated complexes are termed the Gavin Raw and Gavin Curated data sets, respectively.

■ *Ho complexes*: [144] presents another systematic analysis of protein complexes of yeast proteins. This includes 1,577 proteins and 741 protein complexes.

The Gavin and Ho data sets compromise the largest high-throughput protein complex purifications generated by MS technology to date. The binary protein interactions from the Gavin Raw complexes inferred through the spoke and matrix models are referred to as *Gavin Spoke* and *Gavin Matrix*, respectively. Similarly, the binary protein interactions from the *Ho Complex* inferred through the spoke and matrix models are denoted as *Ho Spoke* and *Ho Matrix*, respectively.

Table 2.1 presents the areas of overlap between these yeast PPI data sets. It can readily be seen that there is very limited overlap, both for data sets detected by the same technology (i.e., Ito Full and Uetz data sets, Gavin Spoke and Ho Spoke data sets) and data sets detected by different technologies (i.e., Ito Full and Gavin Spoke).

2.5.2 Public PPI Databases

In addition to these experimental data sets, there are also a number of open databases that provide comprehensive PPI data for several different organisms. There is little standardization among these databases, with each having a unique data structure, format, and mode of description. The data have been curated using various computational methods, which will be discussed in the next chapter. The major open PPI databases will be briefly described as follows:

■ *MIPS*: The Munich Information Center for Protein Sequences (MIPS) [214] is the repository of a significant body of protein information including sequence, structure, expression, and functional annotations. This database also includes PPI data for selected organisms, including *Homo sapiens*. The human PPI data have been manually created and curated on the basis of literature review and include the experimental approach, a description, and the binding regions of interacting partners [237].

- *DIP*: The Database of Interacting Proteins (DIP) [271] has combined data from a variety of sources to create a single, consistent set of PPI. For the yeast PPI data, the core PPIs have been selected from full data by a computational curative process based on the correlation of protein sequence and RNA expression profiles [82].
- *BIND*: The Biomolecular Interaction Network Database (BIND) [8], a component of BOND (the Biomolecular Object Network Databank), includes interactions, molecular complexes as a collection of two or more molecules that together form a functional unit, and pathways as a collection of two or more molecules that interact in a sequence.
- *BioGRID*: The General Repository for Interaction Database (BioGRID) [289] is a unified and continuously updated source of physical and generic interactions. It comprises more than 55,000 nonredundant interactions for yeast, making it the largest database for this organism, and more than 130,000 nonredundant interactions across a total of 22 different organisms.
- *MINT*: The Molecular Interaction Database (MINT) [59] uses expert curators to extract various experimental details from published literature; these are then stored in a structured format. HomoMINT [253] is a separate database of human protein interactions that have been inferred from orthologs in model organisms.
- *IntAct*: IntAct [178] is a database and toolkit for modeling, storing, and analyzing molecular interaction data. In addition to PPI data, it also includes extensive information on DNA, RNA, and small-molecule interactions.
- *HPRD*: The Human Protein Reference Database (HPRD) [219] provides a comprehensive collection of human PPI with protein features such as protein functions, PTMs, enzyme–substrate relationships, and subcellular localization. The human PPI data have been obtained from various experimental methods, including the Y2H systems.

2.5.3 Functional Analysis of PPI Data

It is important to be cognizant of the relationships and functional associations between the interacting protein pairs in these databases. Understanding the functional link, which is established between two interacting proteins, may allow us to assess the reliability of experimentally determined PPI data. Two measurements, functional similarity and functional consistency, can be applied to each interacting protein pair. As a "ground truth," the hierarchically distributed functional categories and their annotations from FunCat [267] in MIPS [214] are used. In this analysis, the PPI data from MIPS, DIP, and BioGRID are compared.

The *functional similarity* of an interacting protein pair is defined as the structural closeness between their functions. The functional categories are typically structured as a hierarchical tree format. The most general function becomes the root of the functional hierarchy. Each function has one or more children categories which correspond to more specific functions. Each protein can be annotated on the functional categories it performs. The set of proteins annotated on a functional category should then be a subset of the proteins annotated on its parent category, and the set of proteins annotated on the root is transitive, which is known as the transitivity property of functional annotations.

Each protein is typically annotated on one or more functional categories because it may perform different functions in different environmental conditions. The functional similarity of two proteins can then be estimated by selecting their most specific functions among the paths from leaf nodes to the root and calculating the average or maximum structural closeness of the pair-wise functions they have.

The most simplest way to calculate the structural closeness of two functions is to measure the path length between them in a hierarchy. It is arrived at by counting the edges of the shortest path between them. However, this method has the assumption that all edges represent the same specificity between a function and its parent function. For the normalization across different structures of the hierarchy, the shortest path length between two functions can be scaled down by the depth of the hierarchical structure. The depth represents the longest path length among all paths from a leaf node to the root. This way may normalize the structural closeness measurements by smoothing the difference of specificity between a longer path length in the hierarchy with a large depth and a shorter path length in the hierarchy with a small depth.

However, these methods do not take into consideration the location of the functional categories to be measured in the hierarchical structure. For example, two general functions having the same root as their parents should have the closeness different from two specific functions which are leaf nodes and have a common parent. To consider this factor, the depth of the most specific common parent should be taken into account. The structural closeness C between two functions F_i and F_j is then calculated by the ratio of the depth of the most specific common function to the average depth of F_i and F_j, where the depth of F_i is the path length from the root to F_i.

$$C(F_i, F_j) = \frac{2 \cdot \text{length}(F_r, F_k)}{\text{length}(F_r, F_i) + \text{length}(F_r, F_j)}, \tag{2.1}$$

where F_r is the root in the functional hierarchy and F_k is the subsuming node of F_i and F_j.

Figure 2–3 provides some examples of structural closeness between two nodes in a hierarchy. Each circle represents a function, and each edge is a general-to-specific relationship between two functions. Selected examples of structural closeness between two functions in the hierarchy are provided in the inset box. The closeness between a parent and a child is greater than that between siblings, and the closeness of siblings on a lower level is greater than that of siblings on a higher level in the hierarchy.

Figure 2–4(a) illustrates the distribution of the interacting protein pairs from the MIPS, DIP, and BioGRID databases with respect to their functional similarity or structural closeness. Significantly, 38% of the interacting pairs in MIPS, 37% in DIP, and 35% in BioGRID have a functional similarity greater than 0.8. The other interacting pairs in the databases have very low rates of similarity, always less than 0.4. Moreover, more than 30% of interacting pairs have a functional similarity of 0, meaning that they share no common functions. It is interesting to note that there are no interacting pairs with a functional similarity in the range between 0.4 and 0.8. The result indicates that more than 60% of the interactions in the databases have not been motivated by a similar function. Some of the functional mismatches might result from false positive interactions caused in the experimental PPI data.

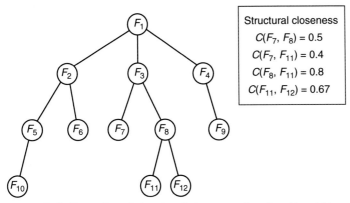

Figure 2–3 Examples of structural closeness in a functional hierarchy.

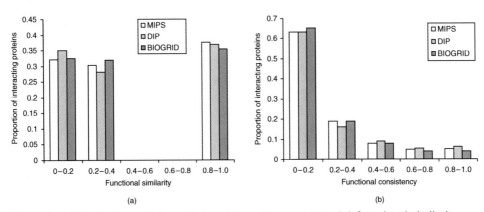

Figure 2–4 Distribution of interacting proteins with respect to (a) functional similarity and (b) functional consistency.

The *functional consistency* of an interacting protein pair is measured by the proportion of their common functions. This measurement assesses the tendency of consistent functional behaviors of two proteins. As already discussed, according to the transitivity property of functional annotations, if a protein is annotated to a function, then it also has more general functions on the paths towards the root in the hierarchical structure. For example, in Figure 2–3, if a protein p_i is annotated to F_5 and F_{12}. the set of functions of p_i is $\{F_1, F_2, F_3, F_5, F_8, F_{12}\}$. The functional consistency is then calculated by the ratio of the number of common functions to the number of all distinct functions of the interacting proteins. Since the smallest number of common functions of any protein pairs is 1 which represents the root, the functional consistency should be greater than 0. If two proteins have the exactly same functions, the functional consistency should be 1 as a maximum.

Figure 2–4(b) shows the distribution of the interacting protein pairs with respect to their functional consistency. Only 18% of the interacting pairs in MIPS, 21% in DIP and 16% in BioGRID have a consistency greater than or equal to 0.4. In contrast, 63% in MIPS and DIP and 65% in BioGRID have the consistency of less than 0.2. Moreover, these common functions are likely to be very general, located on the upper levels in the functional hierarchy. This result thus implies that more than 60% of the interacting proteins do not share any specific functions.

2.6 SUMMARY

In this chapter, we have provided an overview of the experimental generation of PPI data. The materials in this chapter have largely been excerpted from the many publications and web sites that address this topic [113,114,120,121,144,156,187,210, 303,307,346]. As we have seen, the Y2H system, MS, and protein microarrays offer efficient ways to measure PPIs at a large scale. Because it is recognized that two proteins are functionally linked through an interaction, these PPI data become excellent resources for inferring the functions of unknown proteins. However, as we have shown, more than 60% of the interacting proteins generated by these methods do not share any specific functions, significantly degrading the reliability of such inference of protein function. This issue will be further addressed in later chapters.

3

Computational Methods for the Prediction of Protein–Protein Interactions

3.1 INTRODUCTION

The yeast two-hybrid (Y2H) system and other experimental approaches described in Chapter 2 provide useful tools for the detection of protein–protein interactions (PPIs) between specified proteins that may occur in many possible combinations. The widespread application of these methods has generated a substantial bank of information about such interactions. However, as pointed out in Chapter 2, the data generated through these approaches may be unreliable and may not be completely inclusive of all possible PPIs. In order to form an understanding of the total universe of potential interactions, including those not detected by these methods, it is useful to develop approaches to predict the full range of possible interactions between proteins. The accurate prediction of PPIs is therefore an important goal in the field of molecular recognition.

A variety of computational methods have been applied to supplement the interactions that have been detected experimentally. In addition, these methods can assess the reliability of experimentally derived interaction data, which are prone to error. The computational methods for in-silico prediction include genomic-scale approaches [80,98,208,209,235,248], sequence-based approaches [212,287,322, 338], structure-based approaches [10,11,22,95,282], learning-based approaches [42, 43,127,160,236], and network-topology-based approaches [19,62,125,245,269,270]. The individual PPI data can be taken from publicly available databases, such as MIPS [130,214], DIP [271,327], MINT [59,340], IntAct [141,178], BioGRID [289], and HPRD [219,251,252], as described in Chapter 2.

3.2 GENOME-SCALE APPROACHES

The availability of complete genomes for various organisms has enabled the prediction of PPIs at a genomic scale. Genomic-scale approaches typically perform a comparison of gene sequences across genomes and are often justified on the basis of the correlated evolutionary mechanisms of genes. Initial efforts to predict PPIs have been carried out by searches of gene neighborhood conservation [80,235,296]. Dandekar et al. [80] observed the conservation of gene order in several microorganisms and noted that the proteins encoded by the conserved gene pairs appear to physically interact with each other. Overbeek et al. [235] proposed a method to predict functional linkages in a group of genes conserved across different, distantly related genomes. This method searches both homolog pairs and pairs of bidirectional hits within a group of conserved genes.

Gene fusion analysis [98,208] has also been employed to predict PPI at the genomic scale. Two proteins in different organisms or located distantly in a single organism are predicted to interact if they have consecutive homologs in a single organism. The algorithm [98] employed for this analysis includes the following processes. First, all similarities within the query genome are stored in a matrix T. The query genome is also compared with the reference genome and similarities are stored in a matrix Y. The algorithm then identifies those instances in which pairs of query proteins exhibit similarity to a reference protein but not to each other by inspecting these two matrices. A flowchart depicting the gene fusion algorithm is illustrated in Figure 3–1.

In this process, the similarity between genomes is obtained by using the BLAST [13] system for comparing primary biological sequence information. The system includes BLASTN for the comparison of nucleotide sequences and BLASTP for the

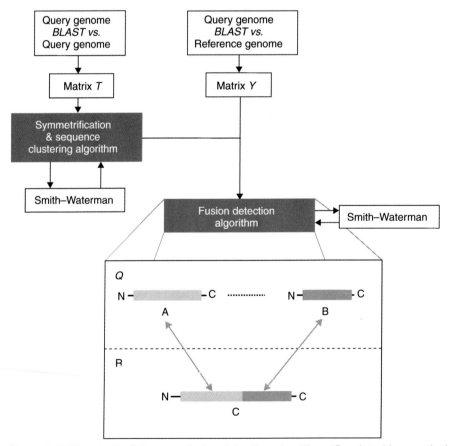

Figure 3–1 Flowchart of the gene fusion detection algorithm. (Reprinted by permission from Macmillan Publishers Ltd: Nature [98], copyright 1999.)

comparison of protein sequences. The search engine compares a query sequence with the sequence database and detects those sequences that fall above a similarity threshold.

Protein phylogenetic profiles [209,248] are useful resources for the prediction of interactions. The phylogenetic profile of a protein is a binary string with a length equal to the number of the genome in question. Each digit in the string is 1 if the genome contains a homolog of the corresponding gene; the digit will be 0 if there is no homolog. These profiles thus provide a means of capturing the evolution of genes across organisms. It has been demonstrated experimentally that proteins having similar phylogenetic profiles are likely to be functionally linked and to interact physically each other [97,248]. Figure 3–2 provides an example of phylogenetic profile analysis applied to four hypothetical genomes, each containing a subset of several proteins

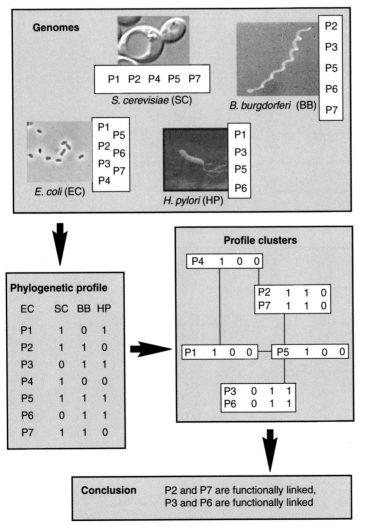

Figure 3–2 Phylogenetic profile analysis to detect functional linkages between proteins. (Reprinted by permission from Macmillan Publishers Ltd: Nature [97], copyright 2000.)

labeled $P1, \ldots, P7$. In a related approach, Pazo and Valencia [242] employed the similarity of phylogenetic trees as the indicator of PPIs. The similarity between two trees was measured by the linear correlation coefficient between two distance matrices containing average homologies for every possible pair of proteins. The process of phylogenetic tree analysis for the prediction of PPIs is shown in Figure 3–3. The phylogenetic trees are constructed by multiple sequence alignments of proteins, and the distance matrices are created using the average homology for every possible pair of proteins.

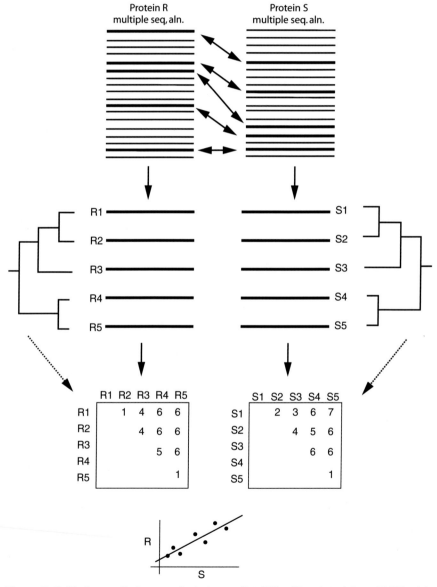

Figure 3–3 Phylogenetic tree analysis to predict PPIs. (Reprinted from [242] with permission of Oxford University Press.)

3.3 SEQUENCE-BASED APPROACHES

Predictions of PPIs have been carried out by integrating evidence of known interactions with information regarding sequential homology. This approach is based on the concept that an interaction generated in one species can be used to predict an interaction in another species. Matthews et al. [212] introduced the term "interologs" to refer to the potential orthologs of known interacting protein partners. A systematic search of interologs can be performed to identify potentially conserved interactions. This research team used BLASTP [13], the protein sequence comparison system mentioned earlier, to search a *Caenorhabditis elegans* database and detect potential orthologs of yeast in *C. elegans*. Their results show that the frequency of detection of interactions through searches for potential interologs is between 600- and 1,100-fold greater than that obtained by conventional two-hybrid screens using random libraries. Yu et al. [338] quantitatively assessed the transfer rate of interologs and verified that PPIs can be transferred when a pair of proteins has a joint sequence identity of greater than 80% or a joint *E*-value [14] of less than 10^{-70}.

Another sequence-based prediction approach proposed by Wojcik and Schachter [322] took into account the domain profiles of proteins. Since interactions typically occur between protein domains, the domain information for each interacting protein in one species may help predict interactions in another species. In this method, PPI data for a source organism is transformed into a domain cluster interaction map. The domain clusters are formed by linking domains that interact with a common region and domains exhibiting high sequence similarity. A domain profile is then constructed from the multiple alignment of the domain sequences in a cluster. Two domain clusters are connected if the number of interactions between them falls above a threshold. In the final step, each domain cluster is mapped to a similar set of proteins in a target organism. The prediction of protein interactions is based on the connectivity between domain clusters.

The pattern of domains appearing in known interacting proteins can also help predict additional PPIs. Sprinzak and Margalit [287] proposed the use of pairs of

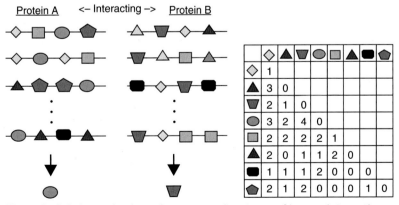

Figure 3–4 Schematic view of sequence signatures of known interacting proteins and their contingency table. (Reprinted from [287], copyright 2001, with permission of Elsevier.)

domains, termed sequence-signatures, that recur frequently in various interacting proteins. They first characterized protein sequences by their sequence-signatures and derived a contingency table. They then identified overrepresented sequence-signature pairs by comparing the observed frequencies to those that would arise randomly. Schematic views of the sequence-signatures of known interacting protein pairs and the corresponding contingency table are illustrated in Figure 3–4. This method relies on the assumption that all interactions occur within well-defined domain–domain interactions.

3.4 STRUCTURE-BASED APPROACHES

The docking method is a classical approach for detecting PPIs by predicting the structure of docked protein complexes. The detection of docked proteins [282] proceeds in two steps. A scoring function is developed that can discriminate between correctly and incorrectly docked orientations, and then a search method is applied to identify correctly docked orientations with reasonable reliability. The docking algorithms themselves involve three steps. First, the algorithm searches for protein complexes by treating proteins as rigid bodies and generating a list of possible docked complexes. Second, these complexes are rescored according to the energy of their association; this includes an evaluation of statistical potentials, electrostatics, and hydrogen bonding. The final, optional third stage introduces flexibility through side-chain rearrangements. In a related approach, Lu et al. [204] extended the concept of threading, a method frequently used to predict the structure of a single protein, into a multimeric threading technique to identify complex protein structures. The algorithm first threads the sequences through a representative structure template library and then uses statistical potentials to compute the energy of interaction between a pair of protein chains.

Protein complexes with known three-dimensional structures offer the best context within which to reliably identify PPIs [95]. However, given the paucity of such known complexes, research has extended to consider homologs proteins. Aloy and Russell [10] presented a method to model putative interactions upon known three-dimensional complex structures and to assess the compatibility of a proposed interaction with the complexes. They first observed that interactions between proteins occur through various main- and side-chain contacts. They then defined the empirical potentials by using a molar-fraction random state model based on the observed tendency of residues to persist on protein surfaces. They obtained homologs of both interacting proteins and applied the empirical potentials to test whether the interactions are preserved. Their experimental results indicate that this method can rank all possible interactions between homologs of the same species on the basis of the known three-dimensional structure of a protein complex and homologs sequences for each interacting protein. In their subsequent work [11], the inferred interaction models are extended from the similarity of sequences to the similarity of structural domains, and the interactions between complexes, termed "cross talk," are taken into consideration.

Similarities in interface surfaces offer an alternative resource for the prediction of interactions. Aytuna et al. [22] proposed an algorithm that starts with a set of structurally known protein interfaces and searches for pairs of proteins having similar residues. The similarity scoring function was defined by integrating structural with evolutionary similarity.

3.5 LEARNING-BASED APPROACHES

Machine learning has been recognized as useful and reliable in a wide spectrum of applications. Various machine-learning techniques can be applied to the prediction of PPIs. Given a database of known interacting pairs, a machine learning system can be trained to recognize interactions based on their specific biological features. An initial attempt along these lines has been made by Bock and Gough [42]. They used a support vector machine (SVM) learning system for training interaction data, with protein sequences and associated physicochemical properties as features. For each protein complex, feature vectors were assembled from encoded representations of tabulated residue properties, including charge, hydrophobicity, and surface tension for each residue in a sequence. Let $\{v_j\}^i$ in L-dimensional real space $\mathbb{R}^L$ denote the feature vector of jth residue in a sequence of length L, where $i \in 1, \ldots, M$ and M is the number of features considered. The lengths of the individual feature vectors $\mathbf{v}$ should be normalized by mapping onto a fixed-length interval K via $\{\mathbf{y}_k\}^i = f(\{\mathbf{v}_j\}^i)$, where the function f is defined by $f : \mathbb{R}^L \rightarrow \mathbb{R}^K$. The full feature vector for a particular protein A is constructed by concatenation of each feature $\mathbf{y}$; that is,

$$\{\varphi_A^+\} = \{\mathbf{y}_k\}^1 \oplus \{\mathbf{y}_k\}^2 \oplus \cdots \oplus \{\mathbf{y}_k\}^M, \tag{3.1}$$

where $\mathbf{a} \oplus \mathbf{b}$ indicates the concatenation of the vectors $\mathbf{a}$ and $\mathbf{b}$. A representation of an interacting pair is formed by concatenating the feature vectors for A and B.

$$\{\varphi_{AB}^+\} = \{\varphi_A^+\} \oplus \{\varphi_B^+\}. \tag{3.2}$$

The vector $\{\varphi_{AB}^+\}$ then becomes a positive training example for the SVM. The experimental results show that approximately four out of five potential interactions were correctly estimated by the system. In their subsequent work [43], Bock and Gough extended the prediction of interactions to the scale of full proteomes by using a phylogenetic bootstrap system.

Gomez et al. [127] proposed a probabilistic approach that learns dynamically from a large collection of data. In their attraction–repulsion model, the interaction between a pair of proteins is represented as the sum of attractive and repulsive forces associated with the features of each protein. The probability of an interaction network $G(V, E)$ is described as

$$P(G) = \prod_{(v_i, v_j) \in E} \hat{p}(v_i, v_j) \prod_{(v_i, v_j) \notin E} [1 - \hat{p}(v_i, v_j)], \tag{3.3}$$

where $\hat{p}(v_i, v_j)$ is the estimated individual edge probability between vertices v_i and v_j. They estimate the probability of observing an interaction between a pair of proteins, one of which has domain ϕ and the other domain ψ, by

$$\hat{p}(\phi, \psi) = \frac{n_{\phi\psi}^{+} + \Psi/2}{n_{\phi\psi}^{+} + \gamma n_{\phi\psi}^{-} + \Psi},$$ (3.4)

where $n_{\phi\psi}^{+}$ and $n_{\phi\psi}^{-}$ are, respectively, the number of times domain pair (ϕ, ψ) appears in interacting and noninteracting proteins. γ is a weighting coefficient such as

$$\gamma = \frac{|E|}{|V|(|V| - 1)/2 + |V| - |E|}.$$ (3.5)

A pseudocount, Ψ, is introduced to account for those instances in which there is an absence of observations, that is, $n_{\phi\psi}^{+} = n_{\phi\psi}^{-} = 0$. The attraction–repulsion model for PPIs is defined by taking the most informative domain–domain probability.

$$\hat{p}(v_i, v_j) = \arg\max |\hat{p}(\phi, \psi) - 0.5|.$$ (3.6)

This approach has the advantage of allowing the incorporation of both positive and negative information regarding interactions.

Many recent studies [115,159,177] have investigated the relationship between mRNA expression levels and PPIs. Jansen et al. [159] used two different methods to analyze two types of available expression data: normalized differences for absolute expression levels and correlation of profiles of relative expression levels. Their experimental results show that a strong corelation exists between expression levels and most permanent protein complexes. Based on this observation, Jansen et al. [160] proposed a Bayesian approach for the prediction of PPIs. The method allows the probabilistic combination of multiple data sets such as experimental interaction data, mRNA expression data, biological function, and essentiality. Figure 3–5 illustrates the process of combining data sources to achieve probabilistic interactomes. This approach assesses each source for interactions by comparison with samples of known positives and negatives, yielding a statistical measure of reliability. The likelihood of possible interactions for every protein pair is then predicted by combing each independent data source, weighted according to its reliability. The predictions were validated by tandem affinity purification (TAP) tagging experiments. It was observed that, at given levels of sensitivity, the predictions were more accurate than the existing high-throughput experimental data sets.

Finally, data-mining techniques that extract useful knowledge from large data sources can be applied to the prediction of interactions. Oyama et al. [236] employed an association rule discovery approach that supports knowledge discovery relating to PPIs. They selected seven features to characterize all yeast proteins: functional category, enzyme number, SWISS-PROT keyword, PROSITE motifs, bias of the amino acids, segment clusters, and amino acid pattern. The association rules of the interacting proteins, such as "proteins having feature 1 interact with proteins having feature 2," were then detected. As input to the experiment, they used the aggregated data from four different sources totaling 4,307 unique protein interaction pairs and derived 5,241 distinct features from the seven categories. After transforming the traditional protein-based transaction data into interaction-based transaction data,

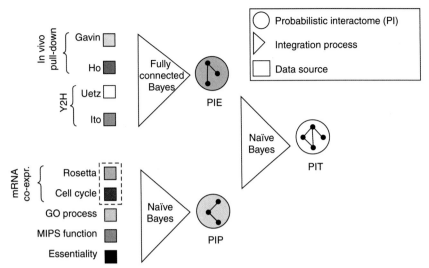

Figure 3–5 Bayesian approach to predicting interactions through the combination of multiple data sources. "(See Color Plate 1.)" (From [160]. Reprinted with permission from AAAS.)

they articulated 6,367 rules. The results confirmed the efficacy of predicting PPIs using data-mining techniques.

3.6 NETWORK TOPOLOGY-BASED APPROACHES

Experimentally determined PPIs in an organism have been used to construct a PPI network. The PPI network is represented as an undirected, unweighted graph $G(V, E)$ with proteins as a set of nodes V and interactions as a set of edges E. $N(v_i)$ denotes the neighbors of a node v_i, comprising a set of nodes connected to v_i. The degree of v_i is then equivalent to the number of neighbors of v_i, $|N(v_i)|$.

The PPI networks generated by known PPIs can be useful resources on which to base the prediction of new interactions or the identification of reliable interactions. Goldberg and Roth [125] proposed the use of topological measurements based on neighborhood cohesiveness. Their mutual clustering coefficients assume that two proteins are more likely to interact if they share many interacting neighbors. The properties of cohesive neighborhoods can be demonstrated in small-world networks; this topic will be addressed in Chapter 4. Figure 3–6 offers an illustration of the property of neighborhood cohesiveness in small-world networks. In Figure 3.6(a), the neighbors of a vertex v are more likely to be neighbors of each other (forming triangles) in a small-world network than in a random graph. In Figure 3.6(b), similarly, the two vertices v and w are more likely to have neighbors in common, also forming triangles. In this figure, the confidence of the interaction (v, w) is increased because they share several interaction partners. For the protein pairs v and w, the mutual clustering coefficient is defined as

$$\text{Jaccard Index:} \quad C_{vw} = \frac{|N(v) \cap N(w)|}{|N(v) \cup N(w)|},$$

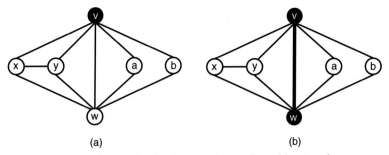

(a)   (b)

Figure 3–6 Neighborhood cohesiveness in small-world networks.

Meet/Min:
$$C_{vw} = \frac{|N(v) \cap N(w)|}{\min(|N(v)|, |N(w)|)},$$

Geometric:
$$C_{vw} = \frac{|N(v) \cap N(w)|^2}{|N(v)| \cdot |N(w)|},$$

Hypergeometric:
$$C_{vw} = -\log \sum_{i=|N(v) \cap N(w)|}^{\min(|N(v)|, |N(w)|)} \frac{\binom{|N(v)|}{i} \cdot \binom{T - |N(v)|}{|N(w)| - i}}{\binom{T}{|N(w)|}},$$

where T represents the total number of proteins in an organism. However, the mutual clustering coefficient measures only the directly interacting neighbors of two proteins without considering the entire complex network topology. Although the authors suggest that protein interactions could be given a confidence weighting instead of taking an "all-or-nothing" view, they do not use such a weighting when calculating these mutual clustering measurements. Instead, they simply treat each interaction as real.

Saito et al. [269] proposed an interaction generality measurement (IG1) based on the idea that interactions involving proteins that have many interacting partners are likely to be false positives but that highly interconnected sets of interactions or interactions forming a closed loop are likely to be true positives. The measurement is defined as the number of proteins that directly interact with a target protein pair, as reduced by the number of proteins interacting with more than one protein. Again, this is a local measurement that considers only the direct neighbors of a protein. In the authors' subsequent work [270], the measure was extended to incorporate the topological properties of interactions beyond the candidate interacting pairs. This extended interaction generality (IG2), illustrated in Figure 3–7, considers five possible topological relationships of a protein C with a candidate interacting pair (A, B) and measures the weighted sum of the five topological components with respect to C. The weights are assigned a priori by performing a principal component analysis on the entire PPI network.

Chen et al. [62] presented the interaction reliability by alternative path (IRAP) approach to measure the reliability of an interaction in terms of the strength of the alternative path. The reversed and normalized interaction generality values ($IG1(v, w)$, $v, w \in V$) are used as the initial edge weights to reflect the local reliability

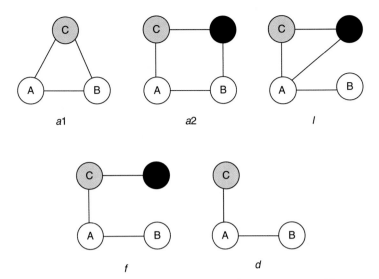

Figure 3–7 Five components of a protein C that interact with a target interacting protein pair (A, B). (This figure is reprinted from [270] with permission of Oxford University Press.)

of each interaction in a PPI network.

$$\text{weight}(v, w) = 1 - \left(\frac{\text{IG1}(v, w)}{\text{IG1}_{\max}} \right), \tag{3.7}$$

where $\text{IG1}_{\max}$ is the maximum interaction generality value among all the vertices in the network. The topological measure for the protein pair (v, w), denoted by $\text{IRAP}(v, w)$, is indicated by the collective reliability of the strongest alternative path of interactions connecting the two proteins in the underlying PPI network:

$$\text{IRAP}(v, w) = \max_{\phi \in \Phi(v, w)} \prod_{(x, y) \in \phi} \text{weight}(x, y), \tag{3.8}$$

where $\Phi(A, B)$ denotes the set of nonreducible paths between vertices v and w. The precision and robustness of this measurement is degraded by considering only the strongest nonreducible alternative path connecting two proteins, which is often an artifact of false positives in the PPI data.

As an alternative means for measuring interaction reliability, Pei and Zhang [245] took into account all possible paths between two proteins. They defined a k-length path strength for each path in a weighted interaction network model. The weight was calculated based on the frequency of each interaction across different databases. Details of their method with formulas will be discussed in Chapter 6.

A probabilistic weighted interaction network model was introduced in [19]. The Bayesian rule is adopted to estimate the posterior probability P^+ that a pair of proteins interact directly and stably; that is, they physically contact one another and are contained within the same protein complex.

$$P^+ = p(y = 1|\mathbf{z}) = \frac{\left(\prod_{i=1}^{T} p(z_i|y = 1)\right) \cdot (y = 1)}{\sum_{j \in \{0,1\}} \left(\left(\prod_{i=1}^{T} p(z_i|y = 1)\right) \cdot (y = 1)\right)}. \tag{3.9}$$

Here, $y = 1$ indicates that the pair of proteins interacts directly and stably, while $y = 0$ otherwise. The vector $\mathbf{z}$ represents the presence or absence of each type of interaction evidence, while T is the number of types of evidence, including two high-throughput Y2H experiments [155,307] and two high-throughput mass spectrometric experiments [113,144]. The reliability of a data set $p(y|z_i)$ is then estimated by optimizing the performance of the algorithm according to a training set of protein complexes. This method uses estimated reliability to maximize the performance of the algorithm instead of taking the initial reliability measure of the data set as input.

3.7 SUMMARY

This chapter has provided an overview of various approaches to the prediction of possible interactions between proteins. We have briefly discussed genomic-scale, sequence-based, structure-based, learning-based, and network-topology-based approaches. These methods have all made major contributions to codifying the PPI databases described in Chapter 2.

4

Basic Properties and Measurements of Protein Interaction Networks

4.1 INTRODUCTION

As discussed in Chapter 1, a protein–protein interaction (PPI) network refers to the sum of PPIs occurring among a set of related proteins. Such networks are typically represented by graphs, in which a set of nodes represents proteins and a set of edges, representing interactions, connects the nodes. Many recent research efforts have involved both empirical and theoretical studies of these PPI networks. Graph theories have been successfully applied to the analysis of PPI networks, and many graph and component measurements specific to this field have been introduced. This chapter will explore the basic terms and measurements used to characterize the graphic representation of the properties of PPI networks.

4.2 REPRESENTATION OF PPI NETWORKS

The computational investigation of PPI network mechanisms begins with a representation of the network structure. As mentioned earlier, the simplest representation takes the form of a mathematical graph consisting of nodes and edges [314]. Proteins are represented as nodes in such a graph; two proteins that interact physically are represented as adjacent nodes connected by an edge. We will first discuss a number of fundamental properties of these graphic representations prior to an exploration of the algorithms.

Graph. Proteins interact with each other to perform a specific cellular function or process. These interacting patterns form a PPI network that is represented by a graph $G = (V, E)$ with a set of nodes V and a set of edges E, where $E \subseteq V \times V$.

$$V \times V = \{(v_i, v_j) \mid v_i \in V, \ v_j \in V, \ i \neq j\}. \tag{4.1}$$

An edge $(v_i, v_j) \in E$ connects two nodes v_i and v_j. The vertex set and edge set of a graph are denoted by $V(G)$ and $E(G)$, respectively. Graphs can be directed or undirected. In directed graphs, each directed edge has a source and a destination vertex. In undirected graphs, the order of the incident vertices of an edge is immaterial, since the edges have no direction. Graphs can be weighted or unweighted; in the latter, each edge can have an associated real-value weight.

4.3 BASIC CONCEPTS

Degree. In an undirected graph, the degree (or connectivity) of a node is the number of other nodes with which it is connected [29]. This is the most elementary characteristic of a node. For example, in the undirected network graphed in Figure 4–1, node A has degree $k = 5$. Let $N(v_i)$ denote the neighbors of node v_i; that is the set of nodes connected to v_i. The degree $d(v_i)$of v_i is then equivalent to the number of neighbors of v_i, or $|N(v_i)|$.

In directed graphs, the out-degree of $v_i \in V$, denoted by $d^+(v_i)$, is the number of edges in E that have origin v_i. The in-degree of $v_i \in V$, denoted by $d^-(v_i)$, is the number of edges with destination v_i. For weighted graphs, all these concepts can be represented as the summation of corresponding edge weights.

Distance Path, Shortest Path, and Mean Path. Many relationships within a graph can be envisioned by means of conceptual "walks" and "paths." A walk is defined as a sequence of nodes in which each node is linked to its succeeding node. A path is a walk in which each node in the walk is distinct. In the path that starts from v_i, passes through v_k, and ends with v_j, $\langle v_i, v_k, v_j \rangle$, v_i and v_j are termed the source node and target node, respectively. The set of paths with source node v_i and target node v_j is denoted by $P(v_i, v_j)$. The length of a path is the number of edges in the sequence of the path. A shortest path between two nodes is the minimal-length path connecting the nodes. $SP(v_i, v_j)$ denotes the set of the distinct shortest paths between v_i and v_j. The distance between two nodes v_i and v_j is the length of the shortest path between them and is denoted by dist(v_i, v_j).

A graph $G' = (V', E')$ is a subgraph of the graph $G = (V, E)$ if $V' \subseteq V$ and $E' \subseteq E$. A *vertex-induced* subgraph is a vertex subset V' of a graph G together with any edges in edge subset E' whose end points are both in V'. The induced subgraph of $G = (V, E)$ with vertex subset $V' \subseteq V$ is denoted by $G[V']$. The *edge-induced* subgraph with edge subset $E' \subseteq E$, denoted by $G[E']$, is the subgraph $G' = (V', E')$ of G, where V' is the subset of V that are incident vertices of at least one edge in E'.

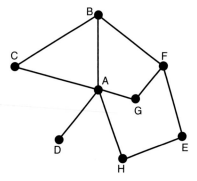

Figure 4–1 A graph in which node A has a degree of 5. (Adapted by permission from Macmillan Publishers Ltd: Nature [29], copyright 2004.)

Degree Distribution. Graph structures can be described according to numerous characteristics, including the distribution of path lengths, the number of cyclic paths, and various measures to compute clusters of highly connected nodes [314]. Barabasi and Oltvai [29] introduced the concept of degree distribution, $P(k)$, to quantify the probability that a selected node will have exactly k links. $P(k)$ is obtained by tallying the total number of nodes $N(k)$ with k links and dividing this figure by the total number of nodes N. Different network classes can be distinguished by the degree distribution. For example, a random network follows a Poisson distribution. By contrast, a scale-free network has a power-law degree distribution, indicating that a few hubs bind numerous small nodes. Most biological networks are scale-free, with degree distributions approximating a power law, $P(k) \sim k^{-\gamma}$. When $2 \leq \gamma \leq 3$, the hubs play a significant role in the network [29]. More details about the scale-free networks will be given later in this chapter.

4.4 BASIC CENTRALITIES

A comprehensive analysis of a complex network starts with an examination of fundamental elements such as vertices and edges. A variety of indices have been developed to quantify the importance of these elements in a graph. Since the introduction of centrality as the earliest of these indices, many extensions have been proposed on both the local and global levels, including degree centrality [256] and feedback centrality [275]. In this section, we will survey some of the more commonly used centrality measurements.

4.4.1 Degree Centrality

The degree centrality of a node, which is simply the degree $d(v)$ of a vertex v, is one of the most simple, useful, and widely applied topological indicators of the importance of vertices in a graph. Degree centrality in a directed graph can be further subdivided into in-degree centrality $d^-(v)$ and out-degree centrality $d^+(v)$ in a directed graph. Degree centrality is a local and static metric, since it considers only the directly connected neighbors of a vertex in a static state. Nonetheless, it serves as a useful indicator of the extent of attachment of a vertex to the graph.

4.4.2 Distance-Based Centralities

Many indices measure the importance of a component on the basis of distance between vertices in a graph. Since information flow in a graph can sometimes be estimated by examining the shortest paths among nodes, shortest paths can be used to measure the topological properties of a graph component. It should be noted, however, that limiting the measurement of information flow to shortest paths is excessively restrictive for a reasonable assessment of some real-world systems. The selection of a metric should be dependent on the nature of the system and the purpose of the analysis.

In the ensuing sections, we will discuss centrality measurements based on shortest paths and random paths. First, we will examine centralities derived from the set of shortest paths in a graph. Shortest-path-based centrality represents the quantity of information that might flow through a graph component under the assumption that the information in a graph travels only along the shortest paths. These centralities can be defined for both vertices and edges.

Stress Centrality. Stress centrality is the simple accumulation of a number of shortest paths between all vertex pairs in a graph that pass through a particular vertex. This index was developed to assist in determining the amount of "work" performed by each vertex in a network [279]. A vertex or an edge traversed by many shortest paths can be considered more central than other graph components.

$$C_S(v) = \sum_{s \neq t \neq v \in V} \rho_{st}(v), \tag{4.2}$$

where $\rho_{st}(v)$ denotes the number of shortest paths passing through v from source s to target t. In determining stress centrality, the shortest paths starting from v or ending at v itself are not included. The stress centrality of a vertex represents the workload the vertex carries in a graph.

Eccentricity. The eccentricity $e(v)$ of a vertex v is the greatest distance between v and any other vertex, $e(v)= \max\{\text{dist}(u, v): u \in V\}$, in a graph. The eccentricity of a vertex represents the distance of a vertex from the center of a graph. Thus, the center of G can be defined as the set of vertices that has minimal eccentricity in a graph. Hage et al. [135] defined a centrality measure as the reciprocal of the eccentricity

$$C_E(v) = \frac{1}{e(v)} = \frac{1}{\max\{\text{dist}(u, v): u \in V\}}. \tag{4.3}$$

Thus, this centrality value for the center of G will have the maximum quantity in the graph.

Closeness. Another centrality measure similar to eccentricity is closeness. Closeness is most simply defined as the reciprocal of the total distance from a vertex v to all the other vertices in a graph:

$$C_C(v) = \frac{1}{\sum_{u \in V} \text{dist}(u, v)}. \tag{4.4}$$

Closeness can also be measured as the mean shortest-path length from a vertex to all other vertices in a graph, thus assigning higher values to more central vertices. As a result, closeness indicates the nearness of a given vertex to the other vertices in a graph. Closeness can be regarded as a measure of the time needed for information to spread from a particular vertex to the others in the network [226]. A number of different closeness-based measures have been developed [36,49,229,268].

Shortest-Path-Based Betweenness Centrality. In [110], betweenness centrality was developed to address the inapplicability of some classical centrality measurements, such as closeness, to unconnected networks. Closeness measurements cannot be developed for disconnected graphs, since graph theory defines the distance between two disconnected vertices as infinity. Betweenness centrality excludes any vertex pair s and t that cannot be reached from the enumeration of shortest paths.

Betweenness centrality is defined as

$$C_B(v) = \sum_{s \neq t \neq v \in V} \frac{\rho_{st}(v)}{\rho_{st}}, \tag{4.5}$$

where ρ_{st} is the number of all shortest paths between vertex s and t, and $\rho_{st}(v)$ is the number of shortest paths passing through a node v out of ρ_{st}. The term inside the summation will be the ratio of the number of shortest paths passing through vertex v to the number of all shortest paths between s and t. Betweenness centrality is a semi-normalized version of stress centrality [110]. While stress centrality counts only the number of shortest paths between all vertex pairs in a graph that pass through a specific vertex, betweenness centrality measures the relative number of shortest paths passing through a vertex for all vertex pairs. Thus, this centrality metric represents the contribution a vertex v makes toward communication between all vertex pair s and t. This may be further normalized by dividing by the number of pairs of vertices that do not include v, that is $(n-1)(n-2)/2, n = |V|$.

4.4.3 Current-Flow-Based Centrality

Shortest-path-based centralities assume that the information in a graph travels only via shortest paths. In most real-world network systems, such a restrictive assumption may be inappropriate, as information may also travel through longer paths. The following section will introduce centrality indices based on electrical current flow theory that do not restrict information flow to the shortest paths.

Electrical Network. Current-flow-based centralities take as their model the flow of electrical current in a network. This model was introduced in [50,226], along with the method for calculating electrical current flow in a network using a matrix format. The current flow of a vertex i is defined as the amount of current that flows through i, averaged over all sources s and targets t. Let V be the voltage vector of an electrical network, for example, V_i is the voltage at vertex i in the network, measured relative to any convenient point. Kirchhoff's law of current conservation states that the total current flow in and out of any vertex is zero

$$\sum_j A_{ij}(V_i - V_j) = \delta_{is} - \delta_{it}, \tag{4.6}$$

where V_i is the voltage at vertex i in the voltage vector V and A_{ij} is an element of the adjacent matrix A as follows:

$$A_{ij} = \begin{cases} 1, & \text{if there is an edge between } i \text{ and } j, \\ 0, & \text{otherwise,} \end{cases} \tag{4.7}$$

and δ_{ij} is the Kronecker δ:

$$\delta_{ij} = \begin{cases} 1, & \text{if } i = j, \\ 0, & \text{otherwise.} \end{cases} \tag{4.8}$$

Noting that $\sum_j A_{ij} = d_i$, the degree of vertex i, we can write Equation (4.6) in matrix form as

$$(D - A) \cdot V = S, \tag{4.9}$$

where A is the adjacency matrix, V is the voltage vector, and D is the diagonal matrix with elements $D_{ii} = d_i$, and the source vector S has elements

$$S_i = \begin{cases} +1, & \text{for } i = s, \\ -1, & \text{for } i = t, \\ 0, & \text{otherwise.} \end{cases} \tag{4.10}$$

To calculate the voltage vector V, we need to solve the linear equation (4.9) for V. It should be noted that we cannot accomplish this by simply inverting the matrix $D - A$. This matrix, which is in the form of a Laplacian graph, is singular. As demonstrated by Newman in [226], removal of any equation from the system results in an invertible matrix. This operation is performed simply by measuring the voltages relative to the corresponding vertex. To illustrate, we would measure voltages relative to some vertex v and, additionally, remove the v_{th} equation from Equation (4.9) by deleting the v_{th} row of $D - A$. Since $V_v = 0$, we can also remove the v_{th} column, giving a square $(n - 1) \times (n - 1)$ matrix, which we denote $D_v - A_v$. Then

$$V = (D_v - A_v)^{-1} \cdot S. \tag{4.11}$$

The voltage of the one missing vertex v is zero. Matrix T is constructed by inserting the v_{th} row and column back into $(D_v - A_v)^{-1}$ and setting to zeros. Then, using Equation (4.10) and (4.11), the voltage at vertex i for source s and target t is given by

$$V_i^{(st)} = T_{is} - T_{it}. \tag{4.12}$$

The current flow passing through a vertex is the half of the currents coming from all incident edges to the vertex:

$$I_i^{(st)} = \frac{1}{2} \sum_j A_{ij} |V_i^{(st)} - V_j^{(st)}| = \frac{1}{2} \sum_j A_{ij} |T_{is} - T_{it} - T_{js} - T_{jt}|, \quad \text{for } i \neq s, t. \tag{4.13}$$

The current flow for the source and target vertices is exactly one unit:

$$I_s^{(st)} = 1, \quad I_t^{(st)} = 1. \tag{4.14}$$

A more detailed description of the electrical current model can be found in [50,226].

Current-Flow Betweenness Centrality. The current-flow betweenness of a vertex v is defined as the amount of current that flows through v in this setup, averaged over all vertex pairs s and t. The current-flow betweenness of a vertex v is the average of the current flow over all source–target pairs:

$$C_{CB}(v) = \frac{\sum_{s \neq t \in V} I_v^{(st)})}{\frac{1}{2}n(n-1)}, \tag{4.15}$$

where $n(n-1)/2$ is a normalizing constant, and $I_v^{(st)}$ is the current flow through node v between source s and sink t. Thus, current-flow betweenness measures the fraction of current flow passing through vertex v between all possible vertex pairs in the network.

A simple random walk from s to t is a walk traveling from source s to target t by taking random intermediate vertices. Current-flow betweenness is shown to be the same as random-walk betweenness [50,226]. In [226], Newman showed that current-flow betweenness and random-walk betweenness are synonymous.

Current-Flow Closeness Centrality. Using a similar technique, the closeness index based on shortest paths can also be transformed to a measure based on electrical current. For the electrical current model set forth in [50], Brandes et al. developed an alternative measure of the distance between two vertices s and t, which is defined as the difference of their electrical potentials. Current-flow closeness centrality is defined by

$$C_{CC}(s) = \frac{n-1}{\sum_{s \neq t} p_{st}(s) - p_{st}(t)} \quad \text{for all } s \in V, \tag{4.16}$$

where $(n-1)$ is a normalizing factor, $p_{st}(s)$ is the absolute electrical potential of vertex s based on the electrical current supply from vertex s to vertex t, and $p_{st}(s) - p_{st}(t)$ corresponds to the effective resistance typically measured as voltage, which can be interpreted as an alternative measure of distance between s and t. A more detailed description of electrical potential p can be found in [50].

Information Centrality. Stephenson and Zelen [290] devised the concept of information centrality. This index incorporates the set of all possible paths between two nodes weighted by an information-based value for each path that is derived from the inverse of its length. Information centrality C_I is defined by

$$C_I(s)^{-1} = nC_{ss}^I + \text{trace}(C^I) - \frac{2}{n}, \tag{4.17}$$

where $C^I = (L+J)^{-1}$ with Laplacian L and $J = 11^T$, and C_{ss}^I is the element on the s_{th} row and the s_{th} column in C^I. It measures the harmonic mean length of paths ending at a vertex s, which is smaller if s has many short paths connecting it to other vertices. Brandes and Fleischer showed that current-flow closeness centrality is equivalent to information centrality [50].

4.4.4 Random-Walk-Based Centrality

As noted previously, it may be unrealistic to assume that information travel in a network will be restricted to the shortest paths. Additionally, in some instances, it may not be possible for a vertex to detect the shortest paths because of the disconnectivity of the graph. Shortest-path-based approaches are not well-suited to such cases. A random-walk-based approach may provide a more realistic solution for these issues. In this approach, information travels via a random path from s to t by selecting the next traveling edge with random probability at each intermediate visiting vertex $i \neq t$. In this section, we will introduce random-walk-based centralities that calculate the importance of a network component on this basis.

Random-Walk Betweenness Centrality. The random-walk betweenness centrality introduced in [226] is based on the idea that information propagated from source s will travel through randomly chosen intermediate visiting nodes to target t. A random walk can be modeled by a discrete-time stochastic process. At initial time 0, vertex s propagates information to one of its neighbors using random probability. This random propagation continues until the target vertex t is encountered. Newman [226] and Brandes et al. [50] showed that random-walk betweenness is equivalent to current-flow betweenness.

Markov centrality. In [320], the centrality of a vertex was defined as the inverse of the mean first passage time (MFPT) in the Markov chain. The MFPT m_{st} from s to t is defined as the expected number of steps starting at node s taken until the first arrival at node t [176]:

$$m_{st} = \sum_{n=1}^{\infty} n f_{st}^{(n)}, \tag{4.18}$$

where n denotes the number of steps taken, and $f_{st}^{(n)}$ denotes the probability that the chain first returns to state t in exactly n steps. MFPTs not only have a natural Markov interpretation but also permit direct computation of a mean first passage matrix giving the MFPTs for all pairs of nodes [320]. The mean first passage matrix is given by

$$M = (I - Z + EZ_{dg})D, \tag{4.19}$$

where I is the identity matrix, and E is a matrix containing all ones. D is the diagonal matrix with elements $d_{vv} = 1/\pi(v)$, where $\pi(v)$ is the stationary distribution (in the Markov chain) of node v. Z is known as the fundamental matrix, and Z_{dg} agrees with Z on the diagonal but is 0 everywhere else. The fundamental matrix is defined as

$$Z = (I - A - e\pi^T)^{-1}, \tag{4.20}$$

where A is the Markov transition probability matrix, e is a column vector of all ones, and π is a column vector of the stationary probabilities for the Markov chain.

The Markov centrality index $C_M(v)$ uses the inverse of the average MFPTs to define the importance of node v

$$C_M(v) = \frac{n}{\sum_{s \in V} m_{sv}}, \tag{4.21}$$

where $n = |R|$, R is a given root set, and m_{st} is the MFPT from s to t. Markov centrality values for vertices show which vertex is closer to the center of mass. More central nodes can be reached from all other nodes in a shorter average time. A more detailed description of Markov centrality is available in [320].

Random-Walk Closeness Centrality. Markov centrality indicates the centrality of a vertex v in a network relative to other vertices. It represents the expected number of steps from v to all other vertices, expressed as an average distance from v to all other vertices, when information propagated from a source s travels via a random path to a target t. Therefore, Markov centrality can be viewed as a kind of random-walk closeness centrality.

4.4.5 Feedback-Based Centrality

Most complex real systems are dynamic, in that the network components are in a constant state of mutual influence and interaction. Static analysis of a network can provide only a limited and local view of such a complex system. To address this inadequacy, feedback centralities take into account the influences among components by iteratively measuring their importance. In feedback centrality, a node becomes more central in tandem with the centrality of its neighbors. Such analyses, which measure the importance of network components, arose initially in the social sciences in the 1950s. The first three measurements discussed below were among those developed to analyze social networks. The last two metrics to be discussed here, PageRank and HITS, were developed to measure the importance of pages in a network that is the set of linked pages in the World Wide Web (WWW). They have subsequently been successfully applied to biological systems. As we will see, all feedback centralities are expressed in a matrix format and determine the importance of components by solving linear systems. Furthermore, most feedback centrality indices are variants of eigenvector centrality.

Katz Status Index. One of the first ventures into the application of the feedback concept was presented by Leo Katz [174] in 1953. The Katz index is a weighted number of walks starting from a given vertex. Each walk is weighted inversely according to its length, that is, a long indirect walk has less weight than a short direct walk. Katz developed the index after observing that consideration of only the direct relationships of a component is insufficient to provide an effective index of importance. Therefore, he also incorporated the indirect influence of distant connected components, as attenuated by their remoteness from the component of interest. The Katz index therefore assigns a high weight to a vertex v that has few direct neighbors but is connected more remotely to highly influential vertices.

To take the distance between a vertex pair into account, a damping factor $\alpha > 0$ is used to weight a walk inversely to its length. The Katz status index is defined by

$$C_K = \sum_{k=1}^{\infty} \alpha^k (A^T)^k \overrightarrow{1},$$ (4.22)

where A is the adjacency matrix of the network, $\overrightarrow{1}$ is the n-dimensional vector in which every entry is 1, and α is a damping factor. We need to restrict α in order to guarantee convergence of Equation (4.22).

Hubbell Index. Hubbell [146] introduced a centrality measurement similar to the eigenvector index (to be discussed below), which is based on the solution of a system of linear equations. This centrality value is defined by means of a weighted and loop-allowed network. The weighted adjacency matrix W of a network G is asymmetric and contains real-valued weights for each edge.

$$C_H = E + W C_H,$$ (4.23)

where $W = (w_{ij})$ is the $n \times n$ adjacency matrix of the network. The column vector C_H is the pattern of status scores $(s_1, s_2, \ldots, s_n)$, and the column vector E is the pattern of exogenous inputs $(e_1, e_2, \ldots, e_n)$. The latter are often referred to as the boundary conditions of the system [146]. If the boundary condition is unknown, $E = \overrightarrow{1}$ may be used. The solution C_H of the above equation is termed Hubbell centrality or the Hubbell Index.

Eigenvector Centrality. Bonacich proposed an approach based on the eigenvectors of adjacency matrices of a graph [46]. It scores the relative importance of all nodes in the network by weighting connections to highly important nodes more than connections to nodes of low importance. As graph G is undirected and loop-free, the adjacency matrix A is symmetric, and all diagonal entries are 0. Eigenvector centrality can be computed by finding the principal eigenvector of the adjacency matrix A.

$$\lambda C_{IV} = A C_{IV},$$ (4.24)

where C_{IV} is a eigenvector. In general, there will be many different eigenvalues λ for which an eigenvector solution exists. However, the additional requirement that all the entries in the eigenvector be positive implies (by the Perron–Frobenius theorem) that only the largest eigenvalue will generate the desired centrality measurement [228]. The ith component of this eigenvector then gives the centrality score of the ith node in the network.

Bargaining Centrality. The feedback centralities introduced to this point have considered only positive feedback. In positive-feedback centralities, the centrality of a vertex is higher if it is connected to other important vertices. Bonacich [47] proposed a feedback centrality that also incorporates negative feedback. For example, in a communication network, positive feedback is relevant because the amount of information available to a component in the network is positively related to the amount of information available to connected components. However, in bargaining situations, it is advantageous to be connected to those who have few options; power comes from being connected to those who are powerless [47]. Being connected to powerful people who have many competitive trading partners weakens one's own bargaining power. Bargaining centrality is defined in matrix form by

$$C_{\mathrm{Bar}} = \alpha(I - \beta A)^{-1} A \vec{1}, \tag{4.25}$$

where α is a scaling factor, β is the influence parameter, A is the adjacency matrix, and $\vec{1}$ is the n-dimensional vector in which every entry is 1.

The parameter α is simply a scaling factor. α is selected so that $\sum_{i=1}^{n} C_{\mathrm{Bar}}(i)^2 = n$, the squared length of $c(\alpha, \beta)$, equals the number of vertices in the network. The second parameter β can be controlled according to the semantics of network relationships. A positive or negative β value can be chosen to represent positive or negative influence, respectively. The choice $\beta = 0$ leads to a trivial centrality where only information regarding direct neighbors is used; larger values will consider a larger range of components. If $\beta > 0$, C_{Bar} is a conventional centrality measurement in which the status of each vertex is positively related to the statuses of the connected vertices. A negative value for β reflects the weakened status of a vertex that accrues from the higher status of directly neighboring vertices in a bargaining situation. The magnitude of β should reflect the degree to which authority or communication is transmitted locally or globally throughout the network as a whole. Small values of β give more weight to the local structure, whereas large values are more cognizant of the position of individuals at the global level. Therefore, a person can be powerful if he or she is in contact with trading partners who have no options or if his or her other optional trading partners themselves also have many other options [47].

PageRank. PageRank [53] is a link analysis algorithm that scores the relative importance of Web pages in a hyperlinked Web network, such as the WWW, using eigenvector analysis. PageRank was developed by Larry Page and Sergey Brin as part of a research project about a search engine. The PageRank of a Web page is defined recursively; a page has a high importance if it has a large number of incoming links from highly important Web pages. PageRank also can be viewed as a probability distribution of the likelihood that a random surfer will arrive at any particular page at certain time.

$$C_{PR}(v) = (1 - d) + d(C_{PR}(t_1)/C(t_1) + \cdots + C_{PR}(t_n)/C(t_n)), \tag{4.26}$$

where $t_i, i = 1, \ldots n$, are the Web pages that point to page v, $C(v)$ is the number of links originated at page v, and d is the damping factor ($d \in [0, 1]$). The PageRank corresponds to the principal eigenvector of the normalized adjacent matrix of the Web. Therefore, PageRank can be viewed as a variant of eigenvector centrality.

Hypertext Induced Topic Selection (HITS). HITS is a link analysis algorithm that rates Web pages for their authority and hub values in a Web page network such as the WWW. Kleinberg introduced the idea of scoring Web pages on the basis of a mutually reinforcing hub and authority relationship. A strong hub is a page that points to many valid authorities; a valid authority is a page that is pointed to by many strong hubs [183]. Authority and hub values are calculated by mutual recursion algorithms. The authority value of a page is defined as the sum of the hub values pointing to that page; similarly, the hub value of a page is defined as the sum of the authority values of the pages linked from that page.

HITS is an iterative algorithm; in its first phase, the search space is reduced based on a search query, and, in the second phase, the hub and authority values are measured within the link structure of the reduced network.

In the first phase of the algorithm, an appropriate subgraph $G[V_\sigma]$ is extracted for a given search query σ, where

- V_σ is relatively small,
- V_σ is rich in relevant pages for the search query σ, and
- V_σ contains most (or many) of the strongest authorities.

The second phase of the algorithm iteratively calculates the hub and authority scores for the Web pages in $G[V_\sigma]$ based on the mutually reinforcing relationship between hubs and authorities. Two iterative operations are defined to update hub and authority values for a Web page:

$$C_{\text{hub}}(p) \longleftarrow \sum_{q:(q,p)\in E} C_{\text{auth}}(q), \tag{4.27}$$

$$C_{\text{auth}}(p) \longleftarrow \sum_{q:(q,p)\in E} C_{\text{hub}}(q), \tag{4.28}$$

where $C_{\text{hub}}(p)$ is a nonnegative authority weight, and $C_{\text{auth}}(p)$ is a nonnegative hub weight for page p. The first and second operations update the authority and hub values for a page, respectively.

4.5 CHARACTERISTICS OF PPI NETWORKS

Small-World Property. PPI networks are highly dynamic and structurally complex. They are thus characterized by the inherent properties of complex systems [5,227,293]. Additionally, PPI networks manifest the properties of small-world networks, meaning that the average shortest-path length between any two nodes in a network is relatively small. In small-word networks, all nodes can be reached quickly from any node via a few hops to its immediate neighbors.

Watts and Strogatz [319] have investigated this phenomenon through experimenting with the random reconnection of a regular network. They have found that the subnetworks in the middle of either a regular network or a random network are

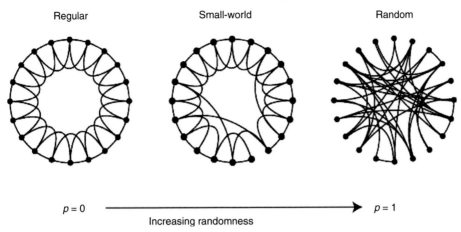

Figure 4–2 Random reconnection procedure of a regular ring graph. (Reprinted by permission from Macmillan Publishers Ltd: Nature [319], copyright 1998.)

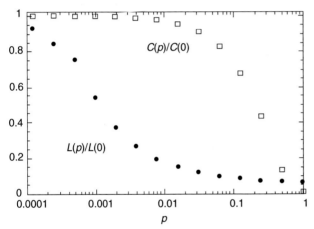

Figure 4–3 The average clustering coefficient $C(p)$ and the average shortest path length $L(p)$ of graphs during the random reconnection procedure with various probabilities p. (Reprinted by permission from Macmillan Publishers Ltd: Nature [319], copyright 1998.)

highly clustered and have short average path lengths between nodes. The procedure for random reconnection of a regular graph is illustrated in Figure 4–2. The procedure starts with a regular ring graph with 20 nodes and four directly connected neighbors for each node. A node and the edge that connects it to its neighbor are chosen, and the edge is reconnected to another node chosen uniformly at random, with probability p. By repeating this process, a disordered random graph is obtained for $p = 1$. For the value of p between 0 and 1, the graph becomes a small-world network. Like a regular graph, it is highly clustered, but it has short path lengths like a random graph. Figure 4–3 illustrates the changes in average shortest path length $L(p)$ and average clustering coefficient $C(p)$ of graphs generated using different probabilities p.

Table 4.1 Statistics for Currently-Available Yeast PPI Networks		
Properties	**DIP**	**MIPS**
Number of proteins	4823	4567
Number of interactions	17471	15470
Density*	0.0015	0.0015
Degree distribution (γ in power law)	1.77	1.64
Average shortest path length	4.14	4.43
Average clustering coefficient*	0.2283	0.2878
* See Chapter 5 for the definitions of density and clustering coefficient.		

As p increases, $L(p)/L(0)$ drops rapidly, while $C(p)/C(0)$ temporarily plateaus at its highest value. As a result, a small-world network with high clustering coefficients (see Chapter 5 for the definition of clustering coefficient) and short path lengths can be detected when p is around 0.01. These small-world characteristics have been observed in many real social and biological networks, including PPI networks.

Yeast PPI networks demonstrate these characteristics. The average shortest path length and average clustering coefficient for these networks extracted from the DIP [271] and MIPS [214] databases are shown in Table 4.1. Although both networks are large and very sparse, with more than 4,500 nodes, the average value of the shortest path lengths between all possible node pairs is very small, at ~4.

Scale-Free distribution. Another special property of PPI networks is their scale-free distribution [29]. Their degree distribution, which refers to the probability that a given node will be of degree k, is approximated by a power law $P(k) \sim k^{-\gamma}$. A scale-free network will have a few high-degree hub nodes, while most nodes will have only a few connections. The structure and dynamics of these networks are independent of the network size as measured by the number of nodes in the network.

Barabasi and Albert [28] have proposed that scale-free networks be defined by two important features, growth and preferential attachment. Networks are continuously expanded by the addition of new nodes with a connection to the nodes already present. As a preferential attachment, the new nodes are likely to be linked to high-degree nodes. Since their topological structure is characterized by a few ultra-high-degree nodes and abundant low-degree nodes, scale-free networks are robust to random attacks but can be vulnerable to a targeted attack on the hubs [7]. Scale-free networks do not possess an inherent modularity, so the average clustering coefficient is somewhat independent [29]. A schematic representation of a scale-free network, a typical degree distribution, and the average clustering coefficients with respect to degree are illustrated in Figure 4–4(b).

Recent studies [161] have examined scale-free distributions in PPI networks. The γ values in the power-law degree distributions of currently available yeast PPI networks are estimated in Table 4.1. These values indicate that the networks follow the scale-free model.

Maslov and Sneppen [211] have observed a disassortativity pattern in PPI networks. Highly connected hub nodes are infrequently linked to each other. This

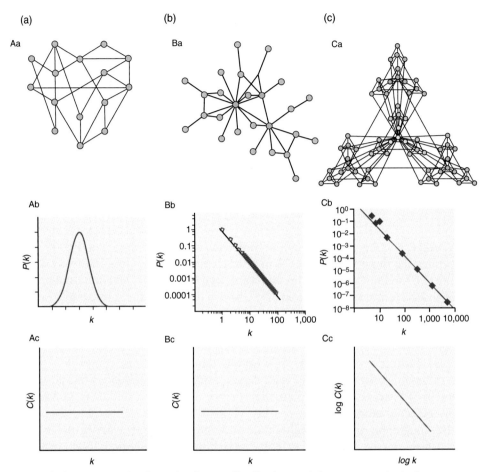

Figure 4–4 A schematic view, the degree distribution and the average clustering coefficient of a random network (a), a scale-free network (b), and a hierarchical network (c). "See Color Plate 2." (Reprinted by permission from Macmillan Publishers Ltd: Nature [29], copyright 2004.)

topological pattern is in contrast to the assortativity nature of social networks, in which well-connected people tend to have direct connections to each other.

Modular and Hierarchical Network. The properties discussed earlier suggest two important topological issues in the analysis of PPI networks: modularity and the presence of hubs. A module in a PPI network is a region with dense internal connections and sparse external interconnections to other regions. Assuming that a PPI network is composed of a collection of modules, we can categorize nodes in the network as *modular nodes*, *peripheral nodes*, and *interconnecting nodes*. Modular nodes are those nodes that form the core of a module. They have a relatively high degree of connectivity to members of the same module. Peripheral nodes are trivial nodes with a low degree of connectivity. They are linked to modular nodes or to the other peripheral nodes in the same module. Interconnecting nodes are connected to the nodes in other modules. We define the edge that connects two nodes in different modules

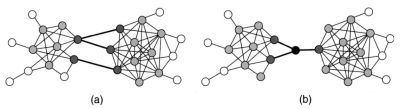

Figure 4–5 Examples of modular networks composed of two modules. (a) Five dark gray nodes represent *interconnecting nodes*. Light gray and white nodes are *modular nodes* and *peripheral nodes*, respectively. Three thick edges are *bridges* connecting two modules. (b) A black node represents *bridging nodes*. Three dark gray nodes are *interconnecting nodes*, and three thick edges are *bridges* connecting from the *bridging node* to each module.

as a *bridge*, and the end nodes of the bridge as *interconnecting nodes*. Figure 4–5(a) illustrates the three types of nodes in a simple network composed of two modules. While two modules are often directly connected by a bridge, an additional bridging node maybe located in the middle of the bridge to support the interconnection. The bridging node is therefore linked to two or more interconnecting nodes located in different modules, as shown in Figure 4–5(b).

The existence of modular structures can be verified by the presence of high average clustering coefficients, which imply that the network comprises a collection of modules. Since hubs are high-degree nodes, a small number of hubs can be found in PPI networks with a power-law degree distribution, and these hubs mainly interconnect to modules.

Building upon this observed module-and-hub structure, Ravasz et al. [261] proposed the hierarchical network model. The architecture of this model is characterized by scale-free topology with embedded modularity. In this model, a few hub nodes are emphasized as the determinants of survival during network perturbation and as the backbone of the hierarchical structure. This model suggests that low-degree nodes are connected to form a small module. A core node within the module interconnects not only with the cores of other small modules but also with a higher-degree node, which, in turn, becomes the core of a larger module consisting of a group of the small modules. By repeating these steps, a hierarchy of modules is structured through the hubs. The degree distribution of hierarchical networks is similar to that of scale-free networks, showing locally disordered effects within modules. However, unlike scale-free networks, the pattern of clustering coefficients in hierarchical networks has an inverse relationship to degree [29]. Therefore, low-degree nodes are clustered better than high-degree nodes, since low-degree nodes are intraconnected within a module, whereas high-degree nodes are typically interconnected between modules. A schematic view of a hierarchical network, degree distribution, and the average clustering coefficients with respect to degree are illustrated in Figure 4–4(c).

The modular and hierarchical network models can reasonably be applied to PPI networks because cellular functionality is typically envisioned as having a hierarchical structure. Extracting these structures from PPI networks may provide valuable information regarding cellular function.

4.6 SUMMARY

This chapter has introduced a graph-based representation for PPI networks and provided a detailed discussion of the basic properties of such graphs. The centrality indices presented will serve as the basis for the an exploration of topological network analysis in the upcoming chapters. As noted, PPI networks have been identified as modular and hierarchical in nature. These properties will be further discussed in the following two chapters. (Some of the material in this chapter is reprinted from [200] with permission of John Wiley & Sons, Inc.)

Modularity Analysis of Protein Interaction Networks

5.1 INTRODUCTION

The component proteins within protein–protein interaction (PPI) networks are associated in two types of groupings: *protein complexes* and *functional modules*. Protein complexes are assemblages of proteins that interact with each other at a given time and place, forming a single multimolecular machine. Functional modules consist of proteins that participate in a particular cellular process while binding to each other at various times and places. The detection of these groupings, known as modularity analysis, is an area of active research. In particular, the graphic representation of PPI networks has facilitated the discrimination of protein clusters through data-mining techniques.

The methods of data mining can be applied to identify various aspects of network organization. For example:

- Proteins located at neighboring positions in a graph are generally considered to share functions ("guilt by association"). On this basis, the functions of a protein may be predicted by examining the proteins with which it interacts and the protein complexes to which it belongs.
- Densely connected subgraphs in the network are likely to form protein complexes that function as single units in a particular biological process.
- Investigation of network topological features can shed light on the biological system [29]. For example, networks may be scale-free, governed by the power law, or of various sizes.

A *cluster* is a set of objects that share some common characteristics. *Clustering* is the process of grouping data objects into sets (clusters); objects within a cluster demonstrate greater similarity than do objects in different clusters. In a PPI network, these sets will be either protein complexes or functional modules. Clustering differs from classification; in the latter, objects are assigned to predefined classes, while clustering defines the classes themselves. Thus, clustering is an unsupervised classification method and does not rely on a training step to place the data objects in predefined classes. Clustering of PPI networks can lead to various analytical insights, including:

- clarification of PPI network structures and their component relationships;
- inference of the principal function of each cluster from the functions of its members; and
- elucidation of the possible functions of cluster members through comparison with the functions of other members.

In this chapter, we will first introduce several basic measurements used to conceptualize and quantify the overall modular topology of a network. We will then present a range of computational approaches for the detection of highly correlated modules.

5.2 USEFUL METRICS FOR MODULAR NETWORKS

As discussed in Chapter 4, many real-world networks, including PPI networks, tend to be modular. Components in a modular network may be grouped by their common properties to explain significant underlying principles. A hierarchical network can be further divided into several subcommunities with some common characteristics. It has also been noted that proteins in PPI networks rarely act alone. Proteins aggregate into protein complexes or functional modules that act as cohesive components of a molecular function. Identification of highly correlated modules should be cognizant of the topological properties and relational semantics among components in a particular domain of the network. The following sections will introduce some common metrics that are used to quantify particular components of a network.

5.2.1 Cliques

A *clique* within a graph is an induced complete subgraph, with constituent vertices that are completely connected to each other. In the algorithm point of view, the identification of all cliques in a graph is very hard since the enumeration of all cliques of a given size k must be considered.

A *maximum clique* is the largest clique among all cliques in a graph G. Finding the maximum clique in a graph is known to be an NP-complete problem [172]. Several faster methods for approximation have been introduced [26,54,58,111].

In a clique, each member shares edges with every other member. A clique C is a *maximal clique* in a graph $G = (V, E)$ if and only if there is no clique C' in G with $C \subset C'$. Alternatively stated, a maximal clique is a complete subgraph that is not contained within any other complete subgraph. The largest maximal clique is the maximum clique. Enumerative algorithms for the identification of cliques were introduced in [45,136,291]. Identification of cliques in most real-world networks can be quickly accomplished in polynomial time, since networks are typically very sparsely connected.

5.2.2 Cores

A *k-core* is a subnetwork of the PPI network within which each protein is connected to at least k proteins of this subnetwork. The concept of k-cores was introduced by Seidman [277] and Bollobas [44] for the purpose of network analysis and visualization. Batagelj et al. defined the k-core in [34] as follows: given a graph $G = (V, E)$, the k-core is an induced subgraph created by removing all vertices and their incident edges with degrees less than k. The vertex v will be also pruned if the degree of vertex v is less than k after removal of all direct neighbors with degrees less than k.

This operation can facilitate the examination of certain properties and the visualization of graphs. For example, the sequence of vertices in sequential coloring can be determined by the descending order of their core numbers. Cores can also be used to localize the search for interesting subnetworks within large networks [34]. The cohesiveness of a graph can be also analyzed through the k-core of a graph. An induced k-core subgraph in a graph G reveals that at least k paths are present between any two pairs of vertices of G.

The *density*, den(G), of G is defined as

$$\text{den}(G) = \frac{2m}{n(n-1)}, \tag{5.1}$$

where n is the number of vertices, and m is the number of edges in graph G.

The density of a graph is the ratio of the number of edges present in a graph to the possible number of edges in a complete graph of the same size. In many real applications, identification of a subgraph of a certain density permits effective examination of the network on both the global and local levels.

5.2.3 Degree-Based Index

The simplest and most commonly used index is based on the degree distribution of vertices. The distribution or average degree measurement is frequently used to visualize the fundamental connectivity of a graph.

The degree distribution $P(k)$, that is, the probability that a selected node will have degree k, of a random graph G is expected to follow the Poisson distribution:

$$P(k) = \frac{(np)^k}{k!} e^{-np}, \tag{5.2}$$

where n is the number of vertices. It has been observed that many real-world network systems follow a power-law degree distribution:

$$P(k) = ck^{-\gamma}, \quad \gamma > 0 \text{ and } c > 0, \tag{5.3}$$

where c is a scaling constant, and γ is a constant exponent. A power-law degree distribution indicates that the probability of finding a highly connected node decreases exponentially with its own degree, which is the number of edges incident to the node. Simply stated, there are many low-degree and few high-degree nodes. Studies of real-world networks, including PPI networks, as discussed in Chapter 4, have shown that $2 \leq \gamma \leq 3$ [6,28,104].

5.2.4 Distance (Shortest Paths)-Based Index

Several metrics characterize a network on the basis of the distance between vertices. The *Wiener index W* is the oldest molecular-graph-based structure-descriptor [321]. It consists of a simple summation of the distances between all vertex pairs, as follows:

$$W(G) = \sum_{u \neq v \in V} \text{dist}(u, v). \tag{5.4}$$

The compactness of a graph G increases as the total distance decreases. In [321], Wiener performed a cross analysis between the total distance of a molecular graph and the boiling point of the molecule that revealed a similar inverse correlation between compactness and boiling point.

The *average path length* APL(G) is the mean of the lengths of the shortest paths between all vertex pairs in a graph G:

$$\text{APL}(G) = \frac{\sum_{u \neq v \in V} \text{dist}(u, v)}{\frac{1}{2}(n^2 - n)}. \tag{5.5}$$

Since shortest paths are well defined only for connected vertex pairs, this index requires management of disconnected components in a manner appropriate to the semantics of each application.

The concept of *reachability* indicates the remoteness of a given vertex from other vertices in a graph. As defined in Chapter 4, the *eccentricity* $e(u)$ of a vertex u is the greatest distance between u and any other vertices, $e(u) = \max\{\text{dist}(u, v) : v \in V\}$. The *radius* rad$(G)$ is the smallest eccentricity value of all vertices:

$$\text{rad}(G) = \min\{e(u) | u \in V\}. \tag{5.6}$$

The *diameter* diam(G) of a graph G is defined as the longest distance value between two arbitrary vertices:

$$\text{diam}(G) = \max\{e(u) | u \in V\}. \tag{5.7}$$

These indices illustrate the extent of scatter or degree of compactness of a graph. A network with a low reachability value will be tightly packed, and any component will be reachable within a small number of steps.

5.3 METHODS FOR CLUSTERING ANALYSIS OF PROTEIN INTERACTION NETWORKS

Clustering proteins on the basis of their protein interaction profiles provides an explorative analysis of the data. Clustering seeks to identify groups of proteins that are more likely to interact with each other than with proteins outside the group. It has been found that proteins can be effectively clustered into these interaction-based groups using computational methods [200]. Considering the large number of proteins and the high complexity of a typical network, decomposition into smaller, more manageable modules is a valuable step toward analysis of biological processes and pathways. Since, as noted, protein clusters may reflect functional modules and biological processes, the function of uncharacterized proteins may be predicted by an examination of other proteins within the same cluster.

There are many different types of clustering approaches available for modularization of PPI networks. An overview of these methods will be presented in the following sections, and ensuing chapters will provide detailed discussion of each.

5.3.1 Traditional Clustering Methods

As noted earlier, clustering can be defined as the grouping of objects in a network based on the similarity of their topological or other natural properties. A variety of graph-theoretic approaches have been employed for identifying functional modules in PPI networks. Following traditional data-mining concepts, graph clustering approaches can be classified as density-based, hierarchical, or partition-based.

Density-based clustering approaches search for densely connected subgraphs. A typical example is the maximum clique algorithm [286] for detecting fully connected, complete subgraphs. To overcome the high level of stringency imposed by this algorithm, relatively dense (rather than complete) subgraphs can be identified by setting a density threshold or optimizing an objective density function [56,286]. A variety of algorithms using alternative density functions have been proposed, including computing the density of k-cores [24], finding k-clique percolation [87,238], tracking the density and periphery of each neighbor [12], and statistically measuring the quality of subgraphs [247]. Recently, several density-based approaches have attempted to uncover overlapping clusters [238,347]. Density-based clustering methods can detect densely connected groups of proteins within a PPI network. However, they are unable to partition entire networks, which, as indicated by the power-law degree distribution, are heavily populated by sparsely connected nodes. These sparse connections decrease the density of clusters, and the relatively isolated nodes are excluded from the clusters generated by density-based methods.

Hierarchical clustering approaches are applicable to biological networks because of the hierarchical nature of their modularity [261,297], as discussed in Chapter 4. These approaches iteratively merge nodes or recursively divide a graph into two or more subgraphs. Iterative merging entails the measurement of the similarity or distance between two nodes or two groups of nodes and the selection of a pair to be merged in each iteration [17,263]. Recursive division involves the selection of the nodes or edges to be cut from the graph. For this purpose, betweenness is an appropriate index to detect the bridges among modules in a network. As defined in Chapter 4, the betweenness of a node or an edge is the sum of the ratio of the number of shortest paths passing through the node or edge to the number of all shortest paths. Iterative elimination of the node or edge with the highest betweenness divides a graph into two or more subgraphs [122,145]. The division can be recursively performed to find modules of a desired size.

Partition-based clustering approaches seek a network partition that accounts for all sparsely connected nodes. One of these approaches, the Restricted Neighborhood Search Clustering (RNSC) algorithm [180], identifies the best partition using a cost function. It starts with random partition of a network and iteratively moves the nodes on the border of a cluster to an adjacent cluster with a goal of decreasing the total cost of clusters. For optimal performance, however, this method requires prior knowledge of the exact number of clusters in a network.

There are additional clustering methods that do not fall within these three major categories. A variety of distance-based approaches will be discussed in Chapter 7. The Markov clustering (MCL) algorithm, presented in detail in Chapter 8, finds clusters using iterative rounds of expansion and inflation that, respectively, promote the strongly connected regions and weaken the sparsely connected regions [308]. Line graph generation [250], also discussed in Chapter 8, transforms the network of proteins connected by interactions into a network of connected interactions and then uses the MCL algorithm to cluster the interaction network.

Such traditional clustering approaches are useful for the global analysis of protein interaction networks. However, their accuracy is limited by the unreliability of interaction data and the complexity of connectivity among modules.

5.3.2 Nontraditional Clustering Methods

In addition to the traditional approaches summarized above, many new clustering methods have been developed for the analysis of PPI networks. In this book, we have classified these approaches into the following categories:

- *Distance-based methods*: These approaches begin by defining the distance or similarity between two proteins in the network, with this distance/similarity matrix then serving as input to traditional clustering algorithms. A variety of distance and similarity measures have been proposed to ensure that the identified modules are biologically meaningful. These measures are based on particular biological characteristics such as protein or gene sequence, protein structure, gene expression, and degree of confidence in an interaction based on frequency of experimental detection. Examples of these metrics include sequence similarity, structural similarity, and the gene expression correlation of the two incident proteins in each interaction. These methods will be discussed in more detail in Chapter 7.
- *Topology-based methods*: These approaches utilize the special topological features of PPI networks, including their scale-free nature, modularity, and hierarchical structure, to formulate modularization algorithms. Typically, these methods first define metrics to quantitatively measure the topological features of interest and then formulate clustering algorithms for modularity analysis. In Chapter 6, we will focus particularly on one such metric, bridging centrality, and its application to modularity analysis.
- *Graph-theoretic methods*: These approaches utilize the methodology of graph theory and convert the process of clustering a PPI network into a graph-theoretical problem. Like topological-based methods, these approaches also take into consideration either the local topology or the global structure of PPI networks. Methods of this type will be discussed in Chapter 8.
- *Flow-based methods*: These approaches offer a novel strategy for analyzing the degree of biological and topological influence exerted by each protein over other proteins in a PPI network. Through simulation of biological or functional flows within the network, these methods seek to model and predict complex network behavior under a realistic variety of external stimuli. They require

sophisticated methods to effectively simulate the stochastic behavior of the system. In Chapter 9, techniques used by these methods will be detailed. We will discuss the compilation of information regarding protein function, the creation and use of a weighted PPI network, and the simulation of the flow of information from each informative protein through the entire weighted interaction network. We will explore the modeling of a PPI network as a dynamic signal transduction system, with each protein acting as a perturbation of the system.

■ *Methods involving knowledge integration*: Clustering approaches can be broadly categorized as supervised, unsupervised, and semi-supervised according to the extent of expert knowledge used in the clustering process. The various methods mentioned above are considered unsupervised, as they simply cluster proteins on the basis of network properties, without any input of additional information. Semi-supervised and fully supervised methods integrate domain knowledge into the clustering process to improve performance. Chapter 11 will present examples of supervised methods that integrate Gene Ontology (GO) [18,302] annotations into the clustering analysis of PPI networks.

5.4 VALIDATION OF MODULARITY

The identification of functional modules within an annotated PPI network can serve as a first step toward the prediction of the functions of unannotated proteins in the network. Chapters 6 and 7 will discuss the details of approaches to the identification of these functional modules. Issues of accuracy assume paramount importance, as disparate results can be generated both by different approaches and by the repeated application of a given approach with different parameters. Therefore, these solutions must be carefully compared with predicted results in order to select the approach and parameters that provide the best outcome. Validation is the process of evaluating the performance of the clustering or prediction results derived from different approaches. This section will introduce several basic techniques used to validate proteomic clustering results.

A survey performed by Jiang et al. [162] of methods for clustering gene expression data revealed three main components to cluster validation: an intuitive assessment of cluster quality, the evaluation of performance based on ground truth, and an assessment of the reliability of the cluster sets. These components are also relevant to the evaluation of clustering performance in proteomics. First, the quality of clusters can be measured in terms of homogeneity and separation on the basis of the definition of a cluster: objects within a cluster are similar to each other, while objects in different clusters are dissimilar. The second aspect of validation involves comparison with some ground truth pertaining to the clusters. The ground truth may be derived from some element of domain knowledge, such as known function families or the localization of proteins. Cluster validation is based on the agreement between clustering results and this ground truth. Validation of the modularity analysis of PPI networks relies principally on this component. The third aspect of cluster validity focuses on the reliability of the clusters, or the likelihood that the cluster structure has not arisen by chance.

5.4.1 Clustering Coefficient

The clustering coefficient of a vertex in a graph measures the extent of the interconnectivity between the direct neighbors of the vertex and is the ratio of the number of edges between the nodes in its direct neighborhood to the number of edges that could possibly exist among them. In many networks, if node A is connected to B and B is connected to C, then A has a high probability of direct linkage to C. Watts and Strogatz [319] quantified this phenomenon via the clustering coefficient to measure the local connectivity around a vertex, thus representing the extent of connectivity of the direct neighbors of the vertex. In their formulation, the clustering coefficient is defined as $CC(v) = 2n_v/k_v(k_v - 1)$, where n_v is the number of links connecting the k_v neighbors of node v to each other. In this coefficient, n_v indicates the number of triangles that pass through node v, and $k_v(k_v - 1)/2$ is the total number of triangles that could pass through node v. For example, in Figure 4–1, $n_A = 1$ and $CC(A) = 1/10$, while $n_F = 0$, $CC(F) = 0$. In a different expression, the clustering coefficient $CC(v)$ of a vertex v can also be described by:

$$CC(v) = \frac{2|\bigcup_{i,j \in N(v)} e(i,j)|}{d(v)(d(v) - 1)}, \quad e(i,j) \in E. \tag{5.8}$$

Following Equation (5.1), the density of a network $G(V, E)$ is generally measured by the proportion of the number of edges to the number of all possible edges. A network G has the maximum density value, 1, when G is fully connected; that is, G is a clique. The effect of a node v_i on density is characterized by the clustering coefficient of v_i [319].

The average degree, average path length, and average clustering coefficient depend on the number of nodes and links in the network. However, the degree distribution $P(k)$ and clustering coefficient $CC(k)$ functions are independent of the size of the network and represent its generic features. These functions can therefore be used to classify various network types [29].

Clustering coefficients can be defined for individual vertices and, at the level of an entire graph, as the average of the clustering coefficients over all vertices. Since this metric quantifies the connectivity ratio among direct neighbors of a vertex, it serves as a measurement of the density in the local region of a vertex.

5.4.2 Validation Based on Agreement with Annotated Protein Function Databases

Clustering results can be compared with ground truth derived from various protein domain databases such as InterPro, the Structural Classification of Protein (SCOP) database, and the Munich Information Center for protein sequences (MIPS) hierarchical functional categories [56,99,186]. These databases are collections of well-characterized proteins that have been expertly classified into families based on their folding patterns and a variety of other information.

Jiang et al. [162] listed several simple validation methods that start with construction of a matrix C based on the clustering results. Given the clustering results of p clusters $\mathcal{C} = \{C_1, \ldots, C_p\}$, we can construct an $n * n$ binary matrix C, where n is the number of data objects, $C_{ij} = 1$ if object pairs O_i and O_j belong to the same cluster, and $C_{ij} = 0$ otherwise. Similarly, we can build a matrix P for the ground truth $\mathcal{P} = \{P_1, \ldots, P_s\}$. The agreement between C and P can be discerned via the following values:

- n_{11} is the number of object pairs (O_i, O_j), where $C_{ij} = 1$ and $P_{ij} = 1$;
- n_{10} is the number of object pairs (O_i, O_j), where $C_{ij} = 1$ and $P_{ij} = 0$;

■ n_{01} is the number of object pairs (O_i, O_j), where $C_{ij} = 0$ and $P_{ij} = 1$;
■ n_{00} is the number of object pairs (O_i, O_j), where $C_{ij} = 0$ and $P_{ij} = 0$.

Several indices [132] have been defined to measure the degree of similarity between C and P; they include:

the Rand index: $\text{Rand} = \dfrac{n_{11} + n_{00}}{n_{11} + n_{10} + n_{01} + n_{00}}$,

the Jaccard coefficient: $\text{JC} = \dfrac{n_{11}}{n_{11} + n_{10} + n_{01}}$,

the Minkowski measure: $\text{Minkowski} = \sqrt{\dfrac{n_{10} + n_{01}}{n_{11} + n_{01}}}$.

The Rand index and the Jaccard coefficient measure the extent of agreement between C and P, while the Minkowski measure embodies the proportion of disagreements to the total number of object pairs (O_i, O_j), where O_i, O_j belong to the same set in P. It should be noted that the Jaccard coefficient and the Minkowski measure do not (directly) involve the term n_{00}. These two indices may be more effective in protein-based clustering because a majority of pairs of objects tend to be in separate clusters, and the term n_{00} would dominate the other three terms in both high- and low-quality solutions. Other methods are also available to measure the correlation between the clustering results and the ground truth [132]. Selection of the optimal index is application-dependent.

In semi-supervised clustering, constraints may ensure the correctness of pairs fixed by the constraints or their closure. In these cases, a modification of the original Rand index may be used to evaluate the decisions that are undetermined by the constraints [182]:

$$\text{CRand} = \frac{\text{\# correct free decisions}}{\text{\# total free decisions}}.$$

Simply counting matches between predicted clusters and complexes in the reference data set does not provide a robust evaluation. In cases where each cluster corresponds to a purification, a maximal number of matches will be found, which leads to maximally-redundant results. Krause et al. [186] defined the following criteria to assess the fit of the clustering results to the benchmark data set:

(1) the number of predicted clusters matching ground truth should be maximal;
(2) each individual complex in the data set should be matched by a single predicted cluster;
(3) each cluster should map to only one complex, as clusters matching more than one complex may be too inclusive; and
(4) complexes should have an average size and size distribution similar to the data set.

Application of these criteria allows a more accurate comparison between clustering results and ground truth, as an one-to-one correspondence is required between predicted clusters and complexes.

These approaches assume that each object belongs to one and only one cluster, an assumption characteristic of classical clustering algorithms. In protein annotation data, however, this is not necessarily the case. One protein may have several functions, act in different localizations of the cell, and participate in multiple pathways and protein complexes. Therefore, accurate cluster validation must be cognizant of these overlapping clusters in the ground truth.

Results obtained from two hierarchical clustering algorithms must be compared at different cutoffs, as cutoffs at different dendrogram levels have different meanings and thus are not directly comparable. In [306], two hierarchical clustering algorithms are compared based on the number of clusters they produced. This approach will tend to be biased toward those algorithms that detect many small clusters. As a result, though tending to be highly homogenous, these clusters cover a small number of proteins and provide limited predictive power.

5.4.3 Validation Based on the Definition of Clustering

Clustering is defined as the process of grouping data objects into sets by degree of similarity. Clustering results can be validated by computing the homogeneity of predicted clusters or the extent of separation between two predicted clusters. The quality of a cluster C increases with higher homogeneity values within C and lower separation values between C and other clusters.

The homogeneity of clusters may be defined in various ways; all measure the similarity of data objects within cluster C.

$$H_1(C) = \frac{\sum_{O_i, O_j \in C, O_i \neq O_j} \text{Similarity}(O_i, O_j)}{|C| \cdot (|C| - 1)}, \tag{5.9}$$

$$H_2(C) = \frac{1}{|C|} \sum_{O_i \in C} \text{Similarity}(O_i, \overline{O}). \tag{5.10}$$

H_1 represents the homogeneity of cluster C by the average pairwise object similarity within C. H_2 evaluates homogeneity with respect to the centroid $\overline{O}$ of the cluster C.

Cluster separation is analogously defined from various perspectives to measure the dissimilarity between two clusters C_1 and C_2. For example:

$$S_1(C_1, C_2) = \frac{\sum_{O_i \in C_1, O_j \in C_2} \text{Similarity}(O_i, O_j)}{|C_1| \cdot |C_2|}, \tag{5.11}$$

$$S_2(C_1, C_2) = \text{Similarity}(\overline{O}_1, \overline{O}_2). \tag{5.12}$$

The *Davies–Bouldin* (DB) index [81] measures the quality of a clustering result exclusively according to such internal information as the diameter of each cluster and the distance between all cluster pairs. The DB index is useful when no reference material is available for comparison. It measures the topological quality of the identified clusters in the intact graph.

$$DB = \frac{1}{k} \sum_{i=1}^{k} \max_{i \neq j} \left[\frac{\text{diam}(C_i) + \text{diam}(C_j)}{\text{dist}(C_i, C_j)} \right], \tag{5.13}$$

where $\text{diam}(C_i)$ is the diameter of cluster C_i, and $\text{dist}(C_i, C_j)$ is the distance between clusters C_i and C_j. A small value of DB indicates that the identified clusters are compact and have widely separated centers. The presence of low DB values therefore indicates a good clustering result.

5.4.4 Topological Validation

The topological properties of modular networks include dense intraconnections and sparse interconnections. As a result, each module should have relatively high density and high separability. The modularity of a network can initially be quantified by the proportion of the average density of the identified modules to the density of the entire network. It can also be measured by the average clustering coefficient of all nodes in the network. A recent study [129] proposed that modularity be assessed through a comparison of the relative density of modules to the random connections of the nodes in the modules of $G(V, E)$:

$$M_{\text{den}} = \frac{1}{n} \sum_{s=1}^{n} \left[\frac{|E'_s|}{|E|} - \left(\frac{d_s}{2|E|} \right)^2 \right], \tag{5.14}$$

where n is the number of modules in the network G, and d_s is the sum of the degree of the nodes in a module $G'_s(V'_s, E'_s)$.

Separability provides another vehicle for assessing the modularity of a network. Assume $G'_s(V'_s, E'_s)$ is a subnetwork of $G(V, E)$, where $V'_s \subseteq V$ and $E'_s \subseteq E$, and d_s is the sum of the degree of nodes in G'_s. The separability of $G'_s(V'_s, E'_s)$ from $G(V, E)$ is generally calculated by the *interconnection rate*, which is defined as the ratio of the number of interconnections between V'_s and $(V - V'_s)$ to the number of all the edges starting from the nodes V'. In practice, the interconnection rate can be calculated by (1- intraconnection rate), where the intraconnection rate is defined as $(2|E'_s|/d_s)^2$. The modularity is then measured by the average separability of the identified modules:

$$M_{\text{sep}} = \frac{1}{n} \sum_{s=1}^{n} \left[1 - \left(\frac{2|E'_s|}{d_s} \right)^2 \right]. \tag{5.15}$$

A higher M_{sep} value indicates that $G'(V', E')$ is more likely to separate from $G(V, E)$ by disconnecting some edges.

The effect of a node v_i on separation can be described by the participation coefficient of v_i [129]. The *participation coefficient* $p(v_i)$ measures the uniformity of distribution of the neighbors of v_i among all modules:

$$p(v_i) = 1 - \sum_{s=1}^{n} \left(\frac{|\{(v_i, v_j)|v_j \in G'_s, i \neq j\}|}{|N(v_i)|} \right)^2, \tag{5.16}$$

where n is the number of modules, and G'_s represents each module. A low $p(v_i)$ value indicates that v_i strongly influences the separation of the network into modules.

5.4.5 Supervised Validation

Modules identified in a PPI network can be validated by comparison to a ground truth comprised of the actual functional categories and their annotations. Assume a module X that is mapped to a functional category F_i. *Recall*, also termed the *true positive rate* or *sensitivity*, is the proportion of proteins common to both X and F_i to the size of F_i. *Precision*, which is also termed the *positive predictive value*, is the proportion of proteins common to both X and F_i to the size of X.

$$\text{Recall} = \frac{|X \cap F_i|}{|F_i|}, \tag{5.17}$$

and

$$\text{Precision} = \frac{|X \cap F_i|}{|X|}. \tag{5.18}$$

In general, larger modules have higher recall values, because a large module X is likely to include many members of F_i. In the extreme case where all the proteins are grouped into one module, the recall value of that module will be maximal. In contrast, smaller modules have higher precision, because the members of these smaller Xs are likely to be homogeneous for a particular function. The extreme example in this instance would designate each protein as a module, and these modules would have maximum precision values. We can thus assess the accuracy of modules with the *f-measure*, which rates the quality of identified modules by comparison with external reference modules. The f-measure is defined as the harmonic mean of recall and precision:

$$f - \text{measure} = \frac{2(\text{Precision} \cdot \text{Recall})}{\text{Precision} + \text{Recall}}. \tag{5.19}$$

5.4.6 Statistical Validation

Modules can be statistically evaluated using the p-value from the hypergeometric distribution, which is defined as

$$P = 1 - \sum_{i=0}^{k-1} \frac{\binom{|X|}{i} \binom{|V| - |X|}{n - i}}{\binom{|V|}{n}}, \tag{5.20}$$

where $|V|$ is the total number of proteins, $|X|$ is the number of proteins in a reference function, n is the number of proteins in an identified module, and k is the number of proteins in common between the function and the module. It is understood as the probability that at least k proteins in a module of size n are included in a reference function of size $|X|$. A low value of p indicates that the module closely corresponds to the function, because it is less probable that the network will produce the module by chance.

5.4.7 Validation of Protein Function Prediction

Leave-One-Out Method. The classification of data may also be assessed using the k-fold cross validation method, which partitions the data set into k subsets. One of these subsets is retained as test data, and the remaining $k - 1$ subsets are used as training data. The validation process is then subjected to k-fold repetition, with each of the k subsets used exactly once as the test data. The results from the k-fold repetition can be averaged to produce a single accuracy estimation.

A special case of k-fold cross-validation is the leave-one-out cross-validation method, which has proven to be more applicable to the assessment of function prediction in PPI networks. This method sets k as the total number of proteins with known functions in the network. One protein is selected, and its functions are hypothetically assumed to be unknown. Functions predicted by a selected method are then compared with the true known functions of the protein. The process is repeated for k known proteins, $P_1, \ldots, P_k$. Let n_i be the number of actual functions of protein P_i, m_i be the number of functions predicted for P_i, and k_i be the overlap between the actual and predicted functions, for $i = 1, \ldots, k$. The recall and precision can be defined as

$$\text{Recall} = \frac{\sum_i^k k_i}{\sum_i^k n_i}, \tag{5.21}$$

$$\text{Precision} = \frac{\sum_i^k k_i}{\sum_i^k m_i}. \tag{5.22}$$

Trials using MIPS and other data sets have produced results that are highly consistent with those of the distributions of expression correlation coefficients and reliability estimations.

5.5 SUMMARY

This chapter has provided an overview of various clustering approaches that have yielded promising results in application to PPI networks. Clustering approaches for PPI networks can be broadly differentiated between the classic distance-based methods and more recent and nontraditional methods, which include graph-theoretic, topology-based, flow-based, statistical, and domain knowledge-based approaches. These nontraditional approaches are gaining acceptance for their ability to provide a more accurate modularity analysis of PPI networks. In general, clustering algorithms are employed to identify subgraphs with maximal density or with a minimum cost of cutoff based on the topology of the network. Clustering a PPI network permits a better understanding of its structure and the interrelationship of constituent components. More significantly, it also becomes possible to predict the potential functions of unannotated proteins by comparison with other members of the same cluster.

6

Topological Analysis of Protein Interaction Networks

With Woo-chang Hwang

6.1 INTRODUCTION

Essential questions regarding the structure, underlying principles, and semantics of protein–protein interaction (PPI) networks can be addressed by an examination of their topological features and components. Network performance, scalability, robustness, and dynamics are often dependent on these topological properties. Much research has been devoted to the development of methods to quantitatively characterize a network or its components. Empirical and theoretical studies of networks of all types – technological, social, and biological – have been among the most popular subjects of recent research in many fields. Graph theories have been successfully applied to these real-world systems, and many graph and component measurements have been introduced.

In Chapters 4 and 5, we provided an introduction to the typical topological properties of real complex networks, including degree distribution, attachment tendency, and reachability indices. We also introduced the scale-free model, which is among the most popular network models. This model exemplifies several important topological properties, which will be briefly summarized here:

- *The small-world property*: Despite the large size of most real-world networks, a relatively short path can be found between any two constituent nodes. The small-world property states that any node in a real-world network can be reached from any other node within a small number of steps. As Erdős and Rényi [100,101] have demonstrated, the typical distance between any two nodes in a random network is the logarithm of the number of nodes, indicating that random graphs are also characterized by this property.
- *Clustering*: A common property of real-world networks is their tendency to be internally organized into highly connected substructures, or clusters. This inherent tendency to clustering is quantified by the clustering coefficient. Watts and Strogatz [319] found that the clustering coefficient in most real networks is much larger than in a random network of equal size. Barabasi et al. [261] showed that the metabolic networks of 43 organisms are organized into many small, highly connected topologic modules that combine in a hierarchical manner into

larger, less cohesive units, with their number and degree of clustering following a power law.

■ *Degree distribution*: In a random network model where edges are randomly placed, the majority of nodes have approximately the same degree, close to the average degree $\langle k \rangle$ of the network. The degree distribution of a random graph is a Poisson distribution. In contrast, recent empirical investigations have shown that the degree distribution of most real-world networks significantly deviates from a Poisson distribution. In real-world complex networks, the degree distribution has a power-law tail $P(k) \sim k^{-\gamma}$.

This chapter will explore the computational analysis of PPI networks on the basis of topological network features.

6.2 OVERVIEW AND ANALYSIS OF ESSENTIAL NETWORK COMPONENTS

In Chapter 4, we discussed the means by which a graph-theoretical representation, together with various topological indices and measurements, can explain or summarize important aspects of a network. These indices have been applied in diverse fields to characterize networks of various kinds, analyze their performance, and identify important network components. The rest of this chapter will demonstrate the application of these metrics to the prediction and analysis of PPI networks.

6.2.1 Error and Attack Tolerance of Complex Networks

Real-world complex systems display a surprising robustness to errors. Barabasi et al. [7] found that the communicative ability of nodes in real-world networks was unaffected even by unusually high failure rates. Their analysis compared the robustness of a scale-free network model with a random network model under conditions that included variations in the diameter and size of the largest cluster, in the average size of isolated clusters, and in the average path length (APL), along with simulated network failures [5,7]. The compactness of a network is often described by its diameter d, defined as the average length of the shortest paths between any two nodes in the network. The diameter characterizes the ability of two nodes to communicate, with a smaller d indicating that any two nodes are separated by only a small number of steps. Most real-world networks have been shown to have a diameter of less than six.

Barabasi's group began their study of the error tolerance of networks by comparing the impact of varying diameter on exponential and scale-free network models; results are presented in Figure 6–1. In the exponential network model, the diameter changed gradually and monotonically with both random failures and targeted attacks on high-degree nodes [illustrated by triangles and diamonds in Figure 6–1(a)]. This behavior arises from the homogeneous degree distribution of the network. Interruptions to randomly chosen nodes and high-degree nodes in the exponential network model were of equal impact on the network diameter. Since all nodes have approximately the same degree, the removal of any individual node will cause the same amount of damage. As a result, both random failures and targeted attacks in an exponential network effected a gradual deterioration in network communication.

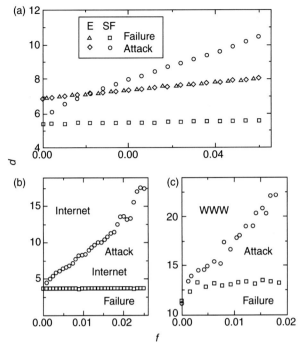

Figure 6–1 Error tolerance of network models. (a) Changes in the diameter d of exponential (E) and scale-free (SF) network models as a function of the fraction f of removed nodes. The triangle and square symbols correspond to the diameter of the E (triangles) and SF (squares) networks when a fraction f of the nodes are randomly removed. The diamond and circle symbols show the response of the E (diamonds) and SF (circles) networks to attacks when the most highly connected nodes are removed. The f-dependence of the diameter was determined for different system sizes ($N = 1,000$; 5,000; 20,000). The obtained curves, apart from a logarithmic size correction, overlap with those shown in (a), indicating that the results are independent of the size of the system. The diameter of the unperturbed ($f = 0$) scale-free network is smaller than that of the exponential network, indicating that scale-free networks use the links available to them more efficiently, generating a more interconnected web. (b) The changes in the diameter of the Internet under random failures (squares) or attacks (circles). Testing used the topological map of the Internet, containing 6,209 nodes and 12,200 links ($\langle k \rangle = 3.4$), collected by the National Laboratory for Applied Network Research (http://moat.nlanr.net/Routing/rawdata/). (c) Error (squares) and attack (circles) survivability of the World Wide Web, measured with a sample containing 325,729 nodes and 1,498,353 links, such that $\langle k \rangle = 4.59$. (Reprinted by permission from Macmillan Publishers Ltd: Nature [7], copyright 2000.)

In contrast, the scale-free network model exhibited dissimilar responses to random failures and targeted attacks; this data is plotted with squares and circles in Figure 6–1(a). Random failures resulted in no change in network diameter, indicating that these interruptions had little impact on network communication. The robustness of scale-free networks to random failures is due to their inhomogeneous degree distribution. The scale-free network model has many low-degree nodes and very few high-degree nodes. The removal of these low-degree nodes does not alter the path structure of the remaining nodes and has no impact on the overall network topology.

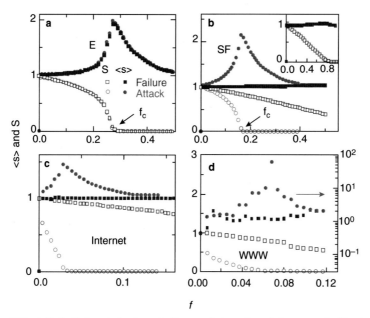

Figure 6–2 Network fragmentation under random failures and attacks. The relative size of the largest cluster S (open symbols) and the average size of the isolated clusters $\langle s \rangle$ (filled symbols) as a function of the fraction of removed nodes f. (a) Fragmentation of the exponential network under random failures (squares) and attacks (circles). (b) Fragmentation of the scale-free network under random failures (blue squares) and attacks (red circles). (c) Fragmentation of the Internet network under random failures (blue squares) and attacks (red circles). (d) Fragmentation of the WWW network under random failures (blue squares) and attacks (red circles). "See Color Plate 3." (Reprinted by permission from Macmillan Publishers Ltd: Nature [7], copyright 2000.)

On the other hand, targeted attacks on high-degree nodes resulted in rapid and dramatic increases in network diameter. For example, when the nodes with degrees in the top 5% were removed, the diameter almost doubled. This vulnerability of scale-free networks to targeted attacks is the negative correlary of their robustness to random failures and arises from the same structural cause. The connectivity of a scale-free network is maintained by the high-degree nodes, and interruptions to these nodes will result in heavy and rapid damage to the network. Figure 6–1(b) and (c) display similar behavior patterns that were observed in real network examples, such as the Internet and the World Wide Web (WWW), showing that these real-world networks are scale-free.

Sequential node removals will damage the structure and cohesion of a network. To better understand the impact of failures and targeted attacks on the network, Barabasi group also investigated this network isolation process. Figure 6–2(a) and (b) illustrate the impacts on the modularity, relative size of the largest cluster (S), and average size of isolated clusters ($\langle s \rangle$) under conditions of random failures and targeted attacks in exponential (E) and scale-free (SF) network models. Modularity in each network model broke down at a point f_c. Here, f represents the fraction of the removed nodes out of the total number of nodes in the network. At small values of

f, only singletons break apart, $\langle s \rangle \simeq 1$, but, as f increases, the size of the fragments that fall off the main cluster grows. At f_c, the system falls apart; the main cluster breaks into small pieces, leading to $S = 0$, and the size of the fragments, $\langle s \rangle$, peaks.

Similar behaviors of S and $\langle s \rangle$ were observed in the exponential network model under conditions of random failures and targeted attacks. As illustrated in Figure 6–2(a), $\langle s \rangle$ peaked and S collapsed to 0 at f_c. Not unexpectedly, the response of the scale-free network model to targeted attacks and random failures was quite different [Figure 6–2(b)]. There was no network breakdown point resulting from random failures in the scale-free model [blue squares in Figure 6–2(b)], indicating again that the scale-free network model is robust to random failures. However, this model showed a very sensitive response to targeted attacks, which resulted in very rapid network dissolution and a steep collapsing process. Figure 6–2(c) and (d) show similar results for the Internet and WWW, both of which demonstrate the behavior characteristic of a scale-free network model.

Another topological metric useful for measuring the compactness of a network is the APL of the network. A well-connected and properly clustered network will have a low APL. Routes or distances among nodes in the network will normally be lengthened when a number of nodes are removed. Thus, analysis of changes in the APL in response to sequential node removals will illustrate the extent that these removals interrupt network communication. The Barabasi group performed a sequential node removal analysis similar to that underlying Figures 6–1 and 6–2 to observe changes in the APL in random and scale-free network models. The relative sizes of the largest component [Figure 6–3(a) and (b)] and the APL [Figure 6–3(c) and (d)] for each network model were observed. Both network models showed similar changes in the size of the largest cluster, but the scale-free model demonstrated an earlier and steeper breakdown process in response to targeted attacks [Figure 6–3(a) and (b)].

The random network model exhibited threshold-like behavior, with targeted attacks producing an earlier and higher peak of the APL than did random failures [Figure 6–3(c)]. The scale-free network model broke down slowly under conditions of random failure, without showing a clear threshold of collapse. Under targeted attack, however, the scale-free model also reached a collapse threshold, beyond which a rapid breakdown occurred [Figure 6–3(d)]. Figure 6–3 indicates that the communications within scale-free networks are more robust against random failures and more vulnerable to targeted attacks than the random network model.

6.2.2 Role of High-Degree Nodes in Biological Networks

Jeong et al. [161] provided quantitative analysis that the phenotypic consequence of a single gene deletion in the yeast (*Saccharomyces cerevisiae*) is strongly affected by the topological position of its protein product in the complex hierarchical network of molecular interactions. They found that high-degree nodes are much more critical to the functioning of the yeast PPI network than nodes of average degree. Deletion of these genes is often lethal to network survival. Although about 93% of all proteins in the network are of low degree, with five or fewer edges, only about 21% of these proteins are lethal. Furthermore, while only 0.7% of the proteins have more than fifteen edges, 62% of these are lethal. This implies that high-degree proteins with a central role in network architecture are three times more likely to be lethal than

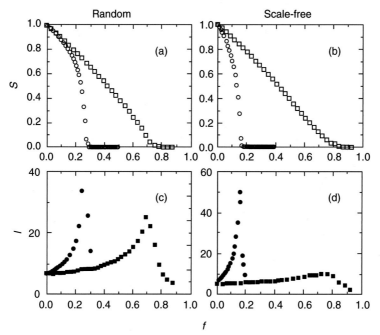

Figure 6–3 The relative size S (a, b) and APL ℓ (c, d) of the largest cluster in an initially connected network when a fraction f of the nodes are removed. (a, c) random network with $N = 10,000$ and $\langle k \rangle = 4$. (b, d) Scale-free network generated by the scale-free model with $N = 10,000$ and $\langle k \rangle = 4$. Squares indicate random node removal, while circles correspond to preferential removal of the most highly connected nodes. (Reprinted with permission from [7], copyright 2002 by the American Physical Society.)

low-degree proteins and supports a strong correlation between the connectivity and indispensability of a given protein. The robustness of yeast against mutations is derived not only from individual biochemical function and genetic redundancy but also from the organization of interactions and the topological positions of individual proteins [161]. This phenomenon was observed in the proteome networks of several organisms including yeast, nematodes, and flies [131,325,336].

Yu et al. also verified that high-degree nodes were much more lethal than low-degree nodes in the yeast PPI network. Essential proteins were found to have approximately twice as many interactions compared with nonessential proteins. About 43% of high-degree nodes in the yeast PPI network were found to be essential; this is significantly higher than the 20% that could be expected by chance [336].

Feeling that previous definitions of essentiality were inadequate, Yu's group introduced a new concept of *marginal essentiality* (M) based on the idea of "marginal benefit" developed by Thatcher et al. [300]. The marginal essentiality of each nonessential gene is calculated by averaging data from four data sets: growth rate, phenotype, sporulation efficiency, and small-molecule sensitivity:

$$M_i = \frac{\sum_{j \in J_i} F_{i,j}/F_{\max,j}}{|J_i|}, \tag{6.1}$$

where $F_{i,j}$ is the value for gene i in data set j, $F_{\max,j}$ is the maximum value in data set j, and J_i is the data sets that have information on gene i.

This analysis indicated that highly marginal essential genes are more likely to be high-degree network nodes. In addition, proteins with higher marginal-essentiality values are more likely to be closely connected to other proteins. Highly marginal essential proteins have a short characteristic path length to other proteins in the network, implying that the effect of that protein on other proteins is more direct [336]. This analysis was extended to several smaller yeast transcriptional regulatory networks which, unlike PPI networks, are topologically and biologically directed and dynamic. This examination revealed that, while transcription factors with many targets tended to be essential, genes that were regulated by many transcription factors were usually not essential [336].

6.2.3 Betweenness, Connectivity, and Centrality

Analysis of essential components in PPI networks has recently moved from a focus on the role of node degrees to other topological issues [103,131,168,337]. Several researchers have asserted that the nodes or edges present on the shortest paths between all node pairs in PPI networks are more essential than the high-degree nodes. This is held to be particularly the case in dynamic networks, such as regulatory or metabolic systems.

Joy et al. analyzed several PPI networks and discovered that nodes with high betweenness and low connectivity (HBLC) can be found in locations between modules. From this observation, they proposed a new *duplication-mutation* (DM) network model that reproduces these HBLC nodes. The DM network model is constructed through two processes. *Gene duplication* replicates the process by which a gene and all its connections are duplicated and which accounts for network growth. The *point mutation* process evolves the structure of a protein to change its interacting partners and, as a result, alter connections within the network. The time-scales involved in these two processes are quite different, with gene duplication proceeding much more slowly than point mutation. Simulation of network growth through this duplication-mutation model led to the evolution of a network that exhibits power-law behavior with HBLC nodes, similar to the yeast PPI network [168]. This structure cannot be predicted by a scale-free model.

In general, Joy's group found that essential proteins in the yeast PPI network had a higher mean betweenness and were associated more frequently with high-betweenness nodes, as illustrated in Figure 6–4. For all proteins, mean betweenness was 6.6×10^{-4}, but the value for essential proteins was 82% higher, at 1.2×10^{-3}. The degree of essential proteins was 77% higher than that of all proteins. Therefore, betweenness was found to be an effective measure of protein lethality, and levels of betweenness were comparable to degree values. The analysis suggested that PPI networks include both highly connected modules and proteins located outside and between these highly connected modules [168].

Yu et al. [337] also investigated high-betweenness and low-degree proteins (bottlenecks) in biological networks. They performed lethality analyses on a variety of network types, including interaction networks, signal transduction networks, and regulatory networks. Nodes were sorted into four categories: hub-bottleneck node

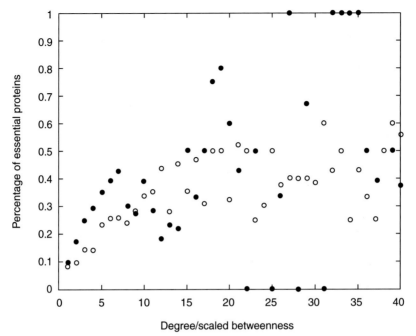

Figure 6–4 Percentage of essential genes with a particular degree (open circle) or betweenness (filled circle). Betweenness is scaled in such a way that the maximum value of betweenness is equal to the maximum degree. The plot was truncated at $k/B = 40$, since the number of essential genes beyond that was below statistical significance. (Reprinted from [168].)

(BH), non-hub-bottleneck node (B-NH), hub-non-bottleneck node (H-NB), and non-hub-non-bottleneck (NB-NH). The lethality of each category was examined in various types of biological networks (see Figure 6–5). Bottlenecks, which are high-betweenness nodes, were shown to be key connectors with surprising functional and dynamic properties. In particular, they are more likely to be essential than low-betweenness nodes. In fact, in regulatory and other directed dynamic networks, betweenness is a better indicator of essentiality than degree. Furthermore, bottlenecks are significantly less coexpressed with their direct neighbors than non-bottleneck nodes. It is evident that, in networks of this type, bottlenecks serve as the connectors among different functional modules [337].

Unlike regulatory networks, PPI networks have undirected edges and demonstrate no obvious information flow. The analysis indicated that the degree of a protein is a better predictor of essentiality in such static, undirected interaction networks. However, betweenness may have biological implications in some subnetworks within PPI networks, particularly in subnetworks involved with signaling transduction or permanent interactions. In these instances, bottleneck proteins are somewhat more likely to be essential [337].

Subgraph centrality offers another means of measuring the essentiality of proteins in PPI networks [102,103]. The subgraph centrality (SC) that accounts for the

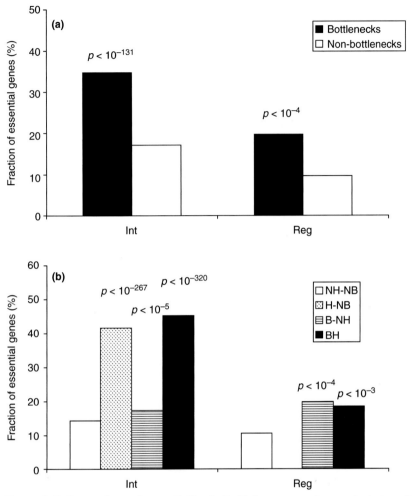

Figure 6–5 Comparison of essentiality (lethality) among various categories of proteins within interaction and regulatory networks (a) Bottlenecks tend to be essential genes in both interaction and regulatory networks. *p*-values measure the statistical significance of the different essentialities between bottlenecks and non-bottlenecks. (b) Essentiality of different categories of proteins: NH-NB (non-hub non-bottlenecks); H-NB (hub-non-bottlenecks); B-NH (non-hub-bottlenecks); BH (hub-bottlenecks). *p*-values measure the statistical significance of the different essentialities between different categories of proteins against non-hub-non-bottlenecks using cumulative binomial distributions. (Reprinted from [337].)

participation of a node i in all subgraphs of the network is defined as follows:

$$SC(i) = \sum_{l=0}^{\infty} \frac{\mu_l(i)}{l!} = \sum_{j=1}^{N} [v_j(i)]^2 e^{\lambda_j}. \tag{6.2}$$

Here, $\mu_l(i)$ is the number of walks starting and ending at node i; that is, closed walks of length l starting at i. $(v_1, v_2, \ldots, v_n)$ is an orthonormal basis of R^N composed by eigenvectors of the adjacency matrix of the network associated with the eigenvalues $\lambda_1, \lambda_2, \ldots, \lambda_N$, and $v_j(i)$ is the ith component of v_j. Accordingly, SC(i) counts the total number of closed walks through which protein i takes part in the PPI network and assigns greater weight to closed walks of short lengths [103]. Thus, *SC* accounts for the number of subgraphs in which a protein participates, giving greater weight to smaller subgraphs, which have been previously identified as important structural motifs in biological networks.

Estrada et al. compared the efficacy of subgraph centrality in identifying lethal proteins to that of the other topological metrics, including degree centrality, closeness centrality, betweenness centrality, eigenvector centrality, and information centrality. As can be seen in Figure 6–6, all centrality measures performed significantly better than the random selection method in selecting essential proteins in the yeast PPI network. Furthermore, subgraph centrality outperformed the other competitive metrics in detecting lethal proteins in the yeast PPI network.

A comparative genomic analysis of centrality and essentiality in three eukaryotic PPI networks (yeast, worm, and fly) was performed by Hahn et al. [131]. These three networks were found to be remarkably similar in structure, in that the number of interactors per protein and the centrality of proteins in the networks had similar

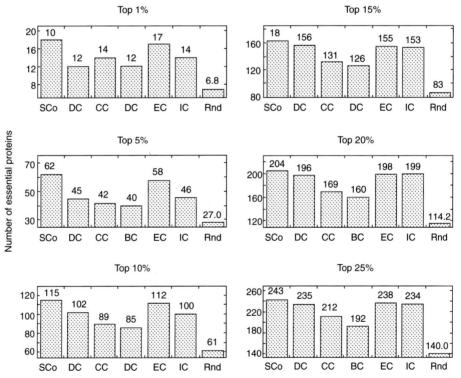

Figure 6–6 Number of essential proteins selected by ranking proteins according to their values of centrality and at random (after 20 realizations). Measurements given are degree centrality (DC), closeness centrality (CC), betweenness centrality (BC), eigenvector centrality (EC), and information centrality (IC). (Reprinted with permission from [102]. Copyright Wiley-VCH Verlag GmbH & Co. KGaA.)

distributions. The lethal protein identification efficacy of the betweenness, degree, and closeness centralities was compared. For all three organisms, all centrality measures indicated that essential genes were more likely to be central in the PPI network. Furthermore, those essential genes evolved more slowly in all three genomes. Proteins that had a more central position in all three networks, regardless of the number of direct interactors, evolved more slowly and were more likely to be essential for survival [131].

6.3 BRIDGING CENTRALITY MEASUREMENTS

Hwang et al. [151,152] introduced a novel *bridging centrality* metric for identifying and assessing "bridges" that play critical linking roles between network sub-modules. The bridging paradigm is intuitive because of its consistency with the everyday notion of bridges in transportation. Their results demonstrate that these metaphorical bridges are critical for modulating information flows and interactions between network modules. Nodes with high bridging centrality are distinctively different from nodes identified on the basis of degree, betweeness centrality, and other measures. Bridging nodes are located in crucial modulating positions among modules in various types of networks. The vulnerability of bridging nodes is unlike that of nodes identified with any of the other centrality metrics, as their removal causes network disruption without dismemberment.

Formally, a *bridge* is a node or an edge that is located between and connects modules in a graph. In other words, a *bridge* is a node v or an edge e that has a high value of bridging centrality. The bridges in a graph are identified on the basis of their high value of bridging centrality relative to other nodes or edges in the same graph. To calculate the bridging centrality of a node v or an edge e, its global importance is computed using betweenness centrality in a graph, conceptually defined as follows:

$$C_B(v) = \sum_{s \neq t \neq v \in V} \frac{\rho_{st}(v)}{\rho_{st}}, \tag{6.3}$$

where ρ_{st} is the number of shortest paths between node s and t, and $\rho_{st}(v)$ is the number of shortest paths passing through a node v out of ρ_{st}.

Betweenness for an edge e can be defined in the same way as for the node in Equation (6.3):

$$C_B(e) = \sum_{s \neq t \in V, \, e \in E} \frac{\rho_{st}(e)}{\rho_{st}}, \tag{6.4}$$

where ρ_{st} is the number of shortest paths between node s and t, and $\rho_{st}(e)$ is the number of shortest paths passing through an edge e out of ρ_{st}.

To obtain a metric capable of identifying bridges, Hwang et al. draw upon the observation that the number of edges entering or leaving the directly neighboring subgraph of a node v relative to the number of edges remaining within the directly neighboring subgraph of node v is high at bridge locations. This property allows us to formulate the concept of a bridging coefficient for both nodes and edges.

Definition 6.1

The bridging coefficient *of a node v is defined as the average probability of edges leaving the directly neighboring subgraph of node v. The* bridging coefficient *of node v is defined by*

$$\Psi(v) = \frac{1}{d(v)} \sum_{i \in N(v), d(i) > 1} \frac{\delta(i)}{d(i) - 1}, \tag{6.5}$$

where $d(x)$ is the degree of a node x, and $\delta(i), i \in N(v)$, is the number of edges leaving the directly neighboring subgraph of node v from each direct neighbor node i. Only the direct neighbor nodes of node v with more than one edge are considered in the bridging coefficient computation.

Figure 6.7 illustrates the above formula, where $\delta(i), i \in N(v)$, includes edge e, which is among the edges incident to node i. Three illustrative examples of the bridging-coefficient computation are presented in Figure 6.7. The number of edges leaving the directly neighboring subgraph is 0 for Figure 6.7(a) and increases in Figure 6.7(b) and (c).

Definition 6.2

The bridging coefficient *of an edge e is defined as the product of the weighted average of the bridging coefficients of two incident nodes i and j for an edge e and the reciprocal of the number of common directly neighboring nodes of nodes i and j. The* bridging coefficient *of an edge e is defined by*

$$\Psi(e) = \frac{d(i)\Psi(i) + d(j)\Psi(j)}{(d(i) + d(j))(|C(i,j)| + 1)}, \quad e(i,j) \in E, \tag{6.6}$$

where nodes i and j are the two incident nodes to edge e, $d(i)$ and $d(j)$ are the degrees of nodes i and j, $\Psi(i)$ and $\Psi(j)$ are the bridging coefficients of nodes i and j, and $C(i,j)$ is the set of common directly neighboring nodes of nodes i and j. The bridging coefficient

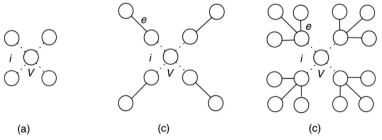

| (a) | (c) | (c) |

Figure 6–7 Illustrative examples of the method for computing the number of edges leaving the directly-neighboring subgraph of node V in the bridging coefficient. The dashed lines represent the edges within the directly-neighboring subgraph of the node marked V, and the solid lines are edges leaving the directly-neighboring subgraph of V. (a), (b), and (c) illustrate three typical cases of local connectivity. The node marked i is a typical direct neighbor node of V, and e is a typical edge leaving the directly-neighboring subgraph of V. (Reprinted from [152].)

of an edge e should be penalized if the direct neighbors of the two incident nodes were well connected each other showing high $|C(i, j)|$.

Bridging centrality is computed using the *rank product* [52], which is defined as the product of the betweenness rank and the bridging coefficient rank. This normalization procedure corrects for the differences in scale among betweenness and the bridging coefficient.

Definition 6.3

The bridging centrality *of a node v is defined by*

$$C_{Br}(v) = R_{C_B(v)} \cdot R_{\Psi(v)}, \tag{6.7}$$

where $R_{C_B(v)}$ *is the betweenness rank of node v, and* $R_{\Psi(v)}$ *is the bridging-coefficient rank of node v.*

In normalizing the rank product, the nodes in a graph are separately ordered according to their measured bridging-coefficient and betweenness scores. The rankings of node *v* are sorted for each metric, and the bridging centrality of node *v* is computed using the product of the rankings in each metric.

Definition 6.4

The bridging centrality *of an edge e is defined by*

$$C_{Br}(e) = R_{C_B(e)} \cdot R_{\Psi(e)}, \tag{6.8}$$

where $R_{C_B(e)}$ *is the betweenness rank of edge e, and* $R_{\Psi(e)}$ *is the bridging-coefficient rank of edge e.*

The first term in Equations (6.7) and (6.8) measures the global importance of a node or an edge by representing the fraction of shortest paths passing through that node or edge. The second term measures the local topological properties around a node or edge, stated as the probability that an edge will leave the directly neighboring subgraph of that node or edge. A bridge is a node *v* or an edge *e* that has a high bridging-centrality value.

Hwang et al. have shown that bridging centrality is capable of identifying nodes or edges that are located between and connect subregions of the network and are therefore potential bottlenecks to information flow between modules.

6.3.1 Performance of Bridging Centrality with Synthetic and Real-World Networks

To obtain an assessment of the underlying network characteristics identified by bridging centrality, Hwang et al. applied two centrality indices (bridging and betweenness) to a synthetic network consisting of 162 nodes and 362 edges, as depicted in Figure 6–8(a) and (b). The network was created by joining three separate synthetic networks and contains such typical key elements as hub nodes, peripheral nodes, and cycles with known bridges. The network was created using the Java Universal Network/Graph Framework (JUNG; see http://jung.sourceforge.net) [234]. The overall

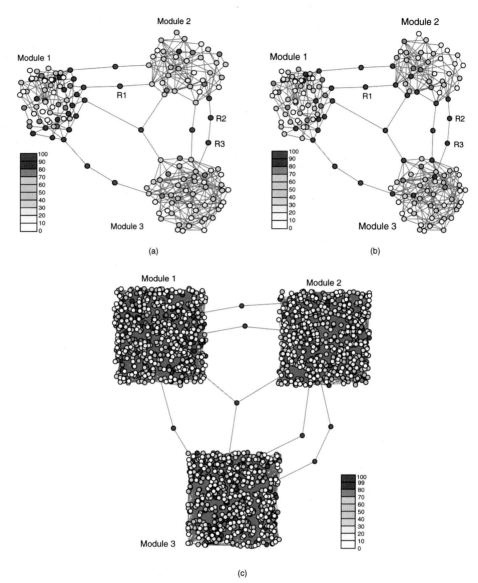

Figure 6–8 Results of applying bridging centrality and betweenness centrality to a synthetic network containing 162 nodes and 362 edges. The network was created by adding bridging nodes to three independently generated subnetworks. The nodes in the upper tenth percentile of bridging-centrality values are depicted by red circles. Nodes in the lowest tenth percentile of bridging-centrality values are depicted by white circles. (a) application of bridging centrality, (b) application of betweenness centrality, (c) the bridging centrality results for a synthetic network in which 500 nodes were added to each subgraph in (a). The bridging nodes remain unchanged from the network in (a). The nodes in the upper tenth percentile of bridging-centrality values are indicated by red circles. "See Color Plate 4." (Reprinted from [152].)

size was kept small to permit easy visual detection of any patterns present. Visual inspection of the synthetic network revealed that the highest values of bridging centrality (red circles in Figure 6–8(a)) occurred in the nodes connecting modules and in highly connected parts of the network. Five bridging nodes emerged within Module 1 and one bridging node in Module 2; four of these nodes were located on the extremity of bridges between modules. Figure 6–8(b) illustrates the application of betweenness centrality to the same network. Betweenness centrality analysis identified some of bridging nodes but failed to identify the major bridges labeled $R1$, $R2$, and $R3$.

To systematically assess whether the bridging centrality metric was robust and capable of effectively identifying bridging nodes in larger networks, networks containing 50, 100, and 500 additional nodes within each of the three subgraphs were generated. The added nodes were connected by the same bridging nodes present in Figure 6–8(a) and (b).

All seven known bridges were present among the top ten (3.2 percentile), eight (1.7 percentile), and seven (0.4 percentile) nodes with the highest bridging-centrality values in the networks with 50, 100, and 500 nodes added to each subgraph, respectively [Figure 6–8(c)]. The number of subgraphs were also increased from three to 30 (2,240 nodes and 5,607 edges), with 62 bridges connecting randomly selected subgraphs. In this scenario, 56 of the bridges (90.3%) were within the upper 5% of bridging centrality values, while only 24 bridges (38.7%) were in the top 5% of betweenness centrality values.

High-throughput assay methodologies, such as microarrays and mass spectrometry, have resulted in the rapid growth of biological network data sets, the analysis of which can potentially yield insights into the mechanisms of human disease and the discovery of new therapeutic interventions [148]. Biological networks can be diverse in structure but often involve ordered sequences of interactions rather than interconnections. In these instances, the majority of proteins in a given functional category do not have a direct physical interaction with other proteins involved in the same functional category [148].

To assess the performance of bridging centrality with a larger, real-world biological network, the metric was applied to the well-studied yeast metabolic network [129], which contains 359 nodes and 435 edges. Results are depicted in Figure 6–9. Again, despite the additional complexity and increased size of the network, nodes involved in bridging between larger modules were selectively identified.

6.3.2 Assessing Network Disruption, Structural Integrity, and Modularity

Ideally, bridging-centrality values could be used to select nodes that truly serve a bridging function. To explore this potential, Hwang et al. used the yeast metabolic network [129] for further analysis. This network has a number of properties characteristic of real-world networks, including a power law distribution, the small-world phenomenon, and high modularity, as well as being sufficiently compact to permit precise observation. In order to investigate the topological locality of the bridging nodes identified by bridging centrality, several network properties were analyzed, including the APL, the average clustering coefficient, the average size of isolated

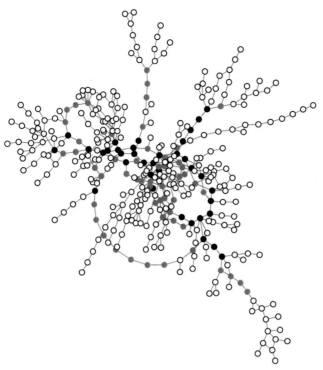

Figure 6–9 Application of bridging centrality to the yeast metabolic network. The nodes in the upper tenth percentile of bridging-centrality values are depicted by black circles; the nodes in the next decile are depicted by gray circles. (Reprinted from [151].)

modules, and the number of singletons. These values were obtained using both bridging and betweenness centrality, and their behavior during sequential node removals was compared. Betweenness centrality was also assessed because it is the only comparable graph metric that is semantically similar to bridging centrality. As depicted in Figure 6–10, the nodes were ordered by each centrality metric and then sequentially removed to observe the changes in network properties.

Figure 6–10(a) depicts the changes in APL resulting from the sequential removal of nodes scoring in the upper tenth percentile for each centrality metric. Incremental changes in the APL resulting from node removal indicate that some nodes are isolated from the main network or that there are some alternative paths that are longer than the removed path. In most intervals, application of betweenness centrality resulted in larger changes in the APL than did bridging centrality. However, an examination of the occurrence of singletons [Figure 6–10(d)] reveals that much of this increase arises from the mass-production by betweenness centrality of singletons in the same interval. The nodes distinguished by betweenness are generally located in the center of modules that have many peripheral nodes with one degree. Therefore, deletion of the nodes identified by betweenness resulted in the isolation of many single nodes and, in turn, the increase in the APL. In contrast, the APL resulting from the deletion of nodes identified by bridging centrality also increased significantly, but far fewer singletons were generated in the same interval. Significantly, the APL increased

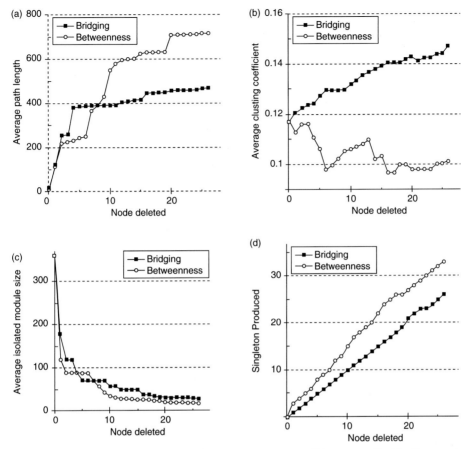

Figure 6-10 Analysis of bridging and betweenness centralities as applied to the yeast metabolic network. Each graph depicts changes in a property resulting from the sequential removal of nodes with centrality scores in the upper tenth percentile.
(a) Changes in the APL, (b) changes in the average clustering coefficient (CC)
(c) changes in the average size of isolated modules, and (d) changes in singletons.
(Reprinted from [151].)

more with bridging centrality than with betweenness in response to the removal of the nine highest-scored nodes. This behavior indicates that interruptions of these bridging nodes resulted in much longer alternative paths or the isolation of larger modules.

Figure 6-10(b) and (c) compare the behavior of the network clustering coefficient and the average size of isolated modules as a result of the consecutive removals of nodes scoring in the upper tenth percentile for betweenness and bridging centrality. The changes demonstrated by these properties provide interesting insights into the features of the nodes identified by the two centrality measures. Again, it is worthwhile to examine the changes in the number of singletons as part of this analysis. Removal of nodes identified by betweenness did not result in monotonic behavior on the part of the clustering coefficients, which decreased by about 20%. The average size of isolated modules also dropped rapidly in the same interval. Furthermore, betweenness produced many more singletons than did bridging centrality in the same intervals. The nodes identified by betweenness were located in the center of modules, and the removal of those nodes damaged the modularity of the network, mass-produced singletons, and lowered the clustering coefficient. Sequential removal of nodes with the highest bridging-centrality scores actually raised the clustering coefficient of the network by about 10% in most intervals while producing fewer singletons. Significantly, therefore, deletion of the high bridging-centrality nodes enhanced the modularity of the network without producing many singletons. This result indicates that the nodes identified by bridging centrality are located between modules and are neither in the center of modules nor on the periphery of the network.

Hwang et al. have also shown that regions of the biological network that connect cliques (e.g., completely connected subgraphs) would be likely locations for bridging nodes. The yeast PPI network [82,327] was used to test this hypothesis.

The topological position of high-scoring (bridging) nodes relative to network subregions was first investigated. As we have discussed in Chapter 5, a *clique* is a complete graph in which each node has edges with every other node. A *maximal clique C* is a clique in a graph $G(V, E)$ if and only if there is no clique C' in G with $C \subset C'$. Alternatively stated, a maximal clique is a complete subgraph that is not contained in any other complete subgraph [4]. Figure 6–11(a) compares the proportion of nodes present in maximal cliques, the *clique affiliation fraction*, for nodes identified via bridging centrality, degree centrality, and betweenness centrality. The profile of the bridging centrality curve differs from the other two metrics, and this method consistently produced the lowest clique affiliation fraction. Of the nodes scored in the upper tenth percentile by degree centrality and betweenness centrality, nearly 80% and 65%, respectively, were members of cliques. The corresponding clique affiliation percentage for bridging centrality was 40%. These results demonstrate that nodes identified by bridging centrality are located outside and between cliques.

A *clique graph* $G' = \{(V', E') | V'$ is the union set of clique nodes and nonclique nodes, E' is the set of edges, an edge $e' = (i, j)$ connects two nodes i and j, $i, j \in V'$, $e' \in E'\}$ is a complex graph generated from an intact graph in which all the nodes in each maximal clique have been merged into a single *clique* node. Two clique nodes are connected by an edge if any two member nodes in the two cliques were connected in the original graph. Each clique node is connected to all nonclique nodes to which its members were connected in the original graph. The edges between the nonclique nodes remain identical to those in the original graph. The *clique betweenness* for a given nonclique node is defined as the proportion of the random paths passing through that node to the random paths between all clique pairs. More simply stated, it represents the fraction of information exchange between all clique pairs in a graph that passes through the node in question. As hypothesized, the clique betweenness for high-scoring bridging nodes was much higher than for highly ranked nodes identified by the degree and betweeness metrics [Figure 6–11(b)]. These results demonstrate that bridging nodes are important mediators of information flows among cliques.

Singletons, the final product of network graph breakdown, are an intuitive measure of the loss of network integrity. Hwang et al. have shown that the sequential removal of nodes with high bridging centrality would generate fewer singletons than the removal of nodes with high degree and betweenness centrality. In fact, bridging

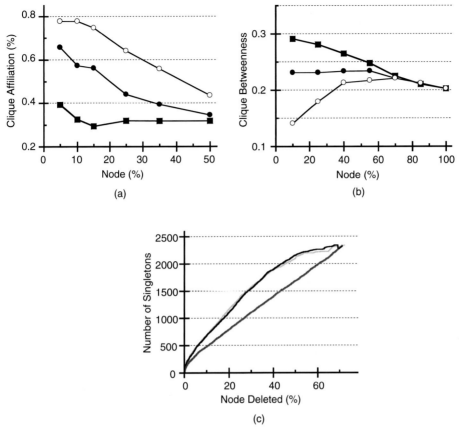

Figure 6–11 Topographical position of high-scoring nodes in the yeast PPI network.
(a) Clique affiliation of the nodes detected by bridging centrality (black squares), degree centrality (open circles), and betweenness centrality (black circles). Maximal cliques were identified in the yeast PPI network and were inspected for the presence of the nodes detected by each method. (b) Random betweenness between detected cliques was measured in the clique graph for bridging centrality (black squares), degree centrality (open circles), and betweenness centrality (black circles). (c) Comparison of the number of singletons that were generated via sequential node deletion by bridging centrality (red line), degree centrality (gray line), and betweenness centrality (blue line). The nodes with the highest values for each of these network metrics were sequentially deleted, and the number of singletons that were produced was enumerated. "See Color Plate 5." (Reprinted from [152].)

centrality did generate the fewest singletons, while degree centrality generated singletons most rapidly [Figure 6–11(c)]. Upon sequential deletion of the nodes in the upper tenth percentile of values, bridging centrality produced 553 singletons, compared to 783 singletons for betweenness centrality and 808 singletons for degree centrality.

Shannon (information) entropy was used to measure the changes to network properties resulting from the sequential removal of nodes [278]. Shannon entropy $H(X)$ is a symmetric, additive information-theoretic measure of the uncertainty of information associated with the discrete random variable X on a finite set

$\chi = \{x_i, \ldots, x_n\}$, with probability distribution function $p(x) = P_r(X = x)$, and is defined by

$$H(X) = -\sum_{x \in \chi} p(x) \log_2 p(x). \tag{6.9}$$

The information entropy is maximal when all the outcomes of a random variable are equally likely. The entropy of a network property can be interpreted as a measure of disorder; the entropy will be large if a network property is heterogeneous and will be zero if the network property becomes monodisperse.

Hwang et al. assessed the effects of sequential node removal on the mean value and entropy of several network-topological properties, including degree distribution. The average degree decreases monotonically as a result of sequential node deletion [Figure 6–12(a)]. There is a very modest initial increase in entropy caused by the generation of singletons, but the entropy decreases monotonically over most of the range [Figure 6–12(b)]. The sequential deletion of nodes based on bridging-centrality values resulted in less degradation of the degree distribution structure than deletion based the other two network metrics. In Figure 6–12, the changes in the average values for each metric are shown in the left column [Figure 6–12(a), (c), (e), and (g)]. The changes in entropy of the distribution of each metric are shown in the right column [Figure 6–12(b), (d), (f), and (h)].

Sequential node removal causes the production of one or more singletons and one or more isolated higher-order subgraphs (modules). Our working hypothesis was that the average size of the isolated modules resulting from the sequential removal of bridging nodes would be larger than the modules resulting from node removal guided by the other metrics.

Figure 6–12(c) and (d) summarize the mean size of isolated modules and the entropy of the size distribution. In Figure 6–12(c), the average-value axis is logarithmically scaled to accommodate the wide size range of isolated modules. The number of isolated modules ranges from the total number of nodes (for the intact network) to one (for a network that has been dismembered into singletons). The average module size produced by bridging centrality decreases more slowly than the other two metrics, indicating that network integrity is robust to the removal of bridging nodes. Nodes in the upper twenty-fifth percentile of values for all three metrics were deleted sequentially. In this scenario, the largest isolated module produced by bridging centrality contained 526 nodes, compared to 116 nodes for betweenness centrality and 22 nodes for degree centrality. The entropy of the isolated module size distribution for each of the metrics exhibits an initial increase and a subsequent decrease. The entropy increase occurs because modules of varying size are generated when nodes are initially removed. Further removal of nodes produces very small subgraphs containing few nodes or singletons, which causes the entropy of the system to decrease. In Figure 6–12(d), sequential removal of bridging nodes results in the slowest increase in entropy.

The average clustering coefficient for degree centrality showed a flat or decreasing trend upon sequential node removal and was distinctly different from that for betweeness centrality and bridging centrality, which exhibited an increasing trend followed by a sharp decrease [Figure 6–12(e)]. The increases for betweenness and

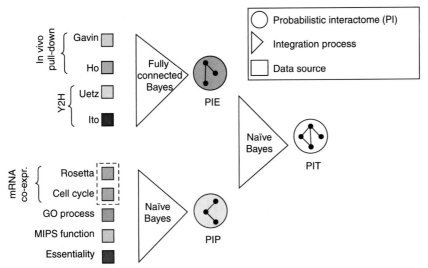

Plate 1: figure 3–5, page 29. Bayesian approach to predicting interactions through the combination of multiple data sources. (From [160]. Reprinted with permission from AAAS.)

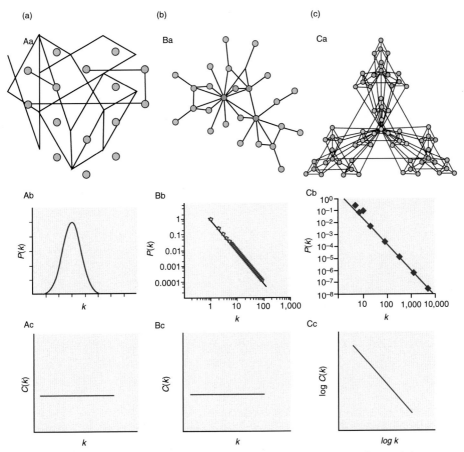

Plate 2: figure 4–4, page 47. A schematic view, the degree distribution and the average clustering coefficient of a random network (a), a scale-free network (b), and a hierarchical network (c). (Reprinted by permission from Macmillan Publishers Ltd: Nature [29], copyright 2004.)

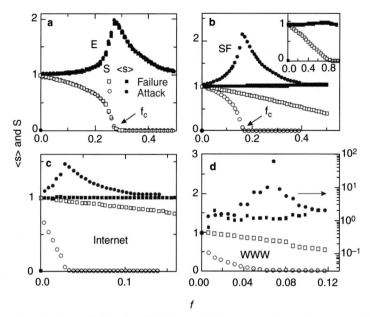

Plate 3: figure 6–2, page 66. Network fragmentation under random failures and attacks. The relative size of the largest cluster S (open symbols) and the average size of the isolated clusters ⟨s⟩ (filled symbols) as a function of the fraction of removed nodes f. (a) Fragmentation of the exponential network under random failures (squares) and attacks (circles). (b) Fragmentation of the scale-free network under random failures (blue squares) and attacks (red circles). (c) Fragmentation of the Internet network under random failures (blue squares) and attacks (red circles). (d) Fragmentation of the WWW network under random failures (blue squares) and attacks (red circles). (Reprinted by permission from Macmillan Publishers Ltd: Nature [7], copyright 2000.)

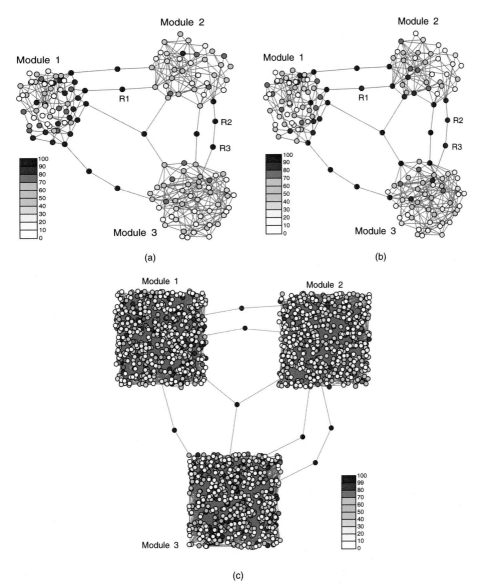

Plate 4: figure 6–8, page 76. Results of applying bridging centrality and betweenness centrality to a synthetic network containing 162 nodes and 362 edges. The network was created by adding bridging nodes to three independently generated subnetworks. The nodes in the upper tenth percentile of bridging-centrality values are depicted by red circles. Nodes in the lowest tenth percentile of bridging-centrality values are depicted by white circles. (a) application of bridging centrality, (b) application of betweenness centrality, (c) the bridging centrality results for a synthetic network in which 500 nodes were added to each subgraph in (a). The bridging nodes remain unchanged from the network in (a) . The nodes in the upper tenth percentile of bridging-centrality values are indicated by red circles. (Reprinted from [152].)

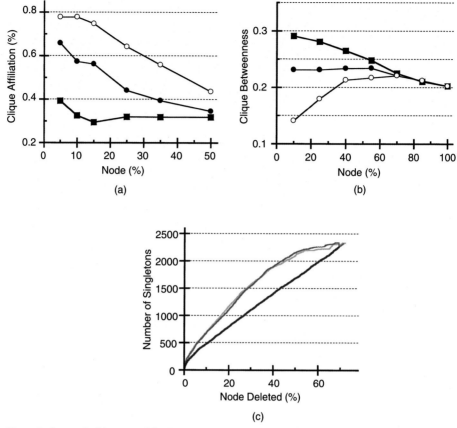

Plate 5: figure 6–11, page 81. Topographical position of high-scoring nodes in the yeast PPI network. (a) Clique affiliation of the nodes detected by bridging centrality (black squares), degree centrality (open circles), and betweenness centrality (black circles). Maximal cliques were identified in the yeast PPI network and were inspected for the presence of the nodes detected by each method. (b) Random betweenness between detected cliques was measured in the clique graph for bridging centrality (black squares), degree centrality (open circles), and betweenness centrality (black circles). (c) Comparison of the number of singletons that were generated via sequential node deletion by bridging centrality (red line), degree centrality (gray line), and betweenness centrality (blue line). The nodes with the highest values for each of these network metrics were sequentially deleted, and the number of singletons that were produced was enumerated. (Reprinted from [152].)

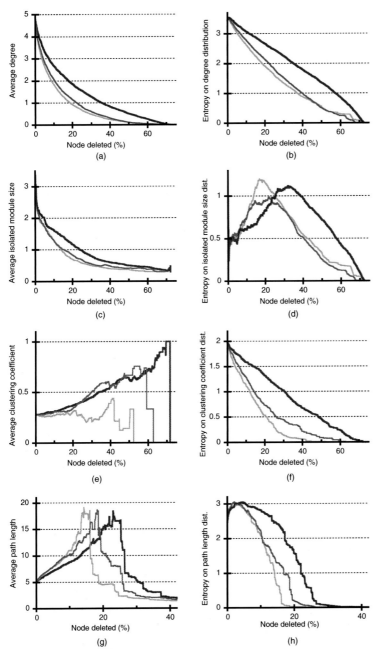

Plate 6: figure 6–12, page 83. Comparison of bridging centrality (red line) with degree centrality (gray line) and betweenness centrality (blue line) applied to node detection in the yeast PPI network data set [82,327]. (a) through (h) The nodes with the highest values of each of these network metrics were sequentially deleted and the effects on the various network properties indicated on the y-axis were computed. (Reprinted from [152].)

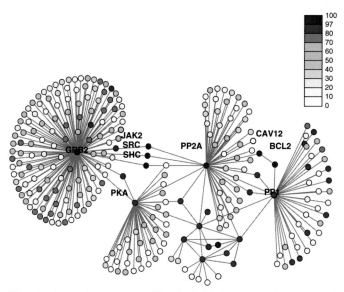

Plate 7: figure 6–15, page 93. The bridging centrality results for the cardiac arrest network. The five nodes with the highest bridging-centrality scores (SHC, SRC, JAK2, CAV12, BCL2) and the hub nodes (GRB2, PKA, PP2A, PP1) for each sub-module are labeled. Nodes in the upper 3% of bridging-centrality values are indicated by red circles. Nodes in the lowest decile of bridging-centrality values are indicated by white circles. The color key to percentile values is shown in the figure. (Reprinted from [152].)

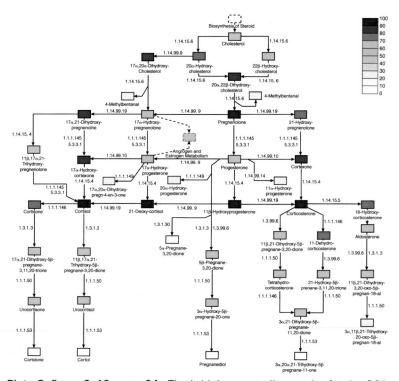

Plate 8: figure 6–16, page 94. The bridging centrality results for the C21-steroid hormone metabolism network. Nodes with bridging-centrality values in the upper tenth percentile are depicted by red circles. Nodes with bridging-centrality values in the lowest tenth percentile are depicted by white circles. (Reprinted from [152].)

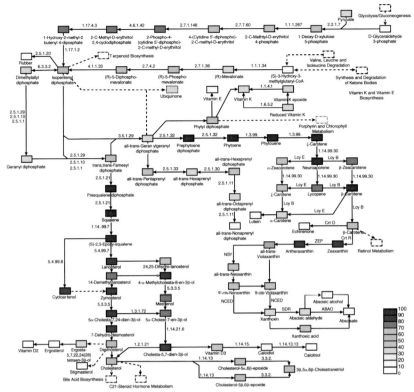

Plate 9: figure 6–17, page 95. The bridging centrality results for the steroid biosynthesis network. Nodes with bridging-centrality values in the upper tenth percentile are depicted by red circles. Nodes with bridging-centrality values in the lowest tenth percentile are depicted by white circles. (Reprinted from [152].)

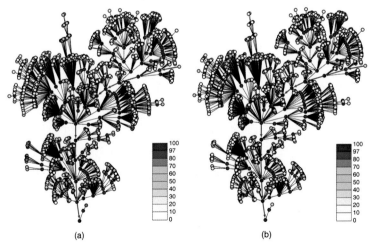

(a)   (b)

Plate 10: figure 6–18, page 96. Application of bridging centrality and Li's dynamic network model to the yeast cell cycle state space network. (a) Dynamic flows passing through nodes as mapped by Li et al. (b) Bridging-centrality scores for each node. The nodes with bridging-centrality values in the upper 3% are depicted by red circles. Nodes with bridging-centrality scores in the lowest tenth percentile are depicted by white circles. The color key to percentile values is shown in the figure. The biological pathway arcs of the yeast cell cycle are shown in blue. (Reprinted from [152].)

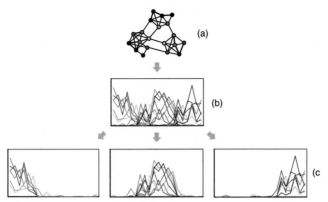

Plate 11: figure 9–21, page 195. Schematic view of functional flow pattern mining. (a) An example of a weighted network and (b) the functional influence patterns generated by flow simulation. (c) Pattern-mining algorithms can effectively identify the coherent patterns as clusters.

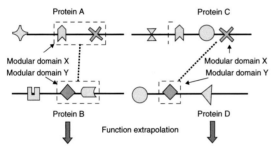

Plate 12: figure 12–1, page 245. Functional annotation scheme based on interacting domain patterns. (Reprinted from [63].)

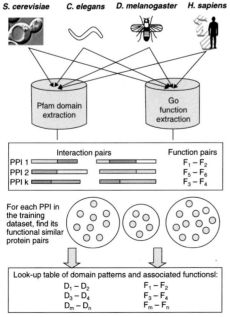

Plate 13: figure 12–2, page 246. Flow chart illustrating CSIDOP method. (Reprinted from [63].)

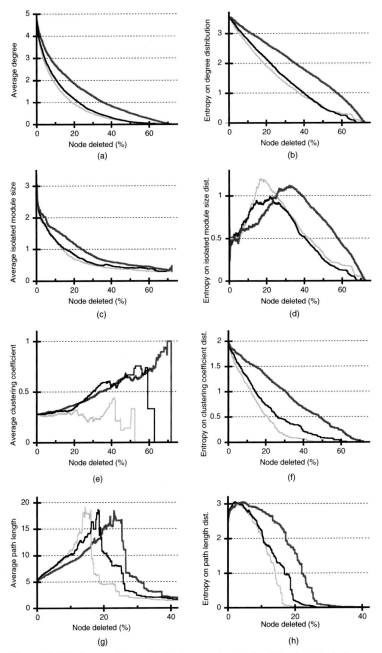

Figure 6–12 Comparison of bridging centrality (red line) with degree centrality (gray line) and betweenness centrality (blue line) applied to node detection in the yeast PPI network data set [82,327]. (a) through (h) The nodes with the highest values of each of these network metrics were sequentially deleted and the effects on the various network properties indicated on the *y*-axis were computed. "See Color Plate 6." (Reprinted from [152].)

bridging centrality demonstrate that nodes scored highly by these metrics are located in sparsely connected regions of the network, while high-degree nodes are more strongly connected. Although the average clustering coefficients for both bridging centrality and betweenness centrality had a broadly similar increasing trend, the point at which complete network breakdown occurred was delayed for bridging centrality. The entropy of the clustering coefficient distribution displayed decreases for all three metrics [Figure 6–12(f)]. However, the curve for bridging centrality was well separated from betweenness centrality in this analysis.

The APL increased more slowly for bridging centrality than for degree and betweenness centrality [Figure 6–12(g)] because sequential deletion of bridging nodes produces larger modules. The APL decreased rapidly when the network disintegrated into numerous small subgraphs with a limited range of path lengths and singletons. The rapid decrease in APL occurred upon removal of the 539th node for bridging centrality, whereas it occurred at the removal of the 377th and 435th nodes for degree and betweenness centrality, respectively. The entropy of the path length distribution increases initially, reflecting the increased path length between nodes, and then decreases upon removal of additional nodes. The slowest decrease in entropy occurred for bridging centrality, demonstrating that removal of bridging nodes disrupts communication without causing as much loss of structural integrity.

These experiments demonstrate that bridging nodes occupy unique locations and are positioned at important junctures between subregions in the network.

6.4 NETWORK MODULARIZATION USING THE BRIDGE CUT ALGORITHM

Bridges are located between modules in a network. Therefore, using identified bridges as module boundaries, a graph can be partitioned into sub-modules. This section will introduce a graph partitioning algorithm that exploits this property of bridging centrality.

The iterative graph clustering algorithm involves three sequential processes:

Process 1: Compute the bridging centrality of all edges in graph G and select the edge e with the highest bridging value.

Process 2: Remove edge e from graph G.

Process 3: Identify a subgraph s as a final cluster: If s is isolated from G and the density of s relative to the original graph G is greater than a selected threshold, remove s from G.

These three sequential steps are repeated until G is empty.

The bridge cut algorithm is described in detail in Algorithm 6.1 [151]. The performance of the algorithm was tested by using it to cluster DIP yeast PPI data set [82,327]. Results were compared to those obtained with six competing clustering approaches: maximal clique [286], quasi clique [56], minimum cut [164], the statistical approach of Samanta and Liang [272], MCL [308], and Rives' method [263].

Results obtained using the DIP PPI data set [82,327] are presented in Table 6.1. The DIP PPI data set contains 2,339 nodes with 5,595 edges. The MIPS complex category data were used as reference modules against which the clustering results were

Table 6.1 Comparative analysis of the bridge cut method and six graph clustering approaches (maximal clique, quasi clique, Rive's method, minimum cut, Markov clustering, and Samanta's method).

Methods	Clusters	Size	MIPS complex (*f*-measure)	DB
Bridge Cut	**114**	**7.6**	**0.53**	**4.78**
Max Cliq	120	4.7	0.49	N/A
Quasi Cliq	103	9.2	0.46	N/A
Rives	74	31	0.33	13.5
Mincut	227	8.7	0.35	7.23
MCL	210	8.4	0.47	6.82
Samanta	138	7.2	0.43	6.8

All methods were applied to the DIP PPI data set. The second column indicates the number of clusters detected. The third column shows the average size of each cluster. The fourth column represents the average *f*-measure of the clusters for MIPS complex modules. The average *f*-measure value of detected modules was calculated by mapping each module to the MIPS complex module with the highest *f*-measure value. The fifth column indicates the Davies–Bouldin cluster quality index. Comparisons are performed for clusters with four or more components.

Algorithm 6.1 BridgeCut(G)

1: G': A clone of graph G
2: ClusterList: the list of final clusters
3: topEdge: the edge with the highest bridging centrality
4: densityThreshold: sub-graph density threshold
5: **while** G != empty **do**
6:     Calculate bridging centrality for all edges in graph G
7:     topEdge = The edge with the highest bridging centrality
8:     Remove topEdge
9:     **if** there is a new isolated module s **then**
10:         **if** Density(s,G') > densityThreshold **then**
11:             ClusterList.add(s)
12:             G.remove(s)
13:         **end if**
14:     **end if**
15: **end while**
16: Return ClusterList

---

measured. This data was considered suitable for this purpose because a group of physically interacting proteins is highly likely to form a protein complex. A sparse network such as the low-density (0.002045) DIP PPI network presents a significant clustering challenge, since most graph clustering methods depend on identifying densely connected regions. Despite this sparse connectivity, the bridge cut algorithm detected more modules with high f-measures, 0.53, in the MIPS complex category and had a lower DB index, 4.78, than the other tested approaches. The maximal clique, MCL, and quasi clique methods produced comparable f-measure scores, at 0.49, 0.47, and 0.46, respectively (see Section 5.4 for the definitions of DB and f-measure.). However, the maximal clique and quasi clique methods produced many small, highly

Table 6.2 Top ten best *f*-measure-valued clusters identified by the bridge cut algorithm.

ID	Size	*F*	Hit (%)	MIPS complex
1	4	1.0	100	AP-3 complex
2	4	1.0	100	CCAAT-binding factor complex
3	5	0.89	80	AP-1 complex
4	4	0.89	100	Gim complexes
5	8	0.86	75	Replication complexes
6	4	0.86	75	Complex Number 482
7	15	0.85	73	Anaphase promoting complex
8	20	0.84	80	20S proteasome
9	7	0.83	71	Tim22p-complex
10	6	0.8	80	Class C Vps protein complex

In order, the columns represent the cluster ID, cluster size, *f*-measure, MIPS complex module matching percentile, and best-matching MIPS complex module.

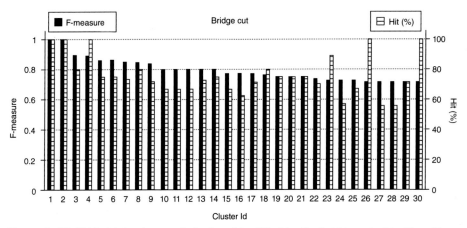

Figure 6–13 Thirty highest-scored clusters identified by the bridge cut algorithm. The *f*-measure values and the percentile of matching proteins with the best-mapping MIPS complex module for the 30 highest *f*-measure-valued clusters are illustrated. (Reprinted from [151].)

overlapping clusters and used only 2.7% and 19.2% of the available nodes, discarding a huge portion of the data set. It is evident that these methods have a limited ability to properly discriminate among detected clusters. DB index values for these two methods cannot be generated for this reason. The MCL method produced an *f*-measure comparable to the bridge cut algorithm, but its DB index result was inferior. Clusters identified by MCL are biologically and topologically weaker, less compact, and more indistinct. The bridge cut method detected more plausible, biologically enriched clusters with greater compactness and stronger topological separability.

Figure 6–13 plots the *f*-measure values and the percentile of proteins matched with the best-mapping MIPS complex module for the thirty highest *f*-measure-valued clusters identified by the bridge cut algorithm. The average *f*-measure value of these proteins is 0.794, and the average likelihood of alignment with the best-matching MIPS complex module is 75.8%. Table 6.2 lists the top ten f-measure-valued clusters and their corresponding sizes, f-measure values, MIPS complex module matching percentile (Hit%), and the name of the best-matching MIPS complex module. The bridge cut algorithm identified plausible modules with high enrichment and a strong likelihood of matching with diverse MIPS complex modules.

6.5 USE OF BRIDGING NODES IN DRUG DISCOVERY

The efficacy, specificity/selectivity, and side-effect characteristics of well-designed drugs depend largely on the appropriate choice of pharmacological target. For this reason, the identification of molecular targets is an early and very critical step in the drug discovery and development process. Target identification could be improved significantly if the large databases of biological information currently available were leveraged using novel analysis approaches. The need for effective target identification is highlighted by the resource- and time-intensive nature of modern pharmaceutical development and the cost of failures. Failures late in the development process, after expensive clinical trials have been undertaken, are significantly more costly than early-stage failures. Several prominent late-stage and post-marketing withdrawals of drugs have occurred in recent years [32,57,169,335].

The goal of the target identification process is to arrive at a very limited subset of biological molecules – preferably one, if possible – that will become the principal focus for the subsequent discovery research, development, and clinical trials. Effective pharmacological intervention with the target protein should significantly impact the key molecular processes in which the protein participates, and the resultant perturbation should be successful in modulating the pathophysiological process of interest. In addition to efficacy and selectivity, side effects are a key consideration. However, the potential for side effects is sometimes deemphasized or deferred during initial target identification in favor of pharmacological activity, in part because it is often assumed that side effects and effect selectivity can implicitly be addressed upon achieving the requisite potency and selectivity of the pharmacological target.

Hwang et al. [152] approached the issue of target identification from a different perspective and with the benefit of information regarding biological pathway networks. In the representation of a biological network, molecules are represented by nodes, and the interactions between molecules are the edges connecting nodes. The degree and betweenness centrality of a node have been proposed as metrics useful for assessing drug targets. As defined in Chapter 4, the degree is the number of edges connecting a node, and betweenness centrality is the fraction of shortest paths passing through a given node [47,110,227,268]. The use of degree and betweenness centrality for drug target identification is based on the observation that proteins with high values of these metrics have a high experimental likelihood of causing lethality when eliminated from a yeast protein network [7,131,134].

Although degree and betweenness centrality can potentially locate targets with strong effect, their major weakness is in their specificity/selectivity of effects and side-effect profiles; lethality cannot be tolerated as an outcome in pharmaceutical development. Furthermore, analysis of several genomes indicates a significant trend toward evolutionary conservation of proteins with high degree and betweeness centrality [131]. Hwang et al. therefore argued that drug targeting with the currently available centrality metric models is likely to prove suboptimal because of the lack of specificity/selectivity of effects and the high risk of side effects.

In this section, we will discuss the use of bridging centrality as an effective drug target identification model. Nodes identified as bridges by their high values of bridging centrality are likely to be good drug targets.

6.5.1 Biological Correlates of Bridging Centrality

In the ideal case, human gene networks would be used to assess target druggability, but such a direct approach is not possible because of the paucity of systematic phenotypic information on human gene networks of therapeutic interest. However, the budding yeast (*S. cerevisiae*) is very amenable to targeted genetic manipulation, and the effect of gene deletions on cell viability has been investigated in this model system. The DIP core yeast PPI data set was obtained from the DIP database [82].

Hwang et al. [152] used the yeast PPI network [82,327] for assessing several biological correlates of bridging centrality.

Lethality is an undesirable attribute in the majority of drug discovery applications, with the possible exception of anticancer drugs. Figure 6–14(a) shows that nodes with the highest bridging-centrality scores are less lethal (with an average lethality of 34%) than nodes with high degree centrality (an average lethality of 48%) and nodes with high betweenness centrality (an average lethality of 42%). These biological correlates are consistent with the critical topological positions of the nodes with the highest bridging-centrality scores.

As expected, the risk of lethality increases with increasing degree and betweenness centrality. However, the lethality risk for nodes in the highest percentiles of bridging centrality differs markedly, and deletions of these nodes are less lethal. Although low-degree nodes have low lethality probabilities, there are numerous low-degree nodes in most networks, severely limiting their value as drug targets.

The biological processes of the nearest-neighbor regions of the six nodes with a degree of 5 or less from the top ten bridging nodes was assessed. The Gene Ontology (GO) [18,302] terms in the "biological process" category was used to assess the functional roles of the nodes in these regions. The most frequent GO terms associated with these neighboring nodes were determined, and the percentage of relevant nodes was calculated. The neighboring region was defined as the subgraph comprised of the nearest neighbor and the nodes directly connected to it. Five levels of the GO biological process hierarchy were analyzed. The proportion of nodes associated with a given GO biological process term was compared to the corresponding proportion in the remainder of the network, using the Z-test for proportions to obtain a p-value. The p-values were expressed as $-$Log p, which is the negative logarithm of the p-value to the base 10. A $-$Log p of 2 is equivalent to a p-value of 0.01.

The results for Gene Ontology levels 4 and 5 (Table 6.3; results for levels 6 and 7 not shown) show that these bridging nodes are located between processes involved in the cell cycle. The frequency of specific biological processes in each region adjacent to a bridging node is higher than the corresponding frequency in the entire yeast

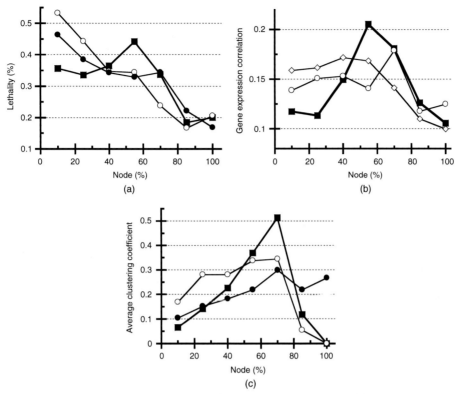

Figure 6–14 Biological characteristics of the nodes ordered by bridging centrality (black squares), degree centrality (open circles), and betweenness centrality (black circles). (a) The lethality of each percentile, (b) the gene expression correlation to the neighbors of each percentile, (c) the average clustering coefficient of each percentile. (Reprinted from [152].)

PPI network, demonstrating relative enrichment for the specific biological process. When a node was adjacent to more than one region, each neighboring region was associated with separate GO terms, indicating that the bridging node was located between different functional subregions. The relative enrichment of function in each neighboring region is maintained across all four levels of the GO hierarchy.

The correlation of bridging nodes with gene expression was measured for the yeast PPI network using the Pearson correlation applied to Spellman cell cycle data [285]. The results [Figure 6–14(b)] indicate that the gene expression correlation of high bridging-centrality nodes is lower than that of nodes identified by the other two metrics. The findings support the premise that bridging nodes are positioned between different functional modules, while the nodes identified by the other two metrics are located within functional modules that have correlated gene expression patterns.

The low lethality and low gene expression correlation of bridging nodes were associated with a lower clustering coefficient [Figure 6–14(c)]. Associations between gene expression and clustering coefficient are expected because highly connected regions of biological networks are rich in functional modules that have correlated

Table 6.3 The GO Biological Process Analysis Results for Top Bridging Nodes with Degree ≤ 5.

Node	Degree	Neighbor	Size	LEVEL 4 GO Term	Hits #	% Hit	% Overall	−Log p
YER120W	2	1	91	G00022403: Cell cycle phase	32	35	10	15
		2	44	G00042254: Ribosome biogen. & assem.	27	61	8	>16
YOR177C	2	1	91	G00022403: Cell cycle phase	32	35	10	15
		2	39	G00044267: Cellular protein meta. process	13	33	23	1.2
		1	56	G00044267: Cellular protein meta. process	11	20	23	0.61
		2	36	G00044267: Cellular protein meta. process	25	69	23	11
YELO34W	5	3	31	G00016070: RNA metabolic process	11	35	25	1.1
		4	45	G00042254: Ribosome biogen. & assem.	18	40	8	15
		5	39	G00044267: Cellular protein meta. process	12	31	23	0.86
YLR430W	2	1	91	G00022403: Cell cycle phase	32	35	10	15
		2	30	G00022413: Rep. pro. in single-celled org.	9	30	6	8.5
YER023W	2	1	56	G00044267: Cellular protein meta. process	12	21	23	0.45
		2	35	G00051649: Est. of cellular localization	14	40	14	5.2
YDR229W	2	1	55	G00016192: Vesicle-mediated transport	14	25	9	5.2
		2	34	G00051649: Est. of cellular localization	16	47	14	7.7

LEVEL 5 GO Term

Node	Degree	Neighbor	Size	GO Term	Hits #	% Hits	% Overall	−Log p′
YER120W	2	1	91	GO:0000074: Regulation of cell cycle	25	27	5	>16
		2	44	GO:0006396: RNA processing	17	39	10	10
YOR177C	2	1	91	GO:0000074: Regulation of cell cycle	25	27	5	>16
		2	39	GO:0006464: Protein modification process	11	28	12	3.2
YELO34W	5	1	56	GO:0030029: Actin filament-based process	6	11	4	2.4
		2	36	GO:0006508: Proteolysis	20	56	5	>16
		3	31	GO:0006396: RNA processing	16	19	10	1.4
		4	45	GO:0042273: Rib. large sub. bio. & assem.	10	22	2	>16
		5	39	GO:0006464: Protein modification process	11	28	12	3.2
YLR430W	2	1	91	GO:0000074: Regulation of cell cycle	25	27	5	>16
		2	30	GO:0008361: Regulation of cell size	8	27	4	11
YERO23W	2	1	56	GO:0030029: Actin filament-based process	6	11	4	2.4
		2	35	GO:0046907: Intracellular transport	14	40	14	5.4
YDR229W	2	1	55	GO:0046908: Neg. reg. of crystal formation	12	22	4	12
		2	34	GO:0046909: Intermembrane transport	16	47	14	8.0

Column headers indicate the following features: "Node" is the identity of the bridging node; "Degree" is the degree of the bridging node; "Neighbor" is the neighboring region assessed; "Size" is the size of the neighboring region; "GO Term" is the Gene Ontology biological process term most frequently associated with the neighboring region; "Hits #" and "% Hits" are the frequency and percentage of occurrence of the GO term in the neighboring region; "% Overall" is the percentage of nodes in the entire yeast PPI network that match the GO term; "−Log p" is the negative logarithm (base 10) of the difference in proportions between the neighboring region and the entire PPI network using the Z-test. A −Log p of 2 corresponds to significance at $p = 0.01$.

gene expression [239]. However, the association of low lethality with low clustering-coefficient values at bridging nodes is unexpected and represents a unique biological correlate of bridging centrality.

Nodes with high clustering coefficients are usually associated with low lethality, because their strong connectivity provides numerous alternate paths around the node [239]. Thus, bridging nodes would be expected to have high lethality due to the lack of alternative paths. Our unexpected findings of low lethality at bridging nodes cannot readily be explained in relationship to clustering-coefficient levels. However, these findings can be rationalized by noting that the removal of bridging nodes disrupts interactions between modules without affecting their structural integrity. The lethality and gene expression results for the yeast PPI network demonstrate that bridging nodes are less lethal and are generally independently regulated in their gene expression. These results are consistent with the possibility that bridging nodes may be attractive as drug targets.

6.5.2 Results from Drug Discovery-Relevant Human Networks

Motivated by the encouraging performance of the bridging centrality metric with the synthetic networks, Hwang et al. [152] evaluated its performance with a network model for the genes involved in human cardiac arrest [16]. The cardiac arrest network, a PPI network of candidate sudden-cardiac-death susceptibility genes, was obtained from [16]. This network (illustrated in Figure 6–15) is simple, highly modular, and has many peripheral nodes. Analysis is simplified by the fact that the majority of its key bridging nodes can be readily identified by visual inspection. The nodes corresponding to SHC, SRC, and JAK2 were ranked first, second, and third in bridging centrality, respectively. These proteins are the three main bridges between the GRB2 and PP2A modules, the two largest modules in the network. CAV12 and BCL2, which are on the bridge between the PP2A and PP1 modules, had the fourth- and fifth-highest values of bridging centrality, respectively. An analysis of the pharmacology literature was used to assess their importance as drug targets in cardiac diseases. Isoproteronol, a β-adrenergic receptor agonist, attenuates phosphorylation of both the SHC and SRC proteins in cardiomyocytes [348]. The angiotensin receptor 2, the target of receptor antagonist drugs such as losartan, also signals via SRC and SHC in cardiac fibroblasts [329]. JAK2 activation is a key mediator of aldosterone-induced angiotensin-converting enzyme expression; the latter is the target of drugs such as captopril, enapril, and other angiotensin-converting enzyme inhibitors [294].

Figure 6–16 summarizes the results of the application of bridging centrality to the C21-steroid hormone network [170]. The metabolites with the highest values of bridging centrality were corticosterone, cortisol, 11 β-hydroxyprogesterone, pregnenolone, and 21-deoxy-cortisol.

Corticosterone and cortisol are produced by the adrenal glands and mediate the flight-or-fight stress response, which includes changes to blood sugar, blood pressure, and immune modulation. Cortisol can be considered a very successful drug target because numerous corticosteroid derivatives have already been approved as immunosuppressive agents; these include hydrocortisone, methylprednisolone sodium succinate, dexamethasone, and betamethasone dipropionate.

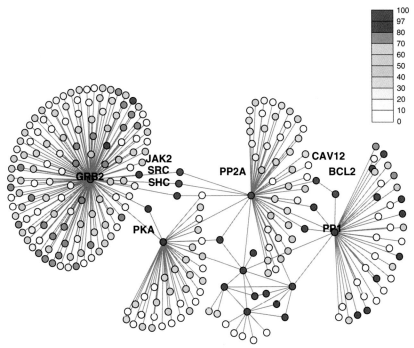

Figure 6–15 The bridging centrality results for the cardiac arrest network. The five nodes with the highest bridging-centrality scores (SHC, SRC, JAK2, CAV12, BCL2) and the hub nodes (GRB2, PKA, PP2A, PP1) for each sub-module are labeled. Nodes in the upper 3% of bridging-centrality values are indicated by red circles. Nodes in the lowest decile of bridging-centrality values are indicated by white circles. The color key to percentile values is shown in the figure. "See Color Plate 7." (Reprinted from [152].)

These drugs are used to treat a wide range of conditions ranging from Addison's disease to allergic rashes, eczema, asthma, and arthritis. In humans, corticosterone is a steroidogenic intermediate, but it is the predominant glucocorticoid in other species. These findings indicate that targeting bridging nodes can yield highly effective and safe drugs.

Similar tests were run using a steroid biosynthesis network; results are presented in Figure 6–17. The C21-steroid hormone metabolism and biosynthesis of steroid networks were obtained from the KEGG database [170]. The metabolites with the highest values of bridging centrality were presqualene diphosphate, squalene, (S)-2,3-epoxysqualene, prephytoene diphosphate, and phytoene.

The conversion of squalene to (S)-2,3-epoxysqualene is mediated by squalene epoxidase. Squalene epoxidase is the primary target of allylamine antifungal agents such as terbinafine and butenafine, which are sold as *LAMISIL*® and *LOTRIMIN*®. These agents exploit the structural differences between human and fungal squalene oxidase [119]. Anti-fungal agents are generally considered difficult to develop because, like humans, these pathogens are eukaryotic and share many biochemical pathways with structurally similar enzymes. Squalene epoxidase is also a promising target for anticholesterol drugs [73], and the anti-cholesterolemic activity of green tea polyphenols is caused by potent selective inhibition of squalene epoxidase [1].

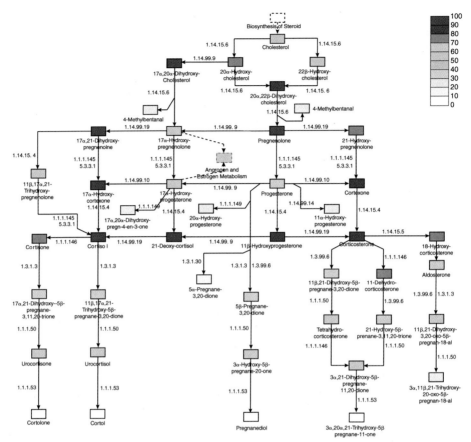

Figure 6–16 The bridging centrality results for the C21-steroid hormone metabolism network. Nodes with bridging-centrality values in the upper tenth percentile are depicted by red circles. Nodes with bridging-centrality values in the lowest tenth percentile are depicted by white circles. "See Color Plate 8." (Reprinted from [152].)

6.5.3 Comparison to Alternative Approaches: Yeast Cell Cycle State Space Network

In this section, Hwang et al. [152] compared the performance of bridging centrality to results obtained by Li et al. [197] using a dynamic network model for the control of the yeast cell cycle. They studied the attractors of the network dynamics of each of the 211 initial protein states and identified a single super-stable state attracting 1,764 protein states [197].

Figure 6–18(a) illustrates the dynamic flows mapped by Li's research. Bridging nodes [Figure 6–18(b)] were found at locations where the dynamic trajectories converged into the biological pathway. The key nodes identified by Li et al. were also highly ranked bridging nodes. These findings indicate that bridging centrality analysis can provide insights that are consistent with more complex, parameter-intensive dynamic models.

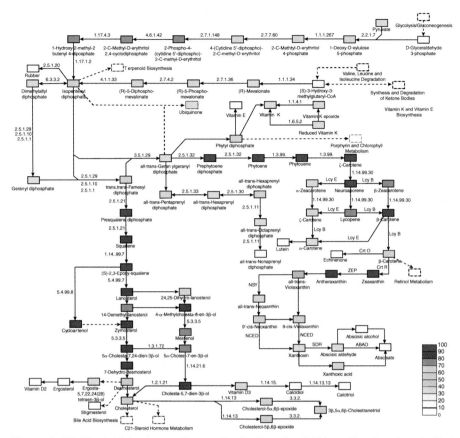

Figure 6–17 The bridging centrality results for the steroid biosynthesis network. Nodes with bridging-centrality values in the upper tenth percentile are depicted by red circles. Nodes with bridging-centrality values in the lowest tenth percentile are depicted by white circles. "See Color Plate 9." (Reprinted from [152].)

6.5.4 Potential of Bridging Centrality as a Drug Discovery Tool

Although computational approaches have been proposed to mine functional modules, protein complexes, essential components, and pathways from PPI data, few computational methods have been investigated for facilitating drug discovery from analyses of biological networks. In this section, we explored the potential of the bridging-centrality metric to selectively identify bridging nodes in biological networks. Bridging centrality is unique because it derives its effectiveness by combining both local and global network properties. Bridging nodes occupy critical sites in networks and connect subregions to each other. The biological characteristics of bridging nodes are consistent with a role in mediating signal flow between functional modules, and the results presented here indicate that many bridging nodes have already been identified as effective drug targets.

It may be desirable to incorporate relative expression levels of specific proteins in different target and nontarget organs into the drug-development analysis, because

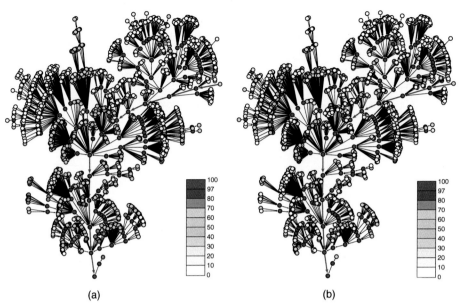

(a)   (b)

Figure 6–18 Application of bridging centrality and Li's dynamic network model to the yeast cell cycle state space network. (a) Dynamic flows passing through nodes as mapped by Li et al. (b) Bridging-centrality scores for each node. The nodes with bridging-centrality values in the upper 3% are depicted by red circles. Nodes with bridging-centrality scores in the lowest tenth percentile are depicted by white circles. The color key to percentile values is shown in the figure. The biological pathway arcs of the yeast cell cycle are shown in blue. "See Color Plate 10." (Reprinted from [152].)

selectivity can also result from mechanisms involving differential expression. The analysis presented here focused principally on topological characteristics, because large-scale system-level network topologies and expression levels for organ systems are not currently available.

The available centrality metrics can be classified as deriving from node connectivity, path, or clustering considerations. Hybrid approaches integrating gene expression, gene ontology, and other data sources have been proposed for functional module detection. In power law networks, the high-degree nodes or hubs are sensitive to targeted attack [7]. In yeast, gene deletion at hubs increases the risk of lethality. Hubs in the yeast interactome network have been picturesquely classified into "date" and "party" hubs by employing gene expression profiles [134]; the network was more vulnerable to targeted attacks at date hubs. However, hub targets may present a wide spectrum of side effects.

Betweenness centrality is a path-based centrality metric. Comparative analysis of the yeast, worm, and fly PPI networks indicates that nodes with high betweenness centrality evolve more slowly and are more likely to be essential for survival [337]. Such nodes are also more likely to be lethal because they are pleiotropic, which limits their usefulness as drug targets. In the yeast metabolic network, a high proportion of nodes lacking alternative paths were found to be lethal in the event of arc deletion [239]. Clustering of the yeast metabolic network has been used to demonstrate that metabolites participating in connecting different modules are conserved more than hubs [129]. In the yeast PIN network, nodes with higher values of subgraph centrality are more likely to be lethal than high-degree nodes [103].

The bridging centrality approach is an intuitive and novel conceptual framework for identifying drug targets with a potential for positive effectiveness and side-effect profiles. Future research will involve analysis of additional networks containing known pharmacological targets to further establish bridging centrality as a criterion for identifying therapeutic targets. Further investigation of disease in animal models, followed by field testing in the pharmaceutical discovery setting, is needed to establish whether the bridging approach can enhance overall success rates in drug discovery.

6.6 PATHRATIO: A NOVEL TOPOLOGICAL METHOD FOR PREDICTING PROTEIN FUNCTIONS

In this section, we present a new topological method for the integration of different data sets, the selection of reliable interactions, and the prediction of potential interactions, which may be overlooked by other approaches. This topological measurement exploits the small-world topological properties of PPI networks to identify reliable interactions and protein pairs with higher function homogeneity. (Most materials in this section are from [245]. Reprinted with permission from IEEE.)

6.6.1 Weighted PPI Network

The probability of the occurrence of any PPI can be assessed either by estimating the probabilities of single interactions or using reliability estimates for entire interaction data sets. The latter approach is considered to provide a more objective estimate for each individual interaction, since it is based on global statistics for the whole data set and is not biased toward any specific protein interaction. Independently estimating the probability of a single interaction requires additional information about related proteins and therefore is intrinsically biased toward those proteins for which information is available.

Pei et al. [245] examined the reliability of such probability estimates using several protein interaction data sets $S = \{S_1, S_2, \ldots, S_n\}$ as input, where each set S_i includes many interactions. S_{combined} is the union of these data sets:

$$S_{\text{combined}} = S_1 \cup S_2 \cdots \cup S_n. \tag{6.10}$$

A probability estimate is then generated for each interaction $(u, v) \in S_{\text{combined}}$. on the basis of the reliability of the full interaction data sets. The probability of each interaction (u, v) that appears in a single data set S_i is equivalent to the reliability of this data set:

$$w(u, v) = r_k \quad \text{for each } (u, v) \in S_k, \tag{6.11}$$

where r_k is the estimated reliability of the PPI data set S_k. An interaction (u, v) may alternatively occur in multiple data sets,

$$(u, v) \in S_{uv1} \cap S_{uv2} \cdots \cap S_{uvm}, \tag{6.12}$$

where $S_{uv1}, S_{uv2}, \ldots, S_{uvm} \in S$ and $m > 1$. In this case, its probability is set to

$$w(u, v) = 1 - (1 - r_{uv1}) * (1 - r_{uv2}) * \cdots * (1 - r_{uvm}), \qquad (6.13)$$

where r_{uvi} is the estimated reliability of S_{uvi}. This formula reflects the fact that interactions detected in multiple experiments are generally more reliable than those detected by a single experiment [23,312].

Estimating the prior probability for each interaction in this manner produces a weighted graph of a PPI network in which vertices are proteins, edges are interactions, and the weights represent our prior knowledge of the probabilities of interactions.

6.6.2 Protein Connectivity and Interaction Reliability

Neighborhood cohesiveness can be defined as the significance of the connections between two vertices. In traditional methods, neighborhood sharing has been confined to the relationship between direct neighbors. Pei et al. [245] extended this concept to indirect neighbors, in recognition of the complex topology of real-world networks.

Figure 6–19 illustrates the various ways in which two proteins may be connected by paths of various lengths. The simplest is the direct connection between two vertices A and B. Other paths may also connect the two vertices; in Figure 6–19, the thick lines represent edges in these paths. In Figure 6–19(a), vertices A and B are connected by two paths of length 2 ($\langle A, C, B \rangle$ and $\langle A, D, B \rangle$). In Figure 6–19(b), vertices A and B are connected by three paths of length 3 ($\langle A, C, D, B \rangle$, $\langle A, E, F, B \rangle$, and $\langle A, C, F, B \rangle$). In (c), vertices A and B are connected by several paths of length 4, one of which is $\langle A, C, D, E, B \rangle$.

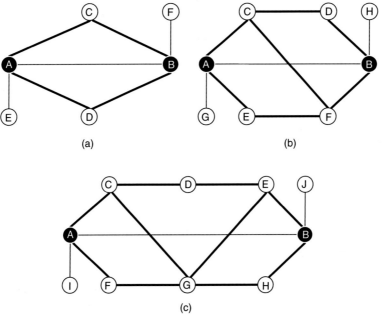

(a)   (b)

(c)

Figure 6–19 Various connections between two proteins.

In a small-world PPI network, high clustering coefficient values suggest that proteins are likely to form dense clusters associated with interactions. Therefore, true positive interactions in protein complexes and tightly coupled networks demonstrate dense interconnections. In [315], Walhout et al. also observed that contiguous interaction connections that form closed loops are likely to increase the biological relevance of the corresponding interactions. Based upon this observation, the significance of the coexistence of two proteins in a dense network can be used as an index of interaction reliability, when corrected for noise-related false positives. The new topological approach presented here evaluates and combines the significance of all k-length paths between two vertices.

6.6.3 PathStrength and PathRatio Measurements

The formulation of this topological measurement begins with a definition of the strength of paths between two vertices.

Definition 6.5

The PathStrength *of a path p, denoted by* PS(p), *is the product of the weights of all the edges on the path:*

$$PS(p) = \prod_{i=1}^{l} w(v_{i-1}, v_i), \tag{6.14}$$

for path $p = \langle v_0, v_1, \ldots, v_l \rangle$.

The k-length PathStrength between two vertices A and B, denoted by $PS^k(A, B)$, is the sum of the PathStrength of all k-length paths between vertices A and B:

$$PS^k(A, B) = \sum_{p=\langle v_0=A, v_1, \ldots, v_k=B \rangle} PS(p). \tag{6.15}$$

The PathStrength of a path captures the probability that a walk along the path will reach its ending vertex. By summing these paths, the k-length PathStrength between two vertices captures the strength of the connections between these two vertices by a k-step walk.

The k-length PathStrength between two vertices is calculated separately for various values of k because paths of different lengths will have diverse impacts on the connection. A larger k-value indicates the presence of more alternative paths and therefore confers less significance on the same PS^k value. To normalize the PathStrength values for paths of different lengths, MaxPathStrength is defined as follows.

Definition 6.6

The k-length MaxPathStrength *between two vertices A and B, denoted by* $MaxPS^k(A, B)$, *is defined as*

$$MaxPS^k(A, B) = \begin{cases} \sqrt{d(A) * d(B)}, & \text{if } k = 2, \\ d(A) * d(B), & \text{if } k = 3, \\ \displaystyle\sum_{P_i \in N(A), P_j \in N(B)} MaxPS^{k-2}(P_i, P_j), & \text{if } k > 3. \end{cases} \tag{6.16}$$

For the weighted PPI network, the degree of a vertex v, denoted as d(v), is the sum of weights of the edges connecting v: $d(v) = \sum_{(u,v)\in E} w(u,v)$. *As defined in Chapter 4, for the unweighted model, the degree of a vertex v is simply the cardinality of N(v):* $d(v) = |N(v)|$.

MaxPathStrength measures the maximum possible PathStrength between two vertices. Since we consider only $PS^k(A, B)$ for $k > 1$, $MaxPS^k(A, B)$ is defined only for the $k > 1$ case. Dividing the PathStrength by this maximum possible value generates a significance measurement for k-length paths.

Definition 6.7

The k-length PathRatio between two vertices A and B, denoted by $PR^k(A, B)$, is the ratio of the k-length PathStrength to the k-length MaxPathStrength between two vertices A and B:

$$PR^k(A, B) = \frac{PS^k(A, B)}{MaxPS^k(A, B)}. \tag{6.17}$$

The final topological measurement is generated by summing the values for all lengths.

Definition 6.8

The PathRatio between two vertices A and B, denoted by PR(A, B), is the sum of the k-length PathRatios between A and B for all possible $k > 1$:

$$PR(A, B) = \sum_{k=2}^{|V|-2} PR^k(A, B), \tag{6.18}$$

where $|V|$ is the number of vertices in the graph.

Since this PathRatio measurement will be used to identify reliable edges, the measurement has been constructed to be independent of $w(A, B)$. Therefore, in the calculation of $PR(A, B)$ the prior probability of (A, B) is hidden by replacing the connection between A and B with a $w(A, B) = 1$ edge.

6.6.4 Analysis of the PathRatio Topological Measurement

Since the PathRatio measurement is composed of PR^k for different k values, each PR^k can be viewed as a component of the measurement. The signal in PathRatio is calculated by the sum of the signals from each of these components. An examination of the components of the measurement reveals several interesting properties.

■ The first PathRatio component, $PR^2(A, B)$, is a generalized form of the square root of the geometric version of the mutual clustering coefficient. If, in the absence of prior reliability information about the edges, each edge is treated equally ($w(u, v) = 1$ for any $(u, v) \in E$), then $PS^2(A, B)$ is the number of shared neighbors of A and B. The degrees of A and B are the number of neighbors of A and B, respectively. Thus, we have

$$PR^2(A, B) = \frac{|N(A) \cap N(B)|}{\sqrt{|N(A)| * |N(B)|}}, \qquad (6.19)$$

which is exactly the square root of the geometric version of the mutual clustering coefficient in [125]. Therefore, the mutual clustering coefficient is incorporated into the PathRatio.

■ The second PathRatio component, $PR^3(A, B)$, measures the ratio of direct connections between the neighbors of vertices A and B. If each vertex in $N(A)$ is connected to each vertex in $N(B)$ with a *weight* $= 1$ edge, the maximum value of $PS^3(A, B)$ is achieved. In this case,

$$PS^3(A, B) = d(A) * d(B). \qquad (6.20)$$

Therefore, the second component of the PathRatio measures the significance of observing length-3 paths, given the degrees of A and B.

■ The $MaxPS^k(A, B)$ for $k > 3$ is defined recursively. The definition of $MaxPS^k(A, B)$ ensures that its value is generally larger for larger k; that is, longer paths. In addition, at higher values of k, it is much more difficult for $PS^k(A, B)$ to achieve the $MaxPS^k(A, B)$ value in a real PPI network. The $MaxPS^4(A, B)$ is defined as the sum of $MaxPS^2$ for each neighbor of A and B. To achieve this maximum value, each neighbor of A and of B should be connected by $MaxPS^2$ paths, each neighbor of A should be connected to A by a *weight* $= 1$ edge, and each neighbor of B should be connected to B by a *weight* $= 1$ edge. These very stringent requirements guarantee that the impact of $PR^k(A, B)$ generally decreases with the increase of k.

One potential problem of this definition is that it requires the enumeration of all k-length paths between two vertices for all values of k. The complexity increases exponentially with the value of k, rendering the calculation computationally prohibitive for large k-values. However, the impact of $PR^k(A, B)$ generally decreases with the increase in k, so the first few components are sufficient to incorporate most signals into the PathRatio. Therefore, a simplified approximation can be made by limiting the calculation to the first several components.

6.6.5 Experimental Results

Experimental results indicate that the PathRatio measurement is capable of finding additional high-confidence interactions that would be overlooked by the mutual clustering coefficient. The PathRatio value for any two proteins in the network can then be used to predict potential protein interactions that have been missed by current biological experiments.

Experiments were conducted using the data sets which comprise all available protein interaction data [93,112,156,223,303,307,327] except those detected by recent high-throughput MS experiments [113,144]. These data sets were combined into a

Table 6.4 Data sets of protein-protein interactions

Data set	Interactions	Proteins	Reliability
Ito	4392	3275	0.17
DIPS	3008	1586	0.85
Uetz	1458	1352	0.47
MIPS	788	469	0.50
Combined	9049	4325	0.47

single PPI data set to create the initial PPI network for these experiments. Table 6.4 lists the four component data sets and their reliabilities. Details of these component data sets are provided in Chapter 2.

Table 6.4 lists the number of interactions and proteins contained in each data set, along with its reliability as estimated by the EPR (*Expression Profile Reliability*) index [82]. This index compares the gene expression data of a given reliable PPI data set with that of a generated random set of protein pairs to make a linear least-square fit of the two sets. For the reliable interaction set needed for this index, we used the subset of DIP interactions that have been identified through one (S) or more (M) small-scale experiments. The Spellman gene expression data [285] was used for the EPR estimate.

From Table 6.4, it is evident that the reliabilities of the data sets range from 0.17 for the Ito data set to 0.85 for small-scale experiments in the DIP database. This justifies the use of weights in combining the different data sets.

Since two interacting proteins are highly likely to share both localization and function and to co-express in a gene microarray experiment, we used measures of the localization homogeneity, function homogeneity, and gene expression distance to validate the reliability of interactions.

6.6.5.1 Calcluation of the PathRatio

The PathRatio has been defined in such a manner that the value of the k-th component will normally drop as k increases, if paths of all lengths exist. Therefore, as noted above, this measurement can be satisfactorily approximated by the first few components. However, it is still necessary to determine the shortest path length that should be considered for one edge. When two vertices have no neighbors in common, but connections do exist between their neighbors, the first nonzero component to be considered is PR^3.

Definition 6.9

An alternative path *between two vertices A and B for $(A, B) \in E$ is a path from A to B with length greater than 1. The* shortest alternative path *(SAP) of an edge (A, B) is defined as the shortest path between A and B after deletion of the edge (A, B).*

Since the intent in [245] was to identify reliable interactions, they considered only those protein pairs for which there is experimental evidence of interactions. The distribution of the shortest alternative path lengths for all edges is listed in

Table 6.5 Shortest alternative path length

SAP	#Edges	Percentage	log(#edges)
2	3075	33.9817	8.0310
3	1824	20.1569	7.5088
4	1461	16.1454	7.2869
5	807	8.91811	6.6933
6	221	2.44226	5.3981
7	37	0.408885	3.6109
8	11	0.12156	2.3979
≥ 9	0	0	/
No alternative path	1613	17.8252	7.3859

Table 6.5. Those results indicate that fewer than 20% of edges are not in a cycle and thus have no alternative paths. No edges have a shortest alternative path length greater than 8, and most have very short alternative path lengths. Fewer than five percent of edges have shortest alternative path lengths greater than 5. On the basis of these observations, the PathRatio can be approximated by its first four components:

$$\text{PR}(A, B) = \sum_{k=2}^{5} \text{PR}^k(A, B). \tag{6.21}$$

The computational complexity of this calculation is $O(|V| * m^5)$, where $|V|$ is the total number of vertices in the graph, and m is the average number of neighbors of a protein. When the properties typical of a real PPI network are considered, this time complexity can be viewed as acceptable. In a typical network, most proteins are connected to only a few other proteins, so m is small. Additionally, according to the many-few property, most highly connected proteins are associated with poorly connected proteins [211]. Therefore, the extreme case in which every vertex on a path has many neighbors rarely arises in practice. In their experiments reported in [245], the PathRatio calculation required only a few minutes using C++ on a Pentium-4 Xeon 2.8 GHz machine with 1 GB memory.

6.6.5.2 Effectiveness of PathRatio Measurement in Assessing Interaction Reliability

The ability of the PathRatio measurement to assess interaction reliability was evaluated by ranking interactions according to their PathRatio values and selecting the highest-valued interactions. The quality of the set of selected interactions was measured using average probability, function homogeneity, localization homogeneity, and average gene expression distance. The average probability of each interaction was calculated as the average value of the initial probabilities of the interactions. This value reflects the composition of interactions from data sets with various reliabilities, with a high average probability indicating a high percentage of reliable interactions. When two interactions were ranked equally, the quality measurements among interactions within the rank were averaged.

The performance of PathRatio was compared with that of IRAP [62] (see Chapter 3 for the discussion of IRAP), the only other method using alternative paths to detect reliable interactions among a given set of interactions. It has been shown that IRAP outperforms IG1 and IG2 measurements [62] (see Chapter 3 for the discussion of IG1) in selecting reliable interactions. The results generated by both PathRatio and IRAP are shown in Figure 6–20.

Figure 6–20 demonstrates that a decrease in PathRatio results in a decrease in the average probability, function homogeneity, and localization homogeneity and an increase in gene expression distance. Therefore, the proposed PathRatio measurement provides a good indication of the reliability of an interaction.

The results provided in Figure 6–20 also indicate that the reliable interactions found by PathRatio have higher values of average probability, function homogeneity, and localization homogeneity and lower gene expression distance than those detected by IRAP. In addition, the IRAP values for interactions are very coarse. In this experiment, the top 1,107 interactions had the same IRAP value of 0.974195. IRAP therefore does not permit the reliability of these interactions to be differentiated. Similarly, the next 295 interactions carried the same IRAP value of 0.961376. This flatness of scoring arises from the use in IRAP of only the strongest alternative path. In fact, many interacting protein pairs are connected by an alternative path of length 2, and both edges on this path have the same lowest-possible IG1 value in the graph. Such protein pairs will have the same highest-possible IRAP value. As a result, IRAP is incapable of distinguishing the reliability of these interactions. In comparison, the PathRatio measurement is very fine-grained and provides a better indication of the reliability of an interaction.

6.6.5.3 Finding Additional High-Confidence Interactions not Detected by the Mutual Clustering Coefficient

Pei et al. [245] hypothesized that PathRatio would have the ability to identify additional high-confidence interactions overlooked by the mutual clustering coefficient. In testing this hypothesis, they considered only those edges with a mutual clustering coefficient of 0, indicating that the two proteins do not have any shared neighbors. They calculated the PathRatio between the two proteins and selected those with the highest PathRatio values. They would expect these interactions to be reliable.

Figure 6–21 presents the average probability of these top-ranked interactions. These results indicate that interactions with a high PathRatio are enriched by reliable interactions. As more interactions are selected, the average PathRatio decreases, resulting in a diminishing percentage of reliable interactions. Therefore, though the geometric version of the mutual clustering coefficient is one component of PathRatio, it is not the only component that is effective in selecting reliable interactions. PathRatio can detect additional high-confidence interactions that are overlooked by the mutual clustering coefficient.

Figure 6–22 provides an example of a real interaction between two proteins that do not share any neighbors but which are strongly connected by paths of length 3. To evaluate the reliability of the interaction (YHR200W,YFR010W), we list all length-3 paths between the two proteins and neighborhoods of the two proteins. The interactions (YHR200W,YGR232W), (YHR200W,YLR421C), (YGR232W,YGL048C), (YLR421C,YGL048C),   (YGR232W,   YKL145W),   (YLR421C,YKL145W),

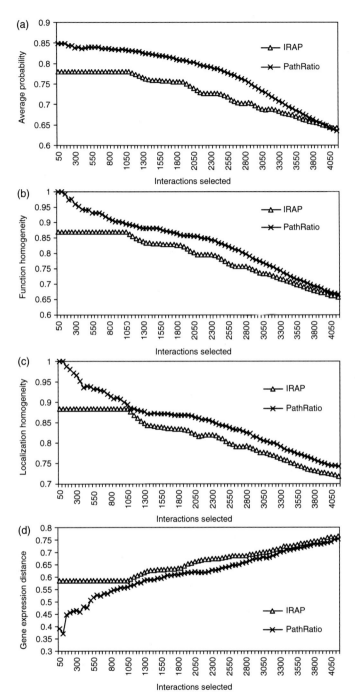

Figure 6–20 Comparison of the performance of PathRatio and IRAP in assessing the reliability of interactions. (a) Average probability, (b) function homogeneity, (c) localization homogeneity, and (d) average gene expression distance.

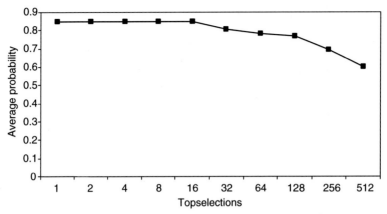

Figure 6–21 Finding additional high-confidence interactions using PathRatio.

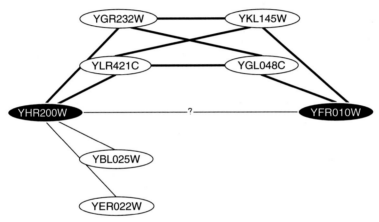

Figure 6–22 An example of a high-confidence interaction.

(YKL145W,YFR010W), and (YGL048C,YFR010W) were all detected by small-scale experiments with the DIP [271]. The interactions (YHR200W,YBL025W) and (YHR200W,YER022W) were detected by Ito's experiments [156]. Though the proteins YHR200W and YFR010W do not have any shared neighbors, they are densely connected by paths of length 3, and the interaction between them, (YHR200W,YFR010W), is very likely to be real. In fact, this interaction has been detected by small-scale experiments with the DIP and was also identified by large-scale experiments with the Gavin protein complex data [113], confirming this prediction. The mutual clustering coefficient in this case, however, is 0, and is therefore unable to detect this high-confidence interaction.

6.6.5.4 Predicting Potential Protein Interactions

Although Pei et al. [245] have focused on the use of PathRatio to select reliable interactions, this measurement can be applied to any two vertices in the PPI network. High-scoring protein pairs can be used as predictors of potential interacting protein pairs [125]. The performance of IRAP, the mutual clustering coefficient [125], and

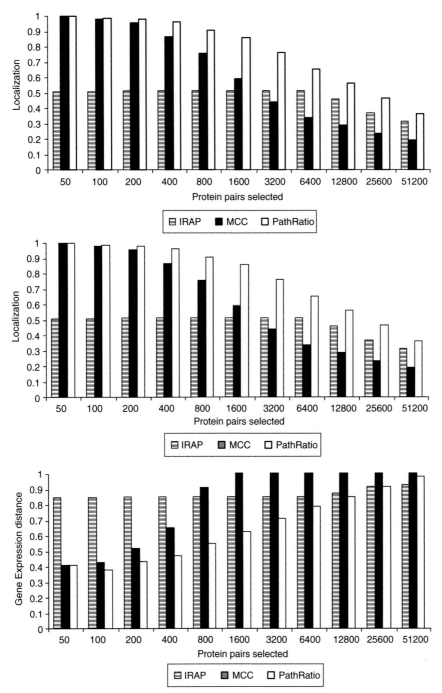

Figure 6–23 Comparison of quality of top protein pairs selected.

PathRatio in selecting protein pairs was evaluated by ranking the scores produced by each method. They then selected the top 50, 100, 200, 400, 800, 1600, 3200, 6400, 12800, 25600, and 51200 pairs ranked by each method. The quality of these selected protein pairs was measured using localization homogeneity, function homogeneity, and average gene expression distance. The results are shown in Figure 6–23 (where MCC refers to the mutual clustering coefficient method [125]).

These results indicate that, at various cutoffs, the top protein pairs selected by the PathRatio method generally have the highest localization homogeneity, the highest function homogeneity, and the lowest average gene expression distance among the three methods. This comparison demonstrates the effectiveness of the PathRatio method in finding potential protein interactions. The performance of the IRAP method was particularly disappointing in this trial. A strikingly large number of protein pairs (10,130) had the same IRAP value of 0.974195, providing little guidance to the identification of interacting pairs.

6.7 SUMMARY

This chapter has discussed several novel approaches to the topological analysis of PPI networks. Experimental trials have demonstrated that such methods offer a promising tool for the analysis of the modularity of PPI networks, prediction of protein interactions, and the prediction of protein functions. As a result, these approaches are now widely used in PPI network analysis.

7

Distance-Based Modularity Analysis

7.1 INTRODUCTION

The classic approaches to clustering follow a protocol termed "pattern proximity after feature selection" [158]. Pattern proximity is usually measured by a distance function defined for pairs of patterns. A simple distance measurement can capture the dissimilarity between two patterns, while similarity measures can be used to characterize the conceptual similarity between patterns. In protein–protein interaction (PPI) networks, proteins are represented as nodes and interactions are represented as edges. The relationship between two proteins is therefore a simple binary value: 1 if they interact, 0 if they do not. This lack of nuance makes it difficult to define the distance between the two proteins. The reliable clustering of PPI networks is further complicated by a high rate of false positives and the sheer volume of data, as discussed in Chapter 2.

Distance-based clustering employs these classic techniques and focuses on the definition of the topological or biological distance between proteins. These clustering approaches begin by defining the distance or similarity between two proteins in the network. This distance/similarity matrix can then be incorporated into traditional clustering algorithms. In this chapter, we will discuss a variety of approaches to distance-based clustering, all of which are grounded upon the use of these classic techniques.

7.2 TOPOLOGICAL DISTANCE MEASUREMENT BASED ON COEFFICIENTS

The simplest of these approaches use classic distance measurement methods and their various coefficient formulas to compute the distance between proteins in PPI networks. As discussed in [123], the distance between two nodes (proteins) in a PPI network can be defined as follows. Let X be a set of n elements and $d_{ij} = \text{dist}(i, j)$ be a nonnegative real function $d : X \times X \to R^+$, which satisfies the following criteria:

(1) $d_{ij} > 0$ for $i \neq j$;
(2) $d_{ij} = 0$ for $i = j$;

(3) $d_{ij} = d_{ji}$ for all i,j, where $\text{dist}(i,j)$ is a distance measure and $D = \{d_{ij}\}$ is a distance matrix. If d_{ij} satisfies the triangle inequality $d_{ij} \leq d_{ik} + d_{kj}$, then d is a metric.

In PPI networks, the binary vectors $X_i = (x_{i1}, x_{i2}, \ldots, x_{iN})$ represent the set of protein purifications for N proteins, where x_{ik} is 1 if the ith protein interacts with the kth protein (the kth protein is presented in the ith purification) and 0 otherwise. If a distance can be determined that fully accounts for known protein complexes, unsupervised hierarchical clustering methods can be used to accurately assemble protein complexes from the data. In [55], the Czekanovski–Dice distance is used:

$$\text{Dice}_{ij} = \frac{|\text{Int}(u) \triangle \text{Int}(v)|}{|\text{Int}(u) \cup \text{Int}(v)| + |\text{Int}(u) \cap \text{Int}(v)|}, \tag{7.1}$$

where $\text{Int}(u)$ and $\text{Int}(v)$ are the sets of proteins u and v together with their interacting partners, while $\triangle$ is the symmetric difference between the two sets. This distance is in the range of $[0..1]$. Two proteins with no shared interacting partners have a distance value of 1, while two proteins that interact with each other and share exactly the same set of interacting partners have a distance value of 0.

Another measurement presented in [272] defines the distance between two proteins u and v as the p-value of observing the number of shared neighbors under the null hypothesis that neighborhoods are independent. The p-value, denoted by PV_{uv}, is expressed using a cumulative hypergeometric distribution:

$$\text{PV}_{uv} = \sum_{i=|N(u) \cap N(v)|}^{\min(|N(u)|,|N(v)|)} \frac{\binom{|N(u)|}{i} \times \binom{|V| - |N(u)|}{|N(v)| - i}}{\binom{|V|}{|N(v)|}}, \tag{7.2}$$

where $N(x)$ represents the set of neighbors of protein x. The p-value is in the range of $[0 \ldots 1]$, with 1 corresponding to a case with no common neighbors. A protein pair with a large number of shared neighbors will have a p-value very close to zero. When two subclusters are merged, the geometric means of the two individual p-values are used to produce the p-value for the merged group. This definition of similarity is closely related to the mutual clustering coefficient defined in [125]. If we define the similarity between proteins u and v as $-\log(PV_{uv})$, the arithmetic means of the two individual similarities can be used to define the new similarity value when merging clusters. The transformed method, which is essentially the UPGMA (Unweighted Pair Group Method with Arithmetic Mean) [216,283] using $-\log(PV_{uv})$ as the similarity measure, is equivalent to the original method.

Frequently, a distance can be easily obtained via a simple matching coefficient that calculates the similarity between two elements. The similarity value S_{ij} between two elements i and j can be normalized between 0 and 1, and the distance can be derived from $d_{ij} = 1 - S_{ij}$. If the similarity value of two elements is high, the spatial distance between them is likely to be short.

Several measures have been proposed for this distance calculation. These include the Jaccard coefficient [125]:

$$S_{mn} = \frac{X_{mn}}{X_{mm} + X_{nn} - X_{mn}}, \tag{7.3}$$

the Dice coefficient [125]:

$$S_{mn} = \frac{2X_{mn}}{X_{mm} + X_{nn}}, \tag{7.4}$$

the Simpson coefficient [125]:

$$S_{mn} = \frac{X_{mn}}{\min(X_{mm}, X_{nn})}, \tag{7.5}$$

the Bader coefficient [24]:

$$S_{mn} = \frac{X_{mn}^2}{X_{mm} \times X_{nn}}, \tag{7.6}$$

the Maryland bridge coefficient [218]:

$$S_{mn} = \frac{1}{2}\left(\frac{X_{mn}}{X_{mm}} + \frac{X_{mn}}{X_{nn}}\right), \tag{7.7}$$

the Korbel coefficient [185]:

$$S_{mn} = \frac{\sqrt{X_{mm}^2 + X_{nn}^2}}{\sqrt{2}X_{mm}X_{nn}}X_{mn}, \tag{7.8}$$

and the correlation coefficient [96]:

$$S_{mn} = \frac{X_{mn} - n\overline{X}_m\overline{X}_n}{\sqrt{(X_{mm} - n\overline{X}_m^2)(X_{nn} - n\overline{X}_n^2)}}, \tag{7.9}$$

where $X_{ij} = X_i \bullet X_j$ (the dot product of two vectors). The value of S_{mn} ranges from 0 to 1. X_{ij} is equal to the number of bits "on" in both vectors, and X_{ii} is equal to the number of bits "on" in one vector. For example, for the case illustrated in Figure 4–1, the matrix X is

$$X = \begin{bmatrix} 0 & 1 & 1 & 1 & 0 & 0 & 1 & 1 \\ 1 & 0 & 1 & 0 & 0 & 1 & 0 & 0 \\ 1 & 1 & 0 & 0 & 0 & 0 & 0 & 0 \\ 1 & 0 & 0 & 0 & 0 & 0 & 0 & 0 \\ 0 & 0 & 0 & 0 & 0 & 1 & 0 & 1 \\ 0 & 1 & 0 & 0 & 1 & 0 & 1 & 0 \\ 1 & 0 & 0 & 0 & 0 & 1 & 0 & 0 \\ 1 & 0 & 0 & 0 & 1 & 0 & 0 & 0 \end{bmatrix}. \tag{7.10}$$

To calculate the distance between A and B, d_{12}, $X_{11} = X_1 \bullet X_1 = 5$, $X_{22} = X_2 \bullet X_2 = 3$, $X_{12} = X_1 \bullet X_2 = 1$. The Jaccard coefficient is calculated as: $S_{12} = 1/(5 + 3 - 1) = 0.1429$; the distance is then $d_{12} = 1 - 0.1429 = 0.8571$.

Various classical clustering algorithms can be applied to perform a modularity analysis based on the calculated distances between proteins. Since these distance-based clustering approaches use classical distance measurements, they are not fully suitable for application to high-dimensional spaces. In such spaces, the distance between each pair of nodes is almost the same as for a large data distribution [38]. Therefore, it is difficult to attain ideal clustering results by using only the simplest distance measurements.

7.3 DISTANCE MEASUREMENT BY NETWORK DISTANCE

There are other definitions based on network distance, which produce more fine-grained distance measurements for protein pairs. As defined in Section 7.2, the distance value will be 0 for any two proteins not sharing an interaction partner. In [263], each edge of the interactions in the network was assigned a length of 1. The length of the shortest path (e.g., distance) between every pair of vertices in the network was calculated to create an all-pairs-shortest-path distance matrix. Each distance in this matrix was then transformed into an *association*, defined as $1/d^2$, where d is the shortest-path distance. This transformation emphasizes local associations (short paths) in the subsequent clustering process. The resulting associations range from 0 to 1. The association of a vertex with itself is defined as 1, while the association of vertices that have no connecting path is defined as 0. Two vertices that are more widely separated in the network will have a longer shortest-path distance and thus a smaller association value. The association value can therefore serve as the similarity measurement for two proteins.

7.3.1 PathRatio Method

In [245], distances were assessed by considering the paths of various lengths between two vertices in a weighted PPI network. The weight of an edge reflects its reliability and lies in the range between 0 and 1. The *PathStrength* of a path is defined as the product of the weights of all the edges on the path. The *k-length PathStrength* between two vertices is then defined as the sum of the PathStrengths of all k-length paths between the two vertices. The PathStrength of a path captures the probability that a walk on the path will reach its ending vertex. By summing these paths, the k-length PathStrength between two vertices captures the strength of connections between these two vertices by a k-step walk. Since paths of different lengths will have different impacts on the connection between two vertices, the k-length PathStrength is normalized by the k-length maximum possible path strength to arrive at the *k-length PathRatio*. Finally, the *PathRatio* measure between two vertices is defined as the sum of the k-length PathRatios between the two vertices for all $k > 1$. Though this measurement is mainly applied in assessing the reliability of detected interactions and predicting potential interactions that are missed by current experiments, it can also be used as a similarity measure for clustering. Further details of the PathRatio metric can be found in Chapter 6.

7.3.2 Averaging the Distances

Another network distance measurement was developed by Zhou [343,344]. He defined the distance d_{ij} from node i to node j as the average number of steps taken by a Brownian particle to reach j from i.

Consider a connected network of N nodes and M edges. Its node set is denoted by $V = \{1,\dots,N\}$ and its connection pattern is specified by the generalized adjacency matrix A. If there is no edge between node i and node j, $A_{ij} = 0$; if there is an edge between those nodes, $A_{ij} = A_{ji} > 0$, and its value signifies the interaction strength. The set of nearest neighbors of node i is denoted by E_i. As a Brownian particle moves throughout the network, it jumps at each time-step from its present position i to a nearest-neighboring position j. When no additional information about the network is known, the jumping probability $P_{ij} = A_{ij}/\sum_{l=1}^{N} A_{il}$ can be assumed. Matrix P is termed the transfer matrix.

The node–node distance d_{ij} from i to j is defined as the average number of steps needed for the Brownian particle to move from i through the network to j. Using simple linear-algebraic calculations, it is obvious that

$$d_{ij} = \sum_{l=1}^{N} \left(\frac{1}{I - B(j)} \right)_{il}, \tag{7.11}$$

where I is the $N \times N$ identity matrix, and matrix $B(j)$ equals the transfer matrix P, with the exception that $B_{lj}(j) \equiv 0$ for any $l \in V$. The distances from all the nodes in V to node j can thus be obtained by solving the linear algebraic equation

$$[I - B(j)]\{d_{1j},\dots,d_{nj}\}^{\mathrm{T}} = \{1,\dots,1\}^{\mathrm{T}}. \tag{7.12}$$

For example, in the network shown in Figure 7–1 with the set of nodes $V = 1, 2, 3, 4$, the adjacency matrix A and transfer matrix P are:

$$A = \begin{bmatrix} 0 & 1 & 1 & 1 \\ 1 & 0 & 1 & 0 \\ 1 & 1 & 0 & 0 \\ 1 & 0 & 0 & 0 \end{bmatrix}, \quad P = \begin{bmatrix} 0 & 1/3 & 1/3 & 1/3 \\ 1/2 & 0 & 1/2 & 0 \\ 1/2 & 1/2 & 0 & 0 \\ 1 & 0 & 0 & 0 \end{bmatrix}.$$

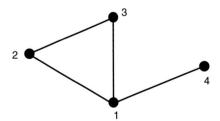

Figure 7–1 Example of distance measurement by the movement of a Brownian particle.

$B(j)$ can be derived from P:

$$B(1) = \begin{bmatrix} 0 & 1/3 & 1/3 & 1/3 \\ 0 & 0 & 1/2 & 0 \\ 0 & 1/2 & 0 & 0 \\ 0 & 0 & 0 & 0 \end{bmatrix}, \quad B(2) = \begin{bmatrix} 0 & 0 & 1/3 & 1/3 \\ 1/2 & 0 & 1/2 & 0 \\ 1/2 & 0 & 0 & 0 \\ 1 & 0 & 0 & 0 \end{bmatrix},$$

$$B(3) = \begin{bmatrix} 0 & 1/3 & 0 & 1/3 \\ 1/2 & 0 & 0 & 0 \\ 1/2 & 1/2 & 0 & 0 \\ 1 & 0 & 0 & 0 \end{bmatrix}, \quad B(4) = \begin{bmatrix} 0 & 1/3 & 1/3 & 0 \\ 1/2 & 0 & 1/2 & 0 \\ 1/2 & 1/2 & 0 & 0 \\ 1 & 0 & 0 & 0 \end{bmatrix}.$$

The distance between any two nodes can be calculated with Equation (7.11):

$$D = \{d_{ij}\} = \begin{bmatrix} 8/3 & 10/3 & 10/3 & 7 \\ 2 & 4 & 8/3 & 9 \\ 2 & 8/3 & 4 & 9 \\ 1 & 13/3 & 13/3 & 8 \end{bmatrix}.$$

Based on the distance measurement, Zhou [344] defined a *dissimilarity index* to quantify the relationship between any two nearest-neighboring nodes. For a graph representing social relationships, nearest-neighboring vertices in the same community tend to have a small dissimilarity index, while those belonging to different communities tend to have high dissimilarity indices.

Given two vertices i and j that are nearest neighbors ($A_{ij} > 0$), the difference in their perspectives of the network can be quantitatively measured. The dissimilarity index $\Lambda(i,j)$ is defined by the following expression:

$$\Lambda(i,j) = \frac{\sqrt{\sum_{k \neq i,j}^{n}(d_{ik} - d_{jk})^2}}{n - 2}. \tag{7.13}$$

According to [343], Equation (7.13) is explained as follows: "If two nearest-neighboring vertices i and j belong to the same community, then the average distance d_{ik} from i to any another vertex $k(k \neq i,j)$ will be similar to the average distance d_{jk} from j to k. This indicates that the perspectives of the network as viewed from i and j are quite similar. Consequently, $\Lambda(i,j)$ will be small if i and j belong to the same community and large if they belong to different communities."

When this approach is applied to a PPI network, clusters of proteins that may be of biological significance can be constructed. Zhou provided three examples of such an application. Most of the proteins in these examples were involved in known functions. It was possible to predict similar biological functions for the few proteins in each cluster that were previously unanalyzed.

7.4 ENSEMBLE METHOD

The use of traditional clustering algorithms for extracting functional modules from PPI data has been hampered by the high false-positive rate of interactions and by particular topological challenges in the network. Three problems commonly encountered in the clustering of PPI data were noted in [20]. First, PPI data sets are inherently noisy. Second, even if the data is assumed to be noise-free, partitioning the network using classical graph partitioning or clustering schemes is inherently difficult. Frequently, PPI networks include a few nodes (hubs) of very high degree, while most other nodes have very few interactions. Applying traditional clustering approaches typically results in an unsatisfactory clustering arrangement, with one or a few giant core clusters and several tiny clusters. Third, some proteins are believed to be multifunctional, and effective strategies for the soft clustering of these essential proteins are needed.

Asur et al. [20] proposed the Ensemble clustering framework to address these issues. Two topology-based distance metrics were introduced to address the high level of noise associated with these data sets. Three traditional graph-partitioning algorithms were used together with two distance metrics to obtain six base clusterings. In the "consensus" stage, these base clusters were pruned to remove redundancies and noise. Final clusters were obtained using two consensus clustering techniques, the agglomerative and the repeated bisections (RBR) algorithms.

7.4.1 Similarity Metrics

As a component of the Ensemble method, Asur et al. introduced two topological similarity metrics to measure the distance between the two incident proteins of each interaction. These metrics are based on the clustering coefficient and shortest-path edge betweenness. The clustering coefficient-based metric captures the local properties of an interaction in the network, while the betweenness-based metric embodies the global characteristics of each edge.

(1) *Clustering coefficient-based metric*: The clustering coefficient [319] is a measure that represents the interconnectivity of the neighbors of a node. As discussed in Chapter 5, the clustering coefficient of a node v with degree k_v can be defined as follows:

$$CC(v) = \frac{2n_v}{k_v(k_v - 1)} \tag{7.14}$$

where n_v denotes the number of triangles that pass through node v.
The clustering coefficient-based similarity of two nodes v and w is calculated by

$$S_{cc}(v, w) = CC(v) + CC(w) - CC'(v) - CC'(w), \tag{7.15}$$

where $CC'(v)$ and $CC'(w)$ are the clustering coefficients of interacting nodes v and w after removal of the interaction between these nodes. The similarity scores are normalized into the range [0−1] using min–max normalization.

(2) *Betweenness-based metric*: Betweenness-based similarity utilizes the shortest-path edge betweenness metric introduced by Newman and Girvan [122].

$$S_{bw}(v, w) = 1 - \frac{SP_{vw}}{SP_{max}}, \tag{7.16}$$

where SP_{vw} is the number of shortest paths passing through edge vw, and SP_{max} is the maximum number of shortest paths passing through an edge in the graph. Scores are again normalized into the range $[0-1]$ using min–max normalization.

7.4.2 Base Algorithms

Asur's group used three conventional graph-clustering algorithms to obtain base clusters. These are

(1) *Repeated bisections (RBR)*: The repeated-bisections algorithm performs $k-1$ bisections iteratively to find the desired k-way clustering solution, where k is the required number of clusters. The input matrix is first partitioned into two groups, after which one of the partitions is selected and further bisected. This bisection process is repeated until the desired number of clusters is found. During each step, a cluster is bisected so that the resulting two-way clustering solution optimizes the $I2$ clustering criterion function, which is given as

$$I2 = \text{maximize} \sum_{i=1}^{k} \sqrt{\sum_{v,u \in S_i} \text{sim}(v,u)} \tag{7.17}$$

where k is the total number of clusters, S_i is the set of objects assigned to the i_{th} cluster, v and u represent two objects, and $\text{sim}(v,u)$ is the similarity between two objects.

(2) *Direct k-way partitioning (direct)*: Direct k-way partitioning computes the desired k-way clustering solution by finding all k clusters simultaneously. Initially, a set of k objects is selected as the seeds of the k clusters. The similarity of each object to these k seeds is computed and assigned to the cluster corresponding to its closest seed. This initial clustering is repeatedly refined to optimize the $I2$ clustering criterion function.

(3) *Multilevel k-way partitioning (Metis)*: Metis (kMetis) is a multilevel partitioning algorithm developed by Karypis and Kumar [173]. It consists of three steps: coarsening, initial partitioning, and refinement. In the coarsening phase, the original graph is transformed into a sequence of smaller graphs. An initial k-way partitioning of the coarsest graph is obtained. The partition is then projected back to the original graph by going through intermediate partitions. Finally, a refinement phase reduces the edge-cut while conserving the balance constraints.

7.4.3 Consensus Methods

The three base-clustering algorithms and the two topological metrics discussed earlier were used to generate six sets of k clusters. These individual clusterings were then combined to produce a meaningful and effective consensus clustering. Given n individual clusterings $(c_1, \ldots, c_n)$, each having k clusters, a consensus function F is a mapping from the set of clusterings to a single, aggregated clustering:

$$F : \{c_i | i \in 1, \ldots, n\} \rightarrow c_{\text{consensus}}. \tag{7.18}$$

For the consensus stage, two alternative techniques, pruning and weighting, were proposed to eliminate noisy clusters from the obtained base clusters.

(1) *PCA-based consensus*: The reliability of a cluster was defined as inversely proportional to its intra-cluster distance, or the distance between nodes in a cluster:

$$\text{Rel}(cl_1) = \frac{|V_{cl_1}| * \text{diam}(G)}{\sum_{(i,j) \in V_{cl_1}} \text{SP}(i,j)} \tag{7.19}$$

where V_{cl_1} represents the nodes in cluster cl_1, and $\text{SP}(i,j)$ represents the shortest path distance in terms of number of edges between nodes i and j. $\text{diam}(G)$ signifies the diameter of the original PPI graph and is used for normalization. In a purification phase, unreliable, weakly connected clusters were pruned on the basis of cluster reliability. The PCA algorithm was used to remove redundancies and noise from the pruned clusters and to reduce the dimensionality. The result of the PCA step is a reduced matrix that contains only discriminatory information, allowing proteins to be easily clustered.

(2) *Weighted consensus*: An alternative approach to pruning involves weighting proteins based on the reliability of the clusters to which they belong. A new weighted graph can be constructed from the base clusters with edges present between proteins if and only if they have been clustered at least once. The weights of these edges are proportional to the reliability of the clusters to which they belong:

$$\text{Weight}(i,j) = \sum_{k=1}^{p} \text{Rel}(cl_k) \times \text{Mem}(i,j,cl_k) \tag{7.20}$$

where $\text{Rel}(cl_k)$ is the reliability score of cluster cl_k, p is the total number of clusters, and $\text{Mem}(i,j,cl_k)$ is the cluster membership function:

$$\text{Mem}(i,j,cl_k) = \begin{cases} 1, & \text{if } f(i,j) \in cl_k, \\ 0, & \text{otherwise.} \end{cases} \tag{7.21}$$

After the pruning or weighting process, either the agglomerative or the RBR algorithm was applied to identify final clusters. The agglomerative hierarchical clustering algorithm starts by assigning each object to a cluster and then repeatedly merges the most similar cluster pair until either the desired number of clusters has been obtained or only one cluster remains. The application of the RBR algorithm proceeds as described in Section 7.4.2. Additionally, soft clustering can be performed to group certain proteins that were associated with multiple clusters. Figure 7–2 provides the overview of the Ensemble framework.

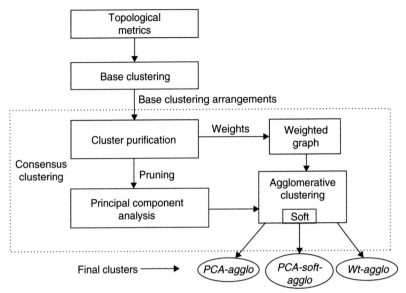

Figure 7–2 Overview of the Ensemble framework. Only the agglomerative algorithm is illustrated here; application of the RBR algorithm proceeds similarly. *PCA-agglo* represents the agglomerative clustering result produced by the PCA-based pruning process. *PCA-soft-agglo* represents the soft clustering result of the PCA-based agglomerative algorithm. *Wt-agglo* represents the agglomerative clustering result produced by the weighting process. (Reprinted from [20].)

7.4.4 Results of the Ensemble Methods

The Ensemble method was applied to the yeast PPI network, and the quality of the clusterings produced was validated using topological, information-theoretic, and domain-based measurements. The PCA-based algorithms generated consensus clusters with high efficiency compared to the other algorithms tested. In addition, the PCA-based soft consensus clustering algorithm proved to be very effective in identifying multiple protein functions. A comparison of the clusters detected by the Ensemble method with those identified by other popular algorithms, such as MCODE [24] and MCL [308], reveals that the Ensemble algorithms can identify larger, denser clusters with improved biological significance. The Ensemble clustering method has two distinct advantages over other classical methods in clustering PPI networks. High robustness to the false positives that are inherent in the PPI dataset is ensured by using pruning techniques to eliminate poor modules and combining several different metrics and methods. Furthermore, the ability of the PCA-based soft consensus clustering algorithm to identify multiple protein functions is a distinct advantage.

7.5 UVCLUSTER

The UVCLUSTER [17] approach to distance measurement is informed by the observation that the shortest path distance between protein pairs is typically not very fine-grained and that many pairs have the same distance value. This method proposes an iterative approach to distance exploration; unlike other distance-based approaches, it converts the set of primary distances into secondary distances. The secondary distance measures the strength of the connection between each pair of proteins when the interactions for all the proteins in the group are considered. Secondary distance is derived by first applying a hierarchical clustering step based on the affinity coefficient to generate N different clustering results. The number of solutions generated that place any two selected proteins in different clusters is defined as the secondary distance between the two proteins. Defined succinctly, the secondary distance represents the likelihood that two selected proteins will not be in the same cluster.

This approach has four steps:

(1) A *primary distance d* between any two proteins in a PPI network is measured by the minimum number of steps required to connect them. Each valid step is a known, physical PPI. Users are allowed to select groups of proteins to be analyzed either by choosing a single protein and establishing a cutoff distance value or by providing the program with a list of proteins.

(2) Next, agglomerative hierarchical clustering is applied to the sub-table of primary distances generated in the first step to produce N alternative and equally-valid clustering solutions. The user specifies a value for N before starting the analysis. UVCLUSTER first randomly samples the elements of the dataset and then clusters them according to the average linkage for the group. The agglomerative process ends when the *affinity coefficient* (AC) is reached. The AC is defined by

$$AC = 100[(P_m - C_m)/(P_m - 1)], \tag{7.22}$$

where C_m (the cluster mean) is the average of the distances for all elements included in the clusters, and P_m (the partition mean) is the average value of distances for the whole set of selected proteins. The AC value is selected by the user at the start of the process.

(3) Once the data set of N alternative solutions has been obtained, the number of pairs of elements that appear together in the same cluster is counted. A *secondary distance d'* between two elements is defined as the number of solutions in which those two elements do not appear together in the same cluster, divided by the total number of solutions (N). In effect, the secondary distance iteratively resamples the original primary distance data, thus indicating the strength of the connection between two elements. Secondary distance represents the likelihood that each pair of elements will appear in the same cluster when many alternative clustering solutions are generated.

(4) After the generation of secondary distance data, the proteins can be clustered using conventional methods such as UPGMA (Unweighted Pair Group Method with Arithmetic Mean) [216,283] or neighbor-joining. The results of an agglomerative hierarchical clustering process in which UPGMA is applied to the secondary distance data are placed in a second UVCLUSTER output file. A third output file contains a graphical representation of the data in PGM (Portable GreyMap) format. To generate the PGM file, proteins are ordered according to the results described in the second output file.

The use of UVCLUSTER offers four significant benefits. First, the involvement of the secondary distance value facilitates identification of sets of closely-linked proteins. Furthermore, it allows the incorporation of previously known information into the discovery of proteins involved in a particular process of interest. Third, guided by the AC value, it can establish groups of connected proteins even when some information is currently unavailable. Finally, UVCLUSTER can compare the relative positions of orthologous proteins in two species to determine whether they retain related functions in both of their interactomes.

7.6 SIMILARITY LEARNING METHOD

In [246], a measurement was introduced that permits an assessment of the similarity between two proteins with only a limited amount of annotation data as input. This method uses a calculation of conditional probability to define the similarity between two proteins based on their protein interaction profiles. (Most materials in this section are from [246]. Reprinted with permission from IEEE.)

As observed in [274], two proteins that interact are typically highly homogeneous in their functional annotations. In [334], it was noted that this homogeneity diminishes as the distance between two proteins increases. The edges in the network act as a means of message-passing through which each protein seeks to propagate its function to neighboring proteins. At the same time, the functions in which each protein engages are influenced by messages received from its neighbors. The final probability of a protein having a specific function is therefore a conditional probability defined by the functional annotation of its neighbors.

Figure 7–3 illustrates the propagation of function from a single protein A as the source of information. The function of A is propagated first to its direct neighbors and then to its indirect neighbors. In this process, the strength of the message diminishes as the distance (path length) increases. In the illustrated example, the function is propagated to protein B via paths $A \rightarrow B$, $A \rightarrow C \rightarrow B$, and $A \rightarrow D \rightarrow B$. Protein B therefore receives messages via several paths and demonstrates a degree of functional homogeneity with the source protein A. Protein C also propagates its function to E, while protein B propagates its function to proteins C, D, and F. Though the PPI network is undirected, the information flow from one vertex (the *source* vertex) to another (the *sink* vertex) can be conveniently represented by a directed graph. For this reason, the terms protein and vertex can be used interchangeably. In the discussion later, the source vertex will be denoted by A and the sink vertex by B. $|V|$ is used to denote the total number of vertices in the network.

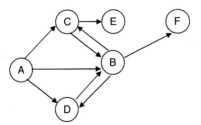

Figure 7–3 Function propagation from source protein *A* to other proteins in the network.

The probability that A will have any selected functional label under consideration is denoted by $P(A)$. The probability of B having this function by propagation from A can then be represented as a conditional probability $P(B|A)$. This conditional probability reflects the likelihood of A's function being transferred to B via the network. Larger values of $P(B|A)$ indicate closer functional homogeneity and therefore greater similarity between two proteins.

The conditional probability measurement is not symmetric, and, in general, $P(A|B) \neq P(B|A)$. Therefore, the similarity between proteins A and B is defined as the product of two conditional probabilities:

$$\text{Similarity}_{AB} = P(A|B) * P(B|A). \tag{7.23}$$

This measurement reflects the functional cohesiveness of the two proteins. This definition permits the measurement of the similarity of two proteins to be recast as the estimation of two conditional probabilities. These probabilities are predicted using a statistical model of topological features.

The probability that the sink protein B will have a particular function is determined by all the messages it receives from its neighbors. A message that favors this functional annotation is termed a *positive message*. A protein that has a functional annotation at a probability higher than a random protein in the network can propagate a positive message to its neighbors. The sink protein also receives messages from other neighboring proteins. The strength of homogeneity will depend both on the sum of positive messages propagated to the vertex, denoted by PM, and the degree of the vertex, denoted by D. The probability of a vertex having a specific function can be expressed as a function of these two values. Using the technique described in [37], we can employ a potential function $U(x; PM, D)$ to express this probability:

$$P(x|PM, D) = \frac{e^{-U(x;PM,D)}}{Z(PM, D)}, \tag{7.24}$$

where x is a binary value $x \in \{0, 1\}$, and 1 indicates that the protein has the function under consideration. The normalization factor $Z(PM, D)$ is the sum of all configurations:

$$Z(PM, D) = \sum_{y=0,1} e^{-U(y;PM,D)}. \tag{7.25}$$

A linear combination of variables is used:

$$U(x; PM, D; \alpha) = (\alpha 0 + \alpha 1 * PM + \alpha 2 * D) * x. \tag{7.26}$$

This model is preferable to the binomial-neighborhood model suggested in [196], as the latter assumes that the neighbors of a vertex behave independently and that the probabilities of a protein having any given function are independent. Since a flexible similarity measurement must be capable of identifying the dense areas of the PPI network, assuming such independence on the part of neighbors would degrade the efficacy of the measurement [37].

The similarity model under discussion here is related to the model proposed in [37]. However, this model, unlike the latter approach, is intended primarily to define the similarity between two proteins. Toward this end, the model always treats only a single protein as annotated and considers proteins beyond the direct neighbors of the source protein.

Each protein B connected with protein A, either directly connected or indirectly via intermediary proteins, has an associated layer comprising the shortest path length between the two proteins, denoted by $\text{dist}(A, B)$. The set of proteins connected to A by a shortest path length k is denoted by $N^{(k)}(A)$:

$$N^{(k)}(A) = \{B | \text{dist}(A, B) = k\}. \tag{7.27}$$

$N^{(1)}(A)$ can be abbreviated as $N(A)$. A protein $B \in N^{(k)}(A)$ is termed a k-step neighbor of A.

The formulation of the similarity metric begins with an iterative calculation of the conditional probability of each protein having the same functional annotation as a source protein A. The calculation of conditional probability starts with the direct neighbors of A. The conditional probability of the direct neighbors of these first neighbors (the two-step neighbors of A) is then calculated on the basis of the first set of probabilities. This iteration continues until a conditional probability for each protein connected with A is generated. Employing the resulting order of conditional probability estimation, a value can be established for the positive message term in Equation (7.24).

This process starts with the direct neighbors of A, which are the proteins belonging to $N^{(1)}(A)$. Since all proteins in this B layer have direct and equally-strong connections to the source protein, the direct connection message $A \rightarrow B$ can be omitted, and only the messages between same-layer neighbors need be considered. Therefore, we can use the number of shared neighbors between A and B as the value of positive messages for protein B.

For the general case of a protein B belonging to $N^{(k)}(A)$ with $k > 1$, only those messages from neighbors in $N^{(k-1)}(A)$ are regarded as positive. Proteins in those layers below $k - 1$ must propagate their information via proteins in $N^{(k-1)}(A)$ to impact the functional annotation of B. Therefore, this information has already been captured in the $(k-1)$-step neighbors of A. Messages propagated from proteins in the same layer are generally weak for $k > 1$, as has been demonstrated experimentally, and can be omitted. The positive messages can be expressed as the sum of the product of two conditional probabilities:

$$PM_{B \leftarrow A} = \sum_{C \in N(B) \cap N^{(k-1)}(A)} P(B|C) * P(C|A), \tag{7.28}$$

where $PM_{B \leftarrow A}$ indicates that the positive message moves from source A to sink B via the network.

The product of two conditional probabilities $P(B|C) * P(C|A)$ measures the probability that the functional annotation of A will be successfully propagated to B via the path $A \rightarrow \cdots \rightarrow C \rightarrow B$. The strength of message propagation from A to B via the network is arrived at by summing these probabilities for all proteins that are both

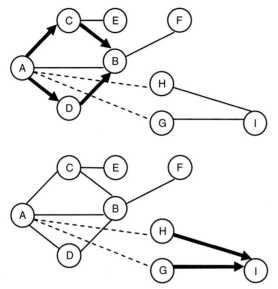

Figure 7–4 Iterative estimation of conditional probabilities.

direct neighbors of B and $(k-1)$-step neighbors of A. The conditional probabilities $P(B|C)$ and $P(C|A)$ were already generated as part of the estimation of $P(Y|X)$ for each X and $Y \in \bigcup_{i=1,\ldots,k-1} N^{(i)}(X)$ in the previous $k-1$ steps.

Figure 7–4 provides an illustration of this function propagation process. In this example, vertex A is the source, and estimation of conditional probabilities starts with its direct neighbors $P(B|A)$, $P(C|A)$, and $P(D|A)$. In Figure 7–4(a), the function propagation messages from A to B appear in the first layer. Messages propagated from vertices C and D to vertex B are depicted by dark lines. Figure7–4(b) illustrates the propagation of function from k-step neighbors H and G to a $(k+1)$-step neighbor I.

The calculated value of positive messages can then be supplied to Equation (7.24) with which the probability can be estimated.

This process provides both a representation of the conditional probability for the two vertices in the graph and the order of estimating the probability. However, at this point, the probability is stated as a function of the model parameters α, rather than as a numerical value. Additional two steps are necessary to quantitatively estimate parameters and calculate the conditional probabilities.

Training samples with known x_i, PM_i, and D_i values are derived from the annotations of proteins with known functions. In the first step (the *model training* step), these training samples become input to the simplex method (the Nelder–Mead algorithm) [255] to estimate the parameters (α) that maximize the joint probability:

$$P = \prod_i P(x_i|PM_i, D_i). \tag{7.29}$$

To increase the accuracy of estimation, these parameters are estimated separately for each layer.

In the second step (the *conditional probability estimation* step), the numerical values of the conditional probabilities are calculated using Equation (7.24) and the parameters (α) estimated in the previous step. An unsupervised clustering method can be applied to the resulting similarity measurements.

7.7 MEASUREMENT OF BIOLOGICAL DISTANCE

As previously noted, PPI data can be represented as a graph in which nodes represent proteins and edges represent interactions among these proteins; however, this model represents only binary relationships among proteins. Many attempts have been made to develop metrics and methods to overcome this shortcoming. The topological distance metrics discussed earlier in this chapter are useful in identifying clusters, but, to ensure that these modules are biologically meaningful, network-partitioning algorithms must also consider functional relationships. The distance between the two proteins involved in an interaction can be also measured by the biological characteristics of the proteins. This measurement can be based on protein or gene sequence, protein structure, gene expression, or degree of confidence in the interaction as indicated by experimental frequency [61,99,140,250,258,304]. Sequence similarity, structural similarity, and gene expression correlation are three common approaches to comparing the biological information available for two proteins participating in an interaction.

7.7.1 Sequence Similarity-Based Measurements

Enright et al. [99] have developed a clustering algorithm, termed TRIBE-MCL, that detects protein families (or clusters) in biological graphs on the basis of protein sequence similarity and the MCL clustering algorithm [308].

Each interaction in a PPI network can be weighted by the *sequence similarity* of the two incident proteins. In Enright's method, sequence similarity is measured by *E*-values generated by BLAST [14]. A FASTA file containing all sequences that are to be clustered into families is assembled, filtered by CAST [257], then compared against its original form using BLAST. The sequence similarities for each interaction generated by this analysis are parsed and stored in a square matrix. Because this method does not operate directly on sequences but on a network that contains similarity information, it avoids the expensive step of sequence alignment. Instead, a global overview of sequence similarity is computed and utilized to cluster the PPI network.

The MCL, initially developed for computational graph clustering, has been adapted for application to biological networks. The MCL method will be discussed in more detail in Chapter 8, but a brief overview will be provided here. Using the sequence similarity between a protein pair, a Markov matrix is constructed, which represents the transition probabilities from any protein in the graph to the other interacting proteins for which a similarity has been detected. The entries in the Markov matrix are probabilities generated from weighted sequence similarity scores. Using this Markov matrix, the MCL clustering algorithm finds clusters in networks through a mathematical bootstrapping procedure. The process simulates random walks through the sequence similarity graph and employs two operators to transform one set of probabilities into another. The algorithm uses iterative rounds of expansion and inflation processes [308] to promote flow within highly connected regions and diminish flow within weakly connected regions. *Expansion* refers to taking the power of a stochastic matrix using the normal matrix product. *Inflation* involves taking the Hadamard power of a matrix, followed by a scaling step, so that the resulting matrix is again stochastic, with the matrix elements in each column corresponding to probability values. The iterative process terminates when equilibrium has been reached. The MCL algorithm is able to identify effective modules because flow tends to remain confined within each cluster, so that a random walk starting at any protein is likely to remain within that cluster. Its computational efficiency is a notable benefit in processing large volumes of data.

In a generic network, expansion involves the traversal of random walks between all pairs of departure and destination nodes, thus associating new probabilities the node pairs. As noted, random walks usually remain within a given cluster rather than moving between clusters. Therefore, the probabilities associated with node pairs contained within the same cluster will be relatively large, as there are many possible routes between these pairs. Inflation increases the probability of intra-cluster walks and demotes inter-cluster walks.

The TRIBE-MCL method is an extension of the MCL algorithm for the assignment of proteins into clusters on the basis of precomputed sequence similarity values. The method has been tested with protein sequence information from various data sets, including Swissprot [25], InterPro [15], SCOP [203], and the draft human genome. Experimental analyses showed that TRIBE-MCL detected highly effective clusters at a much faster speed compared to other tested methods. In addition, it has shown an ability to handle the multi-domain, promiscuous, and fragmented proteins, which typically confound other protein sequence clustering approaches.

7.7.2 Structural Similarity-Based Measurements

Domingues et al. [91] introduced a method for clustering protein structural models according to their backbone structure. The method includes a carbon alpha ($C\alpha$) metric to quantify the distance between two protein structures and the application of two clustering methods, hierarchical clustering [128] and partitioning around medoids (PAM) [175]. Medoids are representative objects of data sets.

In this method, protein structures are classified according to the similarity of backbone structure as represented by a $C\alpha$ distance matrix. The dissimilarity measure used for clustering is based on the Euclidean distance for each pair of $C\alpha$ coordinates. Two filters are applied to improve robustness to a wide range of backbone conformational changes.

Consider the $C\alpha$ coordinates for residue i, (x_i, y_i, z_i). The Euclidean distance between the $C\alpha$ atoms of residues i and j in entry a is defined as $D_{ij}(a) = \sqrt{(x_i - x_j)^2 + (y_i - y_j)^2 + (z_i - z_j)^2}$. The first filter is applied with a cutoff of F_1 to reduce the influence of differences in large distances associated with extensive conformational changes:

$$D'_{ij}(a) = \begin{cases} D_{ij}(a), & D_{ij}(a) \leq F_1, \\ F_1, & D_{ij}(a) > F_1. \end{cases} \tag{7.30}$$

For each pair of entries a and b, the absolute difference is then calculated for each residue pair $\Delta_{ij}(a,b) = |D'_{ij}(a) - D'_{ij}(b)|$. The second filter is then applied with a cutoff of F_2 to restrict the analysis to significant structural differences:

$$\Delta'_{ij}(a,b) = \begin{cases} 0, & \Delta_{ij}(a,b) \leq F_2, \\ 1, & \Delta_{ij}(a,b) > F_2. \end{cases} \tag{7.31}$$

Cutoffs F_1 and F_2 were set to 14.0 and 1.0, respectively. The matrix M is the dissimilarity matrix, where $M(a,b)$ represents the dissimilarity between entries a and b with L aligned residues:

$$M(a,b) = \sum_{i=1}^{L} \sum_{j=1}^{L} \Delta'_{ij}(a,b). \tag{7.32}$$

The hierarchical [128] and PAM [175] clustering methods were then implemented using the dissimilarity matrix M.

PAM is a partitioning algorithm that generalizes K-means clustering to arbitrary dissimilarity matrices. The two-step algorithm starts with a BUILD step in which k initial medoids are sequentially selected. In the SWAP step, the objective function is minimized by iteratively replacing one medoid with another entry. This step is repeated until convergence.

The *silhouette width value* [265] is used to select the best clustering result obtained via the PAM clustering algorithm. Assume that N protein entries have been clustered into k clusters and that an entry a belongs to cluster C of size r. The average dissimilarity between a and all other entries in cluster C is

$$c(a) = \frac{1}{r-1} \sum_{b \in C, b \neq a} M(a,b). \tag{7.33}$$

The average dissimilarity of a to all entries b that belong to another cluster $U \neq C$ of size t is

$$g(a,U) = \frac{1}{t} \sum_{b \in U} M(a,b). \tag{7.34}$$

The dissimilarity between a and the closest cluster that is different from C can be defined as

$$v(a) = \min_{U \neq C} g(a,U). \tag{7.35}$$

The silhouette width $s(a)$ for entry a and the average silhouette width $\bar{s}$ for the set are defined as

$$s(a) = \begin{cases} \frac{v(a) - c(a)}{\max\{c(a), v(a)\}}, & r \neq 1 \text{ and } r \neq N, \\ 0, & r = 1 \text{ or } r = N, \end{cases} \tag{7.36}$$

$$\bar{s} = \sum_{a=1}^{N} s(a). \tag{7.37}$$

Entries with a silhouette value $s(a)$ close to 1.0 are well clustered, and a higher silhouette value indicates that the average distance to entries in the same cluster is smaller than the average distance to the closest neighboring cluster. If the silhouette value is smaller than 0, the entry is not well clustered. PAM clustering is applied to all clusters k numbered between 1 and $N - 1$, and the corresponding average silhouette values $\bar{s}$ are calculated. The best clustering result corresponds to k^* number of clusters $k^* = \text{argmax}_k \bar{s}(k)$.

To test its efficacy, this method was applied to each SCOP [203] species level, and various experimental analyses were performed. The dissimilarity measure of two protein structures used for clustering was then compared with the root-mean-square deviation (rmsd) [78], the average distance between the backbones of superimposed proteins. Clustering results were presented for *D-2-Deoxyribose-5-phosphated aldolase*, *Serum transferrin*, and *Glucose dehydrogenase*. The first and second examples represent two typical cases, with the first having small structural differences and the second having both a large conformational change and a local structural difference. The third example illustrates the use of silhouette width as a measure of cluster quality. A comparative analysis was also made between two hierarchical clustering results with and without the application of filters. These analyses indicated that the backbone structure-based distance metric and clustering method were effective and stable despite the introduction of various structural deviations.

7.7.3 Gene Expression Similarity-Based Measurements

Classical clustering methods have typically focused only on the topological properties of networks. Chen and Yuan [61] have suggested that incorporation of information about both biological and topological relationships is essential to the identification of meaningful modules in biological networks. They formulated a distance metric based on gene expression profiles and an improved Girvan–Newman clustering algorithm extended to select the shortest path on the basis of edge weights.

The method was applied to the measurement of protein similarity in a PPI data set comprised of 265 microarray data sets downloaded from the *Saccharomyces* Genome Database (SGD) [142]. The raw scores were transformed into Z-scores to permit the combination of data from different experiments. The normalized Z-score is found by changing the expression of a given gene g in a microarray experiment m by the ratio r, as follows:

$$Z_g^m = \frac{(r - \mu)}{\sigma}, \tag{7.38}$$

where μ is the experimental mean, and σ is the standard deviation. The edge weight is defined as the average of the Z-score differences over all the experiments. For a given interaction between protein i and protein j, the weight is

$$W_{i,j} = \left| \frac{1}{n} \sum_{m=1}^{n} (Z_i^m - Z_j^m) \right|, \tag{7.39}$$

where n is the total number of microarray experiments in the data set. This weight represents the dissimilarity between the expression profiles of two genes.

The concept of betweenness centrality and its use in a clustering algorithm (the GN algorithm) was first introduced by Girvan and Newman [122]. This measurement assumes that inter-cluster edges are more likely than intra-cluster edges to be on a shortest path. The edges located among clusters in a network can be identified by computing the shortest paths between all node pairs and calculating the number of times each edge is traversed. Hierarchical partitioning of the network can be accomplished by iterative removal of these high-betweenness edges [122].

With the yeast PPI network represented as a weighted graph through the process described earlier, Chen and Yuan extended the GN algorithm so that the shortest path was based on edge weights. They also made additional modifications to the algorithm designed to improve its effectiveness. In the original algorithm, the betweenness of an edge is simply the cumulative number of shortest paths between all node pairs passing through a given edge. Noting that this method of calculating edge betweenness could sometimes lead to unbalanced partitioning, they proposed a nonredundant computational method for edge betweenness. All shortest paths counted for a given edge must have distinct end points. The betweenness of an edge is the maximum number of nonredundant shortest paths between all node pairs that traverse the edge. This modification maintains the intuitive logic of the original algorithm while decreasing the likelihood of generating unbalanced partitions. The maximum bipartite matching algorithm and Floyd–Warshall algorithm were utilized to compute nonredundant edge betweenness; details of these steps are available in [61].

Chen and Yuan applied this modified partitioning algorithm, with its integration of gene expression profiles, to the identification of modules in the yeast PPI network. Results indicate that the algorithm is a useful tool for studying the modularity and organization of biological networks. Genes located within the same functional modules are associated with similar deletion phenotypes. In addition, known protein complexes are typically fully contained within a single functional module, so that module identification may facilitate the process of gene annotation.

7.8 SUMMARY

This chapter has provided a review of a series of approaches to clustering based on topological and/or biological distance. The first category of approaches uses classic distance measurement methods and their various coefficient formulas to compute the distance between proteins in PPI networks. The second class of approaches defines a distance measure based on various network distance factors, including the shortest path length, combined strength of paths of various lengths, and the average number of steps taken by a Brownian particle in moving between vertices. Consensus clustering, the third group of methods, seeks to reduce the noise level in clustering through deployment of several different distance metrics and base-clustering methods. Pruning and consensus techniques are also employed to generate more meaningful clusters. UVCLUSTER exemplifies the fourth category of approach, in which primary and secondary distances are defined to establish the strength of the connection between two elements in relationship to all the elements in the analyzed data set. Similarity learning methods seek to identify effective clusters by incorporating protein annotation data. Finally, three varieties of similarity-based clustering method were presented, all of which draw upon available biological information regarding protein pairs. These methods recognize that the combination of biological and topological information will enhance the identification of effective modules in biological networks. Although each method class has a distinct approach to distance measurement, they all apply classic clustering techniques to the computed distance between proteins. (Some of the material in this chapter is reprinted from [200] with permission of John Wiley & Sons, Inc.)

Graph-Theoretic Approaches
to Modularity Analysis

8.1 INTRODUCTION

Modules (or clusters) in protein–protein interaction (PPI) networks can be identified by applying various clustering algorithms that use graph theory. Each of these methods converts the process of clustering a PPI dataset into a graph-theoretic analysis of the corresponding PPI network. Such clustering approaches take into consideration either the local topology or the global structure of the networks.

The graph-theoretic approaches to modularity analysis can be divided into two classes. One type of approaches [24,238,272,286] seeks to identify dense subgraphs by maximizing the density of each subgraph on the basis of local network topology. The goal of the second group of methods [94,99,138,180,250] is to find the best partition in a graph. Based on the global structure of a network, the methods in this class minimize the cost of partitioning or separating the graph. The approaches in these classes will be discussed in the first two sections of this chapter.

PPI networks are typically large, often having more than 6,000 nodes. In a graph of such large size, classical graph-theoretic algorithms become inefficient. A graph reduction-based approach [65], which enhances the efficiency of module detection in such large and complex interaction networks, will be explored in the third section of this chapter.

8.2 FINDING DENSE SUBGRAPHS

In this section, we will discuss those graph-theoretic approaches that seek to identify the densest subgraphs within a graph; specific methods vary in the means used to assess the density of the subgraphs. Six variations on this theme will be discussed in the following subsections.

8.2.1 Enumeration of Complete Subgraphs

This approach identifies all fully connected subgraphs (termed *cliques*) through complete enumeration [286]. In general, as we have pointed out in Chapter 5, finding all cliques within a graph is a very hard problem. This problem is, however,

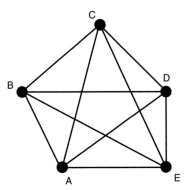

Figure 8-1 Example of a complete subgraph with five nodes.

anti-monotonic; that is, if a subset of set A is not a clique, then set A is also not a clique. Because of this property, dense regions can be quickly identified in sparse graphs. In fact, to find cliques of size n, one needs only to enumerate those cliques that are of size $n - 1$. Assuming the process starts from the least statistically significant number, all possible pairs of edges in the nodes will be considered to find cliques. For example, in the case depicted in Figure 8-1, the starting number will be 4. To examine the edges AB and CD, we should inspect the edges between AC, AD, BC, and BD. If these edges exist, they are considered fully connected, and a clique ABCD is thus identified. If, for protein E, the edges EA, EB, EC, and ED exist, then the clique is expanded to ABCDE. This process eventually generates the list of maximal cliques that are fully and internally connected.

While this approach is simple, it has several drawbacks. The method relies on the basic assumption that a module (or a cluster) is formed as a clique fully and internally connected in a PPI network. Unfortunately, this assumption does not accurately reflect the real structure of protein complexes or functional modules, which are not necessarily fully connected. In addition, many interactions may fail to be detected experimentally and appear as false negative interactions, thus leaving no trace in the form of edges in a PPI network.

8.2.2 Monte Carlo Optimization

Seeking to address the issues that arise in the enumeration of complete subgraphs, Spirin and Mirny [286] introduced a new approach which searches for highly connected rather than fully connected sets of nodes. This was conceptualized as an optimization problem involving the identification of a set of n nodes that maximizes the object function Q, defined as follows:

$$Q(P) = \frac{2m}{n \cdot (n - 1)}, \tag{8.1}$$

where m is the number of edges (interactions) among n nodes in subgraph P. In this formula, the function Q characterizes the density of a cluster [see Equation (5.1) in Chapter 5]. If the subset is fully connected, Q equals 1; if the subset has no internal edge, Q equals 0. The goal is to find a subset with n nodes that maximizes the objective function Q.

A Monte Carlo approach is used to optimize the procedure. The process starts with a connected subset S of n nodes. These nodes are randomly selected from the graph and then updated by adding or deleting selected nodes from S. The remaining nodes increase the value of $Q(S)$. These steps are repeated until the maximum value of $Q(S)$ is identified; this yields an n-node subgraph with high density.

Another quality measure used in this approach is the sum of the shortest distances between selected nodes. A similar Monte Carlo approach is applied to minimize this value. This process proceeds as follows. At time $t = 0$, a random set of M nodes is selected. For each pair of nodes i, j from this set, the shortest path L_{ij} between i and j in the graph is calculated. The sum of all shortest paths L_{ij} from this set is denoted by L_0. At each time step, one of M nodes is randomly selected and replaced by another randomly selected from among its neighbors. To assess whether the original node is to be replaced by this neighbor, the new sum of all shortest paths, L_1, is then calculated. If $L_1 < L_0$, the replacement is accepted with probability 1. If $L_1 > L_0$, the replacement is accepted with probability $\exp^{-(L_1 - L_0)/T}$, where T is the effective temperature. At every tenth time step, an attempt is made to replace one of the nodes from the current set with a node that shares no edges with the current set. This procedure ensures that the process is not caught in an isolated disconnected subgraph. This process is repeated either until the original set converges to a complete subgraph or for a predetermined number of steps. The tightest subgraph, defined as the subgraph corresponding to the smallest L_0, is then recorded. The recorded clusters are merged and redundant clusters are removed. The use of a Monte Carlo approach allows smaller pieces of the cluster to be separately identified rather focusing exclusively on the whole cluster. Monte Carlo simulations are therefore well suited to recognizing highly dispersed cliques.

The experiments conducted by Spirin and Mirny [286] started with the enumeration of all cliques of size 3 and larger in a PPI network with 3,992 nodes and 6,500 edges. In addition, 1,000 random graphs of the same size and degree distribution were constructed for comparison. Using the approach described above, more than 50 protein clusters of sizes from 4 to 35 were identified. In contrast, the random networks contained very few such clusters. This work indicated that real complexes have more interactions than the tightest complexes found in randomly rewired graphs. In particular, clusters in a PPI network have more interactions than their counterparts in random graphs.

8.2.3 Molecular Complex Detection

Molecular complex detection (MCODE), proposed by Bader and Hogue [24], is an effective approach for detecting densely connected regions in large PPI networks. This method weights a vertex by local neighborhood density, chooses a few seeds with a high weight, and isolates the dense regions according to given parameters. The MCODE algorithm operates in three steps: vertex weighting, complex prediction, and optional postprocessing to filter or add proteins to the resulting complexes according to certain connectivity criteria.

In the first step, all vertices are weighted based on their local network density using the highest k-core of the vertex neighborhood. As discussed in Chapter 5, the k-core of a graph is defined as the maximum subgraph if every vertex has at least k links [326]. It is obtained by pruning all the vertices with a degree less than k. Thus, if a vertex v has degree d_v and it has n neighbors with degree less than k, then the degree of v becomes $d_v - n$. It will also be pruned if $k > d_v - n$.

The core-clustering coefficient of a vertex v is defined as the density of the highest k-core of the vertices connected directly to v, together with v itself. Compared with the traditional clustering coefficient, the core-clustering coefficient amplifies the weighting of heavily-interconnected graph regions while removing the many less-connected vertices that are usually part of a PPI network. For each vertex v, the weight of v is

$$w = k \times d, \tag{8.2}$$

where d is the density of the highest k-core graph from the set of vertices including all the vertices directly connected with v and vertex v itself. For example, using the example provided in Figure 4–1, the 2-core weight of node A is $2 \times (2 \times 5)/(5 \times (5 - 1)) = 1$. It should be noted that node D is not included in the 2-core node set because the degree of node D is 1.

The second step of the algorithm is the prediction of molecular complexes. With a vertex-weighted graph as input, a complex with the highest-weighted vertex is selected as the seed. Once a vertex is included, its neighbors are recursively inspected to determine if they are a part of the complex. The seed is then expanded to a complex until a threshold is encountered. The algorithm assumes that complexes cannot overlap (this condition is fully addressed in the next step), so a vertex is not checked more than once. This process stops when, as governed by the specified threshold, no additional vertices can be added to the complex. The vertices included in the complex are marked as having been examined. This process is repeated for the next-highest unexamined weighted vertex in the network. In this manner, the densest regions of the network are identified. The vertex weight threshold parameter defines the density of the resulting complex.

Postprocessing occurs optionally in the third step of this algorithm. Complexes are filtered out if they do not contain at least one 2-core node. The algorithm may be run with the "fluff" option, which increases the size of the complex according to a given fluff parameter between 0.0 and 1.0. For every vertex v in the complex, its neighbors are added to the complex if they have not yet been examined and if the neighborhood density (including v) is higher than the given fluff parameter. Vertices that are added by the fluff parameter are not marked as examined, so the predicted complexes can overlap with the fluff parameter set.

Evaluated using the Gavin [113] and MIPS [214] data sets, MCODE effectively located densely connected regions of a molecular interaction network based solely on connectivity data. Many of these regions correspond to known molecular complexes.

8.2.4 Clique Percolation

Derenyi et al. [87] introduced the novel process of *k-clique percolation*, along with the associated concepts of *k-clique adjacency* and the *k-clique chain*. Two *k*-cliques are adjacent if they share $(k - 1)$ nodes, where k is the number of nodes in the two cliques. A *k*-clique chain is a subgraph comprising the union of a sequence of adjacent *k*-cliques. A *k-clique percolation cluster* is thus a maximal *k*-clique chain. The *k*-clique percolation cluster is equivalent to a regular percolation cluster in the *k*-clique adjacency graph, where the nodes represent the *k*-cliques of the original graph, and there is an edge between two nodes if the corresponding k-cliques are adjacent. Using an heuristic approach, Derenyi et al. found that the percolation transition of k-cliques in random graphs takes place when the probability of two nodes being connected by an edge reaches the threshold $p_c(k)$, where

$$p_c(k) = \frac{1}{[(k-1)N]^{1/(k-1)}},$$ (8.3)

and N is the total number of nodes in a graph.

The key advantage of the clique percolation method is its ability to identify overlapping clusters. A typical PPI network includes overlapping functional modules, so that a protein can be a member of several different functional modules, performing a different function in each. Palla et al. [238] tested the clique percolation approach using the yeast PPI network taken from the core version of the DIP database [271]. They found 82 overlapping modules when $k = 4$. Through this experiment, they determined that the cumulative distribution of module size follows a power law with an exponent of around -1. In addition, they observed that the cumulative distribution of overlap size, which is the number of nodes shared in two modules, is close to a power law with a somewhat larger exponent.

8.2.5 Merging by Statistical Significance

Samanta and Liang [272] took a statistical approach to the clustering of proteins. This approach assumes that two proteins that share a significantly larger number of common neighbors than would arise randomly will have close functional associations. This method first ranks the statistical significance of forming shared partnerships for all protein pairs in an interaction network and then combines the pair of proteins with the greatest significance. The p-value is used to rank the statistical significance of the relationship between two proteins. In the next step, the two proteins with the lowest p-value are combined and are thus considered to be in the same cluster. This process is repeated until a threshold is reached. The steps of the algorithm are described in more detail in the following discussion.

The process begins with the computation of p-values [298] for all possible protein pairs; these are stored in a matrix. The formula for computing the p-value between two proteins is

$$
\begin{aligned}
P(N, n_1, n_2, m) &= \frac{\binom{N}{m}\binom{N-m}{n_1-m}\binom{N-n_1}{n_2-m}}{\binom{N}{n_1}\binom{N}{n_2}} \\
&= \frac{\binom{n_1}{m}\binom{N-n_1}{n_2-m}}{\binom{N}{n_2}} \\
&= \frac{(N-n_1)!\,(N-n_2)!\,n_1!\,n_2!}{N!\,m!\,(n_1-m)!\,(n_2-m)!\,(N-n_1-n_2+m)!},
\end{aligned}
$$ (8.4)

where N is the number of the proteins in the network, each protein in the pair has n_1 and n_2 neighbors, respectively, and m is the number of neighbors shared by both proteins. This formula is symmetric with respect to the interchange of n_1 and n_2. It is a ratio in which the denominator is the total number of ways that two proteins can have n_1 and n_2 neighbors. In the numerator, the first term represents the number of ways in which m common neighbors can be chosen from all N proteins. The second term represents the number of ways in which $n_1 - m$ remaining neighbors can be selected from the remaining $N - m$ proteins. The last term represents the number of ways in which $n_2 - m$ remaining neighbors can be selected with none matching any of the n_1 neighbors of the first protein.

In the second step, the protein pair with the lowest p-value is designated as the first group in the cluster. As illustrated in Figure 8–2, the rows and columns for these two proteins are merged into a single row and column. The probability values for this new group are the geometric means of the two original probabilities (or the arithmetic means of the $\log P$ values). This process is repeated until a threshold is reached, adding elements to increase the size of the original cluster. The protein pair with the second-lowest p-value is selected to generate the next cluster.

A high rate of false positives typically creates significant noise that disrupts the clustering of protein complexes and functional modules. This method overcomes this difficulty by using a statistical technique that forms reliable functional associations between proteins from noisy interaction data. The statistical significance of forming shared partnerships for all protein pairs in the interaction network is ranked.

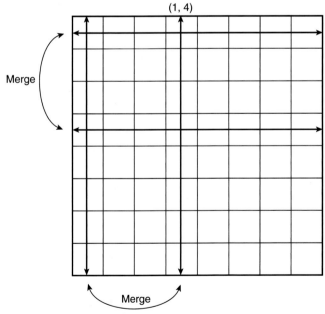

Figure 8–2 If the element (m,n) has the lowest p-value, a cluster is formed with proteins m and n. Therefore, rows/columns m and n are then merged with the new p-value of the merged row/column, using the geometric mean of the separate p-values of the corresponding elements. (Reprinted from [272] with permission from PNAS.)

This approach is grounded on the hypothesis that two proteins with a significantly larger number of common interaction pairs in the measured dataset than would arise randomly will also have close functional links.

To validate this hypothesis, all possible protein pairs were ranked in the order of their probabilities. For comparison, the corresponding probabilities were examined for a random network with the same number of nodes and edges but with different connections. The connections in the random network were generated from a uniform distribution. The comparison suggests that the associations in a real data set contain biologically meaningful information. It also indicates that such low-probability associations did not arise simply from the scale-free nature of the network.

8.2.6 Super-Paramagnetic Clustering

The super-paramagnetic clustering (SPC) method uses an analogy to the physical properties of an inhomogenous ferromagnetic model to find tightly connected clusters in a large graph [39,117,118,299]. Every node on the graph is assigned a Potts spin variable $S_i = 1, 2, \ldots, q$. The value of this spin variable S_i engages in thermal fluctuations, which are determined by the temperature T and the spin values of the neighboring nodes. Two nodes connected by an edge are likely to have the same spin value. Therefore, the spin value of each node tends to align itself with that of the majority of its neighbors.

The SPC procedure proceeds via the following steps:

(1) A q-state Potts spin variable S_i is assigned to each point $\vec{x_i}$.
(2) The nearest neighbors of each point are identified according to a selected criterion, and the average nearest-neighbor distance a is measured.
(3) The strength of the nearest-neighbor interactions is calculated:

$$J_{ij} = J_{ji} = \frac{1}{\hat{K}} \exp\left(-\frac{\|\vec{x_i} - \vec{x_j}\|^2}{2a^2}\right), \tag{8.5}$$

where $\hat{K}$ is the average number of neighbors per site.

(4) An efficient Monte Carlo procedure is applied to calculate the susceptibility χ:

$$\chi = \frac{N}{T}(\langle m^2 \rangle - \langle m \rangle^2), \quad m = \frac{(N_{\max}/N)q - 1}{q - 1}, \tag{8.6}$$

where $N_{\max} = \max\{N_1, N_2, \ldots, N_q\}$ and N_μ is the number of spins with value μ.

(5) The range of temperatures that correspond to the super-paramagnetic phase is identified. The range is bounded by T_{fs}, the temperature of maximal χ, and the (higher) temperature T_{ps} where χ diminishes abruptly. Cluster assignment is performed at $T_{\text{clus}} = (T_{fs} + T_{ps})/2$.
(6) Once the J_{ij} have been determined, the spin–spin correlation function can be obtained by a Monte Carlo procedure. The spin–spin correlation function $\langle \delta_{S_i, S_j} \rangle$ for all pairs of neighboring points $\vec{x_i}$ and $\vec{x_j}$ is measured at $T = T_{\text{clus}}$.

(7) Clusters are identified according to a thresholding procedure. If $\langle \delta_{S_i, S_j} \rangle > \theta$, points $\vec{x_i}$ and $\vec{x_j}$ are defined as "friends." All mutual friends (including friends of friends, etc.) are then assigned to the same cluster.

The SPC algorithm is robust in conditions with noise and initialization errors and has been shown to identify natural and stable clusters with no requirement for pre-specifying the number of clusters. Additionally, clusters of any shape can be identified.

8.3 FINDING THE BEST PARTITION

The graph-theoretic clustering approaches in the second category generate clusters by finding the best partition with which to divide the graph into several subgraphs. The edges to be used as a partition should be the least important in the graph, thus minimizing the informational cost of removing the edges. The importance of an edge is based on the global structure of the graph. Assessing an edge as of lesser importance does not mean that the interaction between two proteins is trivial. Several techniques that employ this means of partitioning will be presented in the following subsections.

8.3.1 Recursive Minimum Cut

The recursive minimum cut, termed in [138] the highly connected subgraph (HCS) detection method, is a graph-theoretic algorithm that separates a graph into several subgraphs by deleting a series of edges at minimum cost. The resulting subgraphs satisfy a specified density threshold. Despite its interest in density, this method differs from approaches discussed earlier, which seek to identify the densest subgraphs. Rather, it exploits the inherent connectivity of the graph and cuts the most unimportant edges as a means for the identification of HCSs.

The definition of some graph-theoretic concepts will be useful at this juncture. The *edge-connectivity* $k(G)$ of a graph G is the minimum number k of edges whose removal results in a disconnected graph. If $k(G) = l$ then G is termed an l-connected or l-connectivity graph. For example, in Figure 8–3, the graph G is a 2-connectivity graph because at least two edges must be cut (shown as dashed lines in graph) to produce a disconnected graph. A HCS is defined as a subgraph whose edge-connectivity exceeds half the number of vertices. For example, in Figure 8–3, graph G_1 is a HCS because its edge-connectivity $k(G) = 3$ is more than half of the number of vertices. A *cut* in a graph is a set of edges whose removal disconnects the graph. A *minimumcut* (abbreviated *mincut*) is a cut with a minimum number of edges. Thus, a cut S is a minimum cut of a nontrivial graph G if and only if $|S| = k(G)$. The length of a path between two vertices consists of the number of edges in the path. The distance $dist(u, v)$ between vertices u and v in graph G is the minimum length of their connecting path, if such a path exists; otherwise $dist(u, v) = \infty$. The diameter of a connected graph G, denoted $diam(G)$, is the longest distance between any two vertices in G. The degree of vertex v in a graph, denoted $d(v)$, is the number of edges incident to the vertex.

The HCS algorithm identifies HCSs as clusters. The algorithm is described below, and Figure 8–3 presents an example of its application. Graph G is first separated into

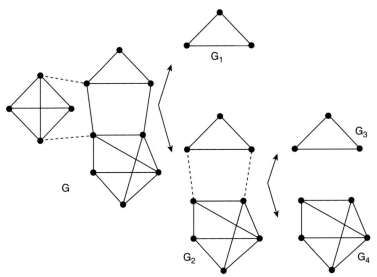

Figure 8–3 An example of applying the HCS algorithm to a graph. Minimum cut edges are depicted as dashed lines. (Adapted from [138] with permission from Elsevier.)

two subgraphs G_1 and G_2, of which G_1 is a HCS, and G_2 is not. Subgraph G_2 is separated into subgraphs G_3 and G_4. This process produces three HCSs G_1, G_3, and G_4, which are considered to be clusters.

HCS$(G(V, E))$ **algorithm**
begin $(H, \overline{H}, C) \leftarrow$ MINCUT (G)
if G is highly connected
then return(G)
else
HCS(H)
HCS$(\overline{H})$
end

The HCS algorithm generates solutions with desirable properties for clustering. The algorithm has low polynomial complexity and is efficient in practice. Heuristic improvements made to the initial formulation have allowed this method to generate useful solutions for problems with thousands of elements in a reasonable computing time.

8.3.2 Restricted Neighborhood Search Clustering (RNSC)

King et al. [180] proposed a cost-based local search algorithm modeled based on the tabu search metaheuristic [124]. In the algorithm, a clustering of a graph $G = (V, E)$ is defined as a partitioning of the node set V. The process begins with an initial random or user-input clustering and defines a cost function. Nodes are then randomly added to or removed from clusters to find a partition with minimum cost. The cost function is based on the number of invalid connections. An invalid connection incident with v is a connection that exists between v and a node in a different cluster, or, alternatively, a connection that does not exist between v and a node u in the same cluster as v.

Consider a node v in a graph G and a clustering C of the graph. Let α_v be the number of invalid connections incident with v. The naive cost function of C is then defined as:

$$C_n(G, C) = \frac{1}{2} \sum_{v \in V} \alpha_v, \tag{8.7}$$

where V is the set of nodes in G. For a vertex v in G with a clustering C, let β_v be the size of the following set: v itself, any node connected to v, and any node in the same cluster as v. This measure reflects the size of the area that v influences in the clustering. The scaled cost function of C is defined as

$$C_n(G, C) = \frac{|V| - 1}{3} \sum_{v \in V} \frac{\alpha_v}{\beta_v}. \tag{8.8}$$

For example, in Figure 8–4, if the eight vertices are grouped into two clusters as shown, the naive cost function $C_n(G, C) = 2$, and the scaled cost function $C_n(G, C) = 20/9$.

Both cost functions seek to define a clustering scenario in which the nodes in a cluster are all connected to one another and there are no other connections between two clusters. The RNSC approach searches for a low-cost clustering solution by optimizing an initial state. Starting with an initial clustering defined randomly or by user input, the method iteratively moves a node from one cluster to another in a random manner. Since the RNSC is randomized, different runs on the same input data will generate different clustering results. To achieve high accuracy in predicting true protein complexes, the RNSC output is filtered according to a maximum p-value selected for functional homogeneity, a minimum density value, and a minimum size. Only clusters that satisfy these three criteria are presented as predicted protein complexes.

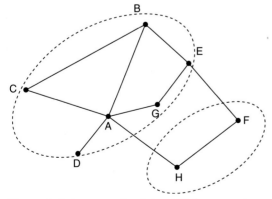

Figure 8–4 An example of the RNSC approach.

8.3.3 Betweenness Cut

As discussed in Chapters 4 and 6, the betweenness centrality measure finds a node or an edge that is likely to be located between modules. The *betweenness* of a node v is defined as

$$C_B(v) = \sum_{s \neq v \neq t \in V} \frac{\rho_{st}(v)}{\rho_{st}}, \tag{8.9}$$

where ρ_{st} is the number of shortest paths between s and t, and $\rho_{st}(v)$ is the number of shortest paths between s and t that pass through node v. In terms of information flow, this measure describes how much flow passes through v. In a similar manner, the betweenness of an edge e can be computed by

$$C_B(e) = \sum_{s \neq t \in V, \, e \in E} \frac{\rho_{st}(e)}{\rho_{st}}, \tag{8.10}$$

where $\rho_{st}(e)$ is the number of shortest paths between s and t that pass through edge e.

The betweenness cut algorithm [94,122] iteratively disconnects the edges with the highest betweenness value and recursively implements the cutting process in each subgraph. It is important that the betweenness value be recalculated for each iteration to ensure that the appropriate edge is cut in the context of the current global structure of the graph. The selection of recursion stopping conditions can be a critical parameter for this method. In general, the density or the size of each subgraph is used as a threshold. If an isolated subgraph created by iterative cutting has a higher density or a smaller number of nodes than a threshold value, then the algorithm stops the recursive process and outputs the set of nodes in the subgraph as a module. With a low density or a high threshold, the average size of output modules becomes large. Thus, the threshold should be carefully set to conform to the expected size of output modules.

Dunn et al. [94] applied this method to yeast and human interaction data sets derived from high-throughput experiments. For the Uetz dataset [307], 327 clusters were identified with an average cluster size of 4.1 by removing 27% of the edges with highest betweenness. For the Gavin dataset [113], 222 clusters were detected with an average cluster size of 4.9 by removing 50% of the edges. For the human interaction data set, the algorithm produced 21 clusters with an average size of 15.6 by removing 14% of the edges. When the clusters were compared to GO terms and their annotations, a significant correlation was found. There was an inverse relationship between the size of clusters generated by this method and the average number of significant annotations. As a critical drawback, the betweenness cut algorithm does not scale well to large networks.

8.3.4 Markov Clustering

The Markov clustering algorithm (MCL) was designed specifically for application to simple and weighted graphs [308] and was initially used in the field of computational graph clustering [309]. The MCL algorithm finds cluster structures in graphs by a mathematical bootstrapping procedure. The MCL algorithm simulates random walks within a graph by the alternation of expansion and inflation operations. Expansion

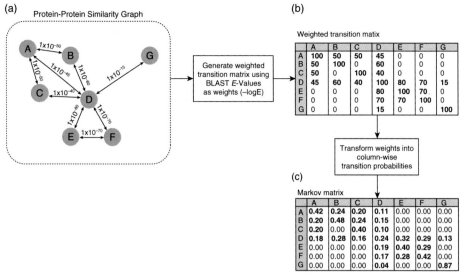

Figure 8–5 (a) Example of a protein–protein similarity graph for seven proteins (A–F). Circles represent proteins (nodes) and lines (edges) represent detected BLASTp similarities with E-values (also shown). (b) Weighted transition matrix for the seven proteins shown in (a). (c) Associated column stochastic Markov matrix for the seven proteins shown in (a). (Reprinted from [99] with permission from Oxford University Press.)

refers to taking the power of a stochastic matrix using the normal matrix product. Inflation corresponds to taking the Hadamard power of a matrix (taking powers entrywise), followed by a scaling step, so that the resulting matrix is again stochastic.

Enright et al. [99] employed the MCL algorithm for the assignment of proteins to families. A protein–protein similarity graph is represented as illustrated in Figure 8–5(a). Nodes in the graph represent proteins that are desirable clustering candidates, while edges within the graph are weighted according to a sequence similarity score obtained from an algorithm such as BLAST [14]. Therefore, the edges represent the degree of similarity between these proteins.

A Markov matrix, as shown in Figure 8–5(b), is then constructed in which each entry in the matrix represents a similarity value between two proteins. Diagonal elements are set arbitrarily to a "neutral" value, and each column is normalized to produce a column total of 1. This Markov matrix is then provided as input to the MCL algorithm.

As noted above, the MCL algorithm simulates random walks within a graph by alternating two operators: expansion and inflation. The structure of the MCL algorithm is described by the flowchart in Figure 8–6. After parsing and normalization of the similarity matrix, the algorithm starts by computing the graph of random walks of an input graph, yielding a stochastic matrix. It then uses iterative rounds of the expansion operator, which takes the squared power of the matrix, and the inflation operator, which raises each matrix entry to a given power and then rescales the matrix to return it to a stochastic state. This process continues until there is no further change in the matrix. After postprocessing and domain correction, the final matrix is interpreted as a set of protein clusters.

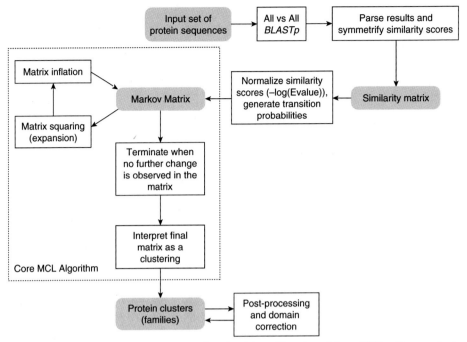

Figure 8–6 Flowchart of the TRIBE-MCL algorithm. (Reprinted from [99] with permission from Oxford University Press.)

As stated in [99], given a matrix $M \in R^{k \times k}$, $M \geq 0$ and a real number $r > 1$, the column stochastic matrix resulting from inflating each of the columns of M with a power coefficient r is denoted by $\Gamma_r M$, and Γ_r represents the inflation operator with power coefficient r. Formally the action of $\Gamma_r : R^{k \times k} \rightarrow R^{k \times k}$ is defined by

$$(\Gamma_r M)_{pq} = (M_{pq})^r \left/ \sum_{i=1}^{k} (M_{iq})^r. \right. \tag{8.11}$$

Each column j of a stochastic matrix M corresponds to node j of the stochastic graph associated with the probability of moving from node j to node i. For values of $r > 1$, inflation changes the probabilities associated with the collection of random walks departing from one particular node by favoring more probable over less probable walks.

Expansion and inflation are used iteratively in the MCL algorithm to enhance the graph where it is strong and to diminish it where it is weak, until equilibrium is reached. At this point, clusters can be identified according to a threshold. If the weight between two proteins is less than the threshold, the edge between them can be deleted. An important advantage of the algorithm is its "bootstrapping" nature, retrieving cluster structure via the imprint made by this structure on the flow process. Additionally, the algorithm is fast and very scalable, and its accuracy is not compromised by edges between different clusters. The mathematics underlying the algorithm is indicative of an intrinsic relationship between the process it simulates and the cluster structure in the input graph.

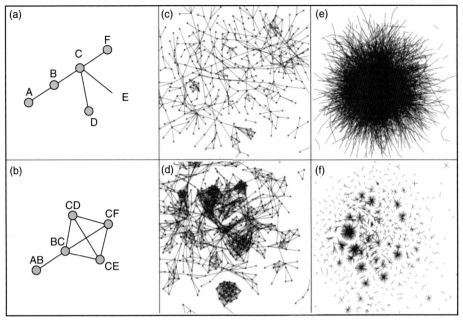

Figure 8–7 Transforming a network of proteins to a network of interactions.
(a) Schematic illustration of a graph representation of protein interactions; nodes correspond to proteins and edges to interactions. (b) Schematic representation illustrating the transformation of the protein graph connected by interactions to an interaction graph connected by proteins. Each node represents a binary interaction and edges represent shared proteins. Note that labels that are not shared correspond to terminal nodes in (a). In this example, these are A, D, E, and F in edges AB, CD, CE, CF. (c) Graph illustrating a section of a protein network connected by interactions. (d) Graph illustrating the increase in structure as an effect of transforming the protein graph in (c) to an interaction graph. (e) Graph representation of yeast protein interactions in DIP. (f) Graph representing a pruned version of (e) with the reconstituted interactions after transformation and clustering. These graphs were produced by using BioLayout. (Reprinted from [250] with permission of Wiley-Liss, Inc., a subsidiary of John Wiley & Sons, Inc. Copyright 2003 Wiley-Liss, Inc.)

8.3.5 Line Graph Generation

Pereira-Leal et al. [250] expressed the network of proteins connected by interactions as a network of connected interactions. Figure 8–7(a) exemplifies an original PPI network graph in which the nodes represent proteins and the edges represent interactions. Periera-Leal's method generates from this an associated line graph, such as that depicted in Figure 8–7(b), in which edges now represent proteins and nodes represent interactions. This simple procedure is commonly used in graph theory.

First, the PPI network is transformed into a weighted network, where the weights attributed to each interaction reflect the degree of confidence attributed to that interaction. Confidence levels are determined by the number of experiments as well by as the number of different experimental methodologies that support the interaction. Next, the network connected by interactions is expressed as a network of interactions, known in graph theory as a line graph. Each interaction is condensed into a node that includes the two interacting proteins. These nodes are then linked by shared protein content. The scores for the original constituent interactions are then averaged and assigned to each edge. Finally, an algorithm for clustering by graph flow simulation, TRIBE-MCL [99], is used to cluster the interaction network and then to reconvert the identified clusters from an interaction–interaction graph back to a protein-protein graph for subsequent validation and analysis.

This technique focuses on the structure of the graph itself and what it represents. It has been included here among the graph-based minimum cutting approaches because it employs the MCL method for clustering. This approach has a number of attractive features. It does not sacrifice informational content, because the original bidirectional network can be recovered at the end of the process. Furthermore, it takes into account the higher-order local neighborhood of interactions. In addition, the graph it generates is more highly structured than the original graph. Finally, it produces an overlapping graph partitioning of the interaction network, implying that proteins may be present in multiple functional modules. Many other clustering approaches cannot place elements in multiple clusters. This represents a significant inability on the part of those approaches to represent the complexity of biological systems, where proteins may participate in multiple cellular processes and pathways.

8.4 GRAPH REDUCTION-BASED APPROACH

To apply the graph-theoretic clustering algorithms to large, complex networks, Cho et al. [65] devised a graph reduction technique. The graph reduction-based approach efficiently identifies modules in such graphs in a hierarchical manner. This approach uses a weighted graph as an input. The weight assigned to each edge in a PPI network can be calculated as a preprocess by using the sequence similarity, structural similarity or expression correlation between interacting proteins as biological distance, following the methods described in Chapter 7. As another measure for the weights of interactions, GO data can be integrated, using the methods to be discussed in Chapter 11. The flowchart of the algorithm is illustrated in Figure 8–8. The details of the algorithm will be discussed in the following two subsections, and performance evaluation results will be offered in the ensuing three subsections. (Most material in this section are from [65]. Reprinted with permission from IEEE.)

8.4.1 Graph Reduction

Graph reduction is the process of simplifying a complex network through removal of nodes without losing the general pattern of connectivity inherent to the network. As illustrated in Figure 8–8, there are two steps to this process of informative node selection and graph reconstruction.

Informative nodes can be selected using any centrality metric for a weighted graph, such as selecting those nodes v_i which have highest values of weighted degree d_i^{wt} or weighted clustering coefficient c_i^{wt} [30].

$$d_i^{\mathrm{wt}} = \sum_{v_j \in N(v_i)} w_{ij}, \tag{8.12}$$

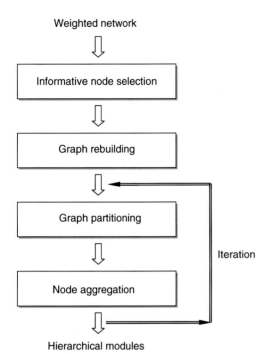

Weighted network

Informative node selection

Graph rebuilding

Graph partitioning

Iteration

Node aggregation

Hierarchical modules

Figure 8–8 Flowchart of the graph reduction-based approach to hierarchical module detection.

where w_{ij} is the weight of the edge $\langle v_i, v_j \rangle$, and

$$c_i^{\text{wt}} = \frac{1}{d_i^{\text{wt}}(d_i - 1)} \sum_{\substack{v_j, v_h \in N(v_i), \\ \langle v_j, v_h \rangle \in E}} \frac{(w_{ij} + w_{ih})}{2}, \tag{8.13}$$

where d_i is the (unweighted) degree of v_i. The number of the informative nodes selected is a user-dependent parameter in this algorithm.

In a weighted graph, *path strength* and *maximum path strength* can be defined. The *path strength* is the product of the weights of all edges on p:

$$S(p) = \prod_{i=1}^{l} w_{(i-1)i}, \tag{8.14}$$

where the path $p = \langle v_0, v_1, \ldots, v_l \rangle$, and $w_{(i-1)i}$ is the weight of the edge $\langle v_{(i-1)}, v_i \rangle$ in the range of $0 \leq w_{(i-1)i} \leq 1$. The *maximum path strength* $S_{\max}(\langle v_0, \ldots, v_l \rangle)$ is the highest value of the path strengths of all paths from v_0 to v_l. It can represent the probability that v_i and v_j are included in the same cluster.

A graph is rebuilt with the selected informative nodes using the *k-hop graph rebuilding* rule. This states that two *informative nodes* v_i and v_j will be connected if there is a path between v_i and v_j within length k in the original graph and there are no informative nodes in the middle of the path. The weight w_{ij} of an edge between v_i and

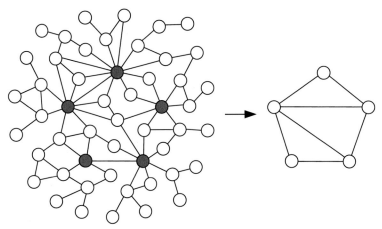

Figure 8–9 An example of graph reduction with an unweighted network where $k = 2$ in k-hop graph rebuilding.

v_j in the reduced graph can be assigned according to the maximum path strength in the original graph. A simple example of graph reduction with an unweighted graph is illustrated in Figure 8–9. Here, the five nodes colored black in the original scale-free network are selected as informative nodes. The reduced graph is composed of the five informative nodes and is rebuilt with new edges that are created with $k = 2$ in the k-hop graph rebuilding rule.

8.4.2 Hierarchical Modularization

As already observed in Chapter 4, PPI networks follow a scale-free and hierarchical network model. In this model, functional modules in a PPI network are hierarchically organized, with a few high-degree nodes and many low-degree nodes. To detect hierarchical modules, this algorithm takes the initialization of a reduced graph as an input and proceeds in a top-down manner. The process consists of graph-partitioning and node-aggregation phases performed iteratively, as illustrated in Figure 8–8.

In the first phase, the reduced graph is optimally partitioned to create preliminary modules, which are the large modules at the highest hierarchical level. A *cut* is a partition that divides a graph into two subgraphs. As with a weighted graph, we define a *cut weight* as the sum of the weights of interconnecting edges between two subgraphs. A *minimum cut* is then the cut with the smallest cut weight. In general, the recursive partitioning of a scale-free network by the minimum cut results in the iterative clipping of peripheral nodes or small outlying branches. Its repeated application eventually identifies only small sets of densely-connected nodes, in the same manner as most bottom-up clustering approaches. Therefore, a *cut ratio* is defined to effectively divide a graph into two subgraphs for this algorithm. The cut ratio $R_c(G)$ for dividing a graph $G(V, E)$ into two subgraphs $G'(V', E')$ and $G''(V'', E'')$ is defined as the cut weight w_c over the size of smaller subgraph:

$$R_c(G) = \frac{w_c}{\min(|V'|, |V''|)}, \tag{8.15}$$

where $w_c = \sum w_{ij}$ for $v_i \in V'$, $v_j \in V''$, and $\langle v_i, v_j \rangle \in E$. To detect the optimal partition of G, this algorithm finds the smallest $R_c(G)$. This optimized minimum cut is recursively performed until the subgraph is smaller than a minimum size threshold, or the weighted density of the subgraph exceeds a maximum density threshold.

The second phase involves the aggregation of noninformative nodes into one of the preliminary modules generated by the previous step. The aggregation of each noninformative node is based on the path strength from it to the members of preliminary modules. The path with the highest maximum path strength between a noninformative node v_n and the node v_i in a preliminary module is identified, and v_n is then aggregated into the module that includes v_i. The number of nodes to be aggregated depends on the minimum threshold that has been set by the user for the maximum path strength.

These graph-partitioning and node-aggregation phases are iterated to build a hierarchy of modules. When the minimum threshold of the maximum path strength is 0, all noninformative nodes are aggregated simultaneously after partitioning the reduced graph, creating the top-level modules in a hierarchy. To produce the second-level modules in the hierarchy, the algorithm aggregates only those noninformative proteins with a maximum path strength exceeding the threshold, partitions the aggregated graphs, and finally aggregates all the other noninformative proteins. In a similar manner, any desired level of hierarchical module can be generated dynamically through the selection of an appropriate maximum path strength threshold for each iterative step.

8.4.3 Time Complexity

The main strength of the graph reduction-based approach is its efficiency. The total time complexity of this algorithm is dependent on the intensity of the graph partitioning step. A minimum cut algorithm recently suggested for partitioning a graph $G(V, E)$ [292] runs in time $O(|V||E| + |V|^2 \log |V|)$. While this deterministic algorithm offers improvements in speed and simplicity of execution over other graph-partitioning algorithms, the size and complexity of the graph remain crucial to overall performance.

Cho et al. [65] analyzed the running time of both the graph reduction-based method and the general minimum cut algorithm without graph reduction and tested on graphs of several different sizes. Nodes were randomly chosen for each graph. The algorithms, coded in Java, were executed on a Sun Ultra 80 workstation with a 450 MHz CPU and 4GB main memory. Table 8.1 indicates that the graph reduction-based algorithm is significantly faster than the alternative. Of particular note is its scalability on very large networks as inputs. Since it reduces the original network to a small and simple graph and aggregates a small number of nodes in each step, the graph reduction-based algorithm has to partition only small graphs.

8.4.4 *k* Effects on Graph Reduction

The value of parameter k in the k-hop graph rebuilding process is a critical factor in the performance of this algorithm. The value k determines the randomness of degree and the modularity of the reduced network. To measure the impact of k,

Table 8.1 Comparison of the running time of the graph reduction-based approach and the general minimum cut algorithm without graph reduction

Number of nodes	Graph reduction-based approach (sec)				General min-cut (sec)
	Graph reduction	Graph partitioning	Node accumulation	Total	
129	0.0	0.3	0.0	0.3	0.7
513	0.0	0.9	0.6	1.5	185.2
926	0.0	1.3	1.2	2.5	2152.0
1428	0.0	1.8	3.1	4.9	16614.4
1867	0.0	2.9	5.4	8.3	56118.9
2463	0.0	3.7	8.7	12.4	—
2983	0.1	4.6	13.7	18.4	—
3607	0.2	11.1	21.6	32.9	—
4183	0.2	12.6	31.1	43.9	—
4770	0.3	12.1	42.3	54.7	—

Cho et al. [65] selected 2% of the nodes from the full set of protein interaction data and implemented the algorithm with the graphs rebuilt by $k = 1$, 2, and 3. They used the Pearson correlation of gene expression profiles for each interacting protein pair to create a weighted interaction network as an input. The Pearson correlation coefficient r between the expression values of two proteins x and y is:

$$r = \frac{\sum_{i=1}^{n}(x_i - \bar{x})(y_i - \bar{y})}{\sqrt{\sum_{i=1}^{n}(x_i - \bar{x})^2}\sqrt{\sum_{i=1}^{n}(y_i - \bar{y})^2}}, \tag{8.16}$$

where n is the number of time points for the expressional profiles. The absolute value of r becomes the weight for the edge between x and y.

First, the degree distributions of the three reduced graphs were investigated. During the graph reduction process, a large portion of the peripheral nodes in a scale-free network are deleted, and the number of highly connected nodes is decreased by the removal of peripheral nodes. Therefore, the degrees of nodes in the reduced graph become randomly distributed. The typical patterns of the degree distributions are described in Figure 8–10. When $k = 2$, the degree distribution was properly randomized. However, it was under-randomized with $k = 1$ and over-randomized with $k = 3$.

Next, the modularity of the three reduced graphs was examined. Table 8.2 shows the weighted density $D(G)$ for each graph G, where the weighted density of a graph is calculated by the ratio of the sum of all edge weights to the number of all possible edges in the graph, and the modularity of a set of modules in a graph is defined as the average weighted density of modules over the weighted density of the graph. Intuitively, a larger k will result in a denser graph. At the end of the process, given a sufficiently large value of k, the graph becomes a clique that is fully connected. The ideal k-value should maximize the modularity of the graph. To generate modules, the optimized minimum cut was employed, using 10 as the minimum size threshold and 0.3 as the maximum density threshold. The average weighted density of all modules and

Table 8.2 Comparison of modularity and average p-score of the reduced graphs where $k = 1, 2,$ and 3

k	Weighted density (D_W)	Average weighted density of modules (D'_W)	Modularity (D'_W/D_W)	Average p-score
1	0.034	0.217	6.30	8.34
2	0.060	0.379	6.35	9.35
3	0.074	0.317	4.27	7.19

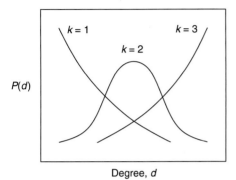

Degree, d

Figure 8–10 Typical patterns of degree distributions $P(d)$ of a graph reduced by different values of k. The degree distribution is well-randomized where $k = 2$.

the modularity of each reduced graph are listed in Table 8.2. The results show that the graph built by $k = 2$ is more modular than the graphs generated by other values of k.

Statistical p-values defined in Equation (5.20) were used to validate the performance. Equation (5.20) is understood as the probability that at least k nodes in a module with size n are included in a particular category with size $|X|$. Low p-value indicates that the module closely corresponds to the category because the network has a rare chance to produce the module. After computing p-value between a module and each functional category on the top level in hierarchy, one major function with the lowest p-value was assigned to the module. p-score is defined for a module as the negative of $\log(P)$ when P is calculated with the assigned function by Formula 5.20. The average p-score of all modules was computed.

8.4.5 Hierarchical Structure of Modules

To identify hierarchical modules, the algorithm started with the informative nodes of the upper 2% of nodes in the weighted degree and aggregated the next 10%, 20%, and 30% of nodes in the weighted degree for each step. The remaining 38%, which are mainly peripheral nodes, were added to the modules at the end. Through this means, modules were generated on four different levels, resulting in a hierarchical structure.

To validate that this algorithm successfully identifies real hierarchical modules within the protein interaction data, the output results were compared to the hierarchical categories of functions [267] from the MIPS database [214]. The statistical

Table 8.3 Statistical results for the identified modules on each level in the hierarchy

Level in hierarchy	Number of modules	Average size of modules	Average p-score	Average of Top 20 p-scores
1 (Top)	8	553.8	11.89	11.89
2	48	95.7	7.26	12.36
3	137	34.3	5.66	13.46
4 (Bottom)	236	20.1	4.73	13.62

results are provided in Table 8.3. The average value of the p-scores decreases as the algorithm moves down the hierarchical structure. In general, smaller modules are correlated with lower average p-scores, since, at these levels, the algorithm is less likely to correctly identify the modules that correspond to the reference sets. However, the average p-score of the twenty most accurate modules gradually increases while the module size decreases. This result indicates that the algorithm successfully identifies some accurate sub-modules from a super-module. This approach explicitly builds a hierarchical structure by identifying the modules that correspond to hierarchical functions.

8.5 SUMMARY

This chapter has introduced a series of graph-theoretic approaches for module detection (clustering) in PPI networks. These approaches fall into three general groups. The first two groups can be more broadly categorized as graph-theoretic approaches to modularity analysis. Under this umbrella, several methods seek to identify dense subgraphs by maximizing the density of the subgraphs. The complete subgraph enumeration method partitions the graph optimally so as to identify fully connected subgraphs within the network. Monte Carlo optimization can enhance efficiency by developing a density function for finding highly connected rather than fully connected subgraphs. The MCODE algorithm assigns each vertex a weight to represent its density in the entire graph and uses the vertex with the highest weight as the seed to generate a dense subgraph. The clique percolation method combines two cliques if there are significant connections between them. Statistical merging combines pairs of proteins with the lowest p-values, indicating that those proteins have a strong relationship. Finally, the SPC technique assigns each node a Potts spin value and computes the spin–spin correlation function. If the correlation between two spins exceeds a threshold, the two proteins are assigned to the same cluster. In general, all approaches in this group use local connectivity to find a dense subgraph within a PPI network.

The second category of graph-theoretic approaches to modularity analysis includes various methods to identify the best partition by minimizing the cost of partitioning or separating a graph. The recursive minimum cut algorithm repeatedly performs a minimum cut until all subgraphs are highly connected. The RNSC algorithm efficiently searches the space of partitions of all nodes and assigns each a cost function related to cutting the edges in the graph. Identification of the lowest-cost partitions becomes synonymous with finding those clusters with minimum cutting. The betweenness cut method iteratively finds the most central edge located between modules and removes these edges until the graph is separated. This iteration is then recursively applied to each subgraph. The MCL algorithm uses iterative rounds of expansion and inflation to promote flow through the graph where it is strong and to remove flow where it is weak. Clusters are then generated via minimum cutting. The line graph generation approach transforms the network of proteins connected by interactions into a network of connected interactions and then uses the MCL algorithm to cluster the interaction network. The approaches in this group consider the global topology of a PPI network.

Graph reduction takes a slightly different approach to the generation of a modular hierarchy. It converts a large, complex network into a small, simple graph and applies the optimized minimum cut to identify hierarchical modules. Experimental results have demonstrated that this approach outperforms classical graph-theoretic methods from the standpoint of efficiency.

9

Flow-Based Analysis of Protein Interaction Networks

9.1 INTRODUCTION

The previous three chapters have discussed in detail the analysis of protein–protein interaction (PPI) networks on the basis of their biological and topological features. As we have noted, these networks are characterized by complex connectivity and elusive interactions, which often compromise the effectiveness of the approaches presented so far. In this chapter, we will examine flow-based approaches, another avenue for the analysis of PPI networks. These methods permit information from other sources to be integrated with PPI data to enhance the effectiveness of algorithms for protein function prediction and functional module detection. Flow-based approaches offer a novel strategy for assessing the degree of biological and topological influence of each protein over other proteins in a PPI network. Through simulation of biological or functional flows within these complex networks, these methods seek to model and predict network behavior under the influence of various realistic external stimuli.

This chapter will discuss several flow-based methods for the prediction of protein function. The first section will address the concept of functional flow introduced by Nabieva et al. [221] and the FunctionalFlow algorithm based on this model. In this approach, each protein with a known functional annotation is treated as a source of functional flow, which is then propagated to unannotated nodes, using the edges in the interaction graph as a conduit. This process is based on simple local rules. A distance effect is formulated that considers the impact of each annotated protein on any other protein, with the effect diminishing as the distance between the proteins increases. In addition, since each edge is defined to have a limited flow capacity and multiple paths between two proteins may result in increased flow between them, network connectivity is exploited. The method obtains a functional score for each protein by simulating the spread of this functional flow through a fixed number of time steps [221]. The number of steps is limited to ensure that flow from a source is restricted to its local neighborhood.

The second section of this chapter will offer a description of CASCADE, a dynamic flow simulation for modularity analysis. The reliability of the predictive results obtained by flow-based methods depends on the deployment of effective simulation methods to capture the stochastic behavior of the system. The CAS-CADE model aggregates information about protein function and applies a weighting strategy to the PPI network. Information flow is simulated starting from each informative protein through the entire weighted interaction network. CASCADE models the PPI network as a dynamic signal transduction system, with each protein acting as a perturbation of the system. The signal transduction behavior of each perturbation should also reflect the topological properties of the network. The overall signal transduction behavior function between any two proteins is formulated to evaluate the biological and topological perturbation caused by a protein on other proteins in the network.

Because a molecule generally performs different biological processes or functions in different environments, real functional modules are typically overlapping. The flow-based approaches can be used to identify overlapping functional modules in a PPI network, while most of the graph clustering approaches previously discussed generate disjoint modules with mutually exclusive sets of proteins. The third section of this chapter will examine a novel functional flow model, which takes a weighted interaction network as input, using a set of pre-selected informative proteins that act as the centroids of the modules. Flow is simulated along paths starting from each informative protein until the influence of flow on a given node falls below a minimum threshold and becomes trivial. The simulation of flow from each informative protein terminates when the flow in the network has been exhausted. A preliminary module is then constituted with the set of proteins under the given influence. Simulating the flow from all informative proteins generates a set of preliminary modules, which may overlap.

9.2 PROTEIN FUNCTION PREDICTION USING THE FUNCTIONALFLOW ALGORITHM

Several researchers have developed flow-based approaches to the prediction of protein function. Using the *Saccharomyces cerevisiae* PPI network, Schwikowski et al. [274] developed the *Majority* method to predict the function of a protein by considering the interactions of its neighbors and adopting the three most frequent annotations. *Neighborhood*, an extension of Majority that was developed by Hishigaki et al. [143], searches all proteins within a particular radius to identify over-represented functional annotations. Karaoz et al. [171] used gene expression data to weight the edges in the *S. cerevisiae* PPI network and based protein function prediction on the network's topological structure.

The FunctionalFlow algorithm introduced by Nabieva et al. [221] was based on the principle of "guilt by association." Each protein with a known functional annotation became the source of *functional flow* for that function. This functional flow was propagated through the surrounding neighborhood, and a weight, or functional score, was then calculated for each protein in the neighborhood. This score represents the amount of functional flow received by the protein for a given function. As noted above, a distance effect was also incorporated to take into account the distance between an annotated protein and other unannotated proteins. The simulation of functional flow generated a score for each function. Each unannotated protein was then associated with its highest-scoring function.

For each function, Nabieva's group simulated the spread of functional flow by an iterative algorithm using discrete time steps. Each node (or protein) was associated with a *reservoir* representing the amount of flow it can transmit to its neighbors in the next iteration. Each edge was similarly tagged with a *capacity constraint* indicating the amount of flow it can convey during a single iteration. The capacity of an edge is its weight. Reservoirs were updated through a series of iterations governed by local rules. The flow residing in the reservoir of a node was rolled over to its neighbors in proportion to the capacity constraint of the corresponding edges. This flow spreads only "downhill" from proteins with fuller reservoirs to nodes with emptier reservoirs. Each source protein can absorb an infinite amount of flow during each iteration.

At the conclusion of all iterations, each protein had a functional score indicating the amount of flow that entered its reservoir. The amount of flow received by each node from each source is inversely proportionate to the distance from the node to the source. Thus, the 1-level (immediate) neighbor of a source receives d iterations of flow, while its 2-level neighbor (two links away from source) receives $d-1$ iterations of flow. The number of iterations determines the maximum shortest path between a source node and a recipient node. In [221], d is set at 6, which is half the diameter of the PPI network of *S. cerevisiae*.

More specifically, $R_t^a(u)$ represents the amount of flow in the reservoir for function a that node u had at time t. At time 0, only function a at annotated nodes:

$$R_0^a(u) = \begin{cases} \infty, & \text{if } u \text{ is annotated with } a, \\ 0, & \text{otherwise.} \end{cases}$$

At each subsequent time step, the method [221] recomputed the reservoir of each protein by considering the amounts of flow that has entered and exited the node:

$$R_t^a(u) = R_{t-1}^a(u) + \sum_{v:(u,v)\in E} (g_t^a(v,u) - g_t^a(u,v)),$$

where $g_t^a(u,v)$ and $g_t^a(v,u)$ represent the flow of function a at time t from protein u to protein v and from protein v to protein u, respectively. The capacity constraints are

$$g_t^a(u,v) = \begin{cases} 0, & \text{if } R_{t-1}^a(u) < R_{t-1}^a(v), \\ \min\left(\omega_{u,v}, \frac{\omega_{u,v}}{\sum_{(u,y)\in E} \omega_{u,y}}\right), & \text{otherwise,} \end{cases}$$

where $\omega_{x,y}$ denotes the weight of the edge between nodes x and y. The total amount of flow that entered node u will be

$$f_a(u) = \sum_{t=1}^{d} \sum_{v:(u,v)\in E} g_t^a(v,u).$$

After d iterations, for each node u will have a functional score for each function. The function for which the highest score was obtained will be treated as the predicted function for each node.

Figure 9–1 illustrates the performance of the Majority [274], Neighborhood [143], GenMultiCut [171] and FunctionalFlow [221] on the PPI network of *S. cerevisiae*,

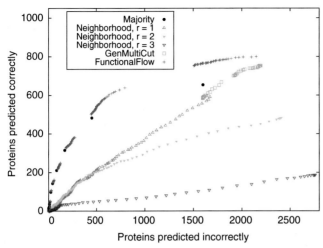

Figure 9-1 ROC analysis of the Majority, Neighborhood, GenMultiCut, and FunctionalFlow algorithms as applied to the *S. cerevisiae* PPI network. (Reprinted from [221] with permission of Oxford University Press.)

using a two-fold cross-validation. The figure uses a variant of receiver operating characteristic (ROC) curves to plot the number of true positives (TPs) as a function of the false positives (FPs) predicted by each method. It is clear that the FunctionalFlow algorithm identifies more TPs than the other three methods over the entire range of FPs. In addition, the FunctionalFlow algorithm outperforms Majority when there are at least three proteins with the same function that do not directly interact. Therefore, FunctionalFlow offers improved performance when considering proteins that interact with few annotated proteins. The Neighborhood and FunctionalFlow algorithms perform similarly in the high-confidence region using a radius 1 or 2; these results correspond to a low FP rate and appear in the left side of the ROC curve. However, the Neighborhood method generates its best results in all regions using a radius of 1, which indicates that its omission of topology is not optimal. In an assessment of the performance of all methods clearing a smaller fraction of the annotated proteins, GenMultiCut has a slight advantage over FunctionalFlow in the very low-confidence region when using 10-fold cross-validation; all other observations are qualitatively the same as for two-fold cross-validation [221].

These results indicate that FunctionalFlow can reliably predict protein function from an examination of PPI networks by integrating information regarding indirect network interactions, network topology, and network distance. While these experiments were confined to the prediction of protein behavior in *S. cerevisiae*, the method is likely to be especially useful when analyzing less characterized proteomes [221].

9.3 CASCADE: A DYNAMIC FLOW SIMULATION FOR MODULARITY ANALYSIS

In [148,149], a statistical simulation model, termed CASCADE, was developed to represent a PPI network as a dynamic signal transduction system. The role played by the signal flow from each protein within the PPI network was treated as a perturbation of signal transduction. The signal transduction behavior of each perturbation reflects the topological properties of the network. An overall signal transduction behavior function between any two proteins was formulated to evaluate the biological and topological perturbation caused by a protein on other proteins in the network. CASCADE provides a novel clustering methodology for PPI networks in which the biological and topological influence of each protein on other proteins is modeled via a concept termed the *occurrence probability*. This represents the probability distribution that the series of interactions necessary to link a pair of distant proteins in the network will occur within a time constant (Most materials in this section are from [148,149].)

9.3.1 Occurrence Probability and Related Models

Occurrence Probability Model. In [148], the Erlang distribution was identified as a parsimonious model for describing PPI networks and other biological interactions [148,165]. Erlang distribution models have been used in pharmacodynamics to model signal transduction and transfer delays in a variety of systems, including the production of drug-induced mRNA and protein dynamics [260] and calcium ion-mediated signaling in neutrophils [133]. In pharmacodynamics, the Erlang distribution has been used to effectively describe the dynamics of signal transduction in systems involving a series of *compartments*. In a biological network, compartments can be any molecular species, such as a protein, a protein complex, or a compound. In these cases, in response to a unit impulse at time $t = 0$, the signal transduction from the compartmental model in Figure 9–2 is equivalent to an Erlang distribution. The application of the Erlang distribution to PPI networks was motivated by several key physicochemical considerations. Sequentially ordered cascades of protein–protein and other biological interactions are frequently observed in biological signal transduction processes. In queuing theory, the distribution of time needed to complete a sequence of tasks in a system with Poisson input is described by the Erlang distribution. Because biological signal transduction can be modeled as a sequence of PPIs, these queuing results can appropriately be applied to the modeling of PPI networks. The Erlang distribution is a special case of the Gamma distribution, and the latter has been shown to describe population abundances fluctuating around equilibrium [86]; this finding is relevant because perturbations to PPI networks will likewise cause alterations in the levels of bound and unbound protein complexes.

The occurrence probability of a sequence of pairwise interactions in the network was modeled using the Erlang distribution and queuing theory, as follows:

$$F(c) = 1 - e^{-\frac{x}{b}} \sum_{k=0}^{c-1} \frac{\left(\frac{x}{b}\right)^k}{k!}, \tag{9.1}$$

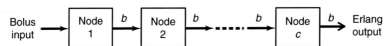

Figure 9–2 An occurrence probability model with an Erlang distribution bolus response. The parameter *b* is the time constant for signal transfer, and *c* is the number of compartments.

where $c > 0$ is the number of edges (the path length) between source and target node, $b > 0$ is the scale parameter, and $x \geq 0$ is an independent variable, usually time. The occurrence probability was applied with $x/b = 1$. The scale parameter b represents the characteristic time required for the occurrence of an interaction between members of a protein pair. Thus, setting the value of x/b to unity assesses the probability that a series of interactions between a source protein and a target protein will occur within this characteristic time scale.

The occurrence probability function is further weighted to reflect network topology. The occurrence probability propagated by the source node is assumed to be proportional to its degree and to follow all possible paths to the target node identified using the Quasi All Paths (QAPs) algorithm.

Quasi All Paths Enumeration Algorithm. From a biological perspective, propagating the interaction signal through all possible paths between paired proteins could be considered a comprehensive approach for evaluating PPI networks. The QAPs enumeration algorithm in CASCADE approximates all possible paths between the node pairs in a network and can be solved in polynomial time. The QAP enumeration algorithm, described in Procedure 9.1, consists of iterative identification of the shortest paths between a node pair. The edges located on the previously identified shortest paths are removed, and the QAP procedure is repeated until the node pair is disconnected. When there is more than one shortest path between a pair of nodes in a network, QAP selects the least-resistant path based on $\prod_{i \in P(v,w)} d(i)$ in Equation (9.2).

The occurrence probability function decreases rapidly with an increasing number of edges between the source and target nodes. Its values at $c = 3$ and $c = 4$ are ~13% and ~3% of its value at $c = 1$, respectively. This suggests that it would be sufficient to compute the occurrence probability based on a maximum of the first four length terms. However, this produces only minor savings in computational effort, and a full implementation of the Erlang distribution provides the stronger corrections for the degree of the downstream nodes required by the topology-weighted probability term.

Topology-Weighted Occurrence Probability Model. As the signal propagates along the path from the source to the target node, the occurrence probability is assumed to dissipate at each intermediate node visited at a rate proportional to the reciprocal of the degree on the path. The overall topology-weighted occurrence probability from node v to node w is defined as

$$S(v \rightarrow w) = \sum_{\rho \in QAP(v,w)} \frac{d(v)}{\prod_{i \in \rho} d(i)} F(c). \tag{9.2}$$

In Equation (9.2), $d(i)$ is the degree of node i, $QAP(v, w)$ is the set of paths identified by QAP between source node v and target node w, ρ is the set of the all nodes visited on a path in the $QAP(v, w)$ from node v to node w, excluding the source node v but including target destination node w, and $F(c)$ is the occurrence probability function [Equation (9.1)].

9.3.2 The CASCADE Algorithm

The CASCADE algorithm involves four sequential processes:

> *Process 1:* Compute the topology-weighted occurrence probability between all node pairs.
> *Process 2:* Select cluster representatives for each node.
> *Process 3:* Form preliminary clusters.
> *Process 4:* Merge preliminary clusters.

The pseudocode for the CASCADE algorithm, which employs the influence quantification function of Equation (9.2), is shown in Algorithm 9.1.

Algorithm 9.1 CASCADE(G)

1: V: set of nodes in graph G
2: $F(c)$: The occurrence probability function
3: $S(v \rightarrow w)$: The occurrence probability arrived from source protein v to target protein w
4: $QAP(v, w)$: list of paths between protein v and w identified by QAP algorithm
5: Clusters: the list of final clusters
6: PreClusters: the list of preliminary clusters
7: **for** each node pair(v, w) $v, w \in V, v \neq w$ **do**
8:    $QAP(v, w) = QAP(G, v, w)$
9:    $S(v \rightarrow w) = \sum_{\rho \in QAP(v,w)} \frac{d(v)}{\prod_{i \in \rho} d(i)} F(c)$
10: **end for**
11: **for** each node $v \in V$ **do**
12:    $v.representative \Leftarrow$ select the best scored node w for node v
13:    **if** $cluster\_w == null$ **then**
14:       Make $cluster\_w$
15:       $cluster\_w.add(v)$
16:       $PreClusters.add(cluster\_w)$
17:    **else**
18:       $cluster\_w.add(v)$
19:    **end if**
20: **end for**
21: Clusters $\Leftarrow$ **Merge**(PreClusters)

Process 1 propagates the topology-weighted occurrence probability from each source node through the QAPs algorithm, described in Procedure 9.1, and accumulates the resulting probabilities associated with each target node for all node pairs according to Equation (9.2). The implementation of Process 1 is shown on lines 7 through 10 of the CASCADE algorithm in Algorithm 9.1. This computation is performed for all node pairs. Then, for each source node, the target nodes with the highest occurrence probability quantity are selected as its representative to the cluster in Process 2. Preliminary clusters are generated in Process 3 by accumulating each node toward its representative. Lines 11 through 20 in Algorithm 9.1 reflect the implementation of Processes 2 and 3. Process 4, summarized in the Merge process in Procedure 9.2, iteratively merges preliminary cluster pairs that have significant

---

Procedure 9.1 QAP(G, *s*, *t*)

1: G: a graph
2: *s*: source node
3: *t*: target node
4: shortest_path(*s*, *t*): a shortest path between a node pair *s* and *t* in graph G
5: edge_list: list of edges
6: QAPs: list of paths
7: **while** node s and node t is connected **do**
8:    Find shortest_path(*s*, *t*)
9:    Add shortest_path(*s*, *t*) to QAPs
10:   Add all edges on shortest_path(*s*, *t*) to edge_list
11:   Remove all edges on shortest_path(*s*, *t*) from graph G
12: **end while**
13: Restore all edges in edge_list into graph G
14: **return** QAPs

Procedure 9.2 Merge(*Clusters*)

1: Clusters: the cluster list
2: MaxPair: the cluster pair(*m*, *n*) with max interconnections among all pairs
3: Max.value: interconnections between cluster pair *m* and *n*
4: MaxPair ⇐ findMaxPair(Clusters,null)
5: **while** *Max.value* ≥ *threshold* **do**
6:    NewCluster ⇐ merge MaxPair *m* and *n*
7:    Replace cluster *m* with NewCluster
8:    Remove cluster *n*
9:    MaxPair ⇐ findMaxPair(Clusters,NewCluster)
10: **end while**
11: **return** Clusters

---

interconnections and overlaps. The findMaxPair method finds the most highly inter-connected pair. The Merge process then merges the pair, updates the cluster list, and repeats until the interconnections and overlaps of all cluster pairs satisfy the predefined threshold.

In the final Merge process described in Procedure 9.2, CASCADE takes intercon-nectivity among detected preliminary clusters into consideration to identify clusters that are more topologically refined. As illustrated in Figure 9–3, CASCADE counts the edges interconnecting members of a preliminary cluster pair. Interconnecting edges between two clusters as illustrated in Figure 9–3 include not only the edges between mutually exclusive nodes but also edges among overlapping and mutu-ally exclusive nodes. The relationship of interconnectivity between clusters to the similarity of two clusters C_i and C_j is defined as

$$\text{Similarity}(C_i, C_j) = \frac{\text{interconnectivity}(C_i, C_j)}{\text{minsize}(C_i, C_j)} \qquad (9.3)$$

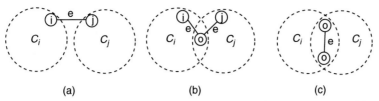

Figure 9–3 Interconnectivity between members of a cluster pair. (a) Interconnecting edge e between two nonoverlapping nodes. (b) Interconnecting edge e between an overlapping node and a nonoverlapping node. (c) Interconnecting edge e between two overlapping nodes.

where interconnectivity(C_i, C_j) is the number of edges between clusters C_i and C_j, and minsize(C_i, C_j) is the size of the smaller of clusters C_i and C_j. The Similarity(C_i, C_j) between two clusters C_i and C_j is the ratio of the number of the edges between them to the size of the smaller cluster. Highly interconnected clusters are iteratively merged based on the similarity of the clusters. The pair of clusters that have the highest level of similarity are merged in each iteration, and the merge process iterates until the highest similarity value among all cluster pairs falls below a given threshold. The cluster pair containing the greatest difference in cluster size becomes the first to be merged if there are several cluster pairs with the same similarity values.

9.3.3 Analysis of Prototypical Data

To illustrate the principles underlying the CASCADE approach, Hwang et al. [149] presented results from the analysis of the simple network shown in Figure 9–4. The four sequential processes discussed briefly in Section 9.3.2 can be restated in more detail, as follows:

Process 1: Propagate the occurrence probability from each node to the other nodes through implementing the QAPs algorithm in the network.

Process 2: Select cluster representatives for each node based on the cumulative occurrence probability value for each node.

Process 3: Form preliminary clusters by aggregating each node into the clusters already formed by the selected representatives.

Process 4: Merge preliminary clusters if they have substantial similarity (interconnectivity).

In the first step, the occurrence probability from each node is propagated to the other nodes through QAPs in the network. For the sake of simplicity, only the occurrence probabilities from nodes A, F, G, H, I, and O are presented in Figure 9–4. Each box in Figure 9–4 contains the weighted occurrence probability, as assessed by Equation (9.2), from nodes A, F, G, H, I, and O to other target nodes. These numerical values illustrate the overall effects of combining network topology with the occurrence probability quantification model. In the second process, those nodes with the highest values of the weighted occurrence probability are selected as representatives. For example, nodes B, C, D, E, and F will choose node A as their

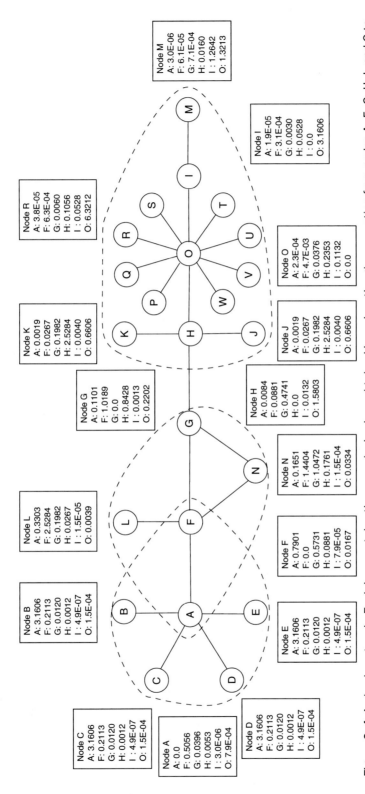

Figure 9–4 A simple network. Each box contains the numerical values obtained based on the given equation from nodes A, F, G, H, I, and O to other target nodes. The values for nodes P, Q, S, T, U, V, and W are the same as those for node R. Results for other nodes are not shown. Final identified clusters are delimited when the merging threshold 2.0 is used.

representative, as A is the highest-scoring node. Similarly, nodes A, G, L, and N will choose node F as their representative. In Process 3, preliminary clusters are formed by accumulating all nodes toward their selected representatives. For example, in Figure 9–4, four preliminary clusters, $C1$ ={A, B, C, D, E, F}, $C2$ ={A, F, G, L, N}, $C3$ ={H, O, J, K}, and $C4$ ={I, H, M, O, P, Q, R, S, T, U, V, W}, are formed based on the choice of representatives. In the final step of the CASCADE algorithm, preliminary clusters are merged if they have significant interconnections.

As noted, the definition of similarity between two clusters employed in Figure 9–3 and in Equation (9.3) encompasses various interconnections, including interconnecting edges between two nonoverlapping nodes, between an overlapping node and a nonoverlapping node, and between two overlapping nodes. As a result, a cluster pair that includes an overlapping node having many edges in each cluster will have a high degree of similarity. For example, in Figure 9–4, $C3$ and $C4$ have a common node O that has one edge in $C3$ and ten edges in $C4$. There are a total of ten interconnecting edges for the cluster pair $C3$ and $C4$, since the edge between H and O is redundant. Here, the similarity value of each cluster pair will be as follows: Similarity($C3$, $C4$)=10/4, Similarity($C1$, $C2$)=8/5, Similarity($C2$, $C3$)=1/4. In this instance, in Process 4, only one merge occurred between clusters $C3$ and $C4$, because this was the only cluster pair with sufficient similarity to satisfy the merge threshold of 2.0. Eventually, two clusters, {A, B, C, D, E, F, G, L, N} and {H, I, J, K, M, O, P, Q, R, S, T, U, V, W}, are obtained after the merge process, using 1.0 as the merge threshold. Three clusters, {A, B, C, D, E, F}, {A, F, G, L, N}, and {H, I, J, K, M, O, P, Q, R, S, T, U, V, W} are obtained and delimited in Figure 9–4 when 2.0 is used as the merge threshold.

9.3.4 Significance of Individual Clusters

The characteristics of all 43 clusters with more than five proteins that were identified in the DIP yeast PPI network [82] using CASCADE are summarized in Table 9.1. For each cluster, this table also provides topological characteristics and assigned molecular functions. The latter was taken to be the most commonly matched functional category from the MIPS functional categories database assigned to the cluster. To facilitate critical assessment, the percentage of proteins that are in concordance with the major assigned function (hits), the discordant proteins (misses), and proteins of unknown status are also indicated.

The largest cluster in Table 9.1 contains 411 proteins, and the smallest cluster contains six. There are an average of 55.1 proteins in a cluster, and the average density of the subgraphs of the clusters extracted from the yeast core PPI network is 0.212. The $-\log p$ values [see Equation (5.20) for the definition of p] of the major functions identified in each cluster are also shown, and these values provide a measure of the relative enrichment of a cluster for a given functional category; higher values of $-\log p$ indicate greater enrichment. The results demonstrate that the CASCADE method can detect both large, sparsely connected clusters as well as small, densely connected clusters. The high values of $-\log p$ (values greater than 2 indicate statistical significance at <0.01) indicate that clusters are significantly enriched for biological function and can be considered to be functional modules.

Table 9.1 Clusters in the yeast PPI network obtained using CASCADE

Cluster	Size	Density	Distribution H	D	U	−log p	Function
1	411	0.0103	17.5	76.4	6.1	19.3	Vesicular transport
2	303	0.0104	33.3	60.0	6.6	19.9	Mitotic cell cycle and cell cycle control
3	240	0.0171	23.3	70.8	5.8	44.1	Nuclear transport
4	176	0.0274	46.0	43.1	10.8	30.8	Transported compounds
5	170	0.0181	32.4	60.0	7.6	19.0	Cytoskeleton
6	104	0.0220	14.8	76.5	8.7	16.3	Conversion to kinetic energy
7	96	0.0450	76.0	19.8	4.2	39.7	mRNA synthesis
8	79	0.0431	58.2	39.2	2.5	33.3	General transcription activities
9	78	0.0416	35.9	62.8	1.3	19.9	Ribosome biogenesis
10	73	0.0353	39.7	58.9	1.5	9.7	Phosphate metabolism
11	70	0.0356	22.9	65.7	11.4	8.1	Ribosome biogenesis
12	69	0.0682	66.7	24.6	8.7	43.9	mRNA processing (splicing, 5′-, 3′-end processing)
13	60	0.0616	23.3	65.0	11.7	13.7	Homeostasis of protons
14	50	0.0637	68.0	30.0	2.0	34.0	rRNA processing
15	37	0.0781	10.8	89.2	0.0	7.2	Cell–cell adhesion
16	29	0.1330	48.3	51.7	0.0	26.8	Peroxisomal transport
17	28	0.1164	28.6	67.9	3.6	6.9	Cytokinesis (cell division)/septum formation
18	23	0.1581	65.2	30.4	4.3	13.6	DNA conformation modification (e.g., chromatin)
19	18	0.1764	72.2	22.2	5.6	18.2	Mitochondrial transport
20	17	0.2206	70.6	29.4	0.0	22.5	Microtubule cytoskeleton
21	17	0.2206	82.4	11.8	5.9	19.1	rRNA synthesis
22	16	0.3000	93.8	6.2	0.0	19.5	Splicing
23	15	0.2190	26.7	73.3	0.0	30.4	Regulation of nitrogen utilization
24	15	0.3047	86.7	13.3	0.0	8.1	Energy generation (e.g., ATP synthase)
25	14	0.3407	85.7	14.3	0.0	14.3	DNA conformation modification (e.g., chromatin)
26	14	0.1978	57.1	28.6	14.3	13.3	Chromosome condensation
27	13	0.5641	76.9	23.1	0.0	17.0	Mitosis
28	13	0.4103	69.2	23.1	7.7	15.4	3′-end processing
29	12	0.3636	58.3	41.7	0.0	14.3	Posttranslational modification of amino acids
30	12	0.1667	16.7	75.0	8.3	2.3	Autoproteolytic processing
31	11	0.2181	54.5	45.4	0.0	2.9	Transcriptional control
32	10	0.4667	80.0	20.0	0.0	14.3	Translation initiation
33	9	0.2500	22.2	77.8	0.0	4.1	S-adenosyl-methionine-homocysteine cycle
34	8	0.3214	50.0	37.5	12.5	5.5	Metabolism of energy reserves
35	8	0.2857	62.5	25.0	12.5	5.2	Vacuolar transport
36	7	0.3333	42.9	57.1	0.0	7.1	DNA damage response
37	7	0.3333	71.4	28.6	0.0	4.3	Modification by ubiquitination, deubiquitination
38	7	0.2857	28.6	71.4	0.0	3.4	Biosynthesis of serine
39	6	0.5333	100.0	0.0	0.0	12.1	Modification with sugar residues (e.g., glycosylation)
40	6	0.4000	100.0	0.0	0.0	10.0	ER to Golgi transport
41	6	0.3333	16.7	16.7	66.6	7.0	Regulation of nitrogen utilization
42	6	0.4667	100.0	0.0	0.0	3.9	DNA recombination and DNA repair
43	6	0.4000	66.6	33.3	0.0	1.9	Intracellular signalling

In this table, the first column is a cluster identifier. The Size column indicates the number of proteins in each cluster. The Density column indicates the percentage of possible protein interactions that are present. The H column indicates the percentage of proteins concordant with the major function indicated in the last column. The D column indicates the percentage of proteins discordant with the major function. The U column indicates the percentage of proteins not assigned to any function. The −log p values for biological function are shown.

Table 9.2 Clusters obtained through the application of CASCADE to three biological network data sets (the yeast DNA damage response network and the Rapamycin and Rich medium gene modules networks)

Data set	Cluster	Size	Density	Distribution H	D	U	−log p	Function
Yeast DDR	1	49	0.063	18.4	81.6	0.0	0.5	DNA repair
network	2	16	0.175	81.3	18.7	0.0	3.6	Cell cycle
	3	9	0.222	44.4	55.5	0.0	3.6	Proteasome
	4	7	0.286	57.1	42.9	0.0	1.7	Metabolism
	5	7	0.286	71.4	28.6	0.0	1.2	Stress response
	6	6	0.333	83.3	16.7	0.0	3.2	Metabolism
Rapamycin	1	19	0.198	42.1	47.4	10.5	2.7	Nitrogen/sulfur metabolism
gene modules	2	12	0.227	33.3	0.0	66.6	1.1	Pheromone response
network	3	9	0.277	77.8	0.0	22.2	5.0	Pheromone response
	4	7	0.285	71.4	28.6	0.0	2.9	AA metabolism/biosynthesis
Rich medium	1	54	0.050	64.8	33.3	1.85	14.1	Cell cycle
gene modules	2	28	0.111	75.0	14.3	10.7	10.2	Ribosome biogenesis
network	3	16	0.179	62.5	12.5	25.0	9.7	Respiration
	4	13	0.222	69.2	30.8	0.0	8.1	Energy/carbohydrate metabolism

In this table, the first column is a cluster identifier. The Size column indicates the number of proteins in each cluster. The Density column indicates the percentage of possible protein interactions that are present. The *H* column indicates the percentage of proteins concordant with the major function indicated in the last column. The *D* column indicates the percentage of proteins discordant with the major function. The *U* column indicates the percentage of proteins not assigned to any function. The −log *p* values for biological function are shown.

Table 9.2 summarizes the characteristics of all clusters with three or more nodes detected by CASCADE using three biological network data sets (the yeast DNA damage response (DDR) network [323] and the Rapamycin and Rich medium gene module networks [27]). It again confirms that CASCADE can detect large, sparsely connected clusters as well as small, densely connected clusters for a range of diverse data sets. Once again, the clusters identified are enriched for certain biological functions and may be considered to be functional modules.

9.3.5 Analysis of Functional Annotation

The functional term distribution of each cluster detected by CASCADE was scrutinized by analyzing the normalized number of MIPS functional terms and the number of proteins that are associated with MIPS functional terms in each cluster.

Table 9.3 assesses the heterogeneity of functional terms from the MIPS database for each cluster detected by CASCADE. The results show that the clusters have a high level of functional homogeneity, even when corrected for cluster size.

Figures 9–5, 9–6, and 9–7 summarize the MIPS functional categories for proteins in the six largest clusters identified by CASCADE. Within each cluster, there was considerable functional homogeneity as assessed by the relatedness among functional categories. For example, Cluster 3 was enriched for RNA transport processes. Furthermore, as would be expected, the largest clusters also contained certain general functions that are required for numerous cellular process; For example, mRNA synthesis was present in Clusters 1, 2, and 3.

Table 9.3 Normalized number of functional terms for each cluster detected by CASCADE (Table 9.1)

Cluster	Size	≥ 3rd hierarchy	≥ 4th hierarchy	≥ 5th hierarchy
1	411	0.38	0.17	0.06
2	303	0.41	0.21	0.07
3	240	0.46	0.21	0.04
4	176	0.39	0.17	0.04
5	170	0.52	0.21	0.05
6	104	0.74	0.29	0.09
7	96	0.50	0.16	0.04
8	79	0.48	0.19	0.04
9	78	0.54	0.18	0.01
10	73	0.81	0.36	0.12
11	70	0.64	0.24	0.07
12	69	0.22	0.06	0.0
13	60	0.67	0.28	0.05
14	50	0.26	0.06	0.0
15	37	0.89	0.30	0.05
16	29	0.24	0.07	0.0
17	28	0.79	0.29	0.04
18	23	0.57	0.13	0.0
19	18	0.33	0.11	0.0
20	17	0.35	0.18	0.06
21	17	0.29	0.06	0.0
22	16	0.25	0.06	0.0
23	15	1.13	0.53	0.20
24	15	0.60	0.13	0.0
25	14	0.79	0.29	0.14
26	14	0.64	0.21	0.0
27	13	0.69	0.31	0.08
28	13	0.54	0.23	0.08
29	12	1.17	0.50	0.17
30	12	0.42	0.17	0.0
31	11	0.82	0.45	0.1
32	10	0.10	0.0	0.0
33	9	0.78	0.44	0.11
34	8	0.50	0.13	0.0
35	8	0.63	0.50	0.25
36	7	1.43	0.29	0.0
37	7	0.86	0.29	0.0
38	7	1.57	0.86	0.29
39	6	1.33	0.50	0.0
40	6	1.00	0.50	0.0
41	6	0.83	0.33	0.0
42	6	0.33	0.17	0.0
43	6	0.0	0.0	0.0

In this table, the first column is a cluster identifier. The Size column indicates the number of proteins in each cluster. The normalized numbers of functional terms in the MIPS functional hierarchy for each identified cluster are presented in the third, fourth, and fifth columns. The number of functional terms per each cluster is normalized by its cluster size. The third column represents the normalized number of functional terms that are more specific than the second-level functional hierarchy. The fourth column represents the normalized number of functional terms that are more specific than the third-level functional hierarchy. The fifth column represents the normalized number of functional terms that are more specific than the fourth-level functional hierarchy.

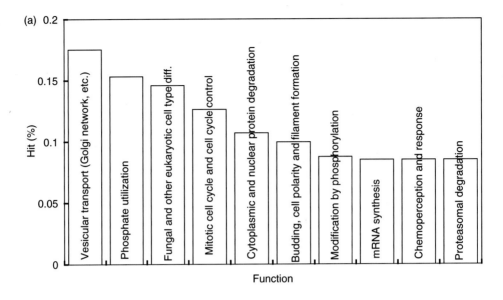

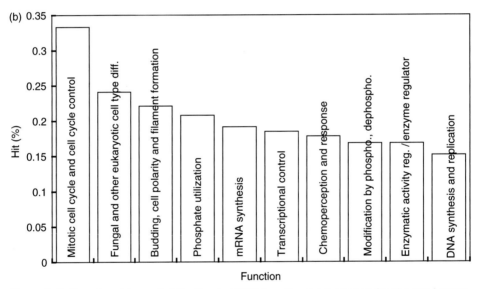

Figure 9–5 Functional term distribution in MIPS functional categories for the top largest clusters in Table 9.1. (a) Cluster 1, size 411. (b) Cluster 2, size 303. Each figure presents the percentile of proteins that are concordant with the top ten best concordant functional terms for each cluster.

Most of the existing network clustering approaches concentrate on densely connected regions, resulting in identification of dense modules of rounded shape. However, this focus limits effective clustering of PPI networks, which are typically very sparsely connected. For this reason, CASCADE has the potential of outperforming the other approaches. Performance was assessed by the analysis of the topological shapes and functional annotations of the clusters detected by

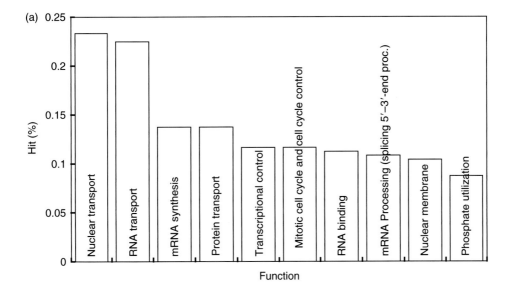

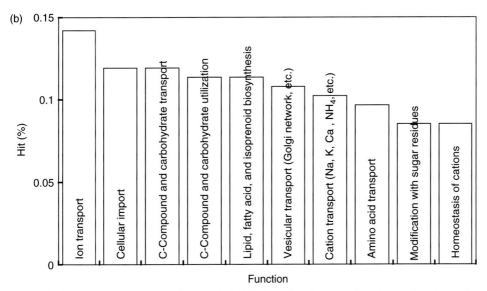

Figure 9–6 Functional term distribution in MIPS functional categories for the top largest clusters in Table 9.1. (a) Cluster 3, size 240. (b) Cluster 4, size 176. Each figure presents the percentile of proteins that are concordant with the top ten best concordant functional terms for each cluster.

CASCADE algorithm, and these results are presented in Figures 9–8, 9–9, and 9–10. This analysis indicates that the densities of the subgraphs for each cluster in the PPI network are low and that the topological shapes are diverse. For example, the modules detected by CASCADE and shown in Figures 9–8, and 9–9 would never have been identified by the other density-based approaches due to their low density. These other methods would discard sparsely connected members in the clustering

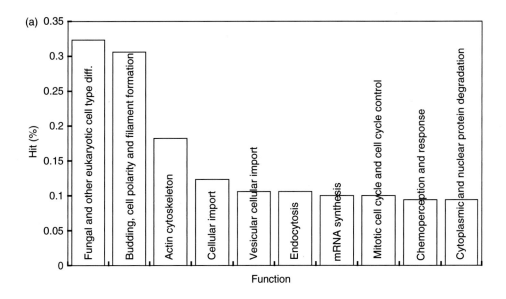

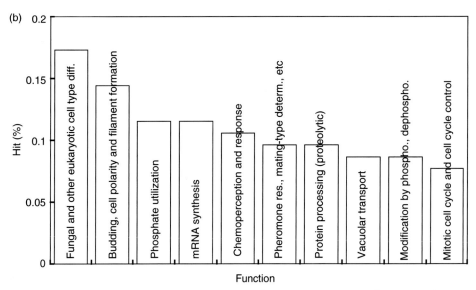

Figure 9–7 Functional term distribution in MIPS functional categories for the top largest clusters in Table 9.1. (a) Cluster 5, size 170. (b) Cluster 6, size 104. Each figure presents the percentile of proteins that are concordant with the top ten best concordant functional terms for each cluster.

process, such as *YGL075C, YKL042W, YLR045C* in Figure 9–8 and *YNL248C, YDR156W,* and *YOR340C* in Figure 9–9, because they have very low connectivity with the other members in the PPI network. However, they are highly enriched by sharing the same functional category with the other members of their cluster, despite the low connectivity within the clusters to which they belong. As illustrated in Figure 9–10, CASCADE detected a cluster with two distinct subregions which,

(a)

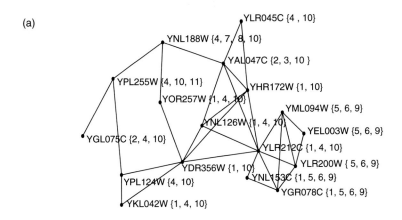

(b)

Fucntion ID	MIPS ID	Function name
1	10.03.01	Mitotic cell cycleand cell cycle control
2	10.03.01.01.11	Mitosis
3	10.03.04.09	Nuclear migration
4	10.03.05.01	Spindle pole body/centrosome and microtubule cycle
5	14.01	Protein folding and stabilization
6	16.01	Protein binding
7	34.11.03.07	Pheromone response, mating-type determination, sex-specific proteins
8	41.01.01	Mating (fertilization)
9	42.04	Cytoskeleton
10	**42.04.05**	**Microtubule cytoskeleton**
11	43.01.03.05	Budding, cell polarity and filament formation

Figure 9–8 Topological shape and functional annotations of Cluster 20 in Table 9.1. (a) Subgraph of Cluster 20 extracted from DIP PPI network. Each protein is annotated by MIPS functional category. (b) MIPS functional IDs and their corresponding literal names. The best assigned functional term is boldfaced.

although connected by only one edge, have excellent functional homogeneity. Other density-based clustering methods would have identified these as two separate modules, and even those would have been recognized only if they had a sufficiently high density. Despite the low density and variable shape of the clusters in these networks, CASCADE was found to identify and assign a high proportion of proteins to the dominant functional category. The performance of competing approaches was affected adversely by weak connectivity.

9.3.6 Comparative Assessment of CASCADE with Other Approaches

To demonstrate the strengths of the CASCADE approach, Hwang et al. [149] compared it to the following ten competing clustering approaches: maximal clique [286], quasi clique [56], minimum cut [164], betweenness cut [122], the statistical approach

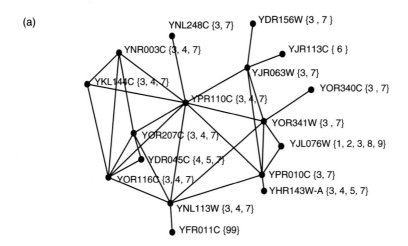

(a)

(b)

Function ID	MIPS ID	Function name
1	10.01.09.05	DNA conformation modication (e.g. chromatin)
2	10.03.0 1	Mitotic cell cycle and cell cycle control
3	**11.02.01**	**rRNA synthesis**
4	11.02.02	tRNA synthesis
5	11.02.03.01	General transcription activities
6	12.01.01	Ribosomal proteins
7	16.03.01	Sugar binding
8	16.03.03	Fatty acid binding (e.g. acyl-carrier protein)
9	42.10.07	Nucleolus
99	99	Unknown

Figure 9–9 Topological shape and functional annotations of Cluster 21 in Table 9.1. (a) Subgraph of Cluster 21 extracted from DIP PPI network. Each protein is annotated by MIPS functional category. (b) MIPS functional IDs and their corresponding literal names. The best assigned functional term is boldfaced.

of Samanta and Liang [272], MCL [308], SPC [39], STM [148], the approaches of Chen [61], and Rives [263]. The clustering results for each method are summarized in Tables 9.4 and 9.5. The $-\log p$ values in Tables 9.4 and 9.5 are the average $-\log p$ values of all clusters detected by each method.

The experimental results for the BioGRID PPI data set [289] are presented in Table 9.4. Performance was measured for each MIPS and GO category. Table 9.4 shows that CASCADE generated lower p-values and outperformed the other methods in each MIPS and GO category. In the MIPS functional category, the clusters identified by CASCADE had p-values that were approximately 2.8- and 1.9-fold lower than those identified by the STM and Rives' approaches, respectively, which were the best-performing alternative clustering methods. In the MIPS localization category, CASCADE identified clusters with p-values that were approximately 1.7- and 2.1-fold lower than those identified by the STM and Rives' approaches,

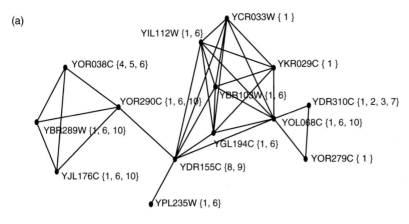

(b)

Function ID	MIPS ID	Function name
1	**10.01.09.05**	**DNA conformation modication (e.g. chromatin)**
2	10.03.01.01	Mitotic cell cycle
3	10.03.01.03	Cell cycle checkpoints (checkpoints of morphogenesis, DNA-damage,-rep.,mitotic phase and spindle)
4	10.03.04.01	Centromere kinetochore complex maturation
5	11.02.03.01	General transcription activities
6	11.02.03.04	Transcriptional control
7	11.02.03.04.03	Transcriptional repressor
8	14.01	Protein folding and stabilization
9	32.01	Stress response
10	34.11.03.07	pheromone response, mating-type determination, sex-specic proteins

Figure 9–10 Topological shape and functional annotations of Cluster 25 in Table 9.1. (a) Subgraph of Cluster 25 extracted from DIP PPI network. Each protein is annotated by MIPS functional category. (b) MIPS functional IDs and their corresponding literal names. The best assigned functional term is boldfaced.

respectively. In the MIPS complex category, the clusters detected by CASCADE had p-values that were ~5-fold and ~3.4-fold lower than those identified by the STM and quasi clique approaches, respectively. Similarly, CASCADE was also found to generate superior clustering results for the Gene Ontology categories. Another important strength of both the CASCADE and STM methods is that they discard only 18.3% of proteins in the process of cluster creation. This is much lower than the other approaches, which have an average discard rate of 33%.

The results presented in Table 9.4 for the DIP yeast PPI data set [82] show that CASCADE generates larger clusters than do other methods. The clusters identified have p-values in MIPS functional categories that are ~6.3- and ~1000-fold lower than those identified by the STM and quasi clique methods, respectively, which are the best-performing alternative clustering methods. The p-values for cellular localization generated by CASCADE are comparable to those of the maximal clique method.

Table 9.4 Comparison of CASCADE to competing clustering methods as applied to two biological network data sets (the BioGRID and DIP yeast PPI networks)

Data set	Method	Cluster Number	Size	Discard (%)	MIPS (−log p) Function	Location	Complex	GO (−log p) mf	cc	bp
BioGRID yeast PPI network	**CASCADE**	**225**	**19.6**	**18.3**	**3.26**	**2.55**	**5.13**	**4.67**	**4.24**	**3.53**
	STM	248	18.1	16.2	2.88	2.37	4.64	4.17	3.98	3.53
	Maximal clique	587	3.6	80.8	2.71	2.21	4.53	3.55	3.47	2.99
	Quasi clique	431	7.4	40.9	2.97	2.03	4.89	4.16	3.88	3.02
	Samanta	289	6.7	64.8	2.63	1.61	4.59	3.48	3.29	3.01
	MCL	617	6.2	29.2	2.58	1.22	3.87	4.02	3.77	2.83
	Chen	577	8.4	10.1	2.61	2.08	4.13	4.36	3.84	3.05
	Rives	217	21.5	13.5	3.04	2.34	4.22	4.14	3.97	3.03
	SPC	85	54.9	13.4	1.33	0.87	2.65	2.11	2.51	2.29
DIP yeast PPI network	**CASCADE**	**50**	**48.1**	**7.3**	**14.1**	**7.84**	**15.8**	**12.1**	**12.8**	**9.09**
	STM	60	40.1	7.8	13.0	7.23	14.2	11.8	11.9	8.04
	Maximal clique	120	5.7	98.3	10.2	7.67	10.0	8.46	10.0	6.57
	Quasi clique	103	11.2	80.8	11.0	6.29	12.0	10.7	11.1	7.69
	Samanta	64	7.9	79.9	8.76	4.74	10.7	9.82	10.8	8.01
	Minimum cut	114	13.5	35.0	7.97	4.58	8.56	8.19	7.87	6.21
	Betweenness cut	180	10.3	21.0	7.89	4.06	8.59	7.02	6.98	4.88
	MCL	163	9.8	36.7	8.08	3.84	9.53	7.81	8.11	6.26
	Chen	141	16.3	1.7	9.12	4.91	9.87	8.28	8.09	6.01
	Rives	42	55.3	7.8	10.1	6.88	9.52	9.61	9.59	7.42
	SPC	5	47.2	6.4	5.27	2.39	5.49	6.23	5.91	5.18

In this table, the Number column indicates the number of clusters identified by each method. The Size column indicates the average number of molecular components in each cluster. Discard (%) indicates the percentage of molecular components not assigned to any cluster. The average −log p values of all detected clusters for MIPS categories (biological function, cellular location, complex) and Gene Ontology (molecular functions (mf), biological process (bp), cellular component (cc)) are shown. Comparisons were performed for clusters with five or more molecular components. The results for minimum cut and betweenness cut for the BioGRID data set are not shown due to limitations of the available implementation.

Table 9.5 Comparison of CASCADE to competing clustering methods as applied to three biological network data sets (the yeast DDR network, the Rapamycin, and the Rich medium gene modules networks)

Dataset	Method	Number	Size	Discard (%)	Function ($-\log p$)
DNA damage response network	**CASCADE**	**6**	**15.7**	**5.0**	**2.28**
	STM	6	16.0	5.2	2.28
	Quasi clique	3	7.0	88.5	0.87
	Samanta	6	6.7	58.3	1.79
	Minimum cut	7	13.1	4.2	1.18
	Betweenness cut	10	8.8	8.3	2.22
	MCL	3	9.3	70.8	2.37
	Chen	7	13.7	0.0	2.66
	Rives	5	18.4	4.1	1.61
	SPC	3	20.3	36.5	2.33
Rapamycin gene modules network	**CASCADE**	**4**	**11.8**	**6.0**	**2.90**
	STM	4	12.5	0.0	2.57
	Quasi clique	13	8.2	0.0	2.17
	Samanta	7	4.9	32.0	1.57
	Minimum cut	8	5.9	6.0	1.82
	Betweenness cut	5	8.0	20.0	2.03
	MCL	6	7.7	8.0	5.48
	Chen	5	10.0	0.0	2.01
	Rives	4	11.0	12.0	1.49
	SPC	3	15.3	8.0	1.47
Rich medium gene modules network	**CASCADE**	**4**	**27.8**	**0.0**	**10.5**
	STM	5	22.4	0.0	8.21
	Quasi clique	5	22.8	0.0	7.81
	Samanta	12	5.3	43.2	4.79
	Minimum cut	10	11.1	0.0	4.41
	Betweenness cut	8	13.9	0.0	6.38
	MCL	23	4.0	4.5	7.29
	Chen	8	13.9	0.0	6.13
	Rives	5	22.2	0.0	5.77
	SPC	5	20.6	7.2	6.80

In this table, the Number column indicates the number of clusters identified by each method. The Size column indicates the average number of molecular components in each cluster. Discard (%) indicates the percentage of molecular components not assigned to any cluster. The average $-\log p$ values of all detected clusters for biological function are shown. Comparisons were performed for clusters with five or more molecular components for the first data set (the DNA damage response network) and for clusters with three or more molecular components for the next two network data sets (the Rapamycin and Rich medium gene module networks). Results for the maximal clique method are not presented because none of the identified clusters has three or more members.

In the MIPS complex category, CASCADE produced the best p-values, superior to those of STM and quasi clique, the best-performing alternative clustering methods. Both CASCADE and STM discarded only 7.3% of proteins in the process of cluster identification. This is much lower than the other approaches, which have an average discard rate of 45%. Similar analyses conducted for clusters with more than nine members obtained qualitatively comparable results. In addition, a comparison was made of the number of proteins in overlapping clusters; that is, clusters with common protein members. With CASCADE, this number was 66 (2.6%). For the maximal clique and quasi clique methods, the corresponding values were 125 (5.0%) and 182 (7.2%), respectively. Other methods were not included in the comparison because they produced only nonoverlapping clusters. CASCADE also performed better in the Gene Ontology category than the two best competing approaches, the STM and quasi clique methods.

These two yeast PPI data sets are relatively modular, and the bottom-up approaches (the maximal clique, quasi clique, and Rives' methods) generally outperformed the top-down approaches (exemplified by the minimum cut, betweenness cut, and Chen methods) in functional enrichment as assessed by $-\log p$. However, since the bottom-up approaches are based on connectivity to dense regions, the percentage of nodes they discard is also higher than CASCADE and the top-down approaches.

The CASCADE results for the yeast DNA damage response (DDR) [323], Rapamycin, and Rich medium network data sets [27] were also compared with those for the competing approaches, and these are presented in Table 9.5. An analysis of the functional data was performed using functional annotations that were acquired manually from the primary literature. The comparisons were performed using clusters with five or more molecular components from the DNA damage response network. For the Rapamycin and Rich medium gene module networks, analysis was performed with clusters with three or more molecular components, because the majority of the competing methods yielded no larger clusters. The maximal clique method yielded no clusters with five or more molecular components for the yeast DDR data set and no clusters with three or more molecular components for the Rapamycin and Rich medium network data sets. For the yeast DDR network, the performance of CASCADE was comparable to that of the betweenness cut and Chen methods, the best-performing alternatives. The MCL method had comparable $-\log p$ values and produced slightly larger clusters than the betweenness cut method, but these benefits were achieved at the cost of a high discard percentage. CASCADE also produced an average 100-fold improvement in performance over the STM approach in p-values for biological function with these three data sets. CASCADE discarded 5.0% of nodes, which is significantly lower than the discard rates of the quasi clique, Samanta and Liang [272], and MCL [308] methods. The percentages of nodes discarded by the betweenness cut and minimum cut method were comparable to CASCADE. The Chen method offered the best performance with $-\log p$ and the lowest discard rate for the yeast DDR data set. However, its performance appears to be sensitive to data set characteristics, since it did not perform as well with other data sets. The yeast DDR data set is relatively sparse and less modular than the yeast PPI network. In this context, top-down approaches such as betweenness cut and minimum cut offer superior performance in comparison to the bottom-up approaches.

The Rapamycin and Rich medium gene module networks have low network density and clustering coefficients, and these extreme topological properties make module identification difficult. Although the quasi clique method offered performance

Table 9.6 Robustness analysis

Noise	Clusters	MIPS Function ($-\log p$)	MIPS Location ($-\log p$)	MIPS Complex ($-\log p$)
0%	50	14.5	8.17	16.5
1%	51	13.8	7.54	15.6
2%	50	14.2	7.66	16.0
3%	49	14.4	7.71	16.7
4%	48	14.3	7.71	16.9
5%	46	14.1	7.67	16.0
10%	42	14.8	8.14	17.5

In this table, the Noise column represents the percentile of random noise added to the DIP PPI data set. The Clusters column tabulates the number of clusters detected. The average $-\log p$ values of all detected clusters for MIPS functional, localization, and complex categories are shown.

comparable to CASCADE with both networks, the density or merge threshold had to be set to unreasonably low values (≤ 0.4) to obtain the best clustering outcome. Because these networks are relatively small in size and have very sparse connectivity, top-down approaches such as betweenness cut perform relatively better in this context.

CASCADE forms a significant enhancement to STM, and these two methods outperformed all others with each of the data sets. Of the remaining nine methods, the quasi clique approach showed the best overall performance, but its results for the sparse, less-modular yeast DDR data set were poor. CASCADE is versatile because it is robust to variations in network topological properties such as density, clustering coefficient, and size.

9.3.7 Analysis of Robustness

To assess robustness, the performance of CASCADE was evaluated through the addition of random interactions to unconnected protein pairs in the DIP PPI data set. Table 9.6 summarizes the number of clusters detected by CASCADE and the corresponding average $-\log p$ values for the MIPS categories. The performance of CASCADE was found to be robust to the addition of random interactions. A small decrease in the number of clusters can be attributed to the increased network connectivity resulting from the addition of edges.

9.3.8 Analysis of Computational Complexity

A comparison of the time complexity of the various methods is summarized in Table 9.7. The total time complexity of CASCADE is bounded by the time for QAP calculations between all pairs of nodes, which is $O(V^3 \log V + V^2 E)$. In almost all biological networks, including PPI networks, $E = O(V \log V)$, which makes the total complexity of CASCADE $O(V^3 \log V)$. Among the competing approaches, the SPC method has the best running-time complexity, $O(V^2)$, and the minimum cut method

Table 9.7 Comparison of computational complexity of CASCADE to competing clustering methods

Method	Complexity
CASCADE	$O(V^3 \log(V))$
STM	$O(V^2 \log(V))$
Maximal clique	NP
Quasi clique	NP
Samanta	$O(V^2 \log(V))$
Minimum cut	$O(V^2 \log(V) + VE)$
Betweenness cut	$O(V^2 + VE)$
MCL	$O(V^2 \log(V))$
Chen	$O(V^2 + VE)$
Rives	$O(V^2 \log(V))$
SPC	$O(V^2)$

has the worst complexity, $O(V^2 \log V + VE)$. CASCADE uses the QAP algorithm to approximate the solution to the all-possible-paths problem, which is algorithmically very hard. From this standpoint, therefore, CASCADE has good and manageable running-time complexity, despite being about V times slower than seven of the other competing approaches. The quasi clique and maximal clique finding problems are both *NP* related problems.

All the experiments described here were executed on four dual-core operon 2.8 GHZ Linux machines. The experiments using the three relatively small data sets (the yeast DDR, Rapamycin, and Rich medium networks) were completed within a few minutes. Running time for the DIP yeast PPI data set was 2.5 h, and a 14.3-h run was needed for the BioGRID yeast PPI data set.

9.3.9 Advantages of the CASCADE Method

As these results indicate, the CASCADE method outperforms competing approaches and is capable of effectively detecting both dense and sparsely connected functional modules of biological relevance with a low discard rate.

As noted, the clustering performance of other algorithms is somewhat degraded as a result of their emphasis on network regions of high intraconnectivity and low interconnectivity. Biological functional modules are typically not sufficiently dense to permit optimal performance by these methods. For example, in the yeast PPI network, an average of only 8.7% of all potential connections between protein pairs are present within a third or greater specific function in the MIPS functional hierarchy. The subgraphs of MIPS functional categories have low density and contain many singletons; some members of functional categories have no direct physical interaction with other members of the same functional category. As a result, effective detection of functional modules in biological interaction data sets can be negatively impacted by an overemphasis on densely connected regions.

Moreover, in the PPI network, the subgraphs of actual MIPS functional categories are generally not closely congregated and tend to be elongated. These subgraphs have an average diameter (defined as the length of the longest path among all pairs of shortest paths) of approximately four interactions in length, which is comparable to the average shortest-paths length of 5.47 for the entire PPI network. The relative bias of other methods toward density and interconnectivity preferences the detection of clusters with relatively balanced, round shapes, negatively impacting performance. In addition, the other algorithms tend to produce incomplete or small clusters, along with singletons. The preference for strongly connected nodes results in the discard of many weakly connected nodes.

The CASCADE method examines the frequencies of individual nodes in each of the clusters it generates (see Figures 9–5 to 9–7 and Table 9.3). In the qualitative assessment presented in Figures 9–5, 9–6, and 9–7, the larger clusters appeared to be more functionally heterogeneous than the smaller clusters. For example, seven of the ten largest clusters contained "mRNA synthesis" as a constituent term, and six of these ten clusters contained the term "fungal eukaryotic cell type differentiation." There also appeared to be substantial functional cohesiveness in each large cluster. For example, Cluster 2, which had 303 genes, included such related terms as "DNA synthesis and replication," "mitotic cell cycle and cell cycle control," "modification by phosphorylation, dephosphorylation," "phosphate utilization," and "fungal and eukaryotic cell differentiation." However, the more systematic and detailed analysis presented in Table 9.3 did not support the premise that the larger clusters were functionally more heterogeneous than smaller clusters. In fact, the proportion of genes in the third and higher levels of the MIPS hierarchy for the larger clusters was similar and unrelated to cluster size. Biologically, the "mRNA synthesis" and "fungal eukaryotic cell type differentiation" terms have broad and pleiotropic effects, and it is unsurprising that they would be required for multiple functional modules. This may better account for their inclusion by CASCADE in several clusters.

In conclusion, the occurrence probability quantification function-based metric employed by CASCADE accounts for both node degree and connectivity patterns. The results of comparative trials have indicated that it offers an effective approach to analyzing biological interactions.

9.4 FUNCTIONAL FLOW ANALYSIS IN WEIGHTED PPI NETWORKS

In [69,70], a functional influence model was developed to simulate the biological influence of each protein on other proteins through a weighted PPI network. A weighted PPI network is formulated by defining the weight of an edge as the reliability of the interaction, or the probability of the interaction being a true positive. The reliability of interactions can be estimated on the basis of known biological information about proteins. We can then quantitatively model the functional flow in weighted PPI networks. (Most materials in this section are from [69,70], with permission of IEEE.)

This functional flow simulation algorithm based on the functional influence model facilitates both the prediction of protein function and the analysis of modularity. Modules can be easily identified as a set of proteins under the functional influence of a source protein. These modules may be either overlapping or disjoint. In addition, the flow simulation can reveal a pattern of functional influence by a source node on other nodes. Using pattern-mining techniques, the set of patterns can be efficiently clustered, and the functions of an unknown protein can be accurately predicted.

9.4.1 Functional Influence Model

The functional influence model assesses the functional influence of a protein on others in a protein interaction network. This model rests on the primary assumption that functional information is propagated through the connections in a network. The reliability of each interaction as a functional link should be assigned into the corresponding edge to generate a weighted graph. The network topology or other function-related resources can be utilized for the calculation of interaction reliability.

The path strength S of a path p in a network is defined as the product of the weights of all the edges on p.

$$S(p) = \frac{\lambda \cdot w_{01}}{\delta} \prod_{i=1}^{n-1} \frac{w_{i(i+1)}}{\delta} \cdot \frac{1}{d_i}, \tag{9.4}$$

where $p = \langle v_0, v_1, \ldots, v_n \rangle$. v_0 is the start node and v_n is the end node of p. $w_{i(i+1)}$ denotes the weight of the edge between v_i and $v_{(i+1)}$. δ is the normalization parameter to make the path strength rated in the range between 0 and 1. d_i is the shape parameter. It represents the degree of connectivity of v_i. λ is the scale parameter which depends on organisms. The path strength of a path p then has inverse relationships with the length of p and the degree of the nodes on p. As the length of p increases, the product of the normalized weights decreases.

The functional influence of a node s on a node t describes the functional impact s has on t. The measurement of functional influence between two proteins is then formulated using the definition of path strength. In a view of discrete paths, the functional influence represents the path strength which is calculated by the single-path-based method or the all-path-based method. The single-path-based strength between two nodes is described as the maximum path strength among all the paths between them. This measurement is computationally efficient. However, it is critical that it does not take into consideration the effect from any alternative paths. The all-path-based strength between two nodes sums up the strength of all possible paths between them. Although this measurement is biologically more reasonable than the single-path-based method, it is not computationally acceptable. In addition, as a weakness of the measurements with discrete paths, the cycling effect by the nodes repeatedly involved should be considerable to achieve potential functional influence between two proteins.

The functional influence model is then advanced on the basis of random walks. The functional influence of a protein on another is measured by the cumulative strength from all possible walks between them. In Figure 9 11, suppose we measure the functional influence $S(v_0, v_n)$ of a node v_0 on a node v_n in a weighted network. Two factors should be considered. One is the prior knowledge of the functional influence of v_0 on the neighbors of v_n, that is, $S(v_0, v_i)$, $S(v_0, v_j)$, and $S(v_0, v_k)$. The other is the weights between v_n and its neighbors, that is, w_{in}, w_{jn} and w_{kn}. In the same way, $S(v_0, v_i)$, $S(v_0, v_j)$ and $S(v_0, v_k)$ requires the prior knowledge of the functional

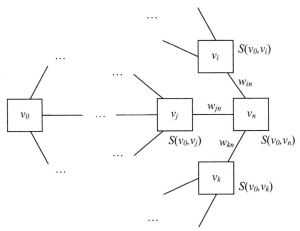

Figure 9–11 Random-walk-based functional influence model. To measure the functional influence of v_0 on v_n, all possible walks are considered, and the strength for each walk can be calculated by Equation (9.4).

influence of v_0 on the neighbors of v_i, v_j and v_k, respectively. Thus, the iterative computation of the functional influence of v_0 on the other nodes can finally estimate the functional influence of v_0 on v_n through any connections in the network.

9.4.2 Functional Flow Simulation Algorithm

The functional flow simulation algorithm is presented to efficiently implement the functional influence model. Functional flow is defined as the propagation of functional influence of a protein over the entire network. The algorithm then simulates functional flow dynamically under the assumption that the flow takes a constant time to traverse each edge. It requires a weighted interaction network as an input, and generates a set of functional influence patterns as an output. For the functional influence of a protein s on a protein t, s and t are called a source node and a target node, respectively. A functional influence pattern of s then represents the distribution of functional influence of s on all the nodes in the network. Thus, it can be accomplished by the flow simulation starting from the source node s to all target nodes.

As notations, $f_s(x \rightarrow y)$ denotes the flow of the functional influence of s as it travels from x to y, where x and y are connected to each other, and $\inf_s(y)$ represents the extent of the functional influence of s on y. Intuitively, $\inf_s(y)$ reaches its maximum value when $y = s$. $\mathcal{P}_s(y)$ is the accumulation of $\inf_s(y)$ throughout the flow.

The initial functional flow delivers the initial rate of functional influence of s to its neighbors, as reduced by the weighting process. The initial rate $\inf_s(s)$ can be a user-specific constant value, such as 1.

$$f_{init}(s \rightarrow y) = w_{s,y} \times \inf_s(s), \tag{9.5}$$

where $w_{s,y}$ is the weight of the edge between s and y, and $0 \leq w_{s,y} < 1$. The functional influence of s on y, $\inf_s(y)$, is then updated by adding the sum of all incoming flow to *y* from its neighbors.

$$\inf_s(y) = \sum_{x \in N(y)} f_s(x \to y). \tag{9.6}$$

The functional influence of *s* traverses all connected edges according to the formula

$$f_s(y \to z) = w_{y,z} \times \frac{\inf_s(y)}{|N(y)|}, \tag{9.7}$$

where $0 \leq w_{y,z} < 1$, and $|N(y)|$ denotes the degree of *y*. Throughout the flow, the amount of functional influence of *s* on each node is repeatedly updated by Equation (9.6), traverses the connected edges according to Equation (9.7), and is collected into $\mathcal{P}_s$. The flow on a path stops if the functional influence reaches a user-dependent minimum threshold $\theta_{\inf}$. The flow simulation starting from *s* terminates when there are no paths along which the functional influence continues to flow.

The functional flow simulation algorithm starting from a node *s* is shown in Algorithm 9.2. The algorithm outputs the functional influence pattern $\mathcal{P}_s$ of *s* on all nodes *t* in the network. The set of target nodes *t* is considered to be the feature space $\mathcal{F}$ in the output format. The output pattern of *s* on $\mathcal{F}$ becomes a specific functional character of *s*. Application of the simulation starting from every node generates the set of functional influence patterns of all components in the network.

Algorithm 9.2 FUNCTIONALFLOWSIMULATION $(G(V,E),s)$

Initialize $\inf_s(s)$
for each $y \in N(s)$ **do**
    Calculate $f_{init}(s \to y)$ and add *y* into a list *L*
end for
while $|L| > 0$ **do**
    for each $y \in L$ **do**
        for each $x \in N(y)$ and $f_s(x \to y) > \theta_{inf}$ **do**
            Compute $\sum f_s(x \to y)$ and add *x* into a list L'
        end for
    end for
    for each $y \in L$ **do**
        Update $\inf_s(y)$ and accumulate it into $\mathcal{P}_s(y)$
    end for
    Replace *L* with L'
end while
return $\mathcal{P}_s$

9.4.3 Time Complexity of Flow Simulation

The run time of functional flow simulation is obviously unrelated to the diameter of the network because of the use of a threshold for stopping functional flow during random walks. Since the threshold is a user-specified criterion, the theoretical

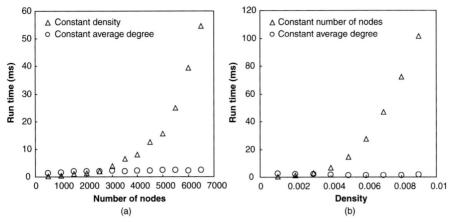

Figure 9–12 The run time of functional flow simulation in synthetic networks. The networks are structured by (a) the change of the number of nodes in a constant density or in a constant average degree, and by (b) the change of density in the constant number of nodes or in a constant average degree.

upper-bound of the run time is unknown. However, there are some factors that manipulate the time complexity of functional flow simulation. To investigate the factors, the algorithm was tested using synthetic networks structured by different features.

The first test has been done by the change of the number of nodes in a constant density and in a constant average degree. First, the networks were created by increasing the numbers of nodes, from 500 to 7000, with the fixed density of 0.002. The density of a network represents the ratio of the number of actual edges to the number of all possible edges. Next, the networks were also created by the same change of the number of nodes but the constant average degree of 5. The results of the average run time of flow simulation starting from randomly selected 200 source nodes in each network are shown in Figure 9–12(a). When the density is constant, the rum time increases as the number of nodes in the network is larger, because of the squared increase of the number of edges. However, when the average degree is constant, the run time is uniform regardless of the network size.

The second test has been done by the change of density in the constant number of nodes and in a constant average degree. The networks were produced by the change of density in the fixed number of nodes to 2000 and in the constant average degree of 5. As shown in Figure 9–12 (b), when the network size is fixed, the run time increases as the density becomes higher. However, when the average degree is constant, the run time is also uniform regardless of the network density. These results indicate that the average degree of networks is a more critical factor for time complexity of flow simulation than the size or density. Since the average degree of protein interaction networks is typically low with power-law degree distribution, the flow simulation algorithm efficiently runs in the networks.

9.4.4 Detection of Overlapping Modules

Overlapping Sub-network Structure Functional modules in a PPI network are typically overlapping, since a given protein may participate in different functional

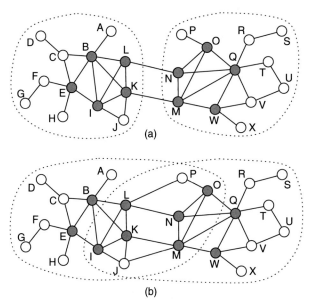

Figure 9–13 Examples of disjoint modules and overlapping modules. (a) This network has two disjoint modules detected by disconnecting two interconnecting edges ⟨L, N⟩ and ⟨K, M⟩. The intraconnection rates of these modules are both 0.89. Each module includes not only core nodes (shaded black) but also peripheral nodes (shown in white). (b) This network has two overlapping modules {A, B,... ,L, M, N, O, P} and {I, J, K, L, M,... ,W, X}. The intraconnection rates of these modules are both 0.87, while those of two disjoint subgraphs created by disconnecting ⟨L, P⟩, ⟨L, N⟩, ⟨K, M⟩ and ⟨J, M⟩ are 0.81. The intraconnection rate represents the proportion of the number of connections among the nodes in a module to the number of all connections starting from the nodes.

activities in various environmental conditions. Despite the frequent sharing of members between modules, the module as an entity retains topological significance, characterized by dense intraconnections and sparse interconnections.

Figure 9–13(a) shows an example of disjoint modules in a network. Two disjoint modules $\{A, B, \ldots, L\}$ and $\{M, N, \ldots, X\}$ are clearly detected by disconnecting two edges $\langle L, N \rangle$ and $\langle K, M \rangle$. Modules can be characterized by the *intraconnection rate*, which is the proportion of the number of connections among the nodes in a module to the number of all connections starting from the nodes. The two modules in Figure 9–13(a) both have a high intraconnection rate of 0.89. Each module contains a combination of highly connected nodes, called *core nodes*, along with sparsely connected nodes, referred to as *peripheral nodes*. In Figure 9–13(a), the core nodes, all of which have a degree greater than 3, are shaded black, and the peripheral nodes are shown in white. Although the peripheral nodes lower the density of modules, it is likely that they have functional correlations with the closely connected core nodes.

The network in Figure 9–13(b) was structured by creating two additional interconnecting edges $\langle L, P \rangle$ and $\langle J, M \rangle$ from the network in Figure 9–13(a). The intraconnection rates of two sets $\{A, B, \ldots, L\}$ and $\{M, N, \ldots, X\}$ are both 0.81. In this network, each set can grow through new connections to generate modules with higher intraconnection rates. For example, the set $\{A, B, \ldots, L\}$ may add nodes $\{M, N, O, P\}$ to form a module $\{A, B, \ldots, L, M, N, O, P\}$. The intraconnection rate of the module is then increased to 0.87. The set $\{M, N, \ldots, X\}$ can also add nodes $\{I, J, K, L\}$ to produce a higher intraconnection rate. The overlap between the two modules thus includes the nodes $\{I, J, K, L, M, N, O, P\}$.

Flow Simulation The flow-based overlapping module detection algorithm [70] includes three phases: informative protein selection, flow simulation to detect preliminary modules and a postprocess to merge similar preliminary modules. This algorithm uses a weighted graph as an input. The weight for each edge in a PPI network can be calculated as a preprocess using sequence similarity, structural similarity or expression correlation between interacting proteins as biological distance, following the procedure described in Chapter 7. GO data can be integrated as another measure for the weights of interactions. The details of these metrics, the definitions of semantic similarity and semantic interactivity, and the process of integration with GO data will be discussed in Chapter 11.

The selection of informative proteins involves identifying the representatives of modules in terms of functionality. They are selected through the topological analysis of PPI networks, generally via the use of centrality metrics. Each informative protein is the core node of a functional module. Various topology-based metrics can be used to select the informative proteins, for example, degree and clustering coefficient. A previous study [29] has observed that the local connectivity of nodes in biological networks plays a crucial role in cellular functions. It means high-degree nodes are possibly the cores in functional modules. The clustering coefficient defined in Equation (5.8) [319] is another useful metric to quantify how well a node affect the local denseness. The node located in the center of a densely connected region can be the core of a functional module. In a weighted network, similar to the discussion in Chapter 8, the degree and clustering coefficient can be extended to the weighted degree d^{wt} and weighted clustering coefficient c^{wt} [30].

$$d_i^{\mathrm{wt}} = \sum_{v_j \in N(v_i)} w_{ij}, \tag{9.8}$$

where w_{ij} is the weight of the edge $\langle v_i, v_j \rangle$, and

$$c_i^{\mathrm{wt}} = \frac{1}{d_i^{\mathrm{wt}}(d_i - 1)} \sum_{\substack{v_j, v_h \in N(v_i), \\ \langle v_j, v_h \rangle \in E}} \frac{(w_{ij} + w_{ih})}{2}, \tag{9.9}$$

where d_i is the (unweighted) degree of v_i. Then the nodes with high weighted degrees or high weighted clustering coefficients are good candidates of informative proteins. The number of the informative proteins selected is a user-dependent parameter in this algorithm.

Flow simulation is based on the functional flow model, discussed above. Functional flow starts from each selected informative protein s. The algorithm computes the cumulative influence on each node throughout the simulation. The cumulative

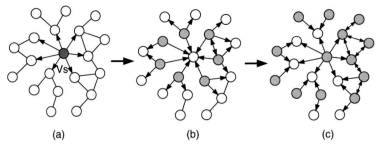

(a)   (b)   (c)

Figure 9–14 An example of information flow. (a) Suppose that V_S represents one of the informative proteins. The information of V_S is transferred from V_S to its neighbors. (b) In the same way, the information the neighbors of V_S received is transferred to their neighbors. (c) Transfer the information of each node to its neighbors is iteratively performed by flow simulation.

influence of s on a node x is a major determinant of whether s and x will be grouped in the same functional module. Since the flow visits all nodes through every possible path, densely connected nodes close to an informative protein s are generally more influenced by s than sparsely connected nodes. Simulating the flow from all informative proteins generates a set of preliminary modules that can potentially overlap. The flow of information is illustrated in Figure 9–14. In that figure, V_s represents one of the selected informative proteins.

Merging Similar Modules As a postprocess, similar preliminary modules should be merged to produce final modules. Two preliminary modules may be similar if two or more informative proteins contribute to the same function. The similarity $S(M_s, M_t)$ between two modules M_s and M_t (M_s and M_t represent a set of nodes.) is measured by the weighted interconnectivity, defined as

$$S(M_s, M_t) = \frac{\sum_{x \in M_s, y \in M_t} c(x,y)}{\min(|M_s|, |M_t|)}, \tag{9.10}$$

where

$$c(x,y) = \begin{cases} 1 & \text{if } x = y, \\ w(x,y) & \text{if } x \neq y \text{ and } \langle x, y \rangle \in E, \\ 0 & \text{otherwise.} \end{cases} \tag{9.11}$$

The modules with greatest similarity as computed by Equation (9.10) are iteratively merged until the greatest similarity falls below a threshold.

Rates of Overlap To test its performance in module detection, the flow-based modularization algorithm was applied to the core PPI data from DIP [271]. Two PPI networks weighted by semantic similarity and semantic interactivity (see Chapter 11 for the definitions) were used as inputs. The algorithm requires two user-dependent parameter values: the number of informative proteins and the minimum amount of flow in a node. The number of modules in an output set depends on the number

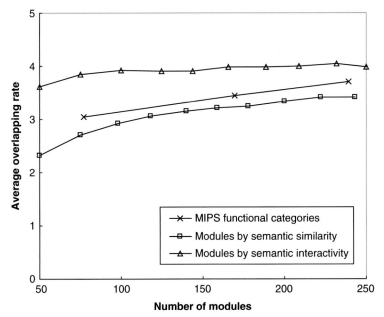

Figure 9–15 The average rate of overlap of proteins with respect to the number of modules in each output set. The average overlap rate represents the average number of occurrences of proteins in the modules. The identified modules have a pattern of overlap similar to the MIPS functional categories.

of selected informative proteins. Conversely, the minimum amount of flow determines the average size of output modules. By varying the two parameter values, we achieved ten different output sets of modules for each weighted interaction network.

The output modules generated by the algorithm shared a large number of common proteins. These overlapping patterns were evaluated by tallying the appearances of each protein within different modules. The average rates of overlap for the sets of identified modules are shown in Figure 9–15. Each set comprises a number of modules in the range between 50 and 250. As expected, the average module size was greater for sets with fewer modules. When the PPI network was decomposed into a larger number of modules, the average rate of overlap increased slightly. For semantic similarity, the rate of overlap was increased by ~10% when the number of generated modules was doubled.

Cho et al. [70] compared the rates of overlap to those of annotated proteins in the hierarchically distributed functional categories from the MIPS database [214]. The database includes seventeen different general functional categories on the top level and 77, 170, and 239 categories on the second, third, and fourth levels, respectively. They calculated the average appearance of proteins in the categories on the second, third, and forth levels. Figure 9–15 shows that the average rate of overlap increased by only 15%, despite the three-fold increase in the number of categories between the second and fourth levels. In general, the modules identified by the flow-based modularization algorithm have a pattern of overlap that is similar to the MIPS functional categories.

Table 9.8 Accuracy of output modules

Weighting Scheme	Modules before postprocessing		Modules after postprocessing	
	$-\log(p\text{-value})$	f-measure	$-\log(p\text{-value})$	f-measure
Semantic similarity	24.10	0.334	24.42	0.337
Semantic interactivity	28.58	0.399	29.05	0.401
Genetic co-expression	17.66	0.268	17.42	0.267

Output modules were generated by the flow-based algorithm with 200 informative proteins. The input was the PPI networks weighted by three metrics. For each metric, the average values of $-\log(p$-value) and the f-measure of the output modules were calculated before and after the postprocessing step to merge similar modules.

Modularization Accuracy Two methods were used to assess the accuracy of modularization. A statistical assessment of the identified modules was performed using the p-value in Equation (5.20). Each module was mapped to a reference function with the lowest p-value, and the negative of $\log(p$-value) was calculated. A low p-value (or a high $-\log(p$-value)) between an identified module and a reference function indicates that the module closely corresponds to the function. The functional categories and their annotations from the MIPS database were used as reference functions. As an alternative assessment, the f-measure as defined in Equation (5.19) was used to directly compare the membership between the identified modules and functional categories.

They monitored the average $-\log(p)$ and f-measure of the output modules before and after postprocessing. Weighting schemes using semantic similarity, semantic inactivity, and gene coexpression were applied to create weighted interaction networks as inputs. Postprocessing involved merging similar modules after completion of the flow simulation. As shown in Table 9.8, postprocessing improved the accuracy of modules generated by the two GO-based weighting methods. In this context, the generation of accurate results via flow-based modularization appears to be dependent on this step, since two or more informative proteins may represent the same functionality. However, with a weighting scheme based on gene coexpression, postprocessing degraded the accuracy of modules. In this case, the merging of modules may have resulted in the creation of larger but less accurate modules.

The p-value is highly dependent on the module size. Figure 9–16 depicts the pattern of the average $-\log(p)$ across different sets of output modules produced by varying parameter values for the number of informative proteins and the minimum flow threshold. Although the average value of $-\log(p)$ increased with average module size, it converged to approximately 34 and 39 with the semantic similarity and semantic interactivity weighting schemes, respectively. In a similar analysis, we found that the average $-\log(p)$ of the output modules generated by the betweenness cut algorithm converged to 20, as shown in Figure 9–16.

False positive interactions in a PPI network may result in miscalculation of betweenness, because the faulty information yields incorrect shortest paths in a network. To address this issue, the betweenness cut algorithm was incorporated into the preprocessing step to filter out potential false positives. Edges with a semantic

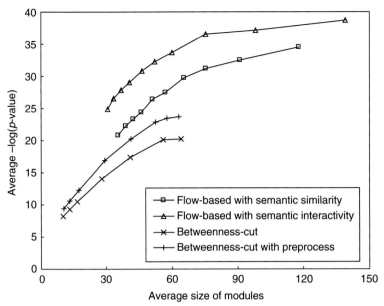

Figure 9–16 Statistical significance with respect to the average size of modules. Four distinct methods were implemented: the flow-based algorithm using either semantic similarity or semantic interactivity, the betweenness cut algorithm, and the betweenness cut algorithm with a preprocessing step to filter out edges with low semantic similarity.

similarity below 0.25 were eliminated, and the refined network was then processed with the betweenness cut algorithm. Figure 9–16 indicates that the overall accuracy of modules was enhanced by this preprocess. This result implies that the betweenness cut algorithm is sensitive to false positive interactions. The average $-\log(p)$ converged to ~23, which is higher than the result achieved by the betweenness cut algorithm without preprocessing.

Figure 9–16 demonstrates that the flow-based modularization algorithm explicitly identified more accurate modules across different output sets than the betweenness cut algorithm. Weighting interactions via semantic similarity enhanced accuracy by 70% over the betweenness cut algorithm and by 50% over the betweenness cut with preprocessing when the average module size was 60. When larger modules were produced by the flow-based algorithm, the average value of $-\log(p)$ was further increased. These results indicate that large modules generated by the flow-based algorithm are enriched for biological function. Furthermore, overlapping modules obtained by the flow-based algorithm have statistically higher associations with functions than the disjoint modules from partitioning methods.

The subset of modules identified by the flow-based algorithm with high values of $-\log(p)$ are listed with their informative proteins and functions in Table 9.9. The input network was weighted by semantic interactivity. Some modules have two informative proteins because they were merged during the postprocessing step. It is likely that the informative protein in each module plays a key role in performing the corresponding function.

Table 9.9 Modules with high values of −log(p-value) identified by the flow-based modularization algorithm

Module ID	Module Size	Informative proteins	Function	−log(p-value)
2	81	YLR147c,YGR091w	mRNA processing – splicing	59.88
3	240	YBR160w	Mitotic cell cycle	35.37
4	63	YER012w	Protein degradation – proteasome	26.48
5	95	YDL140c	mRNA synthesis – general transcription activity	45.23
6	76	YCR093w,YGR134w	mRNA synthesis – transcriptional control	32.23
7	90	YJR022w,YOL149w	mRNA processing – splicing	50.30
13	89	YGR119c	Nuclear transport	48.42
18	67	YDR448w	mRNA synthesis – transcriptional control	42.64
19	21	YJR121w	Energy generation	28.35
24	50	YGR013w	mRNA processing – splicing	57.60
27	74	YOR181w	Actin cytoskeleton	29.85
28	65	YGL172w	RNA transport	44.04
29	30	YLR127c,YDR118w	Protein modification – ubiquitination	29.58
39	65	YLR347c	Nuclear transport	57.92
47	75	YLR229c	Budding and cell polarity	44.52
61	53	YGL092w	Structural protein binding	24.01
63	40	YPR181c	Vesicular transport – ER to Golgi transport	39.22
65	41	YKL145w	Protein modification – proteolytic processing	29.89
71	58	YBL050w	Vesicular transport – vesicle fusion	26.75
76	36	YBR088c	DNA repair	23.09
78	48	YLR335w	Nuclear transport	49.21
83	46	YJL041w	RNA transport	42.93
89	28	YPR041w	Protein synthesis – translation initiation	36.63
95	36	YIL109c	vesicular transport – ER to Golgi transport	41.47
109	52	YER172c	mRNA processing – splicing	53.47
101	24	YGL153w	Peroxisome creation	24.57
111	23	YDR244w	Peroxisomal transport	26.33
122	62	YHR165c	mRNA processing – splicing	59.90
141	24	YBL023c	DNA synthesis – ori recognition	29.35
151	31	YOR076c	Nucleotide metabolism – RNA degradation	31.01
153	39	YDR227w	DNA modification – DNA conformation	24.55
161	28	YLR175w	rRNA processing	21.22
181	33	YOR121w	Transmembrane signal transduction	17.46
183	23	YNL102w	DNA synthesis – polymerization	16.01
185	10	YDR016c	Cell cycle – chromosomal cycle	14.49

The algorithm was implemented with 200 informative proteins and 0.1 as a minimum flow threshold. The input network was weighted by semantic interactivity. Thirty-five output modules are listed with their informative proteins, functions and −log(p-value). Some modules have two informative proteins because they were merged during postprocessing.

9.4.5 Detection of Disjoint Modules

Iterative Centroid Search Flow simulation is also capable of detecting disjoint modules in PPI networks. The process starts by selecting k informative proteins, which are also recognized as the centroids of potential modules. The functional influence from each centroid flows over the entire network. Each node in the network thus has at most k different cumulative influences and votes for the centroid that has the greatest cumulative influence. The PPI network is then partitioned by grouping a centroid with its voting nodes. The accuracy of this approach depends heavily on the proper selection of centroids. If a node on periphery of an actual module is chosen as a centroid, then the simulated flow may cover several different functional groups, and the output module would not be functionally homogeneous.

The iterative centroid search (ICES) algorithm was developed to delineate the optimal positions for centroids and to precisely identify functional modules [69]. It computes the centrality $C(v_i)$ of a node v_i as the sum of the maximum path strengths from v_i to the other nodes in the network.

$$C(v_i) = \sum_{\substack{v_j \in V, \\ i \neq j}} S_{\max}(\langle v_i, \ldots, v_j \rangle). \tag{9.12}$$

The centrality measurement guides the selection of a centroid in each module generated by flow simulation. The node with the highest centrality in a module becomes the centroid. These centroids then become the basis for a new round of flow simulation.

The ICES algorithm iterates between two procedures: the selection of a centroid in each output module and the simulation of flow starting from each centroid to generate a new network partition. Each iterative step identifies a set of centroids progressively closer to the actual cores of the modules. If an initial centroid is located on the periphery of a potential module, the centroid approaches the actual core of the module during the iterations. The algorithm concludes by optimizing the starting position of flow simulation, thus identifying the most appropriate partition of a PPI network.

Enhancement of Accuracy To validate the modules identified by the ICES algorithm, Cho et al. [69] compared them to the hierarchically distributed functional annotations from the MIPS database [214]. For this test, they extracted 61 distinct functions with annotations from the categories on the highest and the second level in a hierarchy. The comparison was performed by means of a supervised method using recall and precision. Overall accuracy was estimated by the f-measure as defined in Equation (5.19). After mapping each module to the function with the highest f-measure value, they calculated the average value of the f-measures of the output modules.

This experiment started with the application of the flow-based modularization algorithm to partition a weighted interaction network of *S. cerevisiae* from DIP [271] built by the integration of GO annotations using semantic interactivity. The top 50 nodes for each degree and weighted degree were selected as centroids, and the flow simulation was applied starting from these 100 nodes. After filtering out modules with a degree less than 5, they obtained 46 initial modules from the degree-based centroids and 37 from the weighted degree-based centroids. The average f-measure values of the modules were 0.19 and 0.23, respectively. Initial modules resulting from the weighted degree-based centroids were more accurate than those generated from the unweighted centroids.

Next, the ICES algorithm was used to optimize the centroid position in each module. Figure 9–17 shows the alteration pattern of the average f-measure of the

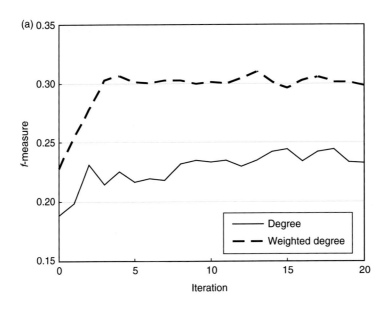

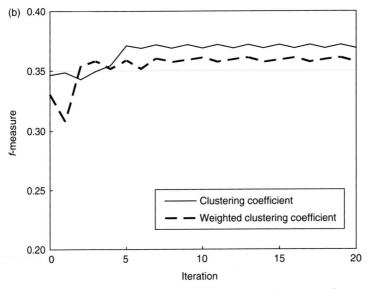

Figure 9–17 The alteration pattern of the average f-measure of output modules over twenty iterations of the ICES algorithm. The initial centroids were selected based on (a) the degree and weighted degree, and (b) the clustering coefficient and weighted clustering coefficient. (Reprinted from [69] with permission of IEEE.)

output modules over twenty iterations. The initial selection of weighted degree-based centroids produced a dramatic increase in the average f-measure during the first three iterative processes, with convergence at ∼0.3. This selection improved overall accuracy by 30%. The selection of unweighted degree-based centroids results in a similar pattern, but with more fluctuation. In this case, the average f-measure gradually increased by around 20% during the iterations.

The ICES algorithm was also implemented with the initial centroids based on the clustering coefficient and weighted clustering coefficient. Again, the process started by filtering out nodes with a degree less than 5. This step excludes components located in small, dense, peripheral sub-networks. The clustering coefficient typically has an inverse relationship to degree in a PPI network [29]. Therefore, many low-degree nodes have high clustering coefficients but do not play an essential role as cores of modules. Figure 9–17 shows the alteration pattern of the average f-measure of output modules over twenty iterations. The f-measure values of the initial modules from clustering-coefficient-based and weighted clustering-coefficient-based centroids were considerably higher, at 0.345 and 0.33, respectively, than those from degree-based or weighted degree-based centroids. Building upon the higher accuracy of the initial modules, further improvement occurred during the subsequent iterations, and they converged to 0.37 and 0.36, respectively. These results indicate that the ICES algorithm enhances the accuracy of functional modules generated by the flow-based method regardless of the metrics of the initial centroid selection.

9.4.6 Functional Flow Pattern Mining

Functional Influence Patterns Flow simulation starting from a source node v can generate a functional influence pattern for v, which describes both the topological and biological relationships of v to the other nodes. The functional influence pattern of v is created by plotting the alteration of the cumulative amount of functional influence of source node v on all target nodes. The set of functional influence patterns for all nodes in the network offers another significant data source for the identification of functional modules and the prediction of function. Cho et al. [70] hypothesized that two molecular components with similar functional influence patterns are highly likely to perform the same function or to share most functions. To validate this hypothesis, they first investigated the relationship of functional influence patterns to functional co-occurrence. For this test, they randomly selected two sets of 450 gene pairs; one set included pairs that co-occurred in the same functional category, while the functions of the pairs in the other set did not co-occur. A functional flow simulation was initiated from each selected node through the core PPI network as described in the previous section. They then calculated the correlation of the two patterns for each pair using the Pearson coefficient and applied a cube root transformation. Figure 9–18 shows the mean values of the correlation; the error bars indicate the standard deviation. The network was weighted using the semantic similarity measure integrated with GO, as discussed in Chapter 11. The results presented in Figure 9–18 indicate that gene pairs that co-occurred in the same function had a higher correlation of functional influence patterns, despite their large variances.

Next, they compared the correlation of functional influence patterns with semantic similarity. The semantic similarity values for interacting proteins were calculated

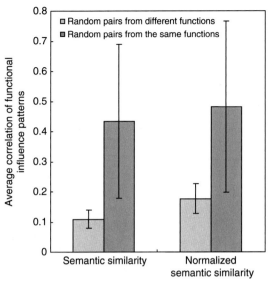

Figure 9–18 Average correlation of functional influence patterns of 450 randomly selected protein pairs, including pairs that do and do not co-occur in the same functional category.

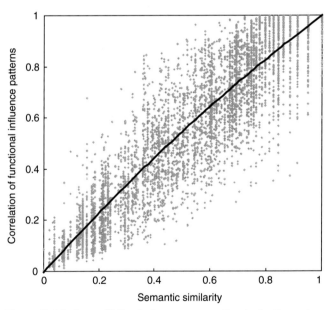

Figure 9–19 Curve fitting between semantic similarity and correlation of functional influence patterns for interacting protein pairs.

using Equation (11.5), and the correlation of the functional influence patterns of each interacting pair was derived using the Pearson coefficient. The values of pattern correlation and semantic similarity for interacting pairs are shown as dot points in Figure 9–19. The polynomial curve fit to this data is nearly linear. This signifies that the similarity of functional influence patterns has a linear relationship with semantic similarity. Just as semantic similarity can measure the functional co-occurrence and functional consistency between molecular components, they observe that functional influence patterns can also estimate these functional associations. This result strongly supports the initial hypothesis stated above. Furthermore, it implies that functional influence patterns are capable of classifying and discriminating molecular components with regard to their functions. As a result, these patterns can be mined to predict functions and detect functional modules.

Function Prediction To employ functional influence patterns as a basis for function prediction, the patterns can be classified using a suitable classification algorithm. In this approach, the target nodes for the influence patterns represent features. In the classification of biological data, a feature selection process [41,88,339] is frequently included because only a small subset of features in the high-dimensional space is informative. Inclusion of noninformative features may degrade the accuracy of classification. However, in the flow-pattern-based algorithm, feature selection is optional, because all target nodes can be informative. Feature selection may be included for efficiency when the dimension of the feature space is extremely large.

Among the feature selection methods for multi-class prediction, the ANOVA F-test is the most prevalent statistic [60].

$$F = \frac{(n-k)\sum n_i(\bar{Y}_i - \bar{Y})^2}{(k-1)\sum(n_i - 1)s_i^2}, \tag{9.13}$$

where

$$s_i^2 = \sum_{j=1}^{n_i} \frac{(Y_{ij} - \bar{Y}_i)^2}{(n_i - 1)}, \tag{9.14}$$

Y_{ij} is the amount of functional influence of the jth object in the ith class, $\bar{Y}_i = \sum_{j=1}^{n_i} Y_{ij}/n_i$, and $\bar{Y} = \sum_{i=1}^{k} n_i\bar{Y}_i/n$. k is the number of classes, n_i is the number of objects in the ith class, and $n = n_1 + n_2 + \cdots + n_k$. However, since the F-test is based on the assumption that the variances are statistically equal across classes, the Brown-Forsythe test statistic

$$B = \frac{\sum n_i(\bar{Y}_i - \bar{Y})^2}{\sum(1 - n_i/n)s_i^2}, \tag{9.15}$$

performs better than the F-test when class variances are heterogeneous [60]. Classification of functional influence patterns was performed with the SVM method using the RBF kernel. The Brown–Forsythe test was used to select the subset of the target nodes. To estimate two parameter values, the penalty parameter C of the error term and γ in the RBF kernel, a grid-search on C and γ using cross-validation in the training data set was conducted, and the values with the highest accuracy were chosen. After a training process involving the functional influence

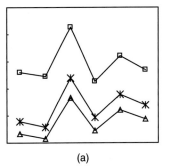 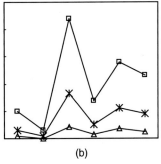

(a)   (b)

Figure 9–20 Examples of (a) shifting and (b) scaling patterns within a cluster.

patterns of known genes, the SVM algorithm predicted the functions of unknown genes.

Detection of Functional Modules The functional influence patterns were then clustered using a pattern-based clustering algorithm. These algorithms [317,331] capture similar patterns in a subspace of features and are differentiated mainly by their consideration of shifting or scaling effects in measuring the similarity between patterns. Simple examples of shifting and scaling patterns within a cluster are depicted in Figure 9–20. This trial employed the pCluster algorithm [317], which addresses the shifting effects by pScore in a 2×2 matrix of the object by feature:

$$\text{pScore}\left(\begin{bmatrix} Y_{xa} & Y_{xb} \\ Y_{ya} & Y_{yb} \end{bmatrix}\right) = |(Y_{xa} - Y_{xb}) - (Y_{ya} - Y_{yb})|, \qquad (9.16)$$

where Y_{xa} is the amount of functional influence of an object x on a feature a. The shifting patterns P can be accepted when $\text{pScore}(P) \leq \delta$. δ is a user-specified threshold. The algorithm also handles scaling effects by transforming the values to a logarithmic form.

A schematic view of the functional influence pattern-mining procedure as applied to a simple example is illustrated in Figure 9–21. Figure 9–21(a) is a synthetic weighted network with twenty nodes. The weight of an edge is described as its thickness. It is readily apparent that the network includes three clusters, as assessed by the connectivity of the nodes. Figure 9–21(b) presents the functional influence patterns generated by flow simulation in the weighted network. Each pattern stands for an object; that is, the representation derived by the functional flow starting from a source node. The x-axis is the feature space $\mathcal{F}$ consisting of the set of target nodes of the functional flow. The y-axis represents the extent of functional influence of a source node on each target node. Figure 9–21(c) presents the clusters identified by searching for coherent patterns.

Prediction Accuracy The flow pattern-based approach to function prediction was tested using an extract from the core version of the yeast PPI network from DIP [271]. The experiments were performed using those proteins that were annotated with any of five top-level functional categories from FunCat in MIPS [267]. To ensure a distinct

Table 9.10 Functional annotation data set used for classification

MIPS ID	Function	# of proteins
10.01	DNA processing	11
10.03	Cell cycle	66
11	Transcription	179
12	Protein synthesis	38
14	Protein fate	206
	Total	500

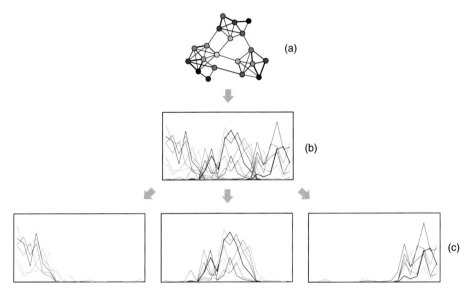

Figure 9–21 Schematic view of functional flow pattern mining. (a) An example of a weighted network and (b) the functional influence patterns generated by flow simulation. (c) Pattern-mining algorithms can effectively identify the coherent patterns as clusters. "See Color Plate 11."

one-to-one correspondence between proteins and functions, any proteins appearing in two or more of these categories were excluded. The functional annotation data sets used as the ground truth are listed in Table 9.10.

Semantic data integration was performed using measurements of semantic similarity generated via Equation (11.5) and of normalized semantic similarity from Equation (11.7). Cases were run both without feature selection and with feature selection via the Brown–Forsythe test as formulated in Equation (9.15). A leave-one-out cross-validation using SVM for multi-class prediction was applied at the end of the process. The classification accuracy for each case is shown in Table 9.11. Use of the semantic similarity measurement resulted in better performance than the normalized semantic similarity, and the feature selection process actually decreased the accuracy of prediction.

Table 9.11 Comparison of classification accuracy

Method	Category	Data integration	Feature selection	Accuracy (%)	Parameters
Functional flow	Flow pattern-based	Semantic similarity	—	82.8	$\theta_{inf} = 0.01$
			Brown-Forsythe	81.0	
		Normalized semantic similarity	—	81.4	
			Brown-Forsythe	77.4	
MRF	Probabilistic	—	—	77.0	
Chi-square	Neighborhood-based	—	—	74.0	$n = 1$

The performance of the flow pattern-based algorithm was compared with that of the most reliable competing methods: a neighborhood-based approach using a chi-square formula [143] and a probabilistic approach in the Markov random field (MRF) model [85]. The neighborhood-based chi-square method searches the functions of the neighbors interacting with an unknown protein and selects the most significant function by a chi-square-like statistical formula. The MRF method inspects the frequency of proteins having the function of interest throughout the entire network. The probability of a protein having the given function was derived from a Gibbs' sampler [264]. A quasi-likelihood approach was used for the parameter estimation in the model. As shown in Table 9.11, the flow pattern-based approach outperforms both the global probabilistic method represented by the MRF model and the local neighborhood-based method.

Accuracy of Module Detection The flow pattern-based approach to functional module detection was tested using a process similar to that described in the previous section, although more specific functional categories were selected, where possible. Proteins were extracted which were annotated with fourth-level functional categories from FunCat [267] related to "cell cycle and DNA processing" as the ground truth. If no fourth-level category was available, then proteins with comparable third-level categorical annotations were used. Details regarding these data sets are presented in Table 9.12. Since any given protein can perform multiple functions, it was expected that clusters would overlap, with some nodes belonging to several different clusters. In fact, each of the eighteen different functional categories contains an average of 40 proteins, while there are only 452 distinct proteins across the eighteen categories.

The statistical evaluation of the output clusters employed the p-value in Equation (5.20). The performance of the flow pattern-based algorithm was assessed in comparison to a selection of methods representative of different techniques. These included the clique percolation method [238] as a representative of the density-based clustering approach and the betweenness cut method [94] as a representative of the hierarchical clustering approach. The clique percolation method searches all k-cliques and iteratively merges adjacent k-cliques that share $k - 1$ nodes. This

Table 9.12 Functional annotation data set used for clustering

MIPS ID	Function	Number of proteins
10.01.03.01	DNA topology	24
10.01.03.03	ORI recognition/Priming complex formation	22
10.01.03.05	Extension/Polymerization activity	27
10.01.05.01	DNA repair	92
10.01.05.03	DNA recombination	42
10.01.09.05	DNA confirmation modification	120
10.01.11	Regulation of DNA processing	4
10.03.01.01	Mitotic cell cycle	111
10.03.01.02	Cell cycle arrest	11
10.03.01.03	Cell cycle check points	46
10.03.02	Meiosis	80
10.03.03	Cel division/septum formation	40
10.03.04.01	Centromere/kinetochore complex maturation	11
10.03.04.03	Chromosome condensation	15
10.03.04.05	Chromosome segregation/division	35
10.03.04.07	Nuclear division	5
10.03.04.09	Nuclear migration	6
10.03.05	Cytoskeleton reorganization	30
Total number of distinct proteins		452

Table 9.13 Comparison of clustering accuracy

Method	Category	Data Integration	# of Clusters	Average cluster size	Accuracy ($-\log P$)	Parameters
Flow pattern clustering	Flow-based	Semantic similarity	14	11.20	5.47	$\theta_{inf} = 0.01$
Betweenness cut	Hierarchical	—	43	9.67	4.62	min density = 0.2
Clique percolation	Density-based	—	52	5.50	3.72	$k = 3$
			16	6.94	4.63	$k = 4$

method is particularly focused on the identification of the overlapping clusters in a network. The betweenness cut algorithm iteratively disconnects the edge with the highest betweenness value until the network is separated into sub-networks. It then recursively implements the cutting process in each sub-network. The clustering results obtained through the three methods are shown in Table 9.13. Although the clique percolation method successfully identified overlapping clusters, it generated numerous small clusters and a few disproportionately large clusters, resulting in poor overall accuracy. The betweenness cut method viewed all isolated sub-networks as individual, disjoint clusters, resulting in a large number of often-inaccurate clusters. In general, the flow pattern-based approach demonstrated better performance than these two competing methods. It properly handled false-positive interactions through integration of semantic data and modeled complex connections by simulation of functional flow. The occurrence of false negatives could be resolved by routing the functional flow through the reliable alternative paths that typically exist in PPI networks.

9.5 SUMMARY

This chapter has discussed several novel approaches to the flow-based analysis of PPI networks. These methods have demonstrated that flow-based techniques can provide a useful tool to analyze the degree of biological and topological influence of each protein on other proteins in a PPI network. Both the prediction of protein function and protein modularity analysis can be performed on the basis of the simulation of flow in PPI networks. Approaches of this type may soon become a mainstream for the analysis of PPI networks.

Statistics and Machine Learning Based Analysis of Protein Interaction Networks

With Pritam Chanda and Lei Shi

10.1 INTRODUCTION

In recent years, the genomic sequencing of several model organisms has been completed. As of June 2006, complete genome sequences were available for 27 archaeal, 326 bacterial, and 21 eukaryotic organisms, and the sequencing of 316 bacterial, 24 archaeal, and 126 eukaryotic genomes was in progress [281]. In addition, the development of a variety of high-throughput methods, including the two-hybrid system, DNA microarrays, genomic SNP arrays, and protein chips, has generated large amounts of data suitable for the analysis of protein function. Although it is possible to determine the interactions between proteins and their functions accurately using biochemical/molecular experiments, such efforts are often very slow, costly and require extensive experimental validation. Therefore, the analysis of protein function in available databases offers an attractive prospect for less resource-intensive investigation.

Work with these sequenced genomes is hampered, however, by the fact that only 50–60% of their component genes have been annotated [281]. Several approaches have been developed to predict the functions of these unannotated proteins. The accurate prediction of protein function is of particular importance to an understanding of the critical cellular and biochemical processes in which they play a vital role. Methods that allow researchers to infer the functions of unannotated proteins using known functional annotations of proteins and the interaction patterns between them are needed.

Machine learning has been widely applied in the field of protein–protein interaction (PPI) networks and is particularly well suited to the prediction of protein functions. Methods have been developed to predict protein functions using a variety of information sources, including protein structure and sequence, protein domain, PPIs, genetic interactions, and the analysis of gene expression. In this chapter, we will discuss several statistics- and machine learning-based approaches to the study of PPIs. We will focus on the prediction of protein functions as inferred from PPI networks.

10.2 APPLICATIONS OF MARKOV RANDOM FIELD AND BELIEF PROPAGATION FOR PROTEIN FUNCTION PREDICTION

A Markov random field (MRF) specifies the joint probability distribution of a set of random variables. It can be depicted as a graph in which each node represents a random variable and each edge represents a dependency between two random variables. The specification of the joint probability distribution is obtained using the fact that every node in the MRF is conditionally independent of every other node given its immediately neighboring nodes. MRF-based methods have been used extensively in applications such as computer vision and image analysis, financial analysis, economics, and sociology.

MRF and Bayesian analyses have been applied in [83,85] for the prediction of protein functions on the basis of information gleaned from PPI networks. As discussed elsewhere in this book, a PPI network consists of a set of proteins, that act as the nodes of the graph; each edge between two nodes represents the presence of an interaction between proteins. A representative network is illustrated in Figure 10–1. Each node

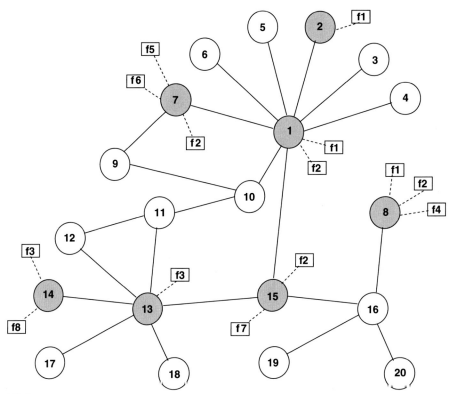

Figure 10–1 Schematic depiction of a representative PPI network. Circles depict proteins (nodes) and edges denote interactions. Proteins with known functional classifications are shaded, while the unclassified proteins are white. Each shaded protein is annotated with several functions depicted by boxes. The nodes and functions are numbered randomly.

(or protein) has an associated probability distribution over the various functions, which can be inferred from the other nodes with which it has edges (interactions) in the network.

Several researchers have developed methods for the generation of such probability distributions. Deng et al. [83,85] used the Gibbs' distribution [199] to define a probability distribution over the protein interaction data. They estimated the MRF model parameters using a pseudo-likelihood analysis [199] and employed a Gibbs' sampler [116] to sample from the distribution and predict the functions of unannotated proteins. Letovsky et al. [196] proposed a binomial model of the local neighbor function and devised a variant of the belief propagation algorithm to assign probabilities of functions to unannotated proteins. MRF-based protein-function prediction methods draw upon the observation that adjacent proteins in a PPI network are more likely to have similar functions than do proteins located at a distance. This phenomenom, termed *local density enrichment* [196], arises from the biological fact that closely interacting proteins tend to have a similar set of functions. The MRF formulation likewise assumes that the probability distribution characterizing the functional labeling of a protein (node) is conditionally independent of all other proteins, given the distribution of its neighboring nodes.

Let us consider a network with $p_1, \ldots, p_N$ proteins and M functional categories $f_1, \ldots, f_M$ that are assigned to these proteins in the network. We will examine a particular functional category $f \in \{f_1, \ldots, f_M\}$. Based on previous studies, assume that m of the proteins in the network have function f and are annotated with f. Assume that $p_1, \ldots, p_n$ are the proteins whose annotations with f are yet to be determined; this will be accomplished on the basis of the known annotations of the remaining set of m proteins $p_{n+1}, \ldots, p_N$. Let X_i be an indicator variable denoting whether protein p_i has the function f (i.e., $X_i = 1$) or not (i.e., $X_i = 0$). If it is not known whether p_i has function f, let $X_i =?$. This generates a functional labeling configuration X where $X = (X_1, \ldots, X_N)$, $X_i \in (0, 1, ?)$. We will denote the observed values of each random variable X_i by x_i. Let $\pi_i = P(\text{protein } p_i \text{ has function } f)$. Assuming equal probabilities for all proteins, let $\pi_i = \pi$. Then

$$P(X = \langle x_1, x_2, \ldots, x_N \rangle) \propto \prod_{i=1}^{N} \pi^{x_i} (1 - \pi)^{(1-x_i)} = \pi^{N_1} (1 - \pi)^{(N-N_1)}, \quad (10.1)$$

where N_1 represents the number of proteins already annotated with function f. Since two proteins are more likely to have similar functions if they interact than if they do not, the belief for the functional labeling of the proteins can be characterized by the Gibbs' distribution and is proportional to

$$\exp(\beta N_{01} + \gamma N_{11} + N_{00}), \quad (10.2)$$

where $N_{t,t'}$ represents the number of interacting protein pairs (p_i, p_j) when $X_i = t$ and $X_j = t'$. In this equation, $N_{t,t'}$ denotes the count of interacting pairs that conform to three cases: neither protein is annotated with function f (N_{00}), one protein is annotated with function f and the other is not (N_{01}), or both proteins are annotated with function f (N_{11}).

Multiplying Equations (10.1) and (10.2), the overall *prior belief* for the functional labeling can be stated by

$$P(X|\theta) = Z^{-1}(\theta)\exp(-U(x)).$$ (10.3)

Here, $U(x)$ is termed the potential function and can be shown to be

$$U(x) = -\alpha N_1 - \beta N_{10} - \gamma N_{11} - N_{00}.$$ (10.4)

$Z(\theta)$ is a normalizing constant (or, in MRF terminology, a partition function) that can be obtained by summing over all the possible functional labeling configurations. $\theta = \{\alpha, \beta, \gamma\}$ are the MRF model parameters with $\alpha = \log(\pi/(1-\pi))$.

The posterior beliefs can be obtained using a Bayesian approach. Let $X_{[-i]}$ denote the configuration $(X_1, X_2, \ldots, X_{i-1}, X_{i+1}, \ldots, X_N)$. Let M_0^i and M_1^i denote the number of interacting neighbors of protein p_i not annotated with function f (labeled 0) and annotated with f (labeled 1), respectively. Considering only the neighboring nodes of p_i when it is assumed to have label 1,

$$P(X_i = 1, X_{[-i]}|\theta) \propto \exp(\alpha N_1 + \beta N_{01} + \gamma N_{11} + N_{00})$$

$$\propto \exp(\alpha N_1 + \beta M_0^i + \gamma M_1^i).$$ (10.5)

This follows from the fact that p_i is labeled 1; therefore, M_0^i and M_1^i count the number of (0, 1) and (1, 1) edges, respectively in the neighborhood of p_i. This is illustrated in Figure 10–2(a).

When p_i is labeled 0,

$$P(X_i = 0, X_{[-i]}|\theta) = P(X_1, X_2, \ldots, X_i = 0, \ldots, X_N|\theta)$$

$$\propto \exp(\alpha(N_1 - 1) + \beta M_1^i + M_0^i)$$ (10.6)

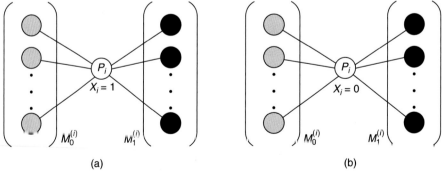

(a)   (b)

Figure 10–2 Protein p_i and its neighbors when (a) p_i is assumed to be annotated with function f and (b) p_i is assumed not to have function f. The neighbors annotated with f are marked in black while those not having function f are marked in gray. In (a) $N_{01} = M_0^i$, $N_{11} = M_1^i$, $N_{00} = 0$. In (b) $N_{00} = M_0^i$, $N_{01} = M_1^i$, $N_{11} = 0$.

Here, since p_i is labeled 0, it follows that there is one less node labeled 1 and M_0^i and M_1^i count the number of $(0, 0)$ and $(0, 1)$ edges, respectively in the neighborhood of p_i. This is illustrated in Figure 10–2(b).

Combining Equations (10.5) and (10.6), it can be shown that the posterior probability is given by

$$P(X_i = 1 | X_{[-i]}, \theta) = \frac{P(X_i = 1, X_{[-i]} | \theta)}{P(X_i = 1, X_{[-i]} | \theta) + P(X_i = 0, X_{[-i]} | \theta)}$$

$$= \frac{\exp(\alpha + (\beta - 1)M_0^i + (\gamma - \beta)M_1^i)}{1 + \exp(\alpha + (\beta - 1)M_0^i + (\gamma - \beta)M_1^i)}. \tag{10.7}$$

Since only the neighboring nodes of p_i are considered here, Equation (10.7) reflects the local dependency of the network. The parameters θ are estimated using a pseudo-likelihood method [199]. This method may often be computed more efficiently than the maximum likelihood over all possible labeling configurations since the latter may require marginalization over a large number of variables. The posterior probability space is then sampled using Gibbs' sampler [264] with a burn-in period of 100 and lag period of 10, until the posterior probabilites are stabilized.

Using the model described above, in [83,85], the authors further explored protein complexes, developed MRF models using multiple sources of PPI information, and integrated protein domain information into their model. As already noted, proteins within a protein complex are more likely to interact and to be functionally similar than are random protein pairs. This characteristic can be used to assign different prior probabilities to each protein, as will be discussed below.

Given a protein p_i in a protein complex, let X_i be the indicator variable denoting the presence or absence of a particular function f for this protein. In Equation (10.1), we assumed that all proteins have an equal prior probability of having function f. However, in the context of protein complexes, the situation can be described by

$$P(X_i = 1 | p_i \text{ is present in a protein complex})$$

$$= \frac{\text{No. of proteins annotated with } f \text{ in the protein complex}}{\text{No. of known proteins in the protein complex}}. \tag{10.8}$$

For proteins that do not belong to any complex, the fraction of the proteins in the entire proteome is used as the prior belief. In these instances, the prior belief about functional labeling can be obtained using the above definition in a manner similar to that set forth in Equation (10.1).

As discussed previously, information regarding PPIs can be derived from multiple information sources: these include gene coexpression data and analysis of mutation-based genetic interactions. An MRF model can be built for each of these information sources and these models can be combined to obtain an overall belief for the functional labeling of proteins in the network. Assuming there are K independent sources of PPI information (each being an independent PPI network), the belief for functional labeling is proportional to

$$\prod_{k=1}^{K} \exp\left(\beta_k N_{01}^{(k)} + \gamma_k N_{11}^{(k)} + N_{00}^{(k)}\right), \tag{10.9}$$

where the term under the product sign is similar to Equation (10.2) with an extra superscript/subscript k denoting the k-th network. Using this and the prior belief described above, an MRF is defined by Gibbs' distribution as before,

$$P(X|\theta) = Z^{-1}(\theta)\exp(-U(x)), \tag{10.10}$$

where the potential function $U(x)$ can be shown to be

$$U(x) = -\sum_{i=1}^{N}(x_i\alpha_i) - \sum_{k=1}^{K}(\beta_k N_{01}^{(k)} + \gamma_k N_{11}^{(k)} + N_{00}^{(k)}) \tag{10.11}$$

with $\alpha_i = \log(\pi_i/(1-\pi_i))$.

In addition, protein function prediction can be enhanced by the integration of domain information since the functions of a protein are largely determined by its domain structure. Assume a given set of domains $D_1, D_2, \ldots, D_M$. For any given protein, let $d_m = 1$ if the protein contains domain D_m, 0 otherwise. Also, let p_{m1} denote the probability that the protein has domain D_m given it has function f and p_{m0} denote the probability that the protein has domain D_m given it does not have function f. Then the joint probability of observing domain D_m and function f is given by

$$P_1(d = \langle d_1, d_2, \ldots, d_M \rangle) \propto \prod_{m=1}^{M} p_{m1}^{d_m}(1-p_{m1})^{(1-d_m)},$$
$$P_0(d = \langle d_1, d_2, \ldots, d_M \rangle) \propto \prod_{m=1}^{M} p_{m0}^{d_m}(1-p_{m0})^{(1-d_m)}. \tag{10.12}$$

These domain probabilities can be multiplied with those in Equation (10.11) to obtain overall prior probabilites of functional assignment. Based on the above model, the posterior probabilities of functional assignment can be shown to be

$$P(X_i = 1|D, X_{[-i]}, \theta)$$
$$= \frac{\exp(\alpha_i + \Sigma_{k=1}^{K}(\beta_k - 1)M_0^i(k) + (\gamma_k - \beta_k)M_1^i(k))}{1 + \exp(\alpha_i + \Sigma_{k=1}^{K}(\beta_k - 1)M_0^i(k) + (\gamma_k - \beta_k)M_1^i(k))} \tag{10.13}$$

which can be sampled using Gibbs' sampler as described above.

MRF-based methods have been applied to the prediction of protein functions in yeast protein databases. In these experiments, the posterior probability of a protein having a particular function of interest was estimated for each unannotated protein. Functions were then assigned to the proteins on the basis of a comparison of the posterior probabilities with some predefined threshold. Protein domain information was then integrated into this approach, drawing upon the Protein Families Database of Alignments and HMM (Pfam domain) and linking this information to the proteins using SWISS-PROT/TrEMBL [231]. The functional categories were obtained from the MIPS (Munich Information Center for Protein Sequences) database [214]. Protein interaction data was obtained from MIPS, while TAP protein complexes and cell cycle gene expression data were derived from [285]. Using a leave-one-out method, the accuracy of these functional predictions can be measured in terms of specificity and sensitivity, following the procedure to be detailed below.

Let n_i be the number of functions known to annotate protein p_i, m_i be the number of functions that annotate p_i using the prediction scheme, and k_i be the number of functions common to the above set of known and predicted functions. Following Equations (5.21) and (5.22), the specificity (sensitivity) can be defined as the fraction of overlap between the known functions and predicted functions over the number of predicted (known) functions for all the proteins considered; that is,

$$\text{Specificity} = \frac{\Sigma_i k_i}{\Sigma_i m_i}, \tag{10.14}$$

$$\text{Sensitivity} = \frac{\Sigma_i k_i}{\Sigma_i n_i}. \tag{10.15}$$

For the functional categories of biochemical function, subcellular localization and cellular role, posterior probability thresholds of 0.13, 0.25, and 0.17 yield maximum specificities and sensitivities of 45%, 64%, and 47%, respectively. Application of these prediction methods to proteins YDR084C and YGL198W, which have vesicular transport functions, achieve a probability of 0.85. The integrated approach combining protein complex data, Pfam domain information, MIPS physical and genetic interactions, gene expression data, and TAP protein complex data results in a joint highest specificity and sensitivity of 76%. Clearly, integration of these other information sources produces a substantial improvement over functional predictions obtained using MIPS interaction data alone.

The application of MRFs in conjunction with functional labels taken from the Gene Oncology GO [137] database has been used in [196] to infer protein functions from the PPI network. Each edge in the network is associated with a random variable $L_{i,t}$ for protein p_i and GO term t. $L_{i,t} = 1$ indicates that p_i has functional label t, with the term equaling 0 if it does not. A neighborhood function for protein p_i is defined by $P(L_{i,t}|N_i, k_{i,t})$ where N_i and $k_{i,t}$ denote the number of neighbors of node p_i in the PPI network and the number of those neighbors that are labeled with GO term t. This neighborhood function can be evaluated as

$$\begin{aligned} P(L_{i,t}|N_i, k_{i,t}) &= \frac{P(k_{i,t}|N_i, L_{i,t})P(L_{i,t}, N_i)}{P(N_i, k_{i,t})} \\ &= \frac{P(k_{i,t}|N_i, L_{i,t})P(L_{i,t})}{P(k_{i,t}|N_i)} \end{aligned} \tag{10.16}$$

by applying Bayes' rule with the independence assumption $P(L_{i,t}, N_i) = P(L_{i,t})P(N_i)$. $P(k_{i,t}|N_i, L_{i,t})$ is the probability of having $k_{i,t}$ nodes labeled with term t that are also neighbors of p_i out of N_i neighbors. This is assumed to have a binomial distribution

$$P(k_{i,t}|N_i, L_{i,t}) = \binom{N_i}{k_{i,t}} q^{k_{i,t}} (1-q)^{N_i - k_{i,t}}, \tag{10.17}$$

where q is the frequency of occurrence of term t in the graph. Since the probability of a protein's neighbors having a particular level will differ depending upon its own label, the neighbors of proteins labeled with t and not labeled with t will have different conditional distributions,

$$P(k_{i,t}|N_i, L_{i,t} = 0) = \binom{N_i}{k_{i,t}} q_0^{k_{i,t}} (1 - q_0)^{N_i - k_{i,t}},$$

$$P(k_{i,t}|N_i, L_{i,t} = 1) = \binom{N_i}{k_{i,t}} q_1^{k_{i,t}} (1 - q_1)^{N_i - k_{i,t}},$$

(10.18)

where $q_{1(0)}$ denotes the probability of the protein having label t (or not having label t) given that its neighboring nodes are labeled with t (or not labeled with t). Examining the other probability terms in Equation (10.16), $P(L_{i,t})$ is simply equal to the frequency of p_i having term t in the PPI network, while $P(k_{i,t}|N_i, L_{i,t})$ is estimated as a weighted average by

$$P(k_{i,t}|N_i) = P(L_{i,t} = 1)P(k_{i,t}|N_i, L_{i,t} = 1) + P(L_{i,t} = 0)P(k_{i,t}|N_i, L_{i,t} = 0)$$

(10.19)

Combining all these, Equation (10.16) can be rewritten as

$$P(L_{i,t}|N_i, k_{i,t}) = \frac{\lambda}{1 + \lambda},$$

(10.20)

where

$$\lambda = \frac{P(L_{i,t} = 1)q_1^{k_{i,t}}(1 - q_1)^{N_i - k_{i,t}}}{P(L_{i,t} = 0)q_0^{k_{i,t}}(1 - q_0)^{N_i - k_{i,t}}}.$$

(10.21)

Since the label probability of a protein depends upon that of its neighbors, and these in turn depend on their neighbors, label probabilities are allowed to propagate iteratively using belief propagation [243,333]. This process involves an initial assignment of functional labels to the nodes, followed by the iterative application of Equation (10.16). This procedure is then repeated for each individual GO term.

This method has been used to analyze the GRID PPI data set, which encompasses 20,985 distinct interactions between 13,607 distinct pairs of proteins. The functional labels were obtained from the 26,551 labels of 6,904 ORFs taken from the 12/01/02 version of the SGD Yeast GO assignments [196]. This process permitted the labeling of 2,573 proteins that were initially unannotated in at least one of the three GO hierarchies (cellular compartment, molecular function, and biological process). In the first step, prior to propagation of labels, 702 new predictions were made for unlabeled proteins. A prediction precision of 85% with a 0.15% false positive rate was achieved for a prediction threshold of 0.8 while reconstructing known labels. During the label propagation phase, 247 additional predictions were made, and a precision of 98.6% with a 0.3% false positive rate was achieved for the same prediction threshold.

Belief propagation using Gibbs' potential [332] has been further explored in [195]. As usual, we represent the PPI network as a graph with vertices denoting proteins and interactions denoted by edges between two nodes. The proteins are denoted by the set $V = \{p_1, p_2, \ldots, p_N\}$ and the functions by the set $F = \{f_1, f_2, \ldots, f_M\}$. Each protein p_i can be characterized by a random variable X_i that can take values from the set F. It is assumed that some proteins in the network are already classified (i.e., their functional labeling is complete); these are denoted by set A. Each protein belonging to set A exerts an external field on the unclassified proteins in its neighborhood. The total field for each unclassified protein in $V \backslash A$ is obtained by combining the individual external fields exerted by each protein in A into a score function defined by

$$E[\{X_i\}_{i=1}^N] = -\sum_{i=1}^N \sum_{j=1}^N \text{Adj}(i,j)\delta(X_i, X_j) - \sum_{i=1}^N h_i(X_i), \quad (10.22)$$

where $\text{Adj}(i,j)$ is the adjacency matrix of the PPI graph with $\text{Adj}(i,j) = 1$ if $i, j \in V \backslash A$ and there is an edge between them, δ is the Kronecker delta function, and $h_i(t)$ counts the number of classified neighbors of protein i that have function t. This score function essentially counts the number of the neighboring nodes that have the same predicted functions over all the interactions in the graph. From this score function, a variational potential, termed Gibbs' potential, is evaluated. This is maximized through belief propagation equations that are solved by a procedure called the cavity method [215]. Given an initial functional assignment for the PPI graph, this method calculates the stationary probabilities of functional labeling of each node by maximizing the Gibbs' potential.

This method has been used to analyze two yeast PPI networks taken from Uetz et al. [307] and Xenarios et al. [327], with functional categories derived from the MIPS database. The network taken from Uetz et al. was comprised of 1,826 proteins, of which 456 were unclassified; there were 2,238 pairwise interactions (edges). The other network contained 4,713 proteins, of which 1410 were unclassified; there were 14,846 interactions. The performance of the method was tested using a *dilution* procedure similar to the leave-one-out method, with two reliability indices and a sharpness criterion. In this procedure, a fraction d of the classified proteins in a given PPI graph, were assumed to be missing; these were referred to as *whitened* proteins. The first reliability criterion was defined as the fraction of whitened proteins for which at least one function was correctly predicted. The second, more stringent reliability criterion was defined as the fraction of correctly predicted functions out of all known functions of a whitened protein in the original PPI graph. The sharpness criterion, which measured the accuracy of the method, was defined as the proportion of correctly predicted functions over all functions predicted. The method achieved high first and second reliability scores that increased with the degree of protein nodes for fixed dilution values. The sharpness measure, however, decreased with the number of significant probability levels (ranks) that were used to make predictions.

10.3 PROTEIN FUNCTION PREDICTION USING KERNEL-BASED STATISTICAL LEARNING METHODS

The past few years have seen the introduction of a number of powerful kernel-based learning methods, including support vector machines (SVMs), Kernel Fisher discriminant (KFD), and Kernel principal component analysis (KPCA). These kernel-based algorithms have been successfully applied to such topics as optical pattern and object recognition, text categorization, time-series prediction, gene expression profile analysis, and DNA and protein analysis [220]. In this section, we will discuss the application of kernel-based statistical learning methods to the prediction of protein function.

Kernel-based statistical learning methods have a number of general virtues as tools for biological data analysis. First, the kernel framework accommodates not only the vectorial and matrix data that are familiar from classical statistical analysis but also the more exotic data characteristic of the biological domain. Second, kernels provide significant opportunities for the incorporation of more specific biological knowledge. Third, the growing suite of kernel-based data analysis algorithms require only that data be reduced to a kernel matrix; this creates opportunities for standardization. Finally, the reduction of heterogeneous data types to the common format of kernel matrices allows the development of general tools for combining multiple data types. Kernel matrices are required only to respect the constraint of positive semidefiniteness; thus the powerful technique of semidefinite programming can be exploited to derive general procedures for combining data of heterogeneous format [220].

Following an experimental paradigm introduced by Deng et al. [85], Lanckriet et al. [191] developed a support vector machine (SVM) approach, which applied a diffusion kernel to a PPI network for the prediction of protein functions. The performance of an SVM method depends on the kernel used to represent the data set. The diffusion kernel K calculates the similarity distance between any two nodes in the network; it is defined as follows:

$$K = e^{\{\tau H\}}, \tag{10.23}$$

where

$$H(i,j) = \begin{cases} 1, & \text{if protein } i \text{ interacts with protein } j, \\ -d_i, & \text{if protein } i \text{ is the same as protein } j, \\ 0, & \text{otherwise,} \end{cases} \tag{10.24}$$

where d_i is the number of interaction partners of protein i, τ is the diffusion constant, and $e^{\{H\}}$ represents the matrix exponential of the adjacent matrix H [194]. Lanckriet et al. [191] showed that the SVM algorithm yields significantly improved results relative both to an SVM trained from any single data type and to the MRF method for all the function categories considered.

Nonetheless, the MRF and SVM approaches each have advantages that should be considered in selecting a prediction methodology. The MRF approach is able to consider the frequency of proteins that possess the function of interest. The SVM method, in contrast, tends to predict protein functions more accurately. Lee et al. [194] combined the advantages of both approaches into a new kernel-based logistic regression model for protein function prediction. Following the approach suggested by Deng et al. [83] in using a diffusion kernel with MRF, they modeled the probability of $X = (X_1, \ldots, X_{n+m})$ as proportional to

$$\exp(\alpha N_1 + \beta_{10} D_{10} + \beta_{11} D_{11} + \beta_{00} D_{00}), \tag{10.25}$$

where $\alpha, \beta_{10}, \beta_{11}$, and β_{00} are constants, and

$$N_1 = \sum_i I\{x_i = 1\},$$

$$D_{11} = \sum_{i<j} K(i,j)I\{x_i = 1, x_j = 1\},$$

$$D_{10} = \sum_{i<j} K(i,j)I\{(x_i = 1, x_j = 0) \text{ or } (x_i = 0, x_j = 1)\},$$

$$D_{00} = \sum_{i<j} K(i,j)I\{x_i = 0, x_j = 0\}.$$

The summations are over all the protein pairs. From Equation (10.25), it can be shown that

$$\log \frac{\Pr(X_i = 1|X_{[-i]}, \theta)}{1 - \Pr(X_i = 1|X_{[-i]}, \theta)} = \alpha + (\beta_{10} - \beta_{00})K_0(i) + (\beta_{11} - \beta_{10})K_1(i),$$

$$(10.26)$$

where

$$K_0(i) = \sum_{i \neq j} K(i,j)I\{x_j = 0\},$$

$$K_1(i) = \sum_{i \neq j} K(i,j)I\{x_j = 1\}.$$

If protein i interacts with protein j, $K(i,j) = 1$; otherwise, $K(i,j) = 0$. Previous researches had used the Markov Chain Monte Carlo (MCMC) approach to estimate the posterior probabilities that an unknown protein would have the function of interest, conditional on the network and the functions of known proteins. In a novel move, Lee et al. [194] developed a simpler *kernel-based logistic regression (KLR) model for one function* based on Equation (10.26). Let

$$M_0(i) = \sum_{j \neq i, x_j \text{known}} K(i,j)I\{x_j = 0\},$$

$$M_1(i) = \sum_{j \neq i, x_j \text{known}} K(i,j)I\{x_j = 1\}.$$

The KLR model is given by

$$\log \frac{\Pr(X_i = 1|X_{[-i]}, \theta)}{1 - \Pr(X_i = 1|X_{[-i]}, \theta)} = \gamma + \delta M_0(i) + \eta M_1(i). \qquad (10.27)$$

By incorporating correlated functions into the model, Lee et al. [194] created the *KLR model for correlated functions*. Assume that there are K functional categories: $C_1, C_2, \ldots, C_K$ and $\sum_{k=1}^{K} \Pr(X_i = C_k) = 1$, and let $\{X_i = C_k\}$ be the instance, in which the i-th protein has function C_K. We can generalize the KLR model as follows:

$$\log \frac{\Pr(X_i = C_k)}{\Pr(X_i = C_K)} = \gamma_k + \sum_{l=1}^{K} \delta_{kl} M_l(i), \tag{10.28}$$

where

$$M_l(i) = \sum_{j \neq i} K(i,j) I\{x_j = C_l\}, \quad l = 1, 2, \ldots, K.$$

$M_l(i)$ is the weighted number of neighbors of protein i having function l with weight $K(i,j)$ for protein j. The presence of a large number of functions may result in high-dimensional parameters. To reduce the number of parameters, Lee et al. [194] use the chi-square test to identify correlated functions for a function of interest. For a protein P_i having a function C_j, the chi-square association value between the function C_j and a function C_l, based on the immediate neighbors of P_i, is defined as

$$\frac{(N_i^{(1)}(l) - N_i^{(1)} Q_l)^2}{N_i^{(1)} Q_i}, \tag{10.29}$$

where $N_i^{(1)}$ is the number of immediate neighbors of P_i, $N_i^{(1)}(l)$ is the number of immediate neighbors of P_i having function C_l, and Q_l is the fraction of known proteins having function C_l. The corresponding quantities are then summed over all proteins in the network having function C_l in the network to obtain an overall statistic:

$$\frac{\left(\sum N_i^{(1)} - \sum N_i^{(1)} Q_l\right)^2}{\sum N_i^{(1)} Q_l}. \tag{10.30}$$

In this model, it is impossible to fit the data to the full framework stated in Equation (10.28). Therefore, for each function only correlated functions with the five highest chi-square values are considered.

It is possible that many other data sources may be usefully drawn upon for the prediction of protein functions. To extend the KLR model to include multiple data sources, Lee et al. [194] created a *KLR model for multiple data sources*. Each data source is first converted to a matrix and is treated in the same manner as physical interaction data. Suppose there are D data sources that have been transformed into kernel matrices. Let $K^{(d)}(i,j)$ be the kernel matrix for the d-th data source. The KLR model with correlated functions [Equation (10.28)] can then further be extended to

$$\log \frac{\Pr(X_i = C_k)}{\Pr(X_i = C_K)} = \gamma_k + \sum_{d=1}^{D} \sum_{l=1}^{K} \delta_{kl}^{(d)} M_l^{(d)}(i), \quad k = 1, 2, \ldots, K - 1.$$

where

$$M_l^{(d)}(i) = \sum K^{(d)}(i,j) I\{X_j = C_l\}, \quad l = 1, 2, \ldots, K.$$

$M_l^{(d)}(i)$ is the weighted number of neighbors of protein i having function l with weight $K^{(d)}(i,j)$ for protein j in the d-th network.

Lee's group followed the experimental protocol established for MIPS physical interaction data to test the MRF approach of Deng et al. [83], the SVM approach of Lanckriet et al. [191], and the KLR models for one function and for correlated functions. These trials indicated that both KLR models generated more accurate predictions than either the MRF or SVM approaches.

10.4 PROTEIN FUNCTION PREDICTION USING BAYESIAN NETWORKS

Bayesian networks have been used for inference and learning in a wide range of fields, including bioinformatics (regulatory networks, protein structure, and gene expression analysis), data fusion, text mining and document classification, image processing, and decision support systems. In this section, we will discuss the application of Bayesian networks to the prediction of protein function. Bayesian methods are particularly valuable in integrative approaches where PPI information from several sources is combined to make useful predictions.

Extending the local density enrichment concept described earlier in this chapter, Chuan et al. [201] has proposed a common-neighbor-based approach, which exploits the small-world property of a network. As defined earlier, this small-world property states that two adjacent nodes are more likely to have common neighbors than would nodes in a random graph [319]. We have seen that the PPI networks are characterized by this property [313]. Therefore, two proteins connected by a true edge in a PPI network should have more common neighbors than those connected by a false positive edge; furthermore, the connected proteins are more likely to have similar functions.

The common-neighbor-based approach can be described in a manner similar to that used in previous sections. Let there be N proteins in the PPI network $p_1, \ldots, p_N$ and assume these belong to M functional categories $f_1, \ldots, f_M$. Considering a particular functional category $f \in \{f_1, \ldots, f_M\}$, assume $p_1, \ldots, p_n$ are proteins annotated with f. The annotation of the remaining set of proteins $p_{n+1}, \ldots, p_N$ is yet to be determined. For an unannotated protein p_i ($n < i \leq N$) and function f, let F_t ($1 \leq t \leq M$) be the indicator variable denoting whether p_i is annotated with f (value 1) or not (value 0). Let $\{p_{t1}, \ldots, p_{tl}\}$ ($1 \leq t1 \leq \cdots \leq tl \leq n$) be the set of proteins annotated with function f and $K_{t1}, K_{t2}, \ldots, K_{tl}$ be random variables indicating the numbers of common neighbors between proteins p_i and p_{tj} ($1 \leq j \leq l$). The conditional probability that p_i will be annotated with function f given the distribution of the annotations of the common neighbors with f is given by

$$
\begin{aligned}
& P(F_t = 1 | K_{t1}, \ldots, K_{tl}) \\
& = \frac{P(K_{t1}, \ldots, K_{tl} | F_t = 1) \cdot P(F_t = 1)}{P(K_{t1}, \ldots, K_{tl})} \\
& = \frac{\prod_{j=1}^{l} P(K_{tj} | F_t = 1) \cdot P(F_t = 1)}{\prod_{j=1}^{l} P(K_{tj} | F_t = 1) \cdot P(F_t = 1) + \prod_{j=1}^{l} P(K_{tj} | F_t = 0) \cdot P(F_t = 0)},
\end{aligned}
$$
(10.31)

where $P(F_t = 1)$ is the prior probability that p_i has function f, $P(K_{t1}, \ldots, K_{tl})$ is the probability that p_i has $K_{t1}, \ldots, K_{tl}$ common neighbors with proteins $p_{t1}, \ldots, p_{tk}$, and $P(K_{t1}, \ldots, K_{tl}|F_t = 1)$ is the conditional probability that p_i has $K_{t1}, \ldots, K_{tl}$ common neighbors with proteins $p_{t1}, \ldots, p_{tk}$ given that p_i has function f. It is also assumed that the number of common neighbors shared by p_i and p_{tj} $(1 \leq j \leq l)$ is independently determined for p_i and p_{tj} $(1 \leq j \leq l)$, so that $P(K_{t1}, \ldots, K_{tl}|F_t = 1) = \prod_{j=1}^{l} p(K_{tj}|F_t = 1)$, where $P(K_{tj}|F_t = 1)$ is the probability that p_i and p_{tj} have K_{tj} common neighbors given that both p_i and p_{tj} have function f.

Let N_t be the total number of proteins annotated with function f. $P(K_{tj}|F_t = 1)$ is assumed to follow a binomial distribution, $B^+(N_t, K_t, p_t)$ where p_t is the probability that two proteins annotated with f share a common neighbor with the same function. However, for a typical PPI network, the average number of N_t $(1 \leq t \leq M)$ is often greater than 100 so the binomial distribution can be approximated by the normal distribution with the same mean and variance:

$$P(K_{tj}|F_t = 1) = \frac{1}{\sqrt{2\pi}\sigma_{t+}} e^{-\frac{(K_{tj}-\mu_{t+})^2}{\sigma_{t+}^2}}, \tag{10.32}$$

where μ_{t+} and σ_{t+}^2 are identical to the mean and variance of the distribution $P(K_{tj}|F_t = 1) = B^+(N_t, K_t, p_t)$.

Similarly, $P(K_{tj}|F_t = 0)$ can be approximated by $\frac{1}{\sqrt{2\pi}\sigma_{t-}} e^{-(K_{tj}-\mu_{t-})^2/\sigma_{t-}^2}$ where μ_{t-} and σ_{t-}^2 are the mean and variance of the distribution $P(K_{tj}|F_t = 0) = B^-(N_t, K_t, p_t)$. Equation (10.31) can then be written as

$$P(F_t = 1|K_{t1}, \ldots, K_{tl}) = \frac{\lambda_t}{\lambda_t + 1}, \tag{10.33}$$

where

$$\lambda_t = \frac{\sigma_{t-}^l}{\sigma_{t+}^l} \cdot e^{-\sum_{j=1}^{l}\left(\frac{(K_{tj}-\mu_{t+})^2}{\sigma_{t+}^2} - \frac{(K_{ti}-\mu_{t-})^2}{\sigma_{t-}^2}\right)} \cdot \frac{P(F_t = 1)}{P(F_t = 0)}. \tag{10.34}$$

$\log(\lambda_t)$ is used as the score to measure the probability that protein p_i will have function f_t. A higher score indicates a greater likelihood that an unannotated protein p_i will have function f_t. This score is used to assign functions to unannotated proteins through the following process. First, for each functional category f_t $(1 \leq t \leq M)$, the means μ_{t-}, μ_{t+} and σ_{t-}, σ_{t+} for conditions $F_t = 0$ and $F_t = 1$, respectively, are estimated using the binomial model as described above. This is followed by the calculation of the functional score for each unannotated protein p_i, taking into consideration the functions that are possessed by those proteins that have at least one common neighbor with p_i. The functions are ranked in descending order of their functional scores, and a maximum of δ functions with the highest scores are assigned to p_i.

Since PPI data are typically incomplete and the number of annotated proteins may be very limited, an unannotated protein may not share common neighbors with any other annotated protein. As in the case of iterative belief propagation [196], discussed earlier, the score functions of unannotated proteins are inferred in an iterative manner. In the initial round of iteration, the functions of some unannoated proteins that are well connected to the annotated proteins are determined. This increases the number of annotated proteins in the network that become input to the next round of iterations. In this manner, all the annotated proteins that are known at any particular round are used to make predictions in the next iterative round. Iteration stops either when the functions of all unannotated proteins have been predicted or when no further predictions can be made.

The common-neighbor-based Bayesian method was tested on the DIP and DIP-Core data sets. The DIP data set contains 4,931 proteins and 17,172 interactions (excluding 285 self-interactions). The DIP-Core data set, which contains 2,547 proteins and 5,949 interactions, has undergone more careful examination and is more reliable. 259 functional categories were obtained from the MIPS database. A leave-one-out cross-validation scheme was employed to test the predictive accuracy of the method using specificity and sensitivity as the measurement criteria as previously described. For a given sensitivity value, this method achieved a high level of specificity; for example, a 50% specificity level was attained at 40% sensitivity. This highlights the effectiveness of the common-neighbor-based method in handling the many false positives and false negatives in PPI data.

10.5 IMPROVING PROTEIN FUNCTION PREDICTION USING BAYESIAN INTEGRATIVE METHODS

As we have seen, additional PPI information can be gleaned from a wide variety of sources and new computational and experimental methods have predicted a number of possible PPIs. Bayesian networks have been employed [160,328] to integrate this extensive range of data and to select the reliable interactions. A Bayesian framework offers many advantages. The Bayesian algorithm is relatively straightforward and can effectively handle heterogeneous data types and missing data. Typically, PPI data sets suffer from low coverage and poor accuracy and reliability is compromised by contradictions between the different data sets [328]. Integration of evidence from these multiple sources of putative interactions is achieved in a Bayesian framework by assesing each source of evidence through comparison against samples of known positive and negative interactions (referred to as "gold standards"). In [160], interaction data from the MIPS complexes catalog is used as the gold standard . The set of negative interactions is synthesized by combining proteins located in different subcellular compartments, since these are the least likely to interact. A pair of proteins is said to interact positively within a data set when both members belong to the same complex. The prior odds of finding such a positive pair are given by

$$O_{\text{prior}} = \frac{P(\text{positive})}{P(\text{negative})}, \tag{10.35}$$

where $P(\text{positive})$ and $P(\text{negative})$ give the fraction of positive and negative pairs in the data set, respectively. The posterior odds are defined after integrating the evidence from N data sets,

$$O_{\text{posterior}} = \frac{P(\text{positive}|e_1 \cdots e_N)}{P(\text{negative}|e_1 \cdots e_N)}$$
$$= L(e_1 \cdots e_N) * O_{\text{prior}}, \tag{10.36}$$

where e_i is a feature or data type used to infer interaction between the proteins and L is the likelihood ratio, defined as

$$L(e_1 \cdots e_N) = \frac{P(e_1 \cdots e_N|\text{positive})}{P(e_1 \cdots e_N|\text{negative})}. \tag{10.37}$$

In [160], a pair of proteins was predicted to interact when $L > L_{\text{cutoff}}$; that is, the likelihood ratio exceeds a particular cutoff (found experimentally to be 600). Experiments were run using four PPI data sets from high-throughput experiments [113,144,155,307] including the probabilistic interactome experimental (PIE) data, mRNA expression levels, and GO biological processes data. The fourth data set, PIP (Probabilistic Interactome Predicted) data, contains information about the indispensability of particular proteins for survival. A naive Bayesian network was initially used to calculate the likelihood of interactions in the PIE data set. A full Bayesian network was then used for a similar calculation with the PIP data set. These two sets of results were integrated again using a naive Bayesian network, since the PIE and PIP data provide independent evidence for the interactions. It was found that likelihood ratios obtained using individual data sources did not exceed the cutoff and had a large number of false positive interactions. However, combining the two data sources using a fully connected naive Bayesian network resulted in 9897 predicted interactions from PIP and 163 from the PIE.

In [328], 27 heterogeneous data sources were integrated to predict PPI in humans using Bayesian networks. The gold-standard positive interactions were obtained from the human protein peferenced database (HPRD) [251], and the gold-standard negative interactions were obtained by pairing nuclear proteins with those from the plasma membrane. For each feature or data type used to infer interaction between the proteins, likelihood ratios were calculated for each protein pair using the gold-standards interactions. When evidence was available from more than one data source, the maximum likelihood ratio value was used for that protein pair. The likelihood ratios that were obtained for the various features considered were integrated using a naive Bayesian network, which generated the final interaction prediction scores.

10.6 SUMMARY

In this chapter, we have examined several statistics- and machine learning-based approaches to the study of PPIs. MRF-based techniques use Bayesian methodology to estimate the posterior probability of a protein having a function of interest. This estimate is made on the basis of the functional labeling status of the neighboring proteins. Once the nodes of a network have been annotated, the method optimizes some global property of all nodes by taking into consideration all the iteration networks and available functional annotations of proteins. These methods perform better than the chi-square [143] and neighbor-counting [274] approaches and have predicted novel functions for proteins in yeast. However, the MRF-based methods do have several drawbacks. Since they consider each function individually, and independently evaluate the probability to be assigned to the proteins in the network, these methods ignore possible correlations between functional assignments. While a protein with a given function may be more likely to also have another similar function, these relationships will be missed when each functional assignment is considered independently. These techniques are also susceptible to the high incidence of false positives, which arise from the unreliability of the protein interaction data.

The local density enrichment based-method introduced by Letovsky [196] uses a binomial distribution function to model the probability of observing a given count of neighboring nodes with a particular functional label. This approach employs a variant of iterative belief propagation to assign stable probabilities of functions to the unannotated proteins. This is in contrast to the MRF approaches, which use Gibbs' distribution for this purpose. Both these methods come under the category of maximum-likelihood methods and perform similarly when applied to common data sets [37]. The message-passing-based prediction method developed by Leone [195] is based upon Gibbs' potential. All these approaches share the drawbacks that also characterize the MRF-based methods. They are susceptible to the high incidence of false positives and false negatives in PPI networks and treat the label assignments of each function independently from the other functions. All assume that two neighboring or nearby proteins are likely to have similar functions.

Kernel-based statistical learning methods represent data by means of a kernel function that defines similarities between pairs of genes or proteins. Such similarities can take the form of quite complex relations, implicitly capturing aspects of the underlying biological machinery. These methods facilitate pattern detection, since the kernel function takes relationships that are implicit in the data and makes them explicit. Each kernel function thus extracts a specific type of information from a given data set, thereby providing a partial description or view of the data. After finding a kernel that best represents all the information available for a given statistical learning task, the methods combine this information via a convex optimization technique known as semidefinite programming (SDP). This SDP-based approach offers a statistically sound, computationally efficient, and robust general methodology for combining many partial descriptions of data [191].

The common-neighbor-based Bayesian method utilizes the small-world property of PPI networks and is more robust to the unreliability and high noise ratio characteristic of PPI networks. However, performance quality depends on the optimal setting of the parameters determining the maximum number of neighbors of each node and the number of highest-ranked functions to be assigned to each node in the network. Each of these methods, as well those discussed elsewhere in this book, offer intriguing possibilities for further improvement in the prediction of the functions of unannotated proteins.

11

Integration of Gene Ontology into the Analysis of Protein Interaction Networks

With Young-rae Cho

11.1 INTRODUCTION

The ability of the various approaches discussed throughout this book to accurately analyze protein–protein interactions (PPIs) is often compromised by the errors and gaps that characterize the data. Their accuracy would be enhanced by the integration of data from all available sources. Modern experimental and computational techniques have resulted in the accumulation of massive amounts of information about the functional behavior of biological components and systems. These diverse data sources have provided useful insights into the functional association between components. The following types of data have frequently been drawn upon for functional analysis and could be integrated with PPI data [276,297,304,305]:

- Amino acid sequences
- Protein structures
- Genomic sequences
- Phylogenetic profiles
- Microarray expressions
- Gene Ontology (GO) annotations

The development of sequence similarity search algorithms such as FASTA [244], BLAST [13], and PSI-BLAST [14] has been a major breakthrough in the field of bioinformatics. The algorithms rest on the understanding that proteins with similar sequences are functionally consistent. Searching for sequential homologies among proteins can facilitate their classification and the accurate prediction of their functions.

The availability of complete genomes for various organisms has shifted such sequence comparisons from the level of the single gene to the genome level [48,97]. As discussed in Chapter 3, several genome-scale approaches have been introduced on the basis of the correlated evolutionary mechanisms of genes. For example, the conservation of gene neighborhoods across different, distantly-related genomes reveals potential functional linkages [80,235,296]. Gene fusion analysis infers pairs of interacting proteins and their functional relatedness [98,208]. Phylogenetic profiles are also useful resources for determining protein function and localization [209,248].

The advent of microarray technology has made it possible to monitor the expression levels of thousands of genes in parallel. The effective analysis of an enormous quantity of gene expression data has resulted in widespread application in the areas of functional genomics and drug discovery over the last several years [96,126,341]. Most of these analyses are based on the concept that the correlated expression profiles of genes can be interpreted as indicating their functional similarity.

The GO Consortium database [18,301] is one of the most comprehensive ontology databases currently available to the bioinformatics community. It is a collaborative effort to address the need for consistent descriptions of genes and gene products. The GO database is a collection of well-defined and structured biological terms that are universal to all organisms. Each term represents a functional class and includes the annotation of genes and gene products. The GO terms and their annotations can contribute significantly to the analysis of PPIs.

In this chapter, we will focus on methods for integrating PPI networks with these GO annotations. First, we will discuss semantic similarity measures used to calculate the reliability of PPIs. Interactivity-based [70] and probabilistic approaches [64] to function prediction and functional module detection will then be detailed.

11.2 GO STRUCTURE

The GO database is composed of GO terms and their relationships. The GO terms represent biological concepts and are grouped into three general categories: biological processes, molecular functions, and cellular components. GO terms are structured by their relationships to each other. For example, "is-a" represents a specific-to-general relationship between terms, while "part-of" represents a part-to-whole relationship. A GO term t_i with an "is-a" relationship to t_j is conceptually more specific than t_j. In this instance, t_i is referred to as a child term of t_j, and t_j is a parent term of t_i.

A directed acyclic graph (DAG) $G = (V, A)$ is then built with the GO terms as a set V of nodes and their relationships as a set A of directed arcs. According to the stipulations of the DAG structure, if t_i is more specific than t_j and t_j is more specific than t_k, then t_i is always more specific than t_k. In other words, if there are directed paths from t_i to t_j and from t_j to t_k in the GO structure, then the path from t_i to t_k should exist, while the path from t_k to t_i should not. A simplified example of the GO structure is illustrated in Figure 11–1. Here, five GO terms as nodes are connected with directed arcs. Apart from the root term, each GO term has one or more parent terms. For example, the parent terms of GO:Node3 are GO:Node1 and GO:Node2.

11.2.1 GO Annotations

The GO database provides annotations for each GO term. Each gene or protein is associated with, or annotated to, one or more GO term(s). Relationships to multiple terms are possible because a given gene or protein can perform different biological processes or functions in different environments. In Figure 11–1, gene $g4$ is annotated to both GO:Node3 and GO:Node4. GO annotations follow the transitivity

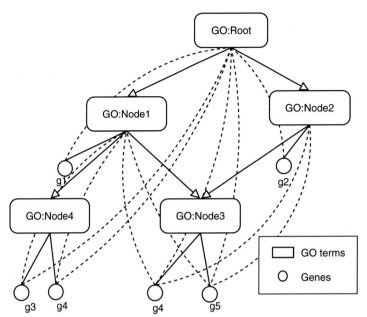

Figure 11–1 The GO structure with GO terms and their annotations. Solid lines between genes and GO terms indicate direct annotation, and dotted lines indicate an annotation inferred through the transitivity property.

property, so that annotating a given gene to a GO term automatically annotates it to more general GO terms on the path towards the root term in the DAG structure. For example, in Figure 11–1, the gene $g4$ is annotated to the term GO:Node4. Consequently, $g4$ will also be annotated to GO:Node1 and GO:Root. The relationship of $g4$ to GO:Node4 is a direct annotation, and its relationship to GO:Node1 and GO:Root are inferred annotations. In Figure 11–1, solid lines connect genes that are direct annotations of the GO terms, and dotted lines indicate annotations inferred by the transitivity property. The set of proteins annotated to the root term is transitive, if all inferred annotations are considered, in that the annotation of the root term includes all genes already characterized.

Suppose G_i and G_j are the sets of proteins annotated to GO terms t_i and t_j, respectively, and t_i is a parent term of t_j. According to the transitivity property of GO annotation, the size of G_i, $|G_i|$ will be greater than or equal to $|G_j|$. Suppose a protein x is annotated to m different GO terms. $G_i(x)$ denotes a set of proteins annotated to GO term t_i, which annotates x, where $1 \leq i \leq m$. In the same way, suppose both x and y are annotated to n different GO terms, where $n \leq m$. In this instance, $G_j(x, y)$ denotes a set of proteins annotated to GO term t_j, which annotates both x and y, where $1 \leq j \leq n$. The minimum size of $G_i(x)$ is always less than or equal to the minimum size of $G_j(x, y)$.

11.3 SEMANTIC SIMILARITY-BASED INTEGRATION

Measuring similarity between concepts in a taxonomy is a common practice in natural language processing. Measurements of semantic similarity can be characterized as

---

Table 11.1 Measurements of semantic similarity between two concepts C_1 and C_2 in the taxonomy

Methods	Formula
Structure-based	
Path-length-based method	$\text{sim}(C_1, C_2) = 1/\text{len}(C_1, C_2)$
Leacock's method	$\text{sim}(C_1, C_2) = -\log(\text{len}(C_1, C_2)/(2 \times \text{depth}))$
Common-parents-based method	$\text{sim}(C_1, C_2) = (\mathcal{P}(C_1) \cap \mathcal{P}(C_2))/(\mathcal{P}(C_1) \cup \mathcal{P}(C_2))$
Wu's method	$\text{sim}(C_1, C_2) = \dfrac{2 \cdot \text{len}(C_{\text{root}}, C_0)}{\text{len}(C_0, C_1) + \text{len}(C_0, C_2) + 2 \cdot \text{len}(C_{\text{root}}, C_0)}$
Information content-based	
Resnik's method	$\text{sim}(C_1, C_2) = -\log P(C_0)$
Lin's method	$\text{sim}(C_1, C_2) = 2 \cdot \log P(C_0)/(\log P(C_1) + \log P(C_2))$
Jiang's method	$\text{sim}(C_1, C_2) = \log P(C_1) + \log P(C_2) - 2 \cdot \log P(C_0)$

$\text{len}(C_1, C_2)$ denotes the shortest path length from C_1 to C_2, and *depth* is the maximum path length from the root to a leaf. C_0 represents the most specific concept that subsumes both C_1 and C_2, and C_{root} is the most general concept that is located in the root of the taxonomy. $\mathcal{P}(C)$ is the set of parent concepts in the taxonomy. $P(C)$ is the probability of C.

---

structure of the taxonomy or information contents of the concepts, as summarized in Table 11.1. These techniques can be applied to measure the degree of similarity between terms in the GO structure. The details of these methods will be discussed in the following subsections.

The semantic similarity measured between two GO terms can be directly converted to a measurement of the similarity between two proteins. Since a protein is annotated to multiple GO terms, several researchers [316] have defined the similarity between two proteins as the average similarity of the GO term cross pairs, which are associated with both interacting proteins. However, this definition may underestimate the reliability of the interaction between these proteins. A particularly strong interaction between the proteins may occur within the function represented by the two most similar GO terms, but this will be ignored in the averaging procedure. To take this effect into consideration, Cho et al. [67,70] computed the reliability of an interaction using the maximum similarity between cross pairs of those GO terms, which are associated with both interacting proteins. Through this means, the reliability of an interaction between two proteins can more accurately be represented by the semantic similarity value.

11.3.1 Structure-Based Methods

Structure-based approaches to the measurement of semantic similarity may be based on the concept of either path length or common parentage. The simplest path length-based similarity measurement is arrived at by counting the edges of the shortest path between two concepts in a taxonomy. Several methods have been suggested, which are based upon this process. Leacock et al. [193] scaled down the shortest path length by the maximum depth of the taxonomy and applied log smoothing. The structural similarity between two concepts may also be measured by counting the number of parent concepts in a taxonomy. Wu et al. [324] considered both path length and common parentage in identifying the structural relationship of two concepts C_1 and C_2 through a global view of the taxonomy. If C_0 is the most specific concept that subsumes both C_1 and C_2, the path lengths from the root concept to C_0, from C_0 to C_1, and from C_0 to C_2 are used for the calculation.

Structure-based methods can be used to estimate the reliability of PPIs. The process starts from the root GO term and moves down an edge created by annotating the child term with at least one of the interacting proteins x and y, selecting the most specific GO terms on each path. Suppose $T(x)$ is the set of the most specific GO terms that are annotated with x. The semantic similarity value of x and y is

$$S_{\text{path}}(x, y) = \frac{1}{\min_{i,j} \text{len}(t_i, t_j) + 1}, \tag{11.1}$$

where $t_i \in T(x)$, $t_j \in T(y)$ and $\text{len}(t_i, t_j)$ is the shortest path length between t_i and t_j. Normalization and log smoothing can be applied.

$$S_{\text{leacock}}(x, y) = -\log \left(\frac{\min_{i,j} \text{len}(t_i, t_j) + 1}{2 \times \text{depth}} \right), \tag{11.2}$$

where *depth* is the maximum path length from the root term to a leaf.

The common parentage of two terms t_i and t_j can be used to measure their similarity:

$$S_{\text{common}}(x, y) = \max_{i,j} \left(\frac{\mathcal{P}(t_i) \cap \mathcal{P}(t_j)}{\mathcal{P}(t_i) \cup \mathcal{P}(t_j)} \right), \tag{11.3}$$

where $\mathcal{P}(t_i)$ is the set of parent terms of t_i. Finally, by considering the path length from the root to the most specific common parent term,

$$S_{wu}(x, y) = \max_{i,j} \left(\frac{2 \cdot \text{len}(t_0, t_{ij})}{\text{len}(t_{ij}, t_i) + \text{len}(t_{ij}, t_j) + 2\text{len}(t_0, t_{ij})} \right), \tag{11.4}$$

is obtained, where t_{ij} is the most specific GO term that subsumes t_i and t_j, and t_0 is the root GO term.

Structure-based methods assume a conceptual similarity between all parent–child term pairs. However, this assumption is unlikely to be correct, as each term in the GO database is independently added and associated with gene products as needed. Therefore, the equality of the similarity values of parent–child term pairs in the GO structure cannot be guaranteed.

11.3.2 Information Content-Based Methods

In information theory, self-information is a measure of the information content associated with the outcome of a random variable. The amount of self information contained in a probabilistic event c depends on the probability $P(c)$ of that event. Events that are less probable will yield a greater amount of self-information if and when these events actually occur. The information content of a concept C in a taxonomy is then defined as the negative log likelihood of C, $-\log P(C)$.

The semantic similarity between two concepts can be measured based on the commonality of their information contents, in that two concepts that share more information are assumed to have greater similarity. Resnik [262] assessed the semantic similarity of the concepts C_1 and C_2 by the information content of the most specific concept C_0 that subsumes both C_1 and C_2. Lin [202] considered not only commonality but also the difference between two concepts by normalizing Resnik's similarity measure with the sum of the individual information content of C_1 and C_2. Jiang et al. [163] combined information content with path length and produced a similarity function, which finds the difference between the individual information content of C_1 and C_2 and the information content of the subsuming concept C_0.

The reliability of PPIs identified by information content-based approaches can be estimated by assessing the annotation size. The annotation size of a GO term t_i, defined as the number of proteins annotated to t_i, can represent its information content. The semantic similarity of the interacting proteins x and y can then be stated as

$$S_{\text{resnik}}(x, y) = -\log[\min_i P_i(x, y)], \tag{11.5}$$

where

$$P_i(x, y) = \frac{|G_i(x, y)|}{|G_0|}. \tag{11.6}$$

$G_i(x, y)$ is a set of proteins annotated to a GO term, which annotates both x and y, and G_0 is the set of proteins annotated to the root GO term. This similarity value can be normalized by incorporating the information content of individual terms. Suppose t_i annotates x and t_j annotates y.

$$S_{\text{lin}}(x, y) = \max_{i,j} \left[\frac{2 \cdot \log P_{ij}(x, y)}{\log P_i(x) + \log P_j(y)} \right], \tag{11.7}$$

where $P_i(x)$ is the proportional relationship between the annotation size of t_i and the maximum annotation size. $P_{ij}(x, y)$ is the proportion of the annotation size of the term subsuming t_i and t_j. Incorporating these terms, the semantic similarity value can be also described as

$$S_{\text{jiang}}(x, y) = \max_{i,j}[\log P_i(x) + \log P_j(y) - 2 \log P_{ij}(x, y)]. \tag{11.8}$$

The reliability of information content-based methods is compromised by the incompleteness of current GO annotations. Genes and proteins are annotated to GO terms as individual experimental results are published. Therefore, any current annotation of a protein cannot be considered to be inclusive of all possible GO terms.

11.3.3 Combination of Structure and Information Content

Hwang et al. [150] attempted to combine the information content-based and structure-based approaches to more accurately identify reliable interactions. This

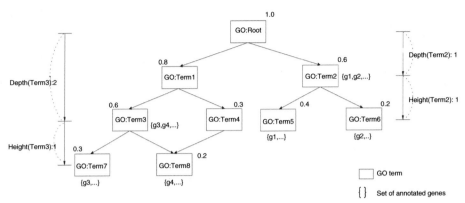

Figure 11–2 The GO structure with GO terms and their annotations. On the left side, the depth and the height of GO:Term3 are shown. On the right side, the depth and the height of GO:Term2 are shown. (Reprinted from [150] with permission of IEEE.)

combined approach defined the concepts of *cardinal specificity* and *structural specificity*. The cardinal specificity of a GO term t_i is the proportion of proteins annotated to t_i.

$$SP_{card}(t_i) = \frac{|T_i|}{|T_0|}, \tag{11.9}$$

where T_i is the set of proteins annotated to t_i and T_0 is the set of proteins annotated to the root term. Structural specificity was assessed on the basis of the depth and height of a term in the GO structure. The depth of t_i is the number of arcs on the shortest directed path to t_i from the root, and the height of t_i is the number of arcs of the shortest directed path from t_i to the farthest leaf node in the GO structure. Examples of this structure are illustrated in Figure 11–2. The structural specificity of t_i was then defined as

$$SP_{struc}(t_i) = \frac{height(t_i) + 1}{height(t_i) + depth(t_i) + 1}. \tag{11.10}$$

The total information content of t_i was described as the sum of the information content with respect to the cardinal specificity of t_i and the structural specificity of t_i.

$$INF(t_i) = -\log(SP_{card}(t_i)) - \log(SP_{struc}(t_i)). \tag{11.11}$$

Finally, the similarity between two proteins x and y was calculated based on the semantic similarity concept normalized by the information content of individual terms, similar to Equation (11.7).

$$S_{hwang}(x, y) = \frac{2 \cdot INF(t_{x,y})}{INF(t_x) + INF(t_y)}, \tag{11.12}$$

where t_x is the most specific GO term, which annotates x, t_y is the most specific GO term, which annotates y, and $t_{x,y}$ is the most common specific GO term, which annotates both x and y.

11.4 SEMANTIC INTERACTIVITY-BASED INTEGRATION

Analysis of a PPI network can be significantly advanced by an understanding of the interaction pattern, or connectivity, of each protein in the network. The interactivity T of a protein x with a set of proteins S_t annotated to a GO term t is defined as

$$T(x, S_t) = \frac{|S_t \cap N(x)|}{|N(x)|}, \tag{11.13}$$

where $N(x)$ is the set of neighbors of x in a PPI network. The semantic interactivity of x with S_t is then the probability that a neighbor of x will be included in S_t, or, alternatively, the probability of x interacting with the proteins in S_t. Considering the functional relatedness of a pair of interacting proteins, $N(x)$ in Equation (11.13) can be replaced with $N(x) \cup \{x\}$.

Cho et al. [68] used the concept of *semantic interactivity* to integrate GO data into a PPI network. Suppose protein x is annotated to GO term t_i and protein y is annotated to GO term t_j. If a large proportion of the interacting partners of x appear in the annotation of t_j and a large proportion of the interacting partners of y appear in the annotation of t_i, then x and y are likely to interact. If x and y are annotated to the same GO term t_i, then the reliability of their interaction increases when more interacting partners of x and y are included in the annotation of t_i.

Suppose $S(x)$ and $S(y)$ are the sets of proteins annotated to those GO terms which are annotated to x and y, respectively. The semantic interactivity T_{sem} of x with the proteins in $S(y)$ is then calculated by

$$T_{\text{sem}}(x, S(y)) = \frac{\max_i |S_i(y) \cap N'(x)|}{|N'(x)|}, \tag{11.14}$$

where $N'(x) = N(x) \cup \{x\}$. Since y can be annotated to k different GO terms, we select the maximum set of $S_i(y) \cap N'(x)$ out of k possible sets. If x and all its neighbors are not included in $S_i(y)$ for any i, then $T_{\text{sem}}(x, S(y))$ is 0. If x and all its neighbors are included in a set $S_i(y)$, then $T_{\text{sem}}(x, S(y))$ is 1. Equation (11.14) thus satisfies the range of $0 \leq P(x, y) \leq 1$. The reliability of the interaction between x and y can be measured by the geometric mean of $T_{\text{sem}}(x, S(y))$ and $T_{\text{sem}}(y, S(x))$.

$$\text{Rel}(x, y) = \sqrt{T_{\text{sem}}(x, S(y)) \times T_{\text{sem}}(y, S(x))}. \tag{11.15}$$

11.5 ESTIMATE OF INTERACTION RELIABILITY

The reliability of interactions predicted by semantic similarity and semantic inter-activity were compared using the core interaction data for *S. cerevisiae* from DIP, the database of interacting proteins [271]. The core data includes 2,526 distinct proteins and 5,949 interactions. The core interactions were selected from the full data set by examination of biological information such as protein sequences and RNA expression profiles [82].

The 2006 version of the GO database [301] contains a total of 21,617 GO terms across three general categories: biological processes, molecular functions, and cellular components. It includes a total of 31,890 annotations for *S. cerevisiae*.

Structure-based semantic similarity was calculated on the basis of the GO terms relating to biological process. Information content-based semantic similarity was derived using GO terms from all three categories. Semantic interactivity was assessed by filtering out excessively specific GO terms, defined as those with fewer than 50 annotated proteins, and using only the terminal GO terms, which were also the leaf nodes in the GO structure. Of these, 129 terminal GO terms with an average annotation size of 73.89 were extracted.

11.5.1 Functional Co-occurrence

The reliability of interactions measured by semantic similarity and semantic interactivity was assessed by ascertaining whether the members of each interacting pair were also annotated to the same functional category in the MIPS database [214]. The interactions were assigned reliability values on a scale from 0 to 1 and were divided into deciles on that basis.

Figure 11–3(a) presents the functional co-occurrence patterns of interacting protein pairs with respect to interaction reliability as measured by structure-based methods. For the edge-counting method, ~40% of interacting protein pairs were co-annotated with GO terms and were thus assigned the maximum reliability value. Seven percent of interacting protein pairs had a one-edge interval between the most specific GO terms annotated with each interacting protein; these pairs had a reliability value of 0.5. As a result, the correlation of reliability with functional co-occurrence was left-shifted. Leacock's similarity measure scaled up the values from the edge-counting method. However, in the reliability range below 0.3, there was no positive correlation between reliability and functional co-occurrence, and there were no interacting pairs with a reliability value below 0.1. Wu's similarity measure performed better than either the edge-counting method or Leacock's method, exhibiting a positive correlation across the full range of reliability values.

Figure 11–3(b) presents the functional co-occurrence patterns of interacting protein pairs with respect to interaction reliability as measured by information content-based methods. Resnik's similarity measure typically under-scored interacting pairs with high reliability values. Using this method, 5% of interacting pairs had reliability values over 0.9, 10% had values from 0.8 to 0.9, and the reliability values of 14% were between 0.7 and 0.8. With the other methods, more than 30% of interacting pairs had reliability values above 0.9. Therefore, interacting pairs with a reliability score above 0.7 by Resnik's measure exhibited no variability in functional co-occurrence. Use of Lin's similarity measure enhanced Resnik's method and resulted in a positive correlation across the full range of reliability values. Using Jiang's similarity measure, 60% of interacting pairs had scores over 0.9. Interestingly, this approach also assigned a reliability score of less than 0.1 to a small number of interacting pairs with relatively high functional co-occurrence rates.

Figure 11–3(c) presents the functional co-occurrence patterns of interacting protein pairs with respect to interaction reliability as measured by their semantic interactivity. These interaction reliability values demonstrated a strong positive correlation with functional co-occurrence. This result indicates that the functional association between two proteins can be better measured by semantic interactivity than by semantic similarity.

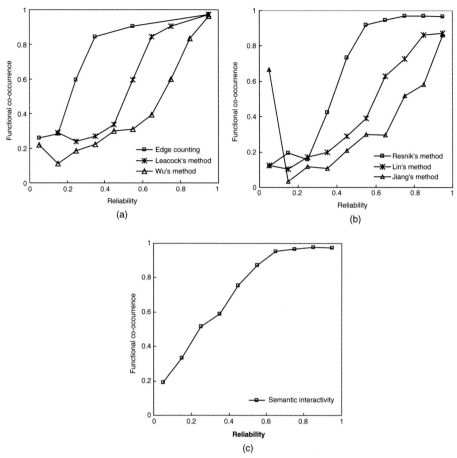

Figure 11–3 Functional co-occurrence patterns of interacting protein pairs with respect to their interaction reliability. Reliability was measured by (a) structure-based semantic similarity, (b) information content-based semantic similarity, and (c) semantic interactivity. (Reprinted from [67] with permission of IEEE.)

11.5.2 Topological Significance

The reliability of interactions can be verified by the interaction properties of the network. A mutual clustering coefficient [125] is a measure of the neighborhood cohesiveness around an edge in a graph. The various measurements of interaction reliability were compared using the Jaccard index as the mutual clustering coefficient. This value indicates the number of common neighbors of interacting proteins as compared to the number of all distinct neighbors. Three reliability measurements that demonstrated good functional co-occurrence were selected for analysis, with each again representing one of the three general methods previously described. The indices chosen were Wu's semantic similarity measure, Lin's semantic similarity measure, and semantic interactivity. As with the previous analysis, the interactions were divided into ten groups according to their reliability values, and the average mutual clustering coefficient for each group was calculated.

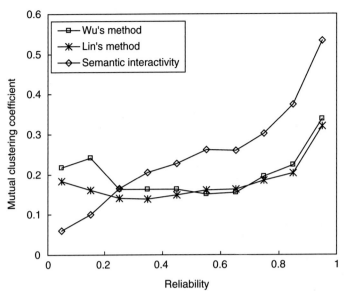

Figure 11–4 Relationship between interaction reliability and the mutual clustering coefficients of interacting proteins. Reliability was measured by structure-based semantic similarity (Wu's method), information content-based semantic similarity (Lin's method), and semantic interactivity. (Reprinted from [67] with permission of IEEE.)

Figure 11–4 illustrates the relationship between interaction reliability and the mutual clustering coefficients of interacting proteins. The plots generated by Wu's and Lin's methods do not show positive correlations. Low-reliability interacting pairs with values under 0.3 had relatively high mutual clustering coefficients. The best results were produced by the semantic interactivity index, which generated reliability values that correlated strongly to the mutual clustering coefficients.

11.5.3 Protein Lethality

The degree of a node can be weighted by summing the weights of the connections to its neighbors in a weighted network. In this case, the weighted interaction network was constructed by assigning each interaction a weight based on its reliability value. Nodes with high weighted degrees in the weighted network represent proteins that interact with many other proteins. Weighted degrees can thus be used to quantify the biological significance of proteins in a PPI network.

This method of identifying biologically significant proteins was used to evaluate the interaction reliability measurements previously discussed. Information from the MIPS database [214] regarding protein lethality was used to indicate the biological essentiality of a protein. Lethality is determined by monitoring the extent of functional disruption within a module when the protein in question is eliminated. Proteins were arranged in a descending order of the weighted degree as measured by Wu's semantic similarity, Lin's semantic similarity, and semantic interactivity. For each case, the cumulative proportion of lethal proteins was consecutively calculated. Figure 11–5 shows the change in lethality when the number of selected proteins is

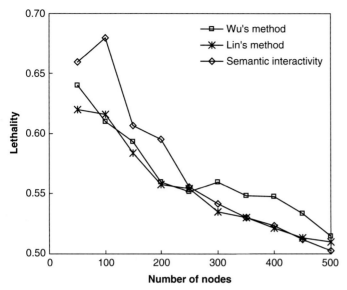

Figure 11–5 Lethality with respect to the cumulative number of proteins ordered by weighted degree. The weight of each edge was measured by structure-based semantic similarity (Wu's method), information content-based semantic similarity (Lin's method), and semantic interactivity. (Reprinted from [67] with permission of IEEE.)

increased. When up to 250 proteins from the highest weighted degree were selected, the semantic interactivity index identified more lethal proteins than the other measurements. This result indicates that biologically essential proteins were correctly selected when semantic interactivity was used as the reliability measure.

11.6 FUNCTIONAL MODULE DETECTION

The reliability of each PPI measured by the semantic interactivity value established in Equation (11.15) can be assigned to the corresponding edge as a weight to build a weighted interaction network. The interactivity measure is produced by integrating evidence of interactions with the functional categories established in the GO database. Using this information to create a weighted interaction network permits more accurate detection of functional modules. Cho et al. [70] used the flow-based method discussed in Chapter 9 to identify functional modules in the weighted interaction network. The performance of this approach was assessed in comparison with that of techniques representing several other approaches.

11.6.1 Statistical Assessment

To test the detection of functional modules, the core *S. cerevisiae* interaction data set from the DIP [271] was used; this data included 2,526 distinct proteins and 5,949 interactions. GO terms with fewer than 50 annotated proteins were removed from the database, and only the terminal GO terms were then selected. The flow-based functional module detection algorithm was applied to the interaction network weighted by semantic interactivity.

Table 11.2 Accuracy of output modules generated by flow-based module detection methods

Weighting scheme	Identified modules before post-processing		Identified modules after post-processing	
	$-\log(p)$	f-measure	$-\log(p)$	f-measure
Semantic similarity	24.10	0.334	24.42	0.337
Semantic interactivity	28.58	0.339	29.05	0.401

The interaction network weighted by semantic interactivity and semantic similarity was taken as the input.

Table 11.3 Performance comparison of modularization methods

Method	Number of modules	Average size of modules	$-\log(p)$	Parameters
Flow-based	189	40.40	29.05	Min flow $= 0.1$
CFinder	57	17.86	12.32	$k = 3$
Betweenness cut	57	41.02	17.44	Max density $= 0.03$

The output modules were generated by the flow-based, CFinder, and betweenness cut. The input was the core protein interaction network from DIP. For the flow-based method, the input network was weighted by semantic interactivity. The performance was statistically evaluated by p-value.

A statistical assessment of the identified functional modules was made using the p-value in Equation (5.20). The set of proteins annotated to each MIPS functional category [214] served as a reference functional module. Each identified module was mapped to a reference functional module, and the negative logarithm of p-value was taken as the accuracy of the identified modules.

Table 11.2 presents the average $-\log(p)$ values of the output modules generated with the two weighting schemes: semantic similarity and semantic interactivity. This table indicates that semantic interactivity resulted in more accurate module detection than semantic similarity. The accuracy of modules generated by the two GO-based weighting methods was further improved through postprocessing to merge similar modules. The postprocessing step appears to be a necessary adjunct to flow-based modularization, because two or more informative proteins having the same function are likely to generate the modules that share many common proteins.

Three competing methods were compared for their accuracy in detecting functional modules. These methods were the CFinder algorithm [238] as a representative of density-based approaches, the betweenness cut algorithm [94,122] as a representative hierarchical approach, and the flow-based algorithm. Table 11.3 presents the parameter values and the results of the output modules for each method. The CFinder algorithm is based on a clique percolation method. Although it was able to identify overlapping modules, it also detected numerous small modules and a few disproportionately large modules. As a result, the average accuracy of CFinder was lower than the other methods. The betweenness cut algorithm iteratively disconnects the edges

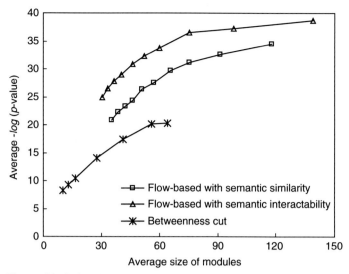

Figure 11–6 Statistical significance of the identified modules with respect to their average size. The functional modules were identified by the flow-based algorithm using semantic similarity and semantic interactivity weighting schemes and the betweenness cut algorithm. (Reprinted from [70].)

with the highest betweenness value and recursively implements the cutting process in each sub-network. Most of the sparsely-connected nodes were included in the output modules. However, because the output modules were disjoint, the betweenness cut algorithm had a lower accuracy than the flow-based method. These results indicate that the flow-based algorithm with a weighted interaction network outperforms other methods in terms of the accuracy of functional module identification.

The p-value is highly dependent on module size. Figure 11–6 shows the pattern of the average $-\log(p)$ across different sets of output modules produced by varying the parameter values for the number of informative proteins and the minimum flow threshold. Although the average value of $-\log(p)$ increased with increases in average module size, it converged to ~ 34 and ~ 39 with input networks weighted by semantic similarity and semantic interactivity, respectively. In a similar analysis, the average $-\log(p)$ of the output modules generated by the betweenness cut algorithm converged to 20, as shown in Figure 11–6. These results indicate that the flow-based modularization algorithm identified more accurate functional modules across different output sets than the betweenness cut algorithm. Furthermore, it is evident that the integration of functional information, such as GO annotations, is necessary for accurate analysis of PPI networks.

11.6.2 Supervised Validation

The identified modules were compared with reference functions by means of a supervised method. As defined in Equation (5.17), recall measures the tendency of the reference function to match the identified module. Precision, as formulated in Equation (5.18), represents the accuracy of the identified module in matching the

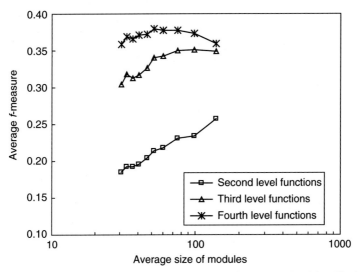

Figure 11–7 The average *f*-measure value of the modules identified by the flow-based method with respect to their average size. The output modules were compared to the annotations on the second-, third-, and fourth-level categories in the MIPS functional hierarchy. (Reprinted from [70].)

reference function. The *f*-measure in Equation (5.19) is calculated using the recall and precision. The average *f*-measure of all modules was calculated by mapping each module to the function with the highest *f*-measure.

The average *f*-measures of the identified modules generated by the flow-based method before and after postprocessing are shown in Table 11.2. As with the results from the statistical assessment using the *p*-value, postprocessing slightly improved the accuracy of modules produced using the two interaction reliability indices. The semantic interactivity value generated better accuracy in modularization than the semantic similarity measure.

The ability of the flow-based algorithm to identify sets of modules on different levels in a functional hierarchy was tested. Ten different output sets generated by the flow-based method with different parameter values were compared to the annotations on the second, third, and fourth levels of the MIPS functional hierarchy [267]. As shown in Figure 11–7, comparison of identified modules to the specific functions on the fourth hierarchical level produced the highest *f*-measures. In contrast, comparison of the modules with the second-level functions, which are general and are associated with many proteins, revealed the largest number of mismatches. An examination of Figure 11–7 indicates that the comparison of identified modules to each functional level produced distinctly dissimilar patterns of accuracy across different output sets. For the second-level functions, those modules with an average size of greater than 100 have the highest accuracy. For the third-level functions, those modules with an average size between 70 and 100 have the highest accuracy. Fourth-level functions compared most accurately to modules with an average size in the range between 40 and 50. These results suggest the possibility of building a hierarchy with the identified modules.

Table 11.4 An example of GO indices

GO Index	Ontological (Functional) description	GO id
9	Cell growth and/or maintenance	GO:0008151
9–25	Cell organization and biogenesis	GO:0016043
9–25–26	Cytoplasm organization and biogenesis	GO:0007028
9–25–26–27	Organelle organization and biogenesis	GO:0006996
9–25–26–38	Ribosome biogenesis and assembly	GO:0042254
9–25–26–38–40	Ribosome biogenesis	GO:0007046
9–25–26–38–40–41	rRNA processing	GO:0006364
9–57	Metabolism	GO:0008152
9–57–89	Nucleobase, ... and nucleic acid metabolism	GO:0006139
9–57–89–96	RNA metabolism	GO:0016070
9–57–89–96–98	RNA processing	GO:0006396
9–57–89–96–98–41	rRNA processing	GO:0006364
9–57–89–102	Transcription	GO:0006350
9–57–89–102–106	Transcription, DNA-dependent	GO:0006351
9–57–89–102–106–107	Transcription from Pol I promoter	GO:0006360
9–57–89–102–106–107–41	rRNA processing	GO:0006364

The GO index provides a hierarchical description of the functions of a protein in the GO structure.

11.7 PROBABILISTIC APPROACHES FOR FUNCTION PREDICTION

11.7.1 GO Index-Based Probabilistic Method

As previously mentioned, the prediction of protein function can be rendered more accurate by the integration of multiple data sources. Toward this end, Chen and Xu [64] proposed a Bayesian probabilistic model that draws upon diverse data sources, with data from each source weighted according to its conditional probability. This approach has the potential of reducing the level of noise in high-throughput data and providing a rich informational context for accurate functional analysis of proteins.

11.7.1.1 Bayesian Probabilistic Model

Chen and Xu's method starts by quantifying the functional similarity between proteins on the basis of the GO index. The GO index represents a sequence of functions assigned to a protein in the GO structure. These functions are encoded by numbers ranked in the hierarchical order staring from the root term in the GO structure. Table 11.4 provides a sample list of GO indices and the corresponding ontological descriptions. Since there are several possible alternative paths between the root term and each GO term, each function can be described with several different GO indices. For example, in Table 11.4, the function "rRNA processing" has three different descriptors: "9–25–26–38–40–41," "9–57–89–96–98–41," and "9–57–89–102–106–107–41."

The functional similarity between two proteins is then expressed as the highest-level function shared by the proteins, in terms of the hierarchical structure of GO indices. For example, suppose a protein p is annotated to the function "RNA metabolism," and a protein q is annotated to the function "RNA processing." The GO indices for p and q are "9–57–89–96" and "9–57–89–96–98," respectively, and the GO index describing the maximum sequence of functions shared by p and q is "9–57–89–96." The functional similarity of p and q is thus 4.

For each binary interaction B, the probability that two interacting proteins will have the same function $P(S|B)$ is computed using the Bayesian formula:

$$P(S|B) = \frac{P(B|S)\, P(S)}{P(B)}, \tag{11.16}$$

where S represents the event that two proteins have the same function at a given GO index level. Thus, $P(S)$ is the prior probability of the proteins having the same function at that level by chance. $P(B|S)$ is the conditional probability of two proteins interacting with each other, given the knowledge that they share the same function. $P(B)$ is the relative frequency of pairs of interacting proteins over all possible pairs in the interaction data set. The integration of multiple data sources can be accomplished in the same manner. For example, for each pair of proteins with correlated gene expression R, and which are members of the same protein complex C, the posterior probability $P(S|R)$ and $P(S|C)$ can be calculated.

Figure 11–8 shows the pattern of functional co-occurrence of interacting proteins with respect to their functional similarity. The probabilities of a pair of interacting proteins sharing functions at the same level of the GO index was normalized by the probabilities of random pairs. Again, the functional similarity of a pair represents the maximum GO index level of the most specific function they share. Interacting proteins sharing more specific functions clearly have a higher posterior probability of functional co-occurrence.

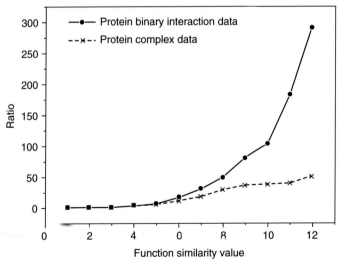

Figure 11–8 The probabilities of a pair of interacting proteins sharing functions in the same GO index level, normalized by the probabilities of random pairs. The functional similarity of a pair represents the maximum GO index level of the most specific function they share. (Reprinted from [64] with permission from Oxford University Press.)

11.7.1.2 Local Prediction of Function

The local prediction of function of an unknown protein by the probabilistic approach assumes that the probability of interacting proteins sharing functions depends on the high-throughput data source of the interactions. The probability that the common functions of the annotated interacting partners can be accurately assigned to the unknown protein is calculated by Equation (11.16). This method is based on the assumption that the events predicting functions of an unknown protein from different high-throughput data sources or different interaction partners are independent.

Suppose an unknown protein x interacts with proteins a, b, and c, and F is a set of functions associated with a, b, and c. The likelihood that function f_l in F will be assigned to x is defined as

$$G(f_l, x) = 1 - (1 - P'(S_l|B)) \times (1 - P'(S_l|C)) \times (1 - P'(S_l|R)), \qquad (11.17)$$

where S_l represents the event that the functions of two proteins have the same GO index level as f_l. $P'(S_l|B)$ is the probability of a pair of interacting proteins having the same function at a given GO index level. $P'(S_l|C)$ and $P'(S_l|R)$ are, respectively, the protein complex membership and the co-expression of a pair of correlated proteins. Since x interacts with one or more annotated protein(s), $P'(S_l|B)$, $P'(S_l|C)$, and $P'(S_l|R)$ in Equation (11.17) can be stated as

$$P'(S_l|B) = 1 - \prod_{i=1}^{n_B}[1 - P_i(S_l|B)], \qquad (11.18)$$

$$P'(S_l|C) = 1 - \prod_{i=1}^{n_C}[1 - P_i(S_l|C)], \qquad (11.19)$$

$$P'(S_l|R) = 1 - \prod_{i=1}^{n_R}[1 - P_i(S_l|R)], \qquad (11.20)$$

where n_B is the number of interaction partners of x, n_C is the number of members in the same protein complex as x, and n_R is the number of co-expressed genes of x. The co-expressed genes were selected based on the microarray gene expression, using a Pearson correlation coefficient r greater than or equal to 0.7. The final prediction results can be sorted for each GO index level by the likelihood score in Equation (11.17).

11.7.1.3 Global Prediction of Function

The information used to predict protein function on a local level is limited to that available from the immediate neighbors of the protein in question. Therefore, local prediction methods cannot predict the functions of an unknown protein if it does not have any annotated interacting partners. In addition, these methods may not be able to incorporate the global properties of PPI networks. In order to raise prediction to a more global level, Chen et al. [64] used the Boltzmann machine to characterize the global stochastic behaviors of a network.

The Boltzmann machine considered a physical system with a set of states α, each of which has energy H_α. In thermal equilibrium, given a temperature T, each possible state α occurs with the probability P_α:

$$P_\alpha = \frac{1}{R} e^{-H_\alpha/K_B T}, \tag{11.21}$$

where the normalizing factor $R = \sum_\alpha e^{-H_\alpha/K_B T}$, and K_B is Boltzmann's constant. In an undirected graph model with binary-valued nodes, each node i has one state value Z, which will be either 0 or 1. In this case, $Z = 1$ means that the corresponding protein has functions that are either known or predicted. The system then goes through a dynamic process from nonequilibrium to equilibrium, which corresponds to the optimization process for the prediction of function. For the state of a node i at time t, the probability of $Z_{t,i}$ being 1, given the inputs from the other nodes at time $t-1$, is

$$P(Z_{t,i} = 1 | Z_{t-1,j \neq i}) = \frac{1}{1 + e^{-\beta \sum_{j \neq i} W_{ij} Z_{t-1,j \neq i}}}, \tag{11.22}$$

where β is a parameter reversely proportional to the annealing temperature, and W_{ij} is the weight of the interaction between i and j. W_{ij} is then calculated by

$$W_{ij} = \delta_j \sum_{k=1}^{12} [1 - (1 - P(S_k|B)) \times (1 - P(S_k|C)) \times (1 - P(S_k|R))], \tag{11.23}$$

where S_k represents the event that two proteins i and j will have the same function at each GO index level k, and 12 is the maximum GO index level. δ_j is a modifying weight:

$$\delta_j = \begin{cases} 1, & \text{if } j \in \text{annotated proteins}, \\ P(Z_{t-1,j} = 1), & \text{otherwise}. \end{cases} \tag{11.24}$$

Figure 11–9 provides a flow chart illustrating the global prediction process.

11.7.1.4 Performance Evaluation

The performance of three versions of the probabilistic approach to protein function prediction was evaluated: local prediction with and without the integration of information pertaining to evolution and localization, and global prediction with the integration of such information. Performance was evaluated using a 10-fold cross-validation. A total of 4,044 annotated proteins in *S. cerevisiae* with known GO indices were labeled into folds 1–10. In each run, one fold was selected as a test data set, and the others were used as training sets. The prior probabilities were calculated in the training sets and applied for function prediction in the test set.

The performance of these three approaches was compared using the measures of specificity (or precision) in Equation (10.14) [or Equation (5.22)] and sensitivity (or recall) in Equation (10.15) [or Equation (5.21)]. Figure 11–10 compares the performance of the three cases using the relationships of specificity and sensitivity. Inclusion of information regarding evolution and localization improved the accuracy of local prediction, and the global prediction approach was superior to local prediction.

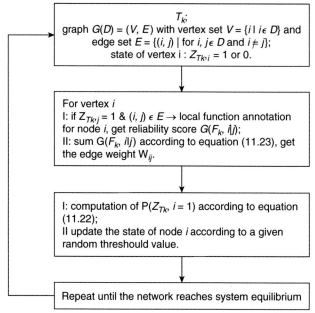

Figure 11–9 Flow chart of the dynamic process for global protein function prediction. (Reprinted from [64] with permission from Oxford University Press.)

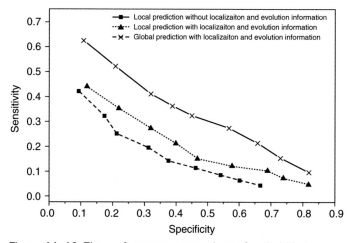

Figure 11–10 The performance comparison of probabilistic approaches for function prediction by specificity-sensitivity (or precision-recall) relationships. (Reprinted from [64] with permission from Oxford University Press.)

11.7.2 Semantic Similarity-Based Probabilistic Method

Protein function prediction via statistical methods using Bayesian networks was discussed in detail in Chapter 10. These methods focus on the common neighbors of unknown proteins for function prediction. The same Bayesian probabilistic method can be used to predict function based on measures of semantic similarity. The integration of semantic similarity and GO information allows this approach to efficiently handle the high rate of false positives in current PPI data and to accurately predict the function of unknown proteins (Some of the materials in this section are from [71]).

11.7.2.1 Bayesian Probabilistic Model

This approach predicts multiple functions for any protein that is functionally uncharacterized but for which there is evidence of interactions. The method employs the Bayesian formula and measures the reliability of interactions in terms of semantic similarity, as discussed in Section 11.3. Assume that a PPI data set contains a set of n distinct proteins $\mathcal{P} = \{p_1, \ldots, p_n\}$. In $\mathcal{P}$, $p_1, \ldots, p_k$ $(k < n)$ are functionally annotated, and $p_{k+1}, \ldots, p_n$ are unannotated. For an unannotated protein p_i, where $k < i \leq n$, let $\mathcal{P}_f = \{p_{f_1}, \ldots, p_{f_m}\}$ be the set of proteins annotated to a function f, and $R_{f_1}, \ldots, R_{f_m}$ be the reliability of the interactions between p_i and p_{f_j}, where $1 \leq j \leq m$, and the reliability is stated as a percentage. If there is no evidence of interaction between p_i and p_{f_j}, then R_{f_j} is 0. According to the Bayes theorem, the conditional probability that p_i will have function f, given $R_{f_1}, \ldots, R_{f_m}$, is defined as

$$P(f = 1 | R_{f_1}, \ldots, R_{f_m}) = \frac{P(R_{f_1}, \ldots, R_{f_m} | f = 1) P(f = 1)}{P(R_{f_1}, \ldots, R_{f_m})}, \tag{11.25}$$

where $P(f = 1)$ is the prior probability that p_i will have function f, $P(R_{f_1}, \ldots, R_{f_m})$ is the probability that p_i will interact with $p_{f_1}, \ldots, p_{f_m}$ with reliability $R_{f_1}, \ldots, R_{f_m}$, and $P(R_{f_1}, \ldots, R_{f_m} | f = 1)$ is the conditional probability that p_i will interact with $p_{f_1}, \ldots, p_{f_m}$ with reliability $R_{f_1}, \ldots, R_{f_m}$, given that p_i has function f. Based on the assumption that the events of the interactions between p_i and $p_{f_1}, \ldots, p_{f_m}$ occur independently,

$$P(R_{f_1}, \ldots, R_{f_m} | f = 1) = \prod_{j=1}^{m} P(R_{f_j} | f = 1). \tag{11.26}$$

Equation (11.25) is then transformed into

$$P(f = 1 | R_{f_1}, \ldots, R_{f_m})$$
$$= \frac{\prod_{j=1}^{m} P(R_{f_j} | f = 1) P(f = 1)}{\prod_{j=1}^{m} P(R_{f_j} | f = 1) P(f = 1) + \prod_{j=1}^{m} P(R_{f_j} | f = 0) P(f = 0)}, \tag{11.27}$$

where $P(f = 0)$ is the probability that p_i will not have function f.

Let M_f be the maximum reliability value stated as a percentage; that is, 100%. The threshold reliability value indicating that p_i and p_{f_j} will share function f is $R_f = M_f - R_{f_j}$. We assume that $P(R_{f_j} | f = 1)$ follows a binomial distribution:

$$P(R_{f_j} | f = 1) = \binom{M_f}{R_f} P_f^{R_f} (1 - P_f)^{M_f - R_f}, \tag{11.28}$$

where P_f is the probability that two proteins will share function f. We can approximate the binomial distribution to a normal distribution with a mean μ and variance σ^2.

$$P(R_{f_j}|f = 1) = \frac{1}{\sqrt{2\pi}\,\sigma_{f+}} e^{-(R_{f_j} - \mu_{f+})^2 / \sigma_{f+}^2}. \tag{11.29}$$

In the same manner,

$$P(R_{f_j}|f = 0) = \frac{1}{\sqrt{2\pi}\,\sigma_{f-}} e^{-(R_{f_j} - \mu_{f-})^2 / \sigma_{f-}^2}. \tag{11.30}$$

Equation (11.27) can be re-written as

$$P(f = 1|R_{f_1}, \ldots, R_{f_m}) = \frac{\lambda_f}{\lambda_f + 1}, \tag{11.31}$$

where

$$\lambda_f = \frac{\sigma_{f-}^m}{\sigma_{f+}^m} \cdot e^{-\sum_{j=1}^m \left(\frac{(R_{f_j} - \mu_{f+})^2}{\sigma_{f+}^2} - \frac{(R_{f_j} - \mu_{f-})^2}{\sigma_{f-}^2} \right)} \cdot \frac{P(f = 1)}{P(f = 0)}. \tag{11.32}$$

μ_{f+} and σ_{f+}^2 are calculated by the reliability values of the interactions between p_i and the proteins annotated to f. Similarly, μ_{f-} and σ_{f-}^2 are calculated by the reliability values of the interactions between p_i and the proteins that are not in the annotation of f. As an alternative to Equation (11.31), $\log(\lambda_f)$ can be computed as the prediction confidence that p_i will be associated with function f.

11.7.2.2 Cross-validation of Function Prediction

The performance of this approach to function prediction was assessed by the leave-one-out cross-validation method, as discussed in Chapter 5. Each annotated protein was assumed to be unannotated, and its functions were predicted using the semantic similarity-based probabilistic approach. Prediction performance was evaluated using the measures of precision in Equation (5.22) and recall in Equation (5.21).

Figure 11–11 plots precision and recall with respect to the threshold of prediction confidence, which is a user-dependent parameter in this algorithm. When this threshold is set at 200, the algorithm predicts no or a very few functions for each protein, but most of the predicted functions are correct when checked against the actual annotations, giving a precision of greater than 0.9. When a lower threshold is used, recall increases, and precision decreases monotonically. Recall values of 0.2 and 0.4 are associated with precision values of ~0.8 and ~0.5, respectively.

11.7.2.3 Comparison of Prediction Performance

The performance of the semantic similarity-based approach to function prediction was compared with that of two competing methods: an approach weighting the functional similarity (FS) of direct and indirect (level-2 neighborhood) neighbors [72]

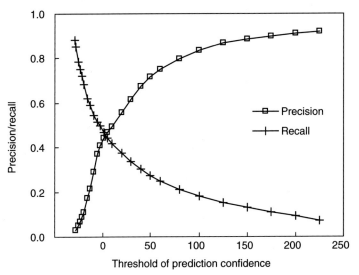

Figure 11–11 The performance of the semantic similarity-based function prediction approach was assessed by leave-one-out cross-validation using proteins that appear in the DIP interaction data and are annotated to MIPS functional categories. As a higher threshold of prediction confidence is used, precision increases and recall decreases.

and a prediction method based on the annotation patterns in the neighborhood [181]. The first of these competing methods computes the likelihood that an unknown protein p will have a given function using the functional similarity weights between p and level-1 or -2 neighbors. The functional similarity weight of two proteins is calculated by the commonality of their neighbors in the PPI network. A threshold value was established for the likelihood of arriving at the output set of predicted functions for each protein. A range of output sets resulted from the application of various thresholds, and these sets increased in size with lower thresholds. The second competing method constructs a set of annotation neighborhood patterns for each function and computes the similarity between the annotation neighborhood patterns of an unknown protein and each function. In this test, the MIPS functional category annotations were used as the ground truth, parameter d was set at 1, and all edge weights were removed and assigned a value of 1. The similarity of annotation neighborhood patterns was used as a threshold. Since the same interaction data from the DIP was used as input for all three tested methods, the reliability of the data source was not a variable.

Figure 11–12 illustrates the precision and recall relationships resulting from application of the three methods. The semantic similarity-based probabilistic approach significantly outperforms the annotation pattern-based method. Because the pattern-based method did not distinguish between general and specific functions, it could not predict general functions with higher confidence than specific functions. Thus, even though it precisely predicted the specific functions, the overall accuracy of the pattern-based method was much lower than that of the other methods. It also resulted in higher precision than the FS weighted method at recall levels over 0.07. At recall

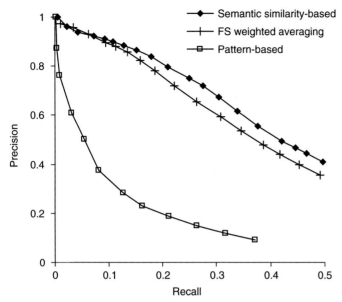

Figure 11–12 Prediction performance assessed via precision-recall for the semantic similarity-based probabilistic approach, the FS weighted averaging method and the annotation pattern-based method. Each method predicted functions with various thresholds of prediction confidence. The semantic similarity-based probabilistic approach outperformed the annotation pattern-based based method and had a higher precision than the FS weighted averaging method when recall levels were greater than 0.07.

values greater than 0.2, the precision of the semantic similarity-based probabilistic approach was more than 0.05 points higher than the FS weighted method. This result indicates that integration of protein interaction data with the GO annotations significantly improves the accuracy of function prediction. Because the other two methods represent interaction connections in a binary manner, they cannot overcome the presence of functionally false positive interactions in the currently available data, although the FS weighted method may partly address the presence of false negatives.

In the above experiment, the function prediction algorithms were implemented using a preset threshold of prediction confidence. Prediction results were not generated for proteins that had low rates of prediction confidence for any function. To make a comprehensive comparison of the prediction accuracy for all proteins, Cho et al. [71] implemented the algorithms a second time using a threshold δ for the number of predicted functions. That is, for each protein, the δ best predicted functions were generated. In addition, the previous experiment used all the functions in the MIPS hierarchical structure. However, predicting very general functions is meaningless when a small number of functions are predicted for each protein. This second evaluation was confined to the functional categories and accompanying annotations from the third level of the functional hierarchy. Prediction accuracy was again evaluated on the basis of precision in Equation (5.22). However, those proteins with fewer than δ actual annotated MIPS functions were assessed using the number of annotated functions, M_i, rather the number of predicted functions,

Table 11.5 The prediction accuracy (precision) of the semantic similarity-based probabilistic approach was compared to three competing methods: the FS weighted averaging method, the chi-square based method, and the neighbor-counting method. δ represents the number of functions predicted for each protein

δ	1	2	3	4	5	6
Semantic similarity based	0.446	0.432	0.434	0.451	0.472	0.490
FS weighted averaging	0.417	0.406	0.415	0.437	0.458	0.479
Annotation pattern-based	0.306	0.311	0.321	0.340	0.362	0.386
Neighborhood-based chi-square	0.294	0.302	0.318	0.343	0.370	0.398

N_i (equivalent to δ). Table 11.5 compares the prediction accuracies of the semantic similarity-based probabilistic approach, the FS weighted averaging method [72], the annotation pattern-based method [181], and the neighborhood-based chi-square method [143]. The semantic similarity-based probabilistic approach outperformed the others at all δ values up to 6. This approach predicted the specific functions of any protein with higher accuracy than the other methods evaluated.

11.7.2.4 Function Prediction of Unknown Proteins

The most recent version of the MIPS functional annotations indicates that a significant number of proteins in *S. cerevisiae* are still uncharacterized. Cho et al. [71] employed the semantic similarity-based probabilistic approach to generate predictions of their functions. Predictions were made only for those unknown proteins with more than three interacting partners in the DIP to avoid the effect of false positive interactions. For each selected protein, the algorithm generated a list of functions with prediction confidence values of $\log(\lambda_f)$, where λ_f is calculated by Equation (11.32). A protein can thus correspond to more than one predicted function at different confidence rates. Table 11.6 lists predicted functions produced with the threshold of prediction confidence set at 32 and the elimination of excessively general functions from the top- or second-level MIPS hierarchical categories. The functions of proteins YJL058C and YGR163W were predicted with a high level of confidence, greater than 100. These results suggest new functional annotations for currently unknown proteins.

11.7.2.5 Prediction of Subcellular Localization

The probabilistic framework can be also applied to the prediction of subcellular localization. This application adopted the same method and parameters as process of function prediction, other than the terms used for calculation of semantic similarity and interaction reliability. Semantic similarity was measured using terms from the cellular component category in the GO database. A total of 556 GO terms and their annotations were employed in this experiment, resulting in a different reliability value for each interaction than in previous experiments. The reliability of pairs derived by this method was much lower than the reliability distribution for functional prediction, with many pairs having a reliability value below 0.2. For each unknown protein, the algorithm generated a list of subcellular components along with

Table 11.6 Functions predicted for unknown proteins by the semantic similarity-based probabilistic approach with a prediction confidence (log λ) over 32. A protein can thus correspond to more than one predicted function with different confidence levels

Unknown	Predicted function		Confidence
	ID in MIPS	Description	
YAL027W	02.16.01	Alcohol fermentation	95.1
YAL053W	01.05	C-compound and carbohydrate metabolism	34.3
YAR027W	20.01.27	Drug/toxin transport	66.0
YBL046W	01.02	Nitrogen, sulfur or selenium metabolism	34.2
YBL046W	14.07.03	Modification by phosphorylation	37.0
YCL028W	01.03.07	Deoxyribonucleotide metabolism	62.7
YFL042C	02.16.01	Alcohol fermentation	46.3
YGL230C	20.01.11	Amine/polyamine transport	32.7
YGR163W	14.13.04	Lysosomal and vacuolar protein degradation	59.9
YGR163W	20.01.01	Ion transport	64.1
YGR163W	34.01.01	Homeostasis of cations	115.2
YHL042W	14.07.02.01	Glycosylation/deglycosylation	49.2
YHR105W	14.07.02.01	Glycosylation/deglycosylation	49.2
YHR140W	20.01.27	Drug/toxin transport	66.0
YJL058C	01.04	Phosphate metabolism	36.0
YJL058C	01.06	Lipid, fatty acid and isoprenoid metabolism	215.7
YJL058C	42.04	Cytoskeleton/structural proteins	42.6
YJL122W	10.03.01.01	Mitotic cell cycle	34.4
YLR376C	10.03.02	Meiosis	36.6
YLR376C	10.03.04	Nuclear or chromosomal cycle	37.1
YKL065C	20.01.11	Amine/polyamine transport	50.3
YKL065C	32.05.01	Resistance proteins	51.9
YPL264C	01.20.19.01	Metabolism of porphyrins	54.9

their prediction confidence. A protein may correspond to more than one predicted subcellular component at different rates of confidence. The localization prediction results are listed in Table 11.7 with 40 as the threshold of prediction confidence. The localizations of YJR033C, JR091C, and YOR076C were predicted with very high levels of confidence, greater than 200.

11.8 SUMMARY

Experimentally determined PPIs are crucial sources of data in the identification of functional modules and the prediction of the functions of uncharacterized proteins. However, it has been observed that only a small portion of pairs of interacting proteins in current interaction databases are related to functional matches. As an essential preprocess, resolving the problem of functionally false positive interactions is required for the successful analysis of PPIs. Measurements of interaction reliability, semantic similarity and semantic interactivity, can be produced by integrating the connectivity of PPI networks with already published annotation data in the GO database. Effective and accurate approaches to protein function prediction

Table 11.7 Subcellular components predicted for unknown proteins by the semantic similarity-based probabilistic approach with prediction confidence (log λ) over 40. A protein can thus correspond to more than one predicted subcellular component with different confidence rates

Unknown	Predicted subcellular localization		Confidence
	ID in MIPS	Description	
YER070W	755	Mitochondria	90.7
YJR033C	750	Nucleus	215.9
YJR091C	722	Integral membrane/endomembranes	49.6
YJR091C	725	Cytoplasm	213.2
YJR091C	770	Vacuole	52.1
YLL038C	705	Bud	50.0
YML023C	722	Integral membrane/endomembranes	119.8
YML023C	750	Nucleus	191.3
YNL293W	705	Bud	81.0
YNL293W	715	Cell periphery	69.6
YNL293W	730	Cytoskeleton	54.3
YOR076C	750.05	Nucleolus	215.8
YOR076C	755	Mitochondria	60.3
YOR231W	705	Bud	168.7
YOR231W	715	Cell periphery	58.0
YOR231W	730	Cytoskeleton	45.3
YOR231W	750	Nucleus	88.0

can also be developed by integrating this annotation data. We have seen that prediction accuracy can be improved by the integration of multiple available data sources. Developing effective models for the incorporation of the rapidly growing amount of heterogeneous biological data is a promising direction for future research.

12

Data Fusion in the Analysis of Protein Interaction Networks

12.1 INTRODUCTION

Computational approaches such as those described in Chapters 6 through 10 analyze protein–protein interaction (PPI) networks on the basis of network properties only, with little integration of information from outside sources. Current conventional methods can predict only whether two proteins share a specific function but not the universe of functions that they share. Their effectiveness is hampered by their inability to take into consideration the full range of available information about protein functions. The discussion in Chapter 11 has demonstrated the effectiveness of integrating Gene Ontology (GO) annotations into such analysis. It has become increasingly apparent that the fusion of multiple strands of biological data regarding each gene or protein will produce a more comprehensive picture of the relations among the components of a genome [191], including proteins, and a more specific representation of each protein. The sophisticated data set, graph, or tree generated through these means can be subjected to advanced computational analysis by methods such as machine learning algorithms. Such approaches have become increasingly widespread and are expected to improve the accuracy of protein function prediction.

In this chapter, we present some of the more recent approaches that have been developed for incorporating diverse biological information into the explorative analysis of PPI networks.

12.2 INTEGRATION OF GENE EXPRESSION WITH PPI NETWORKS

Current research efforts have resulted in the generation of large quantities of data related to the functional properties of genomes; specifically, gene expression and protein interaction data. Gene expression profiles provide a snapshot of the simultaneous activity of all the genes in a genome under a given condition, thus eliminating the need to examine each gene separately. This simultaneous observation of genes offers an insight into their individual functions and the functional associations between them. Gene expression is useful in detecting functional modules because genes that are members of the same module in the co-expression network may have related functions.

In [304], Tornow and Mewes proposed a new method for the detection of protein functional modules, which rests on the observation that genes that are strongly correlated between networks are highly likely to perform the same function. They calculated the strength of the correlation of a group of genes that were detected as members of modules in different networks and compared this strength with the estimated probability that this correlation would arise by chance.

First, a sparse co-expression network was constructed by using the K-mutual nearest-neighbor criterion [3]. A list of K nearest-neighbor profiles was produced for each gene expression profile. The correlation of a certain number of nodes (gene expression profiles) in the network was calculated using the Swendsen–Wang Monte Carlo simulation [295]. A distribution or histogram of the correlation strength of all pairs, triplets, and other node groupings was also calculated. This distribution served as the basis for testing the protein interaction data for significant co-expression. As a result, those portions of the protein interaction network with a significant correlation strength in the co-expression network were identified. The result can be displayed as a substructure of the co-expression network.

12.3 INTEGRATION OF PROTEIN DOMAIN INFORMATION WITH PPI NETWORKS

Protein domains are the structural or functional units of proteins; they are conserved through evolution and serve as the building blocks of proteins. They have been widely used to aid in predicting protein interactions, with a high rate of success [83,208]. Domain-based prediction methods recognize that PPIs are the result of physical interactions between domains. In [179], Park et al. proposed a statistical domain-based algorithm, which they termed a "potentially interacting domain pair" (PID). In [83], Sun et al. proposed a probabilistic approach using the maximum likelihood estimation (MLE).

Recently, Chen et al. [63] introduced the CSIDOP method to predict protein functions on the basis of PPI networks and domain information. This method is based on the hypothesis that two pairs of interacting proteins that contain a common interacting domain pattern are more likely to be associated with similar functions. For example, assume that there are two protein pairs A − B and C − D. Proteins A and C have the same modular domain X, while proteins B and D share modular domain Y. If X and Y interact, then these two pairs share a common interaction domain pattern X − Y. As illustrated in Figure 12–1, proteins A and C are likely to have similar functions, as are proteins B and D.

This novel method also proposes applying data mining to the protein interaction networks of four different species. The data is preprocessed to remove protein pairs lacking domain information, and the method is applied to the remaining pairs. Protein domain information is taken from PFAM [35], and protein molecular function annotations are extracted from the GO database.

An understanding of domain patterns is necessary to properly assign GO functional annotations to proteins. This is achieved by identifying an interaction domain pattern that is uniquely conserved in a group of PPI pairs across different organisms. The CSIDOP method includes an algorithm that uses a new distance similarity metric to find groups of protein interaction pairs with similar functions. Groups of

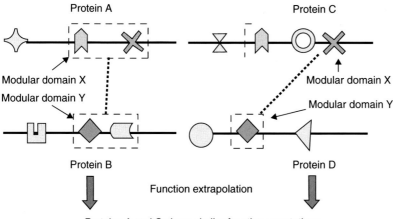

Figure 12–1 Functional annotation scheme based on interacting domain patterns. "See Color Plate 12." (Reprinted from [63].)

functionally similar PPI pairs are constructed, and χ^2 statistics are applied to derive the most meaningful interacting domain patterns from these PPI groups. The χ^2 values are computed using the following formula:

$$\chi^2 = \frac{N \times (\mathrm{AD} - \mathrm{CB})^2}{(\mathrm{A} + \mathrm{C})(\mathrm{B} + \mathrm{D})(\mathrm{A} + \mathrm{B})(\mathrm{C} + \mathrm{D})},$$

where N is the total number of PPI pairs identified, A is the number of PPI pairs in the group that contain the pattern under consideration, and B is the number of remaining PPI pairs outside the group that contain the pattern. C and D are the number of PPI pairs that do not contain the pattern in the group and in the remaining samples outside the group, respectively. The patterns with the highest χ^2 values are identified as the domain patterns of interest.

Figure 12–2 presents a flow chart illustrating the CSIDOP method. Experimental results have indicated that the CSIDOP method produces highly accurate predictions of protein function when compared with other prediction methods [85,196].

12.4 INTEGRATION OF PROTEIN LOCALIZATION INFORMATION WITH PPI NETWORKS

Another important source of information that may be employed to improve protein function prediction is protein localization or the location of the protein within a cell. This information is particularly useful in indicating protein function or filtering noisy PPI data. Taken together with other heterogeneous data, it has been employed in the prediction of PPI networks [160]. The combination of heterogeneous data to predict a functional linkage graph has also been extensively studied [171].

In [222], Kasif and Nariai proposed a Bayesian network structure to capture dependencies between genomic features (PPI data and localization information) and class labels (protein function) for the prediction of protein function. In this

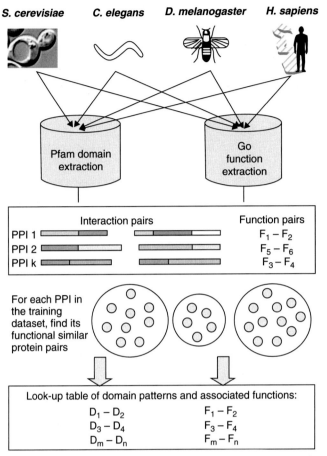

Figure 12–2 Flow chart illustrating CSIDOP method. "See Color Plate 13." (Reprinted from [63].)

model, PPI networks are differentiated into networks between co-localized proteins and networks between differently localized proteins. The method assumes that co-localized PPI networks should be more reliable than networks between differently localized proteins.

The first step in this process involved collection of PPI data pertaining to *S. cerevisiae* from the GRID database [51], localization information from the MIPS database [214] and functional categories from the GO database. For each protein, a feature vector $I = (l_1, l_2, \ldots, l_L)^T$ was defined, where l_i is a random variable indicating localization ($l_i = 1$ if the protein is located in l_i and $l_i = 0$ otherwise), and L is the total number of localization features. A Boolean random variable $f_{i,t}$ was associated with each protein i and the GO term t, where $f_{i,t} = 1$ if protein i is associated with GO term t, $f_{i,t} = 0$ otherwise. Using the collected database information, a functional linkage graph was then constructed. Three network architectures can be identified: co-localized PPI networks (i.e., PPI networks between proteins that share the same localization), cross-localized PPI networks (networks that do not share the same localization), and networks of other types.

The posterior probabilities for all combinations of proteins and GO terms were then calculated using Bayes' theorem:

$$
\begin{aligned}
& P(f_{i,t} = 1 | N_i, k_i, I_i) \\
& = \frac{P(k_i, I_i | f_{i,t}, N_i) \cdot P(f_{i,t} | N_i)}{P(k_i, I_i | N_i)} \\
& = \frac{P(k_i, I_i | f_{i,t}, N_i) \cdot P(f_{i,t} | N_i)}{P(k_i, I_i | f_{i,t}, N_i) \cdot P(f_{i,t}) + P(k_i, I_i | \overline{f_{i,t}}, N_i) \cdot P(\overline{f_{i,t}})} \\
& = \frac{P(k_i | I_i, f_{i,t}, N_i) \cdot P(I_i | f_{i,t}) \cdot P(f_{i,t})}{P(k_i | I_i, f_{i,t}, N_i) \cdot P(I_i | f_{i,t}) \cdot P(f_{i,t}) + P(k_i | I_i, \overline{f_{i,t}}, N_i) P(I_i | \overline{f_{i,t}}) \cdot P(\overline{f_{i,t}})},
\end{aligned}
$$

where $P(f_{i,t} = 1 | N_i, k_i, I_i)$ is the posterior probability associated with the given PPI data and localization information, N_i is the total number of neighbors of protein i in the functional linkage graph (PPI network), k_i is the total number of neighbors of protein i, which are annotated with t, and I_i is a feature vector for localization information of protein i.

The precision of this method is greater than predictions made with the Navie Bayes method [90] or with PPI data alone. It can be concluded that the prediction of protein functions can be enhanced by the inclusion of localization information, as proposed in [222].

12.5 INTEGRATION OF SEVERAL DATA SOURCES WITH PPI NETWORKS

The promising results produced by the methods discussed above suggest that the prediction of protein functions could be further enhanced by integrating several different types of genomic data with PPI data. Each data source will contribute incrementally to the creation of a more comprehensive understanding of the problem at hand. Several research groups have pursued various approaches to the combination of disparate data sources. Troyanskaya et al. [305] proposed a MAGIC (multisource association of genes by integration of clusters) system that uses a Bayesian network to integrate high-throughput biological data from different sources. Chen and Xu [64] also developed a Bayesian model to integrate various data sources, including PPI, microarray data, and protein complex data, into the prediction of protein functions on both local and global levels. Lanckriet et al. [191] developed a kernel method for data fusion. They constructed a kernel matrix for each data source and combined these kernel matrices in a linear form. Tsuda et al. [33] also proposed a kernel method involving the combination of multiple protein networks weighted according to convex optimization. The following two subsections will discuss the use of Bayesian models and kernel-based methods to integrate different types of biological data.

12.5.1 Kernel-Based Methods

Kernel-based statistical learning methods have proven to be of significant utility in bioinformatics applications [273]. These methods use kernel functions to capture the subtle similarities between pairs of genes, proteins, or other biological features and thus embody aspects of the underlying biological structure and function. The kernel representation is both flexible and efficient, can be applied to many different types of data, and permits easy combination of disparate data types.

Kernel-based methods use kernel functions such as $K(x_1, x_2) = \langle \phi(x_1), \phi(x_2) \rangle$, where $\phi(x_1)$ and $\phi(x_2)$ represent embedded forms of data items x_1 and x_2. Such functions make it possible to operate in feature space without computing the coordinates of the data in that space. Instead, it is sufficient to simply compute the inner products between all pairs of data in the feature space. Evaluating the kernel on all pairs of data points yields a symmetric, positive semidefinite matrix K known as the *kernel matrix*, which can be regarded as a matrix of generalized similarity measures among the data points [191].

In [191], Lanckriet et al. used kernel methods to combine disparate data sources and predict protein functions. Each kernel function produces a square matrix representing the similarities between two yeast proteins in each of several related data sets, including gene expression, protein sequence, and PPI data. The formalism of the kernel structure allows these matrices to be combined while preserving the key property of positive semidefiniteness, resulting in a simple but powerful algebra of kernels. As explicated in [191], given a set of kernels $\kappa = K_1, K_2, \ldots, K_m$, the following linear combination can be formed:

$$K = \sum_{i=1}^{m} \mu_i K_i, \tag{12.1}$$

where μ_i is the weight of each kernel. The cost function in the case involving multiple kernels results in a convex optimization problem known as a *semidefinite program* (SDP) [190]:

$$\min_{\mu_i, t, \lambda, \nu, \delta} \ t \tag{12.2}$$

subject to

$$\text{trace}\left(\sum_{i=1}^{m} \mu_i K_i \right) = c,$$

$$\sum_{i=1}^{m} \mu_i K_i \succeq 0$$

$$\begin{pmatrix} \text{diag}(\mathbf{y})(\sum_{i=1}^{m} \mu_i K_i)\text{diag}(\mathbf{y}) & \mathbf{e} + \nu - \delta + \lambda \mathbf{y} \\ (\mathbf{e} + \nu - \delta + \lambda \mathbf{y})^T & t - 2C\delta^T \mathbf{e} \end{pmatrix} \succeq 0, \quad \nu, \delta \geq 0,$$

where c is a constant, C is a regularization parameter, t, λ, ν, δ are all auxiliary variables, $\mathbf{y}$ is a set of labels, and $\mathbf{e}$ is n-vector of ones. Trace( ) refers to the trace of a particular matrix and diag() refers to the diagonals of the corresponding matrix. An SDP can be viewed as a generalization of linear programming where scalar linear inequality constraints are replaced by more general linear matrix inequalities (LMIs). For example, $F(x) \succeq 0$, which requires that the matrix of F be in the cone of positive semidefinite matrices as a function of the decision variables $\mathbf{x}$. An SDP can also be cast as a *quadratically constrained quadratic program* (QCQP) [190], which improves the efficiency of the computation:

$$\max_{\alpha,t} 2\alpha^{\mathrm{T}}\mathbf{e} - ct \qquad (12.3)$$

subject to

$$t \geq \frac{1}{n}\alpha^{\mathrm{T}}\mathrm{diag}(\mathbf{y})K_i\mathrm{diag}(\mathbf{y})\alpha, \qquad i = 1,\ldots,m$$

$$\alpha^T\mathbf{y} = 0,$$

$$C \geq \alpha \geq 0,$$

where α is an auxiliary vector variable. Solving a QCQP leads to the definition of an adaptive combination of kernel matrices and thus to an optimal classification [191]. A classification decision that merges information encoded in the various kernel matrices and weights μ_i that reflect the relative importance of different data types will be obtained.

Experimental trials of this method used information from the MIPS database [214], which is comprised of 13 classes containing 3,588 proteins. Results demonstrated performance superior to the method proposed by Deng et al. [85] and confirmed that kernel methods can successfully integrate disparate data types and improve the accuracy of protein function prediction.

12.5.2 Bayesian Model-Based Method

Diverse sources of biological data may also be integrated into the prediction of protein function using a Bayesian model. In [64], Chen integrated gene expression, protein complexes, PPI data, and GO functional categories [137] to predict protein function. The detail of this approach has been given in Section 11.7.1. Results of experimental trials of this method indicate that the prediction of protein function is enhanced by the use of Bayesian theories to integrate different types of biological data.

12.6 SUMMARY

Systematic and automated prediction of protein functions using high-throughput data represents a major challenge in the post-genomic era. In this chapter, we have provided an overview of several methods for integrating different types of data to enhance the prediction of protein functions. Tornow and Mewes [304] have integrated gene expression with protein interaction networks to detect protein functional modules. Chen et al. [63] combined information about protein domains with the protein interaction networks of four species to assign protein functions across these four networks. Kasif and Nariai [222] integrated protein interaction networks with protein localization information to successfully predict protein functions. To simultaneously integrate biological data from several sources, Troyanskaya et al. [305]

proposed a MAGIC system, which uses a Bayesian network to integrate a variety of high-throughput biological data. Chen and Xu [64] also used a Bayesian model to integrate different kinds of data sources, including PPI, microarray, and protein complex data. Lanckriet et al. [191] constructed a kernel matrix for each data source and combined these kernel matrices in a linear form. Tsuda et al. [33] also proposed a kernel method, which combines multiple protein networks and weights the combination by convex optimization. These methods, along with approaches discussed in previous chapters, suggest that a continued effort to integrate multiple high-throughput data sets into the prediction of the functions of unannotated proteins is likely to be highly fruitful.

13

Conclusion

The generation of protein–protein interaction (PPI) data is proceeding at a rapid and accelerating pace, heightening the demand for advances in the computational methods used to analyze patterns and relationships in these complex data sets. This book has offered a systematic presentation of a variety of advanced computational approaches that are available for the analysis of PPI networks. In particular, we have focused on those approaches that address the modularity analysis and functional prediction of proteins in PPI networks. These computational techniques have been presented as belonging to seven categories:

1. *Basic representation and modularity analysis.* Throughout this book, PPI networks have been represented through mathematical graphs, and we have provided a detailed discussion of the basic properties of such graphs. PPI networks have been identified as modular and hierarchical in nature, and modularity analysis is therefore of particular utility in understanding their structure. A range of approaches has been proposed for the detection of modules within these networks and to guide the prediction of protein function. We have broadly classified these methods as distance-based, graph-theoretic, topology-based, flow-based, statistical, and domain knowledge-based. Clustering a PPI network permits a better understanding of its structure and the interrelationship of its constituent components. The potential functions of unannotated proteins may be predicted by comparison with other members of the same functional module.

2. *Distance-based analysis.* Chapter 7 surveyed five categories of approaches to distance-based clustering. All these methods use classic clustering techniques and focus on the definition of the topological or biological distance or similarity between two proteins in a network. Methods in the first category discussed employ classic distance measurement techniques, and, in particular, rely on a variety of coefficient formulas to compute the distance between proteins. The second class of approaches defines a distance metric based on various network distance factors, including the shortest path length, the combined strength of paths of various lengths, and the average number of steps taken by a Brownian particle in moving between vertices. Consensus clustering, the

third group of methods, seeks to reduce the noise level in clustering through deployment of several different distance metrics and base-clustering methods. The fourth approach type defines a primary and a secondary distance to establish the strength of the connection between two elements in relationship to all the elements in the analyzed data set. Approaches in the fifth category, similarity learning, seek to identify effective clusters by incorporating protein annotation data. Although each method class has a distinct approach to distance measurement, all apply classic clustering techniques to the computed distance between proteins.

3. *Topology-based analysis.* Essential questions regarding the structure, underlying principles, and semantics of PPI networks can be addressed by an examination of their topological features and components. Much research has been devoted to the development of methods to quantitatively characterize a network or its components. In Chapters 4 and 6, we identified several important topological features of PPI networks, including their small-world, modular, and hierarchal properties. We explored the computational analysis of PPI networks on the basis of such topological network features. Experimental trials have demonstrated that such methods offer a promising tool for analysis of the modularity of PPI networks and the prediction of protein functions.

4. *Graph-theoretic approaches.* In Chapter 8, we introduced a series of graph-theoretic approaches for module detection in PPI networks. These approaches can be divided into two classes, one focusing on the identification of dense subgraphs and the other on the designation of the best partition in a graph. In addition, a graph reduction-based approach was proposed to address the inefficiencies inherent in clustering large PPI graphs. This method converts a large, complex network into a small, simple graph and applies the optimized minimum cut to identify hierarchical modules. Graph-theoretic methods have been a particular focus of current research interest.

5. *Flow-based analysis.* Flow-based approaches offer a novel strategy for analyzing the degree of biological and topological influence exerted by each protein over other proteins in a PPI network. Through simulation of biological or functional flows within the network, these methods seek to model and predict complex network behavior under a realistic variety of external stimuli. Flow-based modeling incorporates a factor recognizing the role of proximity in the effect of each annotated protein on all other proteins in the network. In Chapter 9, we discussed three approaches of this type. Details were provided regarding the compilation of information on protein function, the creation and use of a weighted PPI network, and the simulation of the flow of information from each informative protein through the entire weighted interaction network. These simulations model the complex topological properties of PPI networks, including the presence of overlapping functional modules, and thus facilitate the prediction of protein functions. Flow-based techniques can provide a useful tool to analyze the degree of biological and topological influence of each protein on other proteins in a PPI network. Approaches of this type may soon become a standard for the analysis of PPI networks.

6.   *Statistics- and machine learning-based analysis.* Statistical and machine learning has been widely applied in the field of PPI networks and is particularly well suited to the prediction of protein functions. Methods have been developed to predict protein functions using a variety of information sources, including protein structure and sequence, protein domain, PPIs, genetic interactions, and the analysis of gene expression. In Chapter 10, we discussed several statistics- and machine learning-based approaches to the study of PPIs. Approaches of this type form a large proportion of the computational methods available for PPI network analysis.

7.   *Integration of Gene Ontology (GO) into PPI network analysis.* A range of biological information can usefully be integrated into computational approaches to enhance the accuracy of PPI network analysis. Chapter 11 offered a review of the method and benefits of integrating GO annotations into such analysis. Measurements of interaction reliability, semantic similarity, and semantic interactivity can be produced by integrating the connectivity of PPI networks with already-published annotation data in the GO database. Effective and accurate approaches to protein function prediction can also be developed by integrating this annotation data. Prediction accuracy can be improved by the integration of multiple data available sources. Developing effective integration models for incorporating the rapidly growing volume of heterogeneous biological data is a promising direction for future research in the area of functional knowledge discovery.

It has become clear that incorporation of the knowledge and expertise of biologists into the computational analysis of PPI networks can be of significant benefit. Data that can usefully be considered for integration include amino acid sequences, protein structures, genomic sequences, phylogenetic profiles, microarray expressions, and various ontology annotations. A combination of heterogeneous data is often able to provide a more comprehensive view of the biological system. It is hoped that further exploration into these novel conceptual approaches will bring us to a fuller understanding of our genetic constitution and thus to a more sustainable and healthier future.

Bibliography

[1] Abe, I., et al. Green tea polyphenols: novel and potent inhibitors of squalene epoxidase. *Biochemical and Biophysical Research Communications*, 268:767–771, 2000.

[2] Aebersold, R. and Mann, M. Mass spectrometry-based proteomics. *Nature*, 422:198–207, 2003.

[3] Agrawal, H. Extreme self-organization in networks constructed from gene expression data. *Physical Review Letters*, 89:268702–268706, 2002.

[4] Akkoyunlu, E.A. The enumeration of maximal cliques of large graphs. *SIAM Journal on Computing*, 2:1–6, 1973.

[5] Albert, R. and Barabási, A.L. Statistical mechanics of complex networks. *Reviews of Modern Physics*, 74:47–97, 2002.

[6] Albert, R., Jeong, H., and Barabasi, A.L. Diameter of the world wide web. *Nature*, 401:130–131, 1999.

[7] Albert, R., Jeong, H., and Barabasi, A.L. Error and attack tolerance of complex networks. *Nature*, 406:378–482, 2000.

[8] Alfarano, C., et al. The biomolecular interaction network database and related tools 2005 update. *Nucleic Acids Research*, 33:D418–D424, 2005.

[9] Alon, U. Biological networks: the tinkerer as an engineer. *Science*, 301:1866–1867, 2003.

[10] Aloy, P. and Russell, R.B. Interrogating protein interaction networks through structural biology. *Proceedings of the National Academy of Sciences*, 99(9):5896–5901, 2002.

[11] Aloy, P., et al. Structure-based assembly of protein complexes in yeast. *Science*, 303:2026–2029, 2004.

[12] Altaf-Ul-Amin, M., Shinbo, Y., Mihara, K., Kurokawa, K., and Kanaya, S. Development and implementation of an algorithm for detection of protein complexes in large interaction networks. *BMC Bioinformatics*, 7(207), 2006.

[13] Altschul, S.F., Gish, W., Miller, W., Meyers, E.W., and Lipman, D.J. Basic local alignment search tool. *Journal of Molecular Biology*, 215(3):403–410, 1990.

[14] Altschul, S.F., Madden, T.L., Schffer, A.A., Zhang, J., Zhang, Z., Miller, W., and Lipman, D.J. Gapped BLAST and PSI-BLAST: a new generation of protein database search program. *Nucleic Acids Research*, 25(17):3389–3402, 1997.

[15] Apweiler, R., et al. The InterPro database, an integrated documnetation resource for protein families, domains and functional sites. *Nucleic Acids Research*, 29:37–40, 2001.

[16] Arking, D.E., Chugh, S.S., Chakravarti, A., and Spooner, P.M. Genomics in sudden cardiac death. *Circulation Research*, 94:712–723, 2004.

[17] Arnau, V., Mars, S., and Marin, I. Iterative cluster analysis of protein interaction data. *Bioinformatics*, 21(3):364–378, 2005.

[18] Ashburner, M., et al. Gene ontology: tool for the unification of biology. The Gene Ontology Consortium. *Nature Genetics*, 25:25–29, 2000.

[19] Asthana, S., King, O.D., Gibbons, F.D., and Roth, F.P. Predicting protein complex membership using probabilistic network reliability. *Genome Research*, 14:1170–1175, 2004.

[20] Asur, S., Ucar, D., and Parthasarathy, S. An ensemble framework for clustering protein--protein interaction networks. *Bioinformatics*, 23 ISMB/ECCB 2007:i29–i40, 2007.

[21] Auerbach, D., Thaminy, S., Hottiger, M. O., and Stagljar, I. Post-yeast-two hybrid era of interactive proteomics: facts and perspectives. *Proteomics*, 2:611–623, 2002.

[22] Aytuna, A.S., Gursoy, A., and Keskin, O. Prediction of protein–protein interactions by combining structure and sequence conservation in protein interfaces. *Bioinformatics*, 21(12):2850–2855, 2005.

[23] Bader, G.D. and Hogue, C.W. Analyzing yeast protein–protein interaction data obtained from different sources. *Nature Biotechnology*, 20:991–997, 2002.

[24] Bader, G.D. and Hogue, C.W. An automated method for finding molecular complexes in large protein interaction networks. *BMC Bioinformatics*, 4(2), 2003.

[25] Bairoch, A. and Apweiler, R. The SWISS-PROT protein sequence database and its supplement TrEMBL in 2000. *Nucleic Acids Research*, 28:45–48, 2000.

[26] Balan, E. and Yu, C.S. Finding a maximum clique in an arbitrary graph. *SIAM Journal of Computing*, 15:1054–1068, 1986.

[27] Bar-Joseph, Z., Gerber, G., Lee, T., Rinaldi, N., Yoo, J., Robert, F., Gordon, D., Fraenkel, E., Jaakkola, T., Young, R., and Gifford, D. Computational discovery of gene modules and regulatory networks. *Nature Biotechnology*, 21:1337–1342, 2003.

[28] Barabási, A.L. and Albert, R. Emergence of scaling in random networks. *Science*, 286:509–511, 1999.

[29] Barabási, A.L. and Oltvai, Z.N. Network biology: understanding the cell's functional organization. *Nature Reviews: Genetics*, 5:101–113, 2004.

[30] Barrat, A., Barthelemy, M., Pastor-Satorras, R., and Vespignani, A. The architecture of complex weighted netowrks. *Proceedings of the National Academy of Sciences*, 101(11):3747–3752, 2004.

[31] Bartel, P.L., Roecklein, J.A., SenGupta, D., and Fields, S. A protein linkage map of *Escherichia coli* bacteriophage T7. *Nature Genetics*, 12:72–77, 1996.

[32] Barter, P.J., Caulfield, M., Eriksson, M., Grundy, S.M., Kastelein, J.J., Komajda, M., et al. Effects of torcetrapib in patients at high risk for coronary events. *The New England Journal of Medicine*, 357:2109–2122, 2007.

[33] Barutcuoglu, Z., Schapire, R.E., and Troyanskaya, O.G. Hierarchical multi-label prediction of gene function. *Bioinformatics*, 22:830–836, 2006.

[34] Batagelj, V. and Zaversnik, M. Generalized cores. *arXiv:cs/0202039*, 1, 2002.

[35] Bateman, A., Coin, L., Durbin, R., Finn, R.D., and Hollich, V. The Pfam protein families database. *Nucleic Acids Research*, 32:D138–D141, 2004.

[36] Bavelas, A. A mathematical model for group structure. *Human Organizations*, 7:16–30, 1948.

[37] Best, C., Zimmer, R., and Apostolakis, J. Probabilistic methods for predicting protein functions in protein–protein interaction networks. In *German Conference on Bioinformatics, Lecture Notes in Informatics*, pp. 159–168, Bonn, Germany, 2004.

[38] Beyer, K., Goldstein, J., Ramakrishnan, R., and Shaft, U. When Is "Nearest Neighbor" Meaningful? In *ICDT '99: Proceeding of the 7th International Conference on Database Theory*, pp. 217–235, London, UK, 1999. Springer-Verlag.

[39] Blatt, M., Wiseman, S., and Domany, E. Superparamagnetic clustering of data. *Physical Review Letters*, 76:3251–3254, 1996.

[40] Blohm, D.H. and Guiseppi-Elie, A. New developments in microarray technology. *Current Opinion in Biotechnology*, 12:41–47, 2001.

[41] Bo, T.H. and Jonassen, I. New feature subset selection procedures for classification of expression profiles. *Genome Biology*, 3(4):0017.1–0017.11, 2002.

[42] Bock, J.R. and Gough, D.A. Pridicting protein–protein interactions from primary structure. *Bioinformatics*, 17(5):455–460, 2001.

[43] Bock, J.R. and Gough, D.A. Whole proteome interaction mining. *Bioinformatics*, 19(1):125–135, 2003.

[44] Bollobas, B. The evolution of sparse graphs. In *Graph Theory and Combinatorics, Proceeding Cambridge Combinatorial Conference in honor of Paul Erdos*, pp. 35–57, 1984.

[45] Bomze, I.M., Budinich, M., Pardalos, P.M., and Pelillo, M. *The maximum clique problem*, Vol. 4, pp. 1–74. Kluwer Academic Publishers Group, 1999.

[46] Bonacich, P. Factoring and weighting approaches to status scores and clique identification. *Journal of Mathematical Sociology*, 2:113–120, 1972.

[47] Bonacich, P. Power and centrality: a family of measures. *American Journal of Sociology*, 92(5):1170–1182, 1987.

[48] Bork, P., Dandekar, T., Diaz-Lazcoz, Y., Eisenhaber, F., Huynen, M., and Yuan, Y. Predicting function: from genes to genomes and back. *Journal of Molecular Biology*, 283:707–725, 1998.

[49] Botagfogo, R.A., Rivlin, E., and Shneiderman, B. Structural analysis of hypertexts: identifying hierarchies and useful metrics. *ACM Transactions on Information Systems*, 10(2):142–180, 1992.

[50] Brandes, U. and Fleischer, D. Centrality measures based on current flow. In *Proceedings of the 22nd International Symposium on Theoretical Aspects of Computer Science (STACS'05), Lecture Notes in Computer Science (LNCS)*, Springer-Verlag, Vol. 3404, pp. 533–533, 2005.

[51] Breitkreutz, B.J., Stark, C., and Tyers, M. The GRID: the general repository for interaction datasets. *Genome Biology*, 4(3):R23, 2003.

[52] Breitling, R., Armengaud, P., Amtmann, A., and Herzyk, P. Rank products: a simple, yet powerful, new method to detect differentially regulated genes in replicated microarray experiments. *FEBS Letters*, 573:83–92, 2004.

[53] Brin, S. and Page, L. The anatomy of a large-scale hypertextual web search engine. *Computer Networks and ISDN Systems*, 30:107–117, 1998.

[54] Bron, C. and Kerbosch, J. Finding all cliques of an undirect graph. *Communications of the ACM*, 16:575–577, 1973.

[55] Brun, C., Chevenet, F., Martin, D., Wojcik, J., Guenoche, A., and Jacq, B. Functional classification of proteins for the prediction of cellular function from a protein–protein interaction network. *Genome Research*, 5(R6), 2003.

[56] Bu, D., et al. Topological structure analysis of the protein–protein interaction network in budding yeast. *Nucleic Acid Research*, 31(9):2443–2450, 2003.

[57] Burier, M. The safety of rofecoxib. *Expert Opinion on Drug Safety*, 4:491–495, 2005.

[58] Carraghan, R. and Pardalos, P.M. An exact algorithm for the maximum clique problem. *Operations Research Letters*, 9:375–382, 1990.

[59] Chatr-aryamontri, A., Ceol, A., Montecchi-Palazzi, L., Nardelli, G., Schneider, M.V., Castagnoli, L., and Cesareni, G. MINT: the Molecular INTeraction database. *Nucleic Acids Research*, 35:D572–D574, 2007.

[60] Chen, D., Liu, Z., Ma, X., and Hua, D. Selecting genes by test statistics. *Journal of Biomedicine and Biotechnology*, 2:132–138, 2005.

[61] Chen, J. and Yuan, B. Detecting functional modules in the yeast protein–protein interaction network. *Bioinformatics*, 22(18):2283–2290, 2006.

[62] Chen, J., Hsu, W., Lee, M.L., and Ng, S.K. Increasing confidence of protein interactomes using network topological metrics. *Bioinformatics*, 22(16):1998–2004, 2006.

[63] Chen, X., Liu, M., and Ward, R. Protein function assignment through mining cross-species protein protein interactions. *PLoS ONE*, 3(2):e1562, 2008.

[64] Chen, Y. and Xu, D. Global protein function annotation through mining genome-scale data in yeast *Saccharomyces cerevisiae*. *Nucleic Acids Research*, 32(21):6414–6424, 2004.

[65] Cho, Y.-R., Hwang, W., and Zhang, A. Efficient modularization of weighted protein interaction networks using k-hop graph reduction. In *Proceedings of 6th IEEE Symposium on Bioinformatics and Bioengineering (BIBE)*, pp. 289–298, 2006.

[66] Cho, Y.-R., Hwang, W., and Zhang, A. Identification of overlapping functional modules in protein interaction networks: information flow-based approach. In *Proceedings of 6th IEEE International Conference on Data Mining (ICDM) – Workshops*, pp. 147–152, 2006.

[67] Cho, Y.-R., Hwang, W., and Zhang, A. Assessing reliability of protein–protein interactions by semantic data integration. In *Proceedings of 7th IEEE International Conference on Data Mining (ICDM) – Workshops*, pp. 147–152, 2007.

[68] Cho, Y.-R., Hwang, W., and Zhang, A. Modularization of protein interaction networks by incorporating Gene Ontology annotations. In *Proceedings of IEEE Symposium on Computational Intelligence in Bioinformatics and Computational Biology (CIBCB)*, pp. 233–238, 2007.

[69] Cho, Y.-R., Hwang, W., and Zhang, A. Optimizing flow-based modularization by iterative centroid search in protein interaction networks. In *Proceedings of 7th IEEE Symposium on Bioinformatics and Bioengineering (BIBE)*, pp. 342–349, 2007.

[70] Cho, Y.-R., Hwang, W., Ramanathan, M., and Zhang, A. Semantic integration to identify overlapping functional modules in protein interaction networks. *BMC Bioinformatics*, 8(265), 2007.

[71] Cho, Y.-R., Shi, L., Ramanathan, M., and Zhang, A. A probabilistic framework to predict protein function from interaction data integrated with semantic knowledge. *BMC Bioinformatics*, 9(392), 2008.

[72] Chua, H.N., Sung, W.-K., and Wong, L. Exploiting indirect neighbours and topological weight to predict protein function from protein–protein interactions. *Bioinformatics*, 22(13):1623–1630, 2006.

[73] Chugh, A., Ray, A., and Gupta, J.B. Squalene epoxidase as hypocholesterolemic drug target revisited. *Progress in Lipid Research*, 42:37–50, 2003.

[74] Chung, F., and Lu, L. The average distances in random graphs with given expected degrees. *Proceedings of the National Academy of Sciences*, 99:15879–15882, 2002.

[75] Cohen, R., and Havlin, S. Scale-free networks are ultra small. *Physical Review Letters*, 90:058–701, 2003.

[76] Colland, F., Jacq, X., Trouplin, V., Mougin, C., Groizeleau, C., Hamburger, A., Meil, A., Wojcik, J., Legrain, P., and Gauthier, J.M. Functional proteomics mapping of a human signaling pathway. *Genome Research*, 14:1324–1332, 2004.

[77] Conrads, T.P., Issaq, H.J., and Veenstra, T.D. New tools for quantitative phosphoproteome analysis. *Biochemical and Biophysical Research Communications*, 290:885–890, 2002.

[78] Coutsias, E.A., Seok, C., and Dill, K.A. Using quaternions to calculate RMSD. *Journal of Computational Chemistry*, 25(15):1849–1857, 2004.

[79] Cusick, M.E., Klitgord, N., Vidal, M., and Hill, D.E. Interactome: gateway into systems biology. *Human Molecular Genetics*, 14:R171–R181, 2005.

[80] Dandekar, T., Snel, B., Huynen, M., and Bork, P. Conservation of gene order: a fingerprint of proteins that physically interact. *Trends in Biochemical Science*, 23(9):324–328, 1998.

[81] Davies, D. and Bouldin, D. A cluster separation measure. *IEEE Transcation on Pattern Aanlysis and Machine Intelligence*, 1(2):224–227, 1979.

[82] Deane, C.M., Salwinski, L., Xenarios, I., and Eisenberg, D. Protein interactions: two methods for assessment of the reliability of high throughput observations. *Molecular and Cellular Proteomics*, 1.5:349–356, 2002.

[83] Deng, M., Mehta, S., Sun, F., and Chen, T. Inferring domain–domain interactions from protein–protein interactions. *Genome Research*, 12:1540–1548, 2002.

[84] Deng, M., Tu, Z., Sun, F., and Chen, T. Mapping gene ontology to proteins based on protein–protein interaction data. *Bioinformatics*, 20(6):895–902, 2004.

[85] Deng, M., Zhang, K., Mehta, S., Chen, T., and Sun, F. Prediction of protein function using protein–protein interaction data. *Journal of Computational Biology*, 10(6):947–960, 2003.

[86] Dennis, B. and Patil, G.P. The gamma distribution and weighted multimodal gamma distributions as models of population abundance. *Mathematical Biosciences*, 68:187–212, 1984.

[87] Derenyi, I., Palla, G., and Vicsek, T. Clique percolation in random networks. *Physical Review Letters*, 94:160–202, 2005.

[88] Ding, C. and Peng, H. Minimum redundancy feature selection from microarray gene expression data. *Journal of Bioinformatics and Computational Biology*, 223(2):185–205, 2005.

[89] Doherty, J.M., Carmichael, L.K., and Mills, J.C. GOurmet: A tool for quantitative comparison and visualization of gene expression profiles based on gene ontology (GO) distributions. *BMC Bioinformatics*, 7(151), 2006.

[90] Domingos, P. and Pazzani, M. On the optimality of the simple Bayesian classifier under zero-one loss. *Machine Learning*, 29:103–130, 1997.

[91] Domingues, F., Rahnenfuhrer, J., and Lengauer, T. Automated clustering of ensembles of alternative models in protein structure databases. *Protein Engineering, Design and Selection*, 17:537–543, 2004.

[92] Drees, B.L. Progress and variations in two-hybrid and three-hybrid technologies. *Current Opinion in Chemical Biology*, 3:64–70, 1999.

[93] Drees, B.L., et al. A protein interaction map for cell polarity development. *Journal of Cell Biology*, 154:549–576, 2001.

[94] Dunn, R., Dudbridge, F., and Sanderson, C.M. The use of edge-betweenness clustering to investigate biological function in protein interaction networks. *BMC Bioinformatics*, 6(39), 2005.

[95] Edwards, A.M., Kus, B., Jansen, R., Greenbaum, D., Greenblatt, J., and Gerstein, M. Bridging structural biology and genomics: assessing protein interaction data with known complexes. *Trends in Genetics*, 18(10):529–536, 2002.

[96] Eisen, M.B., Spellman, P.T., Brown, P.O., and Botstein, D. Clustering analysis and display of genome-wide expression patterns. *Proceedings of the National Academy of Sciences*, 95:14863–14868, 1998.

[97] Eisenberg, D., Marcotte, E.M., Xenarios, I., and Yeates, T.O. Protein function in the post-genomics era. *Nature*, 405:823–826, 2000.

[98] Enright, A.J., Iliopoulos, I., Kyrpides, N.C., and Ouzounis, C.A. Protein interaction maps for complete genomes based on gene fusion events. *Nature*, 402:86–90, 1999.

[99] Enright, A.J., van Dongen, S., and Ouzounis, C.A. An efficient algorithm for large-scale detection of protein families. *Nucleic Acids Research*, 30(7):1575–1584, 2002.

[100] Erdos, P. and Renyi, A. On random graph. *Publications Mathematica*, 6:290–297, 1959.

[101] Erdos, P. and Renyi, A. On the evolution of random graphs. *Publications of Mathematical Institute of Hungarian Academy of Science*, 5:17–61, 1960.

[102] Estrada, E. Virtual identification of essential proteins within the protein interaction network of yeast. *Proteomics*, 6:35–40, 2006.

[103] Estrada, E. and Velazquez, R. Subgraph centrality in complex networks. *Physical Review E*, 56–103, 2005.

[104] Faloutsos, M., Faloutsos, P., and Faloutsos, C. On power–law relationships of the Internet topology. In *Proceedings of SIGCOMM99*, pp. 251–262, 1999.

[105] Fang, Z., Yang, J., Li, Y., Luo, Q., and Liu, L. Knowledge guided analysis of microarray data. *Journal of Biomedical Informatics*, 39:401–411, 2006.

[106] Fell, D.A. and Wagner, A. The small world of metabolism. *Nature Biotechnology*, 18:1121–1122, 2000.

[107] Fields, S. and Song, O. A novel genetic system to detect protein–protein interactions. *Nature*, 340(6230):245–246, 1989.

[108] Flajolet, M., Rotondod, G., Daviet, L., Bergametti, F., Inchauspe, G., Tiollais, P., Transy, C., and Legrain, P. A genomic approach of the hepatitis C virus generates a protein interaction map. *Gene*, 242:369–379, 2000.

[109] Fransen, M., et al. *Molecular and Cellular Proteomics*, 2:611–623, 2002.

[110] Freeman, L.C. A set of measures of centrality based on betweenness. *Sociometry*, 40:35–41, 1979.

[111] Friden, C., Hertz, A., and De Werra, D. TABARIS: an exact algorithm based on Tabu search for finding a maximum independent set in a graph. *Computers Operations Research*, 17:437–445, 1990.

[112] Fromont-Racine, M., et al. Genome-wide protein interaction screens reveal functional networks involving Sm-like proteins. *Yeast*, 17, 2000.

[113] Gavin, A.C., et al. Functional organization of the yeast proteome by systematic analysis of protein complexes. *Nature*, 415:141–147, 2002.

[114] Ge, H. UPA, a universal protein array system for quantitative detection of protein–protein, protein–DNA, protein–RNA and protein–ligand interactions. *Nucleic Acids Research*, 28(2):e3, 2000.

[115] Ge, H., Liu, Z., Church, G.M., and Vidal, M. Correlation between transcriptome and interactome mapping data from *Saccharomyces cerevisiae*. *Nature Genetics*, 29:482–486, 2001.

[116] Gelman, A., Carlin, J.B., Stern, H.S., and Rubin, D.B. *Bayesian Data Analysis* (first edition). Chapman & Hall; London, 1995.

[117] Getz, G., Levine, E., and Domany, E. Coupled two-way clustering analysis of gene microarray data. *Proceedings of the National Academy of Sciences*, 97:12079–12084, 2000.

[118] Getz, G., Vendruscolo, M., Sachs, D., and Domany, E. Automated assignment of SCOP and CATH protein structure classifications from FSSP scores. *Proteins*, 46:405–415, 2002.

[119] Ghannoum, M.A. and Rice, L.B. Antifungal agents: mode of action, mechanisms of resistance, and correlation of these mechanisms with bacterial resistance. *Clinical Microbiology Reviews*, 12:501–517, 1999.

[120] Gingras, A.C., Aebersold, R., and Raught, B. Advances in protein complex analysis using mass spectrometry. *Journal of Physiology*, 561:11–21, 2005.

[121] Giot, L., et al. A protein interaction map of *Drosophila melanogaster*. *Science*, 302:1727–1736, 2003.

[122] Girvan, M. and Newman, M.E.J. Community structure in social and biological networks. *Proceedings of the National Academy of Sciences*, 99(12):7821–7826, 2002.

[123] Glazko, G., Gordon, A., and Mushegian, A. The choice of optimal distance measure in genome-wide data sets. *Bioinformatics*, 21:iii3–iii11, 2005.

[124] Glover, F. Tabu search. *ORSA Journal on Computing*, 1.190–206, 1989.

[125] Goldberg, D.S. and Roth, F.P. Assessing experimentally derived interactions in a small world. *Proceedings of the National Academy of Sciences*, 100(8):4372–4376, 2003.

[126] Golub, T.R., et al. Molecular classification of cancer: class discovery and class prediction by gene expression monitoring. *Science*, 286:531–537, 1999.

[127] Gomez, S.M., Noble, W.S., and Rzhetsky, A. Learning to predict protein–protein interactions from protein sequences. *Bioinformatics*, 19(15):1875–1881, 2003.

[128] Gordon, D. *Classification*. Chapman & Hall, 1999.

[129] Guimera, R. and Amaral, L.A.N. Functional cartography of complex metabolic networks. *Nature*, 433:895–900, 2005.

[130] Guldener, U., Munsterkotter, M., Oesterheld, M., Pagel, P., Ruepp, A., Mewes, H.-W., and Stumpflen, V. MPact: the MIPS protein interaction resource on yeast. *Nucleic Acids Research*, 34:D436–D441, 2006.

[131] Hahn, M.W. and Kern, A.D. Comparative genomics of centrality and essentiality in three eukaryotic protein-interaction networks. *Molecular Biology and Evolution*, 22:803–806, 2004.

[132] Halkidi, M. and Vazirgiannis, M. Clustering validity assessment: finding the optimal partitioning of a data set. In *Proceedings of the 2001 IEEE International Conference on Data Mining (ICDM)*, pp. 187–194, 2001.

[133] Hallett, M.B. and Pettit, E.J. Stochastic events underlie Ca2+ signalling in neutrophils. *Journal of Theoretical Biology*, 186:1–6, 1997.

[134] Han, J. et. al. Evidence for dynamically organized modularity in the yeast protein–protein interaction network. *Nature*, 430:88–93, 2004.

[135] Harary, F. and Hage, P. Eccentricity and centrality in networks. *Social Networks*, 17:57—63, 1995.

[136] Harary, F. and Ross, I. A procedure for clique detection using the group matrix. *Sociometry*, 20:205–215, 1957.

[137] Harris, M.A., Clark, J., Ireland, A., Lomax, J., Ashburner, M., Foulger, R., Eilbeck, K., Lewis, S., Marshall, B., Mungall, C., et al. The Gene Ontology (GO) database and informatics resource. *Nucleic Acids Research*, 32:D258–D261, 2004.

[138] Hartuv, E., and Shamir, R. A clustering algorithm based graph connectivity. *Information Processing Letters*, 76:175–181, 2000.

[139] Hartwell, L.H., Hopfield, J.J., Leibler, S., and Murray, A.W. From molecular to modular cell biology. *Nature*, 402:c47–c52, 1999.

[140] Hayashida, M., Akutsu, T., and Nagamochi, H. A clustering method for analysis of sequence similarity networks of proteins using maximal components of graphs. *IPSJ Digital Courier*, 4:207–216, 2008.

[141] Hermjakob, H., et al. IntAct: an open source molecular interaction database. *Nucleic Acids Research*, 32:D452–D455, 2004.

[142] Hirschman, J., et al. Genome Snapshot: a new resource at the Saccharomyces Genome Database (SGD) presenting an overview of the *Saccharomyces cerevisiae* genome. *Nucleic Acids Research*, 34:D442–D445, 2006.

[143] Hishigaki, H., Nakai, K., Ono, T., Tanigami, A., and Takagi, T. Assessment of prediction accuracy of protein function from protein–protein interaction data. *Yeast*, 18:523–531, 2001.

[144] Ho, Y., et al. Systematic identification of protein complexes in *Saccharomyces cerevisiae* by mass spectrometry. *Nature*, 415:180–183, 2002.

[145] Holme, P., Huss, M., and Jeong, H. Subnetwork hierarchies of biochemical pathways. *Bioinformatics*, 19:532–538, 2003.

[146] Hubbell, C.H. In input–output approach to clique identification. *Sociometry*, 28:377–399, 1965.

[147] Hvidsten, T.R., Lagreid, A., and Komorowski, J. Learning rule-based models of biological process from gene expression time profiles using Gene Ontology. *Bioinformatics*, 19(9):1116–1123, 2003.

[148] Hwang, W., Cho, Y.-R., Zhang, A., and Ramanathan, M. A novel functional module detection algorithm for protein–protein interaction networks. *Algorithms for Molecular Biology*, 1(24), 2006.

[149] Hwang, W., Cho, Y., Zhang, A., and Ramanathan, M. CASCADE: a novel quasi all paths-based network analysis algorithm for clustering biological interactions. *BMC Bioinformatics*, 9:64, 2008.

[150] Hwang, W., Kim, T., Cho, Y.-R., Zhang, A., and Ramanathan, M. SIGN: reliable protein interaction identification by integrating the similarity in GO and the similarity in protein interaction networks. In *Proceedings of 7th IEEE Symposium on Bioinformatics and Bioengineering (BIBE)*, pp. 1384–1388, 2007.

[151] Hwang, W., Kim, T., Ramanathan, M., and Zhang, A. Bridging centrality: graph mining from element level to group level. In *Proceedings of the 14th ACM SIGKDD International Conference on Knowledge Discovery & Data Mining (KDD08)*, pp. 336–344, 2008.

[152] Hwang, W., Ramanathan, M., and Zhang, A. Identification of information flow-modulating drug targets: a novel bridging paradigm for drug discovery. *Clinical Pharmacology and Therapeutics*, 84(5):563–572.

[153] Ideker, T., Ozier, O., Schwikowski, B., and Siegel, A.F. Discovering regulatory and signalling circuits in molecular interaction networks. *Bioinformatics*, 18:S233–S240, 2002.

[154] International Human Genome Sequencing Consortium. Initial sequencing and analysis of the human genome. *Nature*, 409:860–921, 2001.

[155] Ito, T., Chiba, T., Ozawa, R., Yoshida, M., Hattori, M., and Sakaki, Y. A comprehensive two-hybrid analysis to explore the yeast protein interactome. *Proceedings of the National Academy of Sciences*, 98(8):4569–4574, 2001.

[156] Ito, T., et al. Toward a protein–protein interaction map of the budding yeast: a comprehensive system to examine two-hybrid interactions in all possible combinations between the yeast proteins. *Proceedings of the National Academy of Sciences*, 93(3):1143–1147, 2000.

[157] Ito, T., Ota, K., Kubota, H., Yamaguchi, Y., Chiba, T., Sakuraba, K., and Yoshida, M. Roles for the two-hybrid system in exploration of the yeast protein interactome. *Molecular and Cellular Proteomics*, 1:561–566, 2002.

[158] Jain, A., Murty, M., and Flynn, P. Data clustering: a review. *ACM Computing Surveys*, 31:264–323, 1999.

[159] Jansen, R., Greenbaum, D., and Gerstein, M. Relating whole-genome expression data with protein–protein interactions. *Genome Research*, 12:37–46, 2002.

[160] Jansen, R., Yu, H., Greenbaum, D., Kluger, Y., Krogan, N.J., Chung, S., Emili, A., Snyder, M., Greenblatt, J.F., and Gerstein, M. A Bayesian networks approach for predicting protein–protein interactions from genomic data. *Science*, 302:449–453, 2003.

[161] Jeong, H., Mason, S.P., Barabási, A.-L., and Oltvai, Z.N. Lethality and centrality in protein networks. *Nature*, 411:41–42, 2001.

[162] Jiang, D., Tang, C., and Zhang, A. Cluster analysis for gene expression data: a survey. *IEEE Transactions on Knowledge and Data Engineering (TKDE)*, 16:1370–1386, 2004.

[163] Jiang, J.J. and Conrath, D.W. Semantic similarity based on corpus statistics and lexical taxonomy. In *Proceedings of 10th International Conference on Research in Computational Linguistics*, 1997.

[164] Johnson, D.B. Efficient algorithms for shortest paths in sparse networks. *Journal of the ACM*, 24:1–13, 1977.

[165] Johnson, N.L., Kotz, S., and Balakrishnan, N. *Continuous Univariate Distributions*. John Wiley & Sons, New York, NY, 1994.

[166] Johnsson, N. and Varshavsky, A. Split Ubiquitin as a sensor of protein interactions in vivo. *Proceedings of the National Academy of Sciences*, 91:10340–10344, 1994.

[167] Jones, S. and Thornton, J.M. Principles of protein–protein interactions. *Proceedings of the National Academy of Sciences*, 93:13–20, 1996.

[168] Joy, M., Brock, A., Ingber, D., and Huang, S. High-betweenness proteins in the yeast protein interaction network. *Journal of Biomedicine and Biotechnology*, 2:96–103, 2005.

[169] Juni, P., Nartey, L., Reichenbach, S., Sterchi, R., Dieppe, P.A., and Egger, M. Risk of cardiovascular events and rofecoxib: cumulative meta-analysis. *Lancet*, 364:2011–2019, 2004.

[170] Kanehisa, M. and Goto, S. KEGG: Kyoto encyclopedia of genes and genomes. *Nucleic Acids Research*, 27:29–34, 1999.

[171] Karaoz, U., Murali, T.M., Letovsky, S., Zheng, Y., Ding, C., Cantor, C.R., and Kasif, S. Whole-genome annotation by using evidence integration in functional-linkage networks. *Proceedings of the National Academy of Sciences*, 101(9):2888–2893, 2004.

[172] Karp, R.M. Reducibility among combinatorial problems. In *Complexity of computer computations*, pp. 85–103. Plenum Press, New York, 1972.

[173] Karypis, G., Han, E.-H., and Kumar, V. Chameleon: hierarchical clustering using dynamic modeling. *IEEE Computer: Special Issue on Data Analysis and Mining*, 32: 68–75, 1999.

[174] Katz, L. A new status index derived from sociometric analysis. *Psychometrika*, 18(1):39–43, 1953.

[175] Kaufman, L. and Rousseeuw, P. J. *Finding Groups in Data: An Introduction to Cluster Analysis*. John Wiley & Sons, 1990.

[176] Kemeny, J. and Snell, J. *Finite Markov Chains*. Springer Verlag, 1976.

[177] Kemmeren, P., van Berkum, N.L., Vilo, J., Bijma, T., Donders, R., Brazma, A., and Holstege, F.C.P. Protein interaction verification and functional annotation by integrated analysis of genome-scale data. *Molecular Cell*, 9:1133–1143, 2002.

[178] Kerrien, S., et al. IntAct – open source resource for molecular interaction data. *Nucleic Acids Research*, 35:D561–D565, 2007.

[179] Kim, W.K., Park, J., and Suh, J.K. Large scale statistical prediction of protein protein interaction by potentially interacting domain (PID) pair. *Genome Informatics*, 13:42–50, 2002.

[180] King, A.D., Przulj, N., and Jurisica, I. Protein complex prediction via cost-based clustering. *Bioinformatics*, 20(17):3013–3020, 2004.

[181] Kirac, M. and Ozsoyoglu, G. Protein function prediction based on patterns in biological networks. In *Proceedings of 12th International Conference on Research in Computational Molecular Biology (RECOMB)*, pp. 197–213, 2008.

[182] Klein, D., Kamvar, S., and Manning, C. From instance-level constraints to space-level constraints: Making the most of prior knowledge in data clustering. In *The Nineteenth International Conference on Machine Learning, 2002*, 2002.

[183] Kleinberg, J.M. Authoritative sources in a hyperlinked environment. *Journal of the ACM*, 46(5):604–632, 1999.

[184] Koonin, E.V., Wolf, Y.I., and Karev, G.P. The structure of the rotein universe and genome evolution. *Nature*, 420:218–223, 2002.

[185] Korbel, J.O., Snel, B., Huynen, M.A., and Bork, P. SHOT: a web server for the construction of genome phylogenies. *Trends in Genetics*, 18:159–162, 2002.

[186] Krause, R., Von Mering, C., and Bork, P. A comprehensive set of protein complexes in yeast: mining large scale protein–protein interaction screens. *Bioinformatics*, 19:1901–1908, 2003.

[187] Krogan, N.J., Peng, W.T., Cagney, G., Robinson, M.D., Haw, R., Zhong, G., Guo, X., Zhang, X., Canadien V., et al. High-definition macromolecular composition of yeast RNA-processing complexes. *Molecualr Cell*, 13:225–239, 2004.

[188] Kumar, A. and Snyder, M. Protein complexes take the bait. *Nature*, 415:123–124, 2002.

[189] Kuster, B., Mortensen, P., Andersen, J.S., and Mann, M. Mass spectrometry allows direct identification of proteins in large genomes. *Protemics*, 1:641–650, 2001.

[190] Lanckriet, G.R.G., Cristianini, N., Bartlett, P., Ghaoui, L.E., and Jordan, M.I. Learning the kernel matrix with semi-definite programming. *Proceedings of 19th Internaltional Conf Machine Learning*, pp. 323–330, 2002.

[191] Lanckriet, G.R.G., Deng, M., Cristianini, N., Jordan, M.I., and Noble, W.S. Kernel-based data fusion and its application to protein function prediction in yeast. *Pacific Symposium on Biocomputing*, 9, 2004.

[192] Lasonder, E., et al. Analysis of the *Plasmodium falciparum* proteome by high-accuracy mass spectrometry. *Nature*, 419:537–542, 2002.

[193] Leacock, C. and Chodorow, M. Combining local context and WordNet similarity for word sense identification. In *WordNet: An Electronic Lexical Database*, pp. 265–283. MIT Press, 1998.

[194] Lee, H., Tu, Z., Deng, M., Sun, F., and Chen, T. Diffusion kernel-based logistic regression models for protein function prediction. *OMICS A Journal of Integrative Biology*, 10(1):40–55, 2006.

[195] Leone, M. and Paganim A. Predicting protein functions with message passing algorithms. *Bioinformatics*, 21(2):239–247, 2005.

[196] Letovsky, S. and Kasif, S. Predicting protein function from protein/protein interaction data: a probabilistic approach. *Bioinformatics*, 19:i197–i204, 2003.

[197] Li, F., Long, T., Ouyang, Q., and Tang, C. The yeast cell-cycle network is robustly desinged. *Proceedings of the National Academy of Sciences*, 101:4781–4786, 2004.

[198] Li, S., et al. A map of the interactome network of the metazoan. *Science*, 303:540–543, 2004.

[199] Li, S.Z. *Markov Random Field Modeling in Computer Vision*. Springer-Verlag, Tokyo, 1995.

[200] Lin, C., Cho, Y., Hwang, W., Pei, P., and Zhang, A. Clustering methods in a protein–protein interaction network. In Xiaohua Hu and Yi Pan, eds., *Knowledge Discovery in Bioinformatics: Techniques, Methods and Applications*, pp. 319–351. Copyright by Wiley, 2007.

[201] Lin, C., Jiang, D., and Zhang, A. Prediction of protein function using common-neighbors in protein–protein interaction networks. In *Proceedings of IEEE 6th Symposium on Bioinformatics and Bioengineering (BIBE)*, pp. 251–260, 2006.

[202] Lin, D. An information-theoretic definition of similarity. In *Proceedings of 15th International Conference on Machine Learning (ICML)*, pp. 296–304, 1998.

[203] Lo Conte, L., Ailey, B., Hubbard, T., Brenner, S., Murzin, A.G., and Chothia, C. SCOP: a structural classification of proteins database. *Nucleic Acids Research*, 28:257–259, 2000.

[204] Lu, L., Lu, H., and Skolnick, J. MULTIPROSPECTOR: an algorithm for the prediction of protein–protein interactions by multimeric threading. *PROTEINS: Structure, Function, and Genetics*, 49:350–364, 2002.

[205] MacBeath, G. and Schreiber, S.L. Printing proteins as microarrays for high-throughput function determination. *Science*, 289:1760–1763, 2000.

[206] Mann, M., et al. Analysis of protein phosphorylation using mass spectrometry: deciphering the phosphoproteome. *Trends in Biotechnology*, 20:261–268, 2002.

[207] Mann, M. and Jensen, O.N. Proteomic analysis of post-translational modifications. *Nature Biotechnology*, 21:255–261, 2003.

[208] Marcotte, E.M., Pellegrini, M., Ng, H.-L., Rice, D.W., Yeates, T.O., and Eisenberg, D. Detecting protein function and protein–protein interactions from genome sequences. *Science*, 285:751–753, 1999.

[209] Marcotte, E.M., Xenarios, I., van der Bliek, A.M., and Eisenberg, D. Localizing proteins in the cell from their phylogenetic profiles. *Proceedings of the National Academy of Sciences*, 97(22):12115–12120, 2000.

[210] Markillie, L.M., Lin, C.T., Adkins, J.N., Auberry, D.L., Hill, E.A., Hooker, B.S., Moore, P.A., Moore, R.J., Shi, L., Wiley, H.S., and Kery, V. Simple protein complex purification and identification method for high-throughput mapping of protein interaction networks. *Journal of Proteome Research*, 4:268–274, 2005.

[211] Maslov, S. and Sneppen, K. Specificity and stability in topology of protein networks. *Science*, 296:910–913, 2002.

[212] Matthews, L.R., Vaglio, P., Reboul, J., Ge, H., Davis, B.P., Garrels, J., Vincent, S., and Vidal, M. Identification of potential interaction networks using sequence-based searches for conserved protein–protein interactions or "Interologs." *Genome Research*, 11:2120–2126, 2001.

[213] McCraith, S., Holtzman, T., Moss, B., and Fields, S. Genome-wide analysis of Vaccinia virus protein–protein interactions. *Proceedings of the National Academy of Sciences*, 97:4879–4884, 2000.

[214] Mewes, H.W., et al. MIPS: analysis and annotation of proteins from whole genome in 2005. *Nucleic Acid Research*, 34:D169–D172, 2006.

[215] Mezard, M. and Parisi, G. The Bethe lattice spin glass revisited. *The European Physical Journal B*, 20:217–233, 2001.

[216] Michener, C. and Sokal, R. A quantitative approach to a problem in classification. *Evolution*, 11:130–162, 1957.

[217] Milgram, S. The small world problem. *Psychology Today*, 2:60, 1967.

[218] Mirkin, B. and Koonin, E.V. A top-down method for building genome classification trees with linear binary hierarchies. *Bioconsensus*, 61:97–112, 2003.

[219] Mishra, G.R., et al. Human protein reference database – 2006 update. *Nucleic Acids Research*, 34:D411–D414, 2006.

[220] Muller, K.R., Mika, S., Ratsch, G., Tsuda, K. and Scholkopf, B. An introduction to Kernel-based learning algorithms. *IEEE Transactions on Neural Networks*, 12(2):181–202, 2001.

[221] Nabieva, E., Jim, K., Agarwal, A., Chazelle, B. and Singh, M. Whole-proteome prediction of protein function via graph-theoretic analysis of interaction maps. *Bioinformatics*, 21:i302–i310, 2005.

[222] Nariai, N. and Kasif, S. Context specific protein function prediction. *Genome Informatics*, 18:173–82, 2007.

[223] Newman, J.R., Wolf, E., and Kim, P.S. A computationally directed screen identifying interacting coiled coils from *Saccharomyces cerevisiae*. *Proceedings of the National Academy of Sciences*, 97:13203–13208, 2000.

[224] Newman, M.E. Network construction and fundamental results. *Proceedings of the National Academy of Sciences*, 98:404–409, 2001.

[225] Newman, M.E.J. Scientific collaboration networks: shortest paths, weighted networks and centrality. *Physical Review E*, E64:016132, 2001.

[226] Newman, M.E.J. A measure of betweenness centrallity on random walks. *arXiv:cond-mat*, 1:0309045, Sep. 2003.

[227] Newman, M.E.J. The structure and function of complex networks. *SIAM Review*, 45(2):167–256, 2003.

[228] Newman, M.E.J. The mathematics of networks. *The New Palgrave Encyclopedia of Economics,* 2nd edition, 2006.

[229] Nieminen, U.J. On the centrality in a directed graph. *Social Science Research*, 2:371–378, 1973.

[230] Nooren, I. and Thornton, J.M. Diversity of protein–protein interactions. *EMBO Journal*, 22:3486–3492, 2003.

[231] O'Donovan, C., Martin, M.J., Gattiker, A., Gasteiger, E., Bairoch, A., and Apweiler, R. High-quality protein knowledge resource: Swiss-Prot and TrEMBL. *Briefings in Bioinformatics*, 3(3):275–284, 2002.

[232] Ofran, Y. and Rost, B. Analysing six types of protein–protein interfaces. *Journal of Molecular Biology*, 325(2):377–387, 2003.

[233] Oliver, S. Guilt-by-association goes global. *Nature*, 403:601–603, 2000.

[234] O'Madadhain, J., Fisher, D., and White, S. JUNG: Java Universal Network/Graph Framework. *sourceforge.net*, 2007.

[235] Overbeek, R., Fonstein, M., D'Souza, M., Pusch, G.D., and Maltsev, N. The use of gene clusters to infer functional coupling. *Proceedings of the National Academy of Sciences*, 96:2896–2901, 1999.

[236] Oyama, T., Kitano, K., Satou, K., and Ito, T. Extraction of knowledge on protein–protein interaction by association rule discovery. *Bioinformatics*, 18(5):705–714, 2002.

[237] Pagel, P., et al. The MIPS mammalian protein–protein interaction database. *Bioinformatics*, 21(6):832–834, 2005.

[238] Palla, G., Derenyi, I., Farkas, I., and Vicsek, T. Uncovering the overlapping community structure of complex networks in nature and society. *Nature*, 435:814–818, 2005.

[239] Palumbo, M., Colosimo, A., Giuliani, A., and Farina, L. Functional essentiality from topology features in metabolic networks: a case study in yeast. *Federation of European Biochemical Societies Letters*, pp. 4642–4646, 2005.

[240] Pandey, A. and Mann, M. Proteomics to study genes and genomes. *Nature*, 405:837–846, 2000.

[241] Patterson, S.D. and Aebersold, R.H. Proteomics: the first decade and beyond. *Nature Genetics*, 33:311–323, 2003.

[242] Pazos, F. and Valencia, A. Similarity of phylogenetic trees as indicator of protein–protein interaction. *Protein Engineering*, 14(9):609–614, 2001.

[243] Pearl, J. *Probabilistic Reasoning in Intelligent Systems: Networks of Plausible Inference*. Morgan Kaufmann, 1988.

[244] Pearson, W.R. and Lipman, D.J. Improved tools for biological sequence comparison. *Proceedings of the National Academy of Sciences*, 85(8):2444–2448, 1988.

[245] Pei, P. and Zhang, A. A topological measurement for weighted protein interaction network. In *Proceedings of 16th IEEE Computational Systems Bioinformatics Conference (CSB)*, pp. 268–278, 2005.

[246] Pei, P. and Zhang, A. A two-step approach for clustering proteins based on protein interaction profile. In *Proceedings of Fifth IEEE International Symposium on Bioinformatic and Bioengineering (BIBE 2005)*, pp. 201–209, 2005.

[247] Pei, P. and Zhang, A. A "seed-refine" algorithm for detecting protein complexes from protein interaction data. *IEEE Transactions on Nanobioscience*, 6(1):43–50, 2007.

[248] Pellegrini, M., Marcotte, E.M., Thompson, M.J., Eisenberg, D., and Yeates, T.O. Assigning protein functions by comparative genome analysis: protein phylogenetic profiles. *Proceedings of the National Academy of Sciences*, 96:4285–4288, 1999.

[249] Peng, J., Elias, J.E., Thoreen, C.C., Licklider, L.J., and Gygi, S.P. Evaluation of multidimensional chromatography coupled with tandem mass spectrometry (LC/LC-MS/MS) for large-scale protein analysis: the yeast proteome. *Journal of Proteome Research*, 10:1021, 2002.

[250] Pereira-Leal, J.B., Enright, A.J., and Ouzounis, C.A. Detection of functional modules from protein interaction networks. *Proteins*, 54:49–57, 2004.

[251] Peri, S., et al. Development of human protein reference database as an initial platform for approaching systems biology in humans. *Genome Research*, 13:2363–2371, 2003.

[252] Peri, S., et al. Human protein reference database as a discovery resource for proteomics. *Nucleic Acids Research*, 32:D497–D501, 2004.

[253] Persico, M., Ceol, A., Gavrila, C, Hoffmann, R., Florio, A., and Cesareni, G. Homon-MINT: an inferred human network based on orthology mapping of protein interactions discovered in model organisms. *BMC Bioinformatics*, 6:S21, 2005.

[254] Phizicky, E.M. and Fields, S. Protein–protein interactions: methods for detection and analysis. *Microbiological Reviews*, 59:94–123, 1995.

[255] Press, W.H., Teukosky, S.A., Vetterling, W.T., and Flannery, B.P. *Numerical Recipe in C: The Art of Scientific Computing*. Cambridge University Press, New York, 1992.

[256] Proctor, C.H. and Loomis, C.P. *Analysis of sociometric data*, pp. 561–586. Dryden Press, 1951.

[257] Promponas, J., Enright, J., Tsoka, S. Krell, P., Leory, C., Hamodrakas, S., Sander, C., and Ouzounis, A. CAST: an iterative algorithm for the complexity analysis of sequence tracts. *Bioinformatics*, 16:915–922, 2000.

[258] Rahat, O., Yitzhaky, A., and Schreiber, G. Cluster conservation as a novel tool for studying protein–protein interactions evolution. *Proteins*, 71:621–630, 2008.

[259] Rain, J.C., Selig, L., De Reuse, H., Battaglia, V., Reverdy, C., Simon, S., Lenzen, G., Petel, F. and Wojcik, J., Schachter, V., Chemama, Y., Labigne, A., and Legrain, P. The protein–protein interaction map of *Helicobacter pylori*. *Nature*, 409:211–215, 2001.

[260] Ramanathan, M. A dispersion model for cellular signal transduction cascades. *Pharmaceutical Research*, 19:1544–1548, 2002.

[261] Ravasz, E., Somera, A.L., Mongru, D.A., Oltvai, Z.N., and Barabási, A.-L. Hierarchical organization of modularity in metabolic networks. *Science*, 297:1551–1555, 2002.

[262] Resnik, P. Using information content to evaluate semantic similarity in a taxonomy. In *Proceedings of 14th International Joint Conference on Artificial Intelligence*, pp. 448–453, 1995.

[263] Rives, A.W. and Galitski, T. Modular organization of cellular networks. *Proceedings of the National Academy of Sciences*, 100(3):1128–1133, 2003.

[264] Robert, C.P. and Casella, G. *Monte Carlo Statistical Methods* (2nd edition). Springer-Verlag, New York, 2004.

[265] Rousseeuw, P.J. Silhouettes: a graphical aid to the interpretation and validation of cluster analysis. *Journal of Computational and Applied Mathematics*, 20:53–65, 1987.

[266] Rual, J.F., et al. Towards a proteome-scale map of the human protein–protein interaction network. *Nature*, 437:1173–1178, 2005.

[267] Ruepp, A., et al. The FunCat: a functional annotation scheme for systematic classification of proteins from whole genomes. *Nucleic Acid Research*, 32(18):5539–5545, 2004.

[268] Sabidussi, G. The centrality index of a graph. *Psychometrika*, 31:581–603, 1966.

[269] Saito, R., Suzuki, H., and Hayashizaki, Y. Interaction generality, a measurement to assess the reliability of protein–protein interaction. *Nucleic Acids Research*, 30(5):1163–1168, 2002.

[270] Saito, R., Suzuki, H., and Hayashizaki, Y. Construction of reliable protein–protein interaction networks with a new interaction generality measure. *Bioinformatics*, 19(6):756–763, 2003.

[271] Salwinski, L., Miller, C.S., Smith, A.J., Pettit, F.K., Bowie, J.U., and Eisenberg, D. The database of interacting proteins: 2004 update. *Nucleic Acid Research*, 32:D449–D451, 2004.

[272] Samanta, M.P. and Liang, S. Predicting protein functions from redundancies in large-scale protein interaction networks. *Proceedings of the National Academy of Sciences*, 100(22):12579–12583, 2003.

[273] Scholkopf, B., Tsuda, K., and Vert, J.P. *Support Vector Machine Applications in Computational Biology*. MIT Press, 2004.

[274] Schwikowski, B., Uetz, P., and Fields, S. A network of protein–protein interactions in yeast. *Nature Biotechnology*, 18:1257–1261, 2000.

[275] Seeley, J.R. The net of reciprocal influence. *Canadian Journal of Psychology*, III(4):234–240, 1949.

[276] Segal, E., Wang, H., and Koller, D. Discovering molecular pathways from protein interaction and gene expression data. *Bioinformatics*, 19:i264–i272, 2003.

[277] Seidman, S.B. Network structure and minimum degree. *Social Networks*, 5:269–287, 1983.

[278] Shannon, C.E. A mathematical theory of communication. *Bell System Technical Journal*, 27:379–423, 1948.

[279] Shimbel, A. Structural parameters of communication networks. *Bulletin of Mathematical Biophysics*, 15:501–507, 1953.

[280] Sigman, M. and Cecchi, G.A. Global organization of the Wordnet lexicon. *Proceedings of the National Academy of Sciences*, 99:1742–1747, 2002.

[281] Sivashankari, S. and Shanmughavel, P. Functional annotation of hypothetical proteins – A review. *Bioinformation*, 1(8):335–338, 2006.

[282] Smith, G.R. and Sternberg, M.J.E. Prediction of protein–protein interactions by docking methods. *Current Opinion in Structural Biology*, 12:28–35, 2002.

[283] Sneath, P. and Sokal, R. *Numerical Taxonomy*. Freeman, San Francisco, 1973.

[284] Sole, R.V., Pastor-Satorras, R., Smith, E., and Kepler, T.B. A model of large-scale proteome evolution. *Advances in Complex Systems*, 5:43–54, 2002.

[285] Spellman, P., Sherlock, G., Zhang, M., Iyer, V., Eisen, M., Brown, P., et al. Comprehensive identification of cell cycle-regulated genes of the yeast *Saccharomyces cerevisiae* by microarray hybridization. *Molecular Biology of the Cell*, 9:3273–3297, 1998.

[286] Spirin, V. and Mirny, L.A. Protein complexes and functional modules in molecular networks. *Proceedings of the National Academy of Sciences*, 100(21):12123–12128, 2003.

[287] Sprinzak, E. and Margalit, H. Correlated sequence-signatures as markers of protein–protein interaction. *Journal of Molecular Biology*, 311:681–692, 2001.

[288] Sprinzak, E., Sattath, S., and Margalit, H. How reliable are experimental protein–protein interaction data? *Journal of Molecular Biology*, 327:919–923, 2003.

[289] Stark, C., Breitkreutz, B.-J., Reguly, T., Boucher, L., Breitkreutz, A., and Tyers, M. BioGRID: a general repository for interaction datasets. *Nucleic Acids Research*, 34:D535–D539, 2006.

[290] Stephenson, K.A. and Zelen, M. Rethinking centrality: methods and examples. *Social Networks*, 11:1–37, 1989.

[291] Stix, V. Finding all maximal cliques in dynamic graphs. *Computational Optimization and Applications*, 27(2):173–186, 2004.

[292] Stoer, M. and Wagner, F. A simple min-cut algorithm. *Journal of the ACM*, 44(4):585–591, 1997.

[293] Strogatz, S.H. Exploring complex networks. *Nature*, 410:268–276, 2001.

[294] Sugiyama, T., et al. Aldosterone induces angiotensin converting enzyme gene expression via a JAK2-dependent pathway in rat endothelial cells. *Endocrinology*, 146:3900–3906, 2005.

[295] Swendsen, R.H. and Wang, J.S. Nonuniversial critical dynamics in Monte Carlo simulations. *Physical Review Letters*, 58:86–88, 1987.

[296] Tamames, J. Evolution of gene order conservation in prokaryotes. *Genome Biology*, 2(6), 2001.

[297] Tanay, A., Sharan, R., Kupiec, M., and Shamir, R. Revealing modularity and organization in the yeast molecular network by integrated analysis of highly heterogeneous genomewide data. *Proceedings of the National Academy of Sciences*, 101(9):2981–2986, 2004.

[298] Tavazoie, S., Hughes, D., Campbell, M.J., Cho, R.J., and Church, G.M. Systematic determination of genetic network architecture. *Nature Genetics*, pp. 281–285, 1999.

[299] Tetko, I.V., Facius, A., Ruepp, A., and Mewes, H.W. Super paramagnetic clustering of protein sequences. *BMC Bioinformatics*, 6(82): 2005.

[300] Thatcher, J., Shaw, J., and Dickinson, W. Marginal fitness contributions of nonessential genes in yeast. *Proceedings of the National Academy of Sciences*, 95:253–257, 1997.

[301] The Gene Ontology Consortium. The Gene Ontology (GO) project in 2006. *Nucleic Acids Research*, 34:D322–D326, 2006.

[302] The Gene Ontology Consortium. The Gene Ontology project in 2008. *Nucleic Acids Research*, 36:D440–D444, 2008.

[303] Tong, A.H., et al. A combined experimental and computational strategy to define protein interaction networks for peptide recognition modules. *Science*, 295:321–324, 2002.

[304] Tornow, S. and Mewes, H.W. Functional modules by relating protein interaction networks and gene expression. *Nucleic Acids Research*, 31(21): 6283–6289, 2003.

[305] Troyanskaya, O.G., Dolinski, K., Owen, A.B., Altman, R.B. and Botstein, D. A Bayesian framework for combining heterogeneous data sources for gene function prediction (in *Saccharomyces cerevisiae*). *Proceedings of the National Academy of Sciences*, 100(14):8348–8353, 2003.

[306] Ucar, D., Parthasarathy, S., Asur, S., and Wang, C. Effective pre-processing strategies for functional clustering of a protein–protein interactions network. In *IEEE 5th Symposium on Bioinformatics and Bioengineering (BIBE05)*, pp. 129–136, 2005.

[307] Uetz, P., et al. A comprehensive analysis of protein–protein interactions in *Saccharomyces cerevisiae*. *Nature*, 403:623–627, 2000.

[308] Van Dongen, S. A new cluster algorithm for graphs. Technical Report INS-R0010, Center for Mathematics and Computer Science (CWI), Amsterdam, 2000.

[309] Van Dongen, S. Performance criteria for graph clustering and markov cluster experiments. Technical Report INS-R0012, Center for Mathematics and Computer Science (CWI), Amsterdam, 2000.

[310] Venter, J.C., et al. The sequence of the human genome. *Science*, 291:1304–1351, 2001.

[311] Vidal, M. *The Two-Hybrid System*, p. 109. Oxford University Press, 1997.

[312] Von Mering, C., et al. Comparative assessment of large-scale data sets of protein–protein interactions. *Nature*, 417:399–403, 2002.

[313] Wagner, A. The yeast protein interaction network evolves rapidly and contains few redundant duplicate genes. *Molecular Biology and Evolution*, 18:1283–1292, 2001.

[314] Wagner, A. How the global structure of protein interaction networks evolves. *Proceedings. Biological sciences/The Royal Society*, 270:457–466, 2003.

[315] Walhout, A.J., Sordella, R., Lu, X., Hartley, J.L., Temple, G.F., Brasch M.A., Thierry-Mieg, N., and Vidal, M. Protein interaction mapping in C. elegans using proteins involved in vulval development. *Science*, 287:116–122, 2000.

[316] Wang, H., Azuaje, F., Bodenreider, O., and Dopazo, J. Gene expression correlation and gene ontology-based similarity: an assessment of quantitative relationships. In *Proceedings of IEEE Symposium on Computational Intelligence in Bioinformatics and Computational Biology (CIBCB)*, pp. 25–31, 2004.

[317] Wang, H., Wang, W., Yang, J., and Yu, P.S. Clustering by pattern similarity in large data sets. In *Proceedings of ACM SIGMOD International Conference on Management of Data*, pp. 394–405, 2002.

[318] Washburn, M.P., Wolters, D., and Yates, J.R. Large-scale analysis of the yeast proteome by multidimensional protein identification technology. *Nature Biotechnology*, 19:242–247, 2001.

[319] Watts, D.J. and Strogatz, S.H. Collective dynamics of 'small-world' networks. *Nature*, 393:440–442, 1998.

[320] White, S. and Smyth, P. Algorithms for estimating relative importance in networks. In *Proceedings of the 9th ACM SIGKDD International Conference on Knowledge Discovery and Data Mining (KDD03)*, pp. 266–275, 2003.

[321] Wiener, H. Structural determination of paraffin boiling points. *Journal of the American Chemical Society*, 69:17–20, 1947.

[322] Wojcik, J. and Schachter, V. Protein–protein interaction map inference using interacting domain profile pairs. *Bioinformatics*, 17:S296–S305, 2001.

[323] Workman, C.T., Mak, H.C., McCuine, S., Tagne, J.B., Agarwal, M., Ozier, O., Begley, T.J., Samson, L.D., and Ideker, T. A systems approach to mapping DNA damage response pathways. *Science*, 312:1054–1059, 2006.

[324] Wu, Z. and Palmer, M. Verb semantics and lexical selection. In *Proceedings of 32th Annual Meeting of the Association for Computational Liguistics*, pp. 133–138, 1994.

[325] Wuchty, S. Interaction and domain networks of yeast. *Proteomics*, 2:1715–1723, 2002.

[326] Wuchty, S. and Almaas, E. Peeling the yeast protein network. *Proteomics*, 5:444–449, 2005.

[327] Xenarios, I., Salwinski, L., Duan, X.J., Higney, P., Kim, S.-M., and Eisenberg, D. DIP, the Database of Interacting Proteins: a research tool for studying cellular networks of protein interactions. *Nucleic Acid Research*, 30(1):303–305, 2002.

[328] Xia, K., Dong, D., and Han, J.J. IntNetDB v1.0:an integrated protein–protein interaction network database generated by probabilistic model. *BMC Bioinformatics*, 7(508): 2006.

[329] Yamazaki, T., Komuro, I., Shiojima, I., and Yazaki, Y. The molecular mechanism of cardiac hypertrophy and failure. *Annals of the New York Academy of Sciences*, 874:38–48, 1999.

[330] Yanagida, M. Functional proteomics; current achievements. *Journal of Chromatography. B, Analytical Technologies in the Biomedical and Life Sciences*, 771:89–106, 2002.

[331] Yang, J., Wang, W., Wang, H., and Yu, P.S. δ-clusters: capturing subspace correlation in a large data set. In *Proceedings of the 18th International Conference on Data Engineering (ICDE)*, pp. 517–528, 2002.

[332] Yeang, C.H. and Jaakkola, T. Physical network models and multi-source data integration. In *Proceedings of Seventh Annual International Conference on Research in Computational Molecular Biology (RECOMB 2003), Berlin, April 10–13*, pp. 312–321, 2003.

[333] Yedidia, J., Freeman, W., and Weiss, Y. Understanding belief propagation and its generalizations. In *Exploring Artificial Intelligence in the New Millennium*, pp. 239–269. Morgan Kaufmann Publishers Inc. San Francisco, CA, 2003.

[334] Yook, S.H., Oltvai, Z.N., and Barabasi A.L. Functional and topological characterization of protein interaction networks. *Proteomics*, 4:928–942, 2004.

[335] Yousry, T.A., Major, E.O., Ryschkewitsch, C., Fahle, G., Fischer, S., Hou, J. et al. Evaluation of patients treated with natalizumab for progressive multifocal leukoencephalopathy. *The New England Journal of Medicine*, 354:924–933, 2006.

[336] Yu, H., Greenbaum, D., Lu, H., Zhu, Z., and Gerstein, M. Genomic analysis of essentiality within protein networks. *Trends in Genetics*, 20:227–231, 2004.

[337] Yu, H., Kim, P., Sprecher, E., Trifonov, V., and Gerstein, M. The importance of bottlenecks in protein networks: correlation with gene essentiality and expression dynamics. *PLoS Computational Biology*, 3:713–720, 2007.

[338] Yu, H., Luscombe, N.M., Lu, H.X., Zhu, X., Xia, Y., Han, J.-D.J., Bertin, N., Chung, S., Vidal, M., and Gerstein, M. Annotation transfer between genomes: protein–protein interologs and protein–DNA regulogs. *Genome Research*, 14:1107–1118, 2004.

[339] Yu, L. and Liu, H. Redundancy based feature selection for microarray data. In *Proceedings of 10th ACM SIGKDD International Conference on Knowledge Discovery and Data Mining*, pp. 737–742, 2004.

[340] Zanzoni, A., Montecchi-Palazzi, L., Quondam, M., Ausiello, G., Helmer-Citterich, M., and Cesareni, G. MINT: a Molecular INTeraction database. *FEBS Letters*, 513:135–140, 2002.

[341] Zhang, A. *Advanced Analysis of Gene Expression Microarray Data*. World Scientific Publishing Co. Pte. Ltd., 2006.

[342] Zhang, B., Kraemer, B., SenGupta, S., Fields, S., and Wickens, M. Yeast three-hybrid system to detect and analyze interactions between RNA and protein. *Methods in Enzymology*, 306:93–113, 1999.

[343] Zhou, H. Distance, dissimilarity index, and network community structure. *Physical review. E, Statistical, Nonlinear, and Soft Matter Physics*, 67:061901, 2003.

[344] Zhou, H. Network landscape from a Brownian particle's perspective. *Physical Review E*, 67:041908, 2003.

[345] Zhu, H. and Snyder, M. Protein chip technology. *Current Opinion in Chemical Biology*, 7:55–63, 2003.

[346] Zhu, H., et al. Global analysis of protein activities using proteome chips. *Science*, 293:2101–2105, 2001.

[347] Zotenko, E., Guimaraes, K.S., Jothi, R., and Przytycka, T.M. Decomposition of overlapping protein complexes: a graph theoretical method for analyzing static and dynamic protein associations. *Algorithms for Molecular Biology*, 1(7): 2006.

[348] Zou, Y., et al. Isoproterenol activates extracellular signal-regulated protein kinases in cardiomyocytes through calcineurin. *Circulation*, 104:102–108, 2001.

Index

Printed in the United States
by Baker & Taylor Publisher Services